MW00635913

The Seed

A COSMIC DANCE WITH SYNCHRONICITY

Samantha Lyn
with Sulannaya AM~RA

GODDESS PUBLISHING
SEDONA, ARIZONA

Copyright © 2019 by Samantha Lyn.

All rights reserved. No part of this publication may be reproduced, distributed or transmitted in any form or by any means, including photocopying, recording, or other electronic or mechanical methods, without the prior written permission of the publisher, except in the case of brief quotations embodied in critical reviews and certain other noncommercial uses permitted by copyright law. For permission requests, write to the publisher, addressed "Attention: Permissions Coordinator," at the address below.

Goddess Publishing LLC
1001 S Main St Ste 5129
Kalispell, MT 59901
www.readtheseedbook.com

MEDIA: please contact media@goddesspublishing.org

SALES: for bulk purchases, please contact support@goddesspublishing.org

Book Layout ©2017 BookDesignTemplates.com

Cover Art By Mynzah

The Seed/ Samantha Lyn -- 1st ed.
ISBN 978-0-578-61125-9

"For a seed to achieve its greatest expression, it must come completely undone. The shell cracks, its insides come out and everything changes. To someone who doesn't understand growth, it would look like complete destruction."

~ Cynthia Occelli

"So many of the events that you call 'random' are actually scripted and guided by higher intelligence, that it would bring your mind to fathomless depths to even be able to conceive of the level of planning and forethought that is actually going on."

~ David Wilcock – "The Synchronicity Key"

Sandi's Message

Congratulations, dear readers for choosing this powerful book, and embarking on a personal journey with Samantha!

I have had the wonderful experience of editing this empowering, insightful and thought provoking book.

Samantha has opened her heart and followed her inner guidance to share this personal journey with all of you in the grand hope there will be those of you that will connect with her journey and gain wisdom and the knowledge that you are not alone!

I can truly attest to this very kind and loving person who exists through the guidance from her heart.

It has been an absolute joy to be asked to be a small part of the completion of this great book.

Dear readers, you will not be disappointed!

Sandi O'Connor
Clarkdale, Arizona
September 6, 2016

Piece of the Galactic Puzzle

As I sit here in Samantha's home in Arizona, editing her book, I am amazed and awed at Sam's brave and courageous spirit to choose to come to earth to do this work. She is a powerful woman and I am forever changed since having the opportunity to not only help edit, but to witness the birthing of this material.

I was first made aware of Sam's book by Selene, when I met her at the Crystal Quest event in Arkansas in the autumn of 2014. It was also the first time I met Sam. When I first laid eyes on her, there was an instant tugging in my heart, not just of remembrance, but of Knowingness. I KNEW her. Not just Sam from this lifetime, but her soul. Her imprint was palpable. Warm, earthy, motherly, giving, kind, wickedly funny, completely present and the ultimate energy of Love. The more time we spent together in Arkansas during our first Crystal Quest together, the easier it was to find ourselves sitting in the ease of the energy of Sisterhood from many lifetimes of galactic adventures.

The only difficult thing about our week at the Crystal Quest was that she was unable to share much about herself, as it was the basis of this book. Selene had advised Sam prior to her embarking on the trip that, under no circumstances should she share any bit of the material with others. And I know this was hard for her, because it prevented her from strongly bonding with some of her soul family.

After sharing with Sam an experience I had been through, I could clearly see in her eyes the recognition of her own story in mine. Something of my own experience paralleled hers and she seemed very much wanting to share it with me. But in a second, her eyes would move away from me. She wanted so much to show me just how much we had been through the same experiences and to help provide some clarity for me. But she knew she couldn't share just yet.

This was how committed she was to her work, as isolating as it may have been at times for her. You have Big Lady Balls, SiStar! I applaud you!

At the end of our time together in the Natural State, Selene asked the group if there were any editors in the room that would help Sam with her book. I instantly heard from my inner voice that I was to raise my hand. Yet I didn't. While I have written and edited hundreds of research and investigation reports in my daily work, I would not have considered myself a professional writer. And to be honest, at that time I was still trying to hide from myself, which included ALL of my talents and abilities.

I had at least two other opportunities during the end of our week in Arkansas to raise my hand for the job, again publicly, and was always pushed by this voice to offer my services. Yet, I did nothing. I silently hushed that inner voice by saying that if no one had offered once we got home from the trip, I would put my name on it.

Once we returned home, I connected with Sam through emails, and she had mentioned that the right person had not yet stepped up to edit the book. Imagine my surprise when I heard my own voice say that if it felt right to her, I would love to edit her book. After confirming with both herself and Selene, Sam granted me this Great Task.

Once Spirit brings you in touch with your mission, it will rarely let you dodge it successfully.

This information has been kept highly secret, and you will soon see why. The risk was just too great to get into the wrong hands, not only to Sam and her family, but to all with whom she may have shared her story.

Not to say I am alone in this endeavor. I have been monitored throughout this process. Yes, a being has been present with me, guiding me on the how-tos of editing this information so that it is handled in just the right way. I strongly sense He is from Samantha's galactic team, and that Selene has her hand in this in some way.

My responsibility as the galactic editor has been to become the bridge through telepathic thought-form communication with this being. I am obviously not the one in charge here, and am but a humble servant to this work.

I am to read the material and hear it in my mind, which He is also able to telepathically hear. I am then given back a telepathic thought-form of a comment or question or grammar change. All of this, of course has just been explained by Him in telepathic thought-form in my head. As weird as all this may sound to some of you, I am constantly amused and grateful by this beautiful process and the beings behind all of these grand experiences; my galactic family in the skies.

My message to you, the reader, is simple: read this book. Take your time with it, as it will be challenging for some of you to embrace all that this knowledge has to offer you. As much as Samantha's galactic occurrences may seem difficult to relate to, I implore you to keep an open mind. While what she has gone through may seem fantastical and beyond your own scope of abilities, know this... this book is threading many mysteries together and nudging you to remember your own experiences that have long since been forgotten.

My hope is that this helps you find the pieces you have been hiding from yourself.

Now is the time, my dear friends. Remember.

Thank you, Goddess SiStar Sam, for helping me find mine.

Jennifer Alexander
March 19, 2015
Cottonwood, Arizona, U.S.A

CHAPTER 1

"The Remembering" – July 2011:

I am barefoot on the earth, standing, my arms outstretched, palms and face lifted, worshipping the infinite sky above me. I feel a rush of white light pour down from the cosmos through the crown of my head and it fills my body. I begin to consciously expand, my aura reaching out farther and farther until I realize that I am floating upward toward the sky.

I enjoy this sensation of flying through the clouds. It is very familiar to me. I see a silver cord attached to my chest and it leads to "the beyond;" beyond where I can see with my naked eye. I choose to follow this cord and move wherever it takes me, in complete surrender to the journey. I rise higher and higher until I notice that I am now outside of Earth's atmosphere, and I am floating through space. It is so quiet and peaceful here. I see debris soar by me and around me. It is truly fascinating!

From this perspective, I notice something very interesting. I begin to recognize an energetic aura around every single thing I see. Nothing is exempt from this. I also notice that each of the auras are interconnected, all are a part of The Infinite Oneness of Existence.

I have never seen this before, but it has become so clear to me, instantly, and I am exhilarated. Everywhere I look, there is another link in this cosmic chain.

I celebrate by dancing and flying freely. Everything imaginable is a part of this beautiful connection. Finally, after several minutes of this wondrous journey, I begin my descent back to Earth. As I arrive, I again notice that even nothing here is exempt from this mystical phenomenon.

I notice a little squirrel scampering up a tree. This sweet squirrel is one of the links, the tree another. I am another. Every single living thing is a part of this. I look down upon such a magnificent sight with a bird's eye view and I am breathless. We are all a living representation of the Divine Sacred Geometric pattern of The Flower of Life. This powerful symbol is alive within us all, in all the trillions of cells; it is alive in everything in Existence.

We are IT, every single one of us. We are The Universal Seeds. The Universal Seeds of Life.

CHAPTER 2

Synchronicity Embraced

This is not your ordinary book.

This lifetime alone for me has included multiple incarnations to date, and I still have a lot of time left for who knows how many more. For me, life has been one series of events after another - some ordinary, *many* extraordinary - each one equally significant in their own unique way for setting me gracefully (and sometimes not so gracefully) on my Divine Path. This is a path towards empowerment through the full alignment and merging of my physical self, sitting here writing this book, and my True Cosmic Self that reaches far beyond time and space, and is infinite.

The common thread connecting many of these life events, especially the ones that have led me clearly on my spiritual path, is the very real concept which so many refer to as "coincidence," or "chance," but that I have come to Know deep within my Heart and Soul as "*synchronicity.*"

Every single experience in this life for me has been part of a Sacred Road—not always visible or easy to follow, often lonely, yet always beautiful nonetheless—tirelessly leading me one step at a time closer toward ultimately waking up to the essence of my True Self, my Soul resonance—my unique cosmic Divine Frequency which I'd lost in translation somewhere along the way in this crazy game of life here on Earth.

You see, I have been guided and watched over by off-planet beings residing in alternate dimensions of time and space, and celestial forces my entire life. In fact, in the spirit of full disclosure, I would say that I too am not entirely what one might term "from here," and I assure you, I am not the only one. There are so many more of us here now, other starseeds and beings of a more cosmic heritage, just like me. It is as common as anything else on the planet, many of us simply haven't been privy to this information yet. The term "starseed," means we were seeded here on the physical plane by way of other celestial forces, planets and dimensions, for a highly specific mission.

This is a very real phenomenon that is occurring, as we are all walking amongst "them"—*us* every single day, in our families, our circle of friends, our places of employment. It does not make those of us carrying these frequencies any more special or for that matter, any less human from the perspective of the heart and our love of the Earth. We simply have come here on special assignment to complete certain missions, all in service to support the shifting of the consciousness on the planet which is taking place as we speak.

Some of us will complete our assignments, and some of us will fall off track, and not remember who we are or what we're doing here. Some of us are simply too sensitive, and lack the support we need in order to become fully empowered and self-realized enough to complete what we came here to do.

Some of us experience such levels of high strangeness that, without the resources needed in order to understand what we are going through, it can become too much to bear. We squelch our gifts, in an attempt to survive and try to become "normal," to fit in, just to be able to function in our daily lives enough to relate with our family and friends. This actually has the opposite effect, sadly. Many are lost before their full light ever becomes realized, especially by themselves. This is not an easy or glamourous path to have chosen, and is truly not for the faint-hearted spirit.

Some starseeds are driven so far off the deep end by the often overwhelming feelings of intense Knowingness, to where loneliness, confusion, or isolation kick in, they are led to develop addictions or other self-destructive coping mechanisms simply to make it through the days of their lives here on the planet. We often numb ourselves through addictions of all kinds. Some even resort to suicide out of utter desperation, when it feels like there is no light at the end of this endlessly long and arduous tunnel.

This is such a sad truth, as well as the greatest inspiration behind this book—to help us *all* to know and understand that we are never alone, and if we only knew how many of us are really out there, having these same or similar experiences, it may just save someone's life, metaphorically, or even, dare I say, literally.

This book is as much for me as it is for anyone else, and I know this.

So, in light of this, Here and Now, I choose to reclaim my unique Soul frequency, that of my Higher Self. I hereby reclaim fully my Cosmic Essence.

~The resonant frequency of my Soul holds the sound vibration of 'Sulannaya AM-RA'~

This name translates as "The Seed of the Sun" according to my Higher Self, my "Twin," who resides aboard ship and is one of the main guiding celestial forces in my life. I had asked for clarification on the meaning of this name during a Quantum Healing regression session I'd had with a trained Dolores Cannon apprentice on December 7, 2012, almost one year to the date of being downloaded with it spontaneously (without asking) through meditation.

My life this time around was always meant to be this way. I regret nothing and cherish every single moment of my glorious experience here on this fascinating, though often frustrating planet at this most auspicious time in the history of All That Is.

This has no doubt been a magical, beautiful life journey so far for me, and I would change nothing about it, not even the challenges I was absolutely certain were going to kill me, including writing this very book which you hold in your hands.

Well, "they" didn't kill me. The mysterious and elusive "they." I am still very much here, intact, and fully alive. And I am sharing this story, *my story*, as it is and always has been the grand design for this particular assignment. It is all part of a divinely orchestrated plan, and it is needed, especially Now. I know without a shadow of a doubt that this story, this book, was always going to be written, and that I agreed long before coming here to be the one to write it.

My profound wish is that in the sharing of my story, you, the reader, may realize a greater sense of purpose in your own life. May it inspire you. May it even, at times, entertain you. May it intrigue you to dig deeper into your own greater mysteries. May it be a catalyst for the changes you have been praying for in your own life. May it bring you a greater sense of inner peace, and help give you solace or clarity where there may still be confusion or isolation. May it help clean up and sharpen your own discernment skills. May it give you hope, seeing that even in the ultimate depths of darkness, we can always find our way back to the Light again. May my story touch your Heart and Soul in a way that challenges, and even changes, how you view yourself and the world around you, and beyond, forever. May it open you up in ways beyond your wildest dreams.

I have no expectations for any precious outcome here; only that it reach the ones who are waiting for it, the ones who seek it. Because I know you are out there.

I have no investment in whether you believe any of it or not. I am not here to convince anyone of anything. I already know that these stories and experiences are real—I have lived them firsthand. Believe me, many times, I'd wished I hadn't. I did not yet see the gift in any of them as they were happening to me. My reason for writing about these experiences is not to receive popularity votes or attention. Most of the time I quite feared the opposite stepping forward with such naked truths about myself—and feared the great risk of losing everyone and everything I hold sacred and dear to my heart.

Frankly, I wrote this book because I had no other choice. In truth, I tried not to write this book. Many times, I tried not to be who I am. And it nearly killed me.

So now, I surrender. I surrender to completing my assignments here on this planet because I know for a fact that whatever scheme I could cook up in my own head to avoid it, were I to even try (which for the record, I have done multiple times but gave up long ago), is beyond the scope of my conscious imaginative ability.

There's no way that five, ten, or 20 years ago I would have ever guessed this is where I would be now, and what I would be doing. If anyone had tried to tell me I'd be writing a book about my experiences with extraterrestrials and other paranormal experiences, I would have laughed in their face and said no chance in hell. I never would have believed anyone who told me that by 2016 I would be announcing to the world, and risking it all—all the love, support and respect I have received throughout my life from friends, family and people who care about me—that I walk with one foot in both worlds, and I always have. The worlds of the seen and the unseen. The physical, and the cosmic. That I am in some senses a double agent. Or, to paraphrase Judy Carroll, I am "*Human by day, and ET by night.*"

Yet, here I am, stating precisely this. And when I look back in hindsight, each and every single twist and turn in this unpredictable road of life has brought me to *this* moment, *right here.*

I'm now choosing to step out of that closet, and reclaim my own personal power, no longer ashamed of or confused about who I am. My heart is still the same heart. My Love is still as strong and powerful as ever, if not more so. My sense of compassion and caring for my fellow humans, Earthly and Galactic alike, is still intact and beaming brightly. I have simply given up the games. Given up trying to be "normal," something I am *not* and never will be. I have given up trying to fit myself into boxes that I just don't fit into. I have given up the fight, which all along was really only against myself.

So thank you, from the depths of my Heart and Soul, for walking this Earth with me right Now, as our paths intersect through the bridge that connects us either physically or by way of this book, and even beyond.

We all have a voice, a message and a purpose. Let us always lift one another up, rather than tear one another down. We are here to stand together in this.

Let us all accept and support one another, and walk together in peace. This is my profound wish for the life of this book.

Because *Now* is The Time.

CHAPTER 3

The Seed is Planted

I grew up in a small town in Southern Ontario named Thorold. At the end of my street, Thorold turned in to St. Catharines, which is the town where I was born during a full moon on the 24th of May, 1975.

We lived on the border between the two towns, a metaphor that would become one of the most defining aspects of my life here in this present incarnation on the planet. Borders and bridges are some of my life's most prominent themes, it seems.

I have realized since writing this book that everywhere I have ever lived in Canada, I was always within a few miles of a major US border. I have now resided in the United States, in Sedona, Arizona, since 2008, which I never thought in a million years I would ever do, but my team upstairs obviously had other plans for me. You see, I've been in contact with, and have been led by these ETs, or Extraterrestrial beings, my entire life.

This book is like a "coming out" for me, something I'd never personally planned to do, yet now see clearly that I was being prepared for this moment since before I was born. Early on, I was at peace with it, and didn't realize it might seem unusual to others. As I grew and started to relate more to the world outside of my own safe little bubble, I shut my inner Knowing down, for fear of being misunderstood or condemned. I now know I have lived many lifetimes burnt at the stake for being who I am, so revealing it, even to myself, had always terrified me. I became closely acquainted with this paralyzing fear, and felt that telling people these things about myself may not be the safest thing to do.

As I grew older, and became accustomed to shutting down the more mystical sides of me, I began to forget them myself, and so I lost access to these abilities. I became a victim, and for the life of me didn't understand why "they"—the ETs for instance—seemed to "choose" *me* of all people to "do stuff" to, or why I had to *feel* everything everyone else felt, or how or why I "Knew" things before they happened, so that when they *would* come to pass I would blame myself for "making" them happen. I lived in a kind of silent torture no one knew about. I was so good, I even hid it from myself most of the time, until one day I would snap over the most ridiculous thing. Then no one would understand how such a rage could come over a sweet child or person like me. It was the big mystery.

These gifts often felt like a curse. I know many who identify as empathic, as well as people who work with ETs, who say the same thing. It's about coming around to the realization that we signed up for this on some level of the Soul, at least most if not *all* the time. These experiences are no coincidence and definitely no accident. As insensitive or harsh as that may sound, I have come to Know this as the Truth.

It took me a while to understand that one, but finally, and thankfully, I did. In doing so, I also began to see that on the other side of this cursed coin, was "The Gift." Once I flipped that coin around and saw its other side clearly, my life, my world, started to make sense, probably for the first time ever, thanks to Selene and her gift of Galactic Tracking that turned the lights back on for me. I finally began to unravel the truth of Who I Really Am and what exactly it is I am doing here. I discovered the path of my many missions, and was able to release that nagging and unrelenting sense of forgetting my purpose, which I'd been aching to remember since I was a young child.

It truly all started to make sense.

I am here to help bridge the Worlds, as I have come to know them. The conscious and the unconscious. Earth and Sky. Human and ET. I walk with one foot in each world, on the balancing beam of Knowingness and Love.

Endearingly termed "Little Italy" by its residents, Thorold is a small town, sometimes with a bad rap for being a little too rough, tough, crazy and wonderfully Italian. I loved growing up there.

I had no sense in my younger years of the strong mafia presence there, but I'm almost certain now it was all around me. I would have never guessed it though, as this culture is one of the warmest there is, and if you are their friend, you are also considered their family. When this is the case, you know someone has always got your back, no matter what.

Located between St. Catharines and Niagara Falls, Canada, Thorold is often also referred to as "the armpit" of the Niagara Region. With its high population of Italian families and culture, many of my friends' parents growing up in the 80s and

90s spoke only Italian in their households, and barely any English, or it was broken and minimal at best.

I adored growing up in this culture. I loved hearing the fast-talking "Ma's" and "Nona's" outside my bedroom window at 6 am, perpetually sounding like they were yelling at everyone around them; or the shuffling slippers of the "Nono's" and "Pa's" as they hocked up phlegm and spat it to the ground, slapping onto the paved driveways, that they spray down with a hose several times a day anyway, so no big deal. These, believe it or not, were comforting sounds to me from the warmth of my bed as the sun rose each morning. I loved every bit of it. It was home.

I also loved being invited over to my neighbours' home across the street. Their youngest daughter, Cathy, was my friend, and we went years where we were nearly inseparable, especially in the long, lazy days of summer. During these times, I would occasionally be asked to stay for dinner, and it was always a wondrous and exciting event for me.

Homemade pasta with sauce made right from their own garden-fresh tomatoes, homemade meatballs, and true authentic cheeses right from their special markets in town with imported everything straight from Italy. All prepared in their downstairs kitchen. Italians have two kitchens. The regular kitchen we all know about and have on the main level of the home (which I am convinced for them is just for show), and then the basement kitchen, *where all the magic happens*.

It was truly divine decadence for me, especially since I was accustomed to eating meals of frozen pizza pockets, bologna sandwiches, Minute Rice, Shake and Bake chicken, and Kraft Dinner.

It became a running joke among Cathy's older brothers (she had three of them, and an older sister) that they could always tell when Sam was full. Every single time, when I couldn't possibly eat another bite even if I'd wanted to, I would inevitably lean back as far as I could in my chair, with my pants either undone or pulled down over my uncomfortably full and bulging belly. Everyone would laugh once I got to that point, all knowing that I was truly done once the pants were down, yet always offering me just one last helping.

I loved being a part of these dinner tables. To me, it was magical and joyful, and I always stuffed in every single morsel of food my tiny frame could handle, which was much more than it looked like it could, thankfully. These dinners ruined me for jarred pasta sauce forever. To this day, I can only eat the highest quality sauces, and only homemade.

Donato Setacci, Cathy's father, was a gentle, kind soul with a twinkle in his eye who barely spoke English. He was an older man; Cathy being the fifth and youngest child in the family. By the time we were young best friend kids, some of Cathy's eldest siblings were already married with children.

Mr. Setacci loved his garden and loved to stroll to the end of his yard, and up the street. He really had the whole "take it easy" sort of attitude to life down pat, though he was by far not a lazy man. Quite to the contrary, he was always doing something in his garden or yard, he just never seemed stressed about anything. He was one of the sweetest presences in the neighbourhood, smiling, and greeting everyone who passed.

He also took a bit of a shining to me for some reason. I remember one day when I was about nine or ten, we were having one of our pleasant, broken-up attempts at a conversation. We really did both enjoy this connection we shared, and were willing to ignore the communication challenges, doing our best to chat whenever our paths crossed which was often in my earlier years.

This particular day, out of nowhere he says to me in his thick Sicilian accent, "Seeds. I'm going to call you 'Seeds' from now on."

"Oh. Okay. Why? What does that mean?" I asked him, curiously.

"That is what your name means. Samantha (pronounced in his endearing accent as "cement") means 'Seeds.' That is your name. You are 'Seeds.' You plant, you love, you grow." He continued to smile, with a distinct little twinkle in his eye, and from that day forth, I knew myself as "Seeds" whenever I was around Mr. Setacci, and it somehow seemed right.

Cathy has since told me that her father and mother would still talk about me from time to time, even years after I had moved away. She said, "He could see that you were so full of life at such a young age, but he also knew that you were brought here to love and help others grow."

WOW. I did not expect to hear that, but it warmed my heart, and helped confirm for me that my connection with Mr. Setacci went much deeper than a third-dimensional neighbour status.

Somehow, even as a child, I felt seen by this man in a way others did not appear to see me. I knew this new name fit me perfectly somehow, even if I didn't understand why, and I welcomed our conversations and connection even more so after that.

I could not comprehend then, in any conscious way, the enormity of the Initiation this quiet, twinkly-eyed, grey-haired Italian man bestowed upon me that day, and I am eternally grateful to him for imparting his wisdom unto me. It would be decades before I would make the connection and solve this piece of the puzzle, but it was well worth the wait, and I honour him as The Divine Cosmic Messenger of this key puzzle piece, whether he was aware of what he was doing or not.

Mr. Setacci passed on from this world to the next on June 17th, 2014. He is now, quite fittingly in my opinion, a star in the sky, twinkling as brightly as his mischievous, warm, and wisdom-filled eyes. I have no doubt about this. I think of him often and it always brings a smile to my face and joy in my heart. He was a treasure of a man and I will always remember and miss him.

Since living here in Sedona, I have come into conscious contact with many others from my soul family. It was after meeting Sierra in a food preparation class in the summer of 2011 that one of the most significant pieces to my own puzzle came in to view for me.

Sierra connected me with a very significant woman, one from my intimate soul family, who would end up becoming my spiritual, or rather, *galactic* mentor of sorts, helping me shift my life and my focus, through self-empowerment. She helped me to begin to see the truth of who I really am and what exactly I am doing here, the bigger picture of my birth and this present incarnation.

My connection with this incredible woman, Selene, helped me begin to piece together the experiences and events from my life in a very precise tapestry through her mastery of natal and galactic astrology, combined with her own sort of internal tracking device that allows her and everyone she counsels in this way to trace very clearly all the way back to their childhood, and further back even. For me specifically, the journey began before I came to the planet. I was able to see clearly then my life on earth as a coherent journey, carrying a much-needed Galactic Message for this world.

It is shared in this book you are reading, for starters.

No longer are the events of my life random or chaotic. No longer am I in the dark about my Truth. Finally, experiences that had plagued me or confused me in the webs of their mystery, some for decades, which I had been afraid of ever confessing to or sharing with anyone; suddenly all of these seemingly random events were connected by a common thread, and now made perfect sense to me.

The first time I spoke with Selene, I felt like I was being fully recognized for the very first time in my life, like an invisible veil that had been concealing the real me was finally lifted and exposed to the Light.

It was overwhelming, and incredibly freeing. I could finally see more clearly connections with others whom I am here to serve with as well. Specifically, one particular soul incarnate who currently inhabits a persona in the public eye.

This connection, which I was never able to understand, and which I had tried for nearly 20 years to deny and run away from, questioning my own sanity more times than I care to admit, was a very hard one for me to come to terms with on a good day, let alone trust or surrender to. Suddenly, after meeting Selene, I was able to understand it so much more deeply.

First of all, her absolute validation of the truth of this connection was huge for me; receiving confirmation of the reality and greater depth and purpose of my connection with this soul was what I sorely needed clarity on, and for which I am eternally grateful. It's easy to trust oneself when we are within the realms everyone else plays in, but when treading into unseen, cosmic territory, especially when these adventures and experiences involve public figures, it can be a bit of a difficult pill to swallow.

I knew in my blood and bones though, that Selene was the one who would be able to tell me once and for all if I was off my rocker or not when it came to this aspect of my life story. I knew she would tell me if I needed to have my head examined, even though deep inside, I already knew the truth, and knew I was playing with a full deck. Maybe even more so. But these just aren't the kinds of things one talks about in every day interactions with people. Believe me. I learned that lesson the hard way.

If nothing else, this woman is no nonsense and tells it like it is. She doesn't play around and has absolutely nothing to prove to anyone. She carries a Galactic Wisdom beyond any I have ever heard of or met, and she has the highest sense of spiritual integrity I have ever witnessed in anyone.

I knew it was balls out to even broach the subject with her. But I had to know. I mean, who else could I trust to give it to me straight and shoot from the hip? I knew she might tell me something I did not want to hear, yet I was at a point in my life, after having gone through some quite serious health issues, and a failing marriage, where I needed to only seek the truth, and to make absolutely certain I was moving about my life in full alignment with my highest self and purpose. I knew it was the only way I was going to be able to continue on in this life. That's how critical this time was for me. It was quite literally a choice of life or death.

I was terrified of what I might hear from someone I held in such high regard, and I prepared myself for the worst. If nothing else, I am courageous and even when the truth stings a little (or a lot), I would rather know and move from a place of knowing, than not knowing and moving about in ignorance and confusion like an idiot.

I knew without a doubt that Selene was the outside, objective eye that I needed in order to finally understand the connection I shared with this mysterious man. I knew I would either gain a deeper understanding of its purpose in my conscious awareness so I might be able to do something with it all, or put it to rest–forever. That is where I was at. I was so done playing (and running) if it was not going to serve me, and ultimately, my higher purpose.

All of her information confirmed my connection with this Soul in a much more grounded and profound way than I could have even imagined. It helped me begin to piece all of my mysterious experiences with him together in a very masterfully clarified way. I was able to make sense of the tracking I had naturally been doing for years leading up to this conversation with her. I was finally able to see and understand the connection multi-dimensionally from a place of Galactic Service, and less personally, which made all the difference for me.

The realization was actually what knocked me in the head and made me able to see clearly, for the first time, what my mission here on this planet truly was, and the importance of it becoming manifest in the physical realm, Now.

I finally began to see the truth, and not because someone was telling me what the truth was, but because the synchronization was finally present where someone was there who knew these same truths that I did, yet who also held the cosmic experience and galactic wisdom to explain it to me, as she had gone through the rigorous training and lived through much of the same hell of forgetting and then remembering as I had, and then some. She was helping others like me to begin embracing our own truths, to begin learning how to function in this physical world by empowering us to get moving on with what we actually came here to do, dropping all other nonsensical distractions and removing all attempts from our lives to cancel out us and our Missions.

It was time to stop hiding from myself and to step into my personal power, roll up my sleeves, and get the real work done. This can be said for all of us at this time, really.

Since meeting Selene, my life has shifted drastically, and I have finally begun to grab the torch carrying my name and signature, and run with it. I see very clearly now what I came here to do at this time. I own it, am leveling up, and making it manifest in my life with the gifts I have been given, in order to be of service to others and fulfill the promises of my soul. It is a continuous process.

I have never felt more empowered or sure of anything in my life. This book practically wrote itself, in a very short time. I began it (for a third time) in August 2013, and three weeks later, the first draft was birthed, editing and all. As soon as I got out of the way, my own fears and self-judgments cleared and let go completely.

Then new fears arose. After a few more years of riding the waves of what I have written about in this book might mean for me and all others, grappling with the responsibility of how it may affect those I care about the most, and those who have yet to realize their significant roles in this story, I am finally able to birth this book and share its message, for those with the ears to hear.

Because, I understand Now is most definitely The Time.

My wish is that what I share may serve as either confirmation of your own experiences that have as of yet remained unexplainable, or that it may help open up your minds to new ways of seeing the world around you, knowing that indeed, reality is not always just what we see in front of us. That sometimes, oftentimes, what we don't see, or aren't yet willing to see, is where Truth is hidden, patiently awaiting our discovery of it.

The journey within is the most powerful journey we will ever embark upon.

You are not reading this book by accident.

In loving honour of your own divine service, whatever that may be, simply being you, hearing and following honestly the unique call of your own soul. Thank you for being you, for being here, for shining your light. I salute you and honour you from the deepest cosmic well in my heart.

Thank you for being on this planet, Now.

Infinite Gratitude, Love, and Grace as We Journey Onward...

Sulannaya AM~RA

"The Seed of the Sun"

***Please Note: In this book, whenever I am speaking of my experiences using the term "they," which is indicative of the outdated thoughtform "us vs. them," it is for clarity's sake in order to give a more accurate account of where I was at while having the experience. This thoughtform clearly illustrates my past feelings and ways of viewing my reality, and is no longer how I experience my reality since awakening to my inner Truth. I now know and have experienced the Truth of my Oneness with All That Is, and thus view all of my experiences simply as Divine Mirrors of my Self.*

****Also please note that some names have been changed out of respect and in order to honour the privacy of those who may not wish to be associated with this transmission.*

CHAPTER 4

The Portal Home

I had some interesting habits as a child. I ate very little, unless it was made of chocolate, then my stomach was neverending it seemed. I slept from day one as a newborn all night long without any need for night feedings. At first my mother worried about me and would try to wake me, but quickly realized that she had struck gold, and counted her lucky stars, as her first baby, my sister, had been colicky and fussy from the get-go; quite the opposite experience.

To this day, my mother describes me as the absolute easiest baby and child she had ever seen.

I am left-handed and my natural tendency has always been to read and write from the right side of the page to the left. I read books from the end to the beginning as a child, and still read magazines this way.

I was into anything artistic–music, drawing, painting, dancing. I even made up my own language as a child. I was social and loved people but I was also very content with being alone. I even preferred it much of the time.

I always walked around with a pep in my step and always, *always* was on some sort of mission, no matter what it was.

My mother would try to dress me up like a doll, bless her heart. She would do my hair all pretty, put frilly dresses on me. Inevitably, I would walk by her shortly thereafter, my hair sticking up, pony tail to the side, half out, and my pretty little dress full of dirt or the bow to the side and untied, in the midst of some kind of focused creation or solo adventure.

I didn't fit into most molds very well or for very long. But I also didn't care if she tried to fit me into one, at least when I was very young. I didn't even seem to notice it then; I had more important things on the go. I just went on with my business and didn't fuss about any of it.

I also developed a habit of sitting in closets for hours at a time. I remember doing this, and I would have been less than five, since I wasn't in school yet. My mother tells me of the first time she noticed I was missing and how she ran around the house frantically looking for me, thinking I'd somehow escaped and was really missing. I don't think I came out when she called me either. I know now why I didn't.

Because I wasn't there.

I would go sit in the closet, and I remember feeling a familiar presence with me, always. It was comforting and I was not the least bit afraid of it. In fact, I enjoyed it and chose to be there rather than any other place. I had no concept of time, but my mother says I would stay in that closet for hours sometimes, "quietly playing."

I knew that I was not alone in that closet. And it was always the same closet, which happened to be in the "haunted room" as my sisters and I used to call it. We referred to it as such after we witnessed the dimmer light knob turn on its own one night, making the room brighter and dimmer as it turned one way, then the other, while we were having a little slumber sleep together. These kinds of things were common in this home, especially in the room with "the closet."

What I didn't know then but is so clear to me now was that in fact, when I would go into that closet, I was actually entering a portal in which I was able to have access to the ships and my sky family aboard it whenever I was inside.

I loved that closet so much, and I was such a creative child that, when I went through a phase with my sisters of making up bedtime games, most of which they embraced, when I created a game that required we sleep all night in the closet, well, that one didn't seem to fly with them so well. We never really did it. All the other games, we played. I find that interesting.

They had no problems playing hamburger or hotdog, where we would pile on top of each other and pretend we were the top and bottom buns and the meaty middle of the burger or dog, and chat and giggle together while we did so; they had no problem pretending to be cigarettes in a cigarette package. The bed was the package, the blanket was the foil wrap, and we would lie pin straight, like three cigarettes, and talk and laugh together, without moving a muscle other than our faces.

Yet the closet sleeping game, which I believe I named "Grimace" after the MacDonald's character, didn't get picked up as a favourite, and in fact, never really happened. I suppose I can't exactly blame them. I think we might have tried it for a few minutes once, and quickly decided it was not going to work.

I thought then that maybe it was just too squishy (which of course, it undoubtedly was), but now wonder if there may have been more to their reluctance. They wouldn't even sleep *next* to the closet with me if I recall correctly.

Why would I have wanted to sleep there in the first place? Perhaps because it was a special place for me, and one where I felt at home, and perhaps I was attempting to share this experience with my sisters. Who knows?

We quickly forgot about "Grimace" and were content with Cigarette and Hot Dogs and Hamburgers, and always managed to have fun no matter what we were doing or where we were together.

God Bless silly sisterly love. It helped me stay grounded in this reality, and I am so grateful for all of our fun and ridiculous adventures together.

CHAPTER 5

Aboard Ship

This is an excerpt from one of my regression sessions in 2013, on why I spent so much time in my closet as a young child:

I am waiting in the closet. This feels familiar to me. A doorway opens in one of the walls inside.

It is a portal.

I see the legs of a very large parental figure standing in the portal entrance. This being reaches down and takes my hand. The feeling is that of a Mother/Father, though not an Earth human.

This is a Venusian being, very tall, with blue skin.

I love going with these beings, and look forward to it. It is something I have done many times before.

They take me onto the ship for my classes, and to visit with my family there. This ship feels like home to me. I am happy and jovial and excited when I get to be here.

Inside the ship, which is very large, I see a control board to my left. There is a being standing there doing something with this control board filled with purple and green lights. It seems like no big deal to any of the others that I am there. This tells me that my feeling of having been here many times before is true.

I am here to spend time with my family by connecting physically with them. I am also here to take my classes. I have a school that I attend here regularly.

As soon as I enter the ship, I am taken to a room. In this room, there is a scanner which has a green laser-type light that scans me thoroughly, and resets my frequencies if anything is off as a natural result of my Earthly experiences. These scans clear any energetic debris, and can also cause instantaneous healing of the physical Earth body if that is in the Highest Interest of the one who is being scanned. Once scanned and reset, you are able to visit or study aboard ship freely with the others.

There are many from my sky family here. Many other children, all types and races of beings. The Teacher teaches the classes. This is what we call this being: "The Teacher".

There is a blackboard beside The Teacher, which is a screen, floating in mid-air. When The Teacher points at it, lasers appear on the board, displaying the symbolic language of the lesson.

We are learning galactic mathematics; specifically, a class pertaining to the mathematics of the inner workings of the biological Earth body. It is very much like a science class with all the equations, shapes, numbers, grids, and designs.

These are not like any numbers I recognize from Earth. They are different. These numbers and lessons being taught by The Teacher are connected specifically with the mathematics of the Earth Body. We all learn these lessons, as well as the lessons pertaining to ET bodies and how they function. We all learn one another's processes, and this unites us.

We are taught that ET bodies are different than Earth human bodies. They look similar in ways, such as we have many of the same body parts from an outer perspective, but there are differences in the equations of the cellular and DNA makeup of our bodies, which makes their vessels sometimes vastly different than ours from an inner perspective.

The Earth body experiences certain processes differently than the ET body. The ET body processes are often amplified frequency-wise "to the power of__," and we are learning about this from The Teacher. ET bodies are attuned to higher frequencies than human bodies.

This day, we are learning about the mathematical equations that the frequencies of the bodies undergo during the hybridization process.

For instance, there is a faster spin frequency for the ETs who take part in this equation, whereas an Earth body undergoing a physical hybridization experiment experience will spin differently. They will observe a slower frequency than the ETs.

This is simply because the ETs hold a steadier, more consistent light quotient, and so, in general, their spin is consequently quicker than a human's.

The Teacher is teaching me how to sustain my Earth body at a frequency that is able to successfully house and hold, to contribute physically to, the creation of these hybrid beings from and within my Earth body. The Teacher is teaching me specifically what frequency I need to maintain to remain healthy in my Earth body during hybridization.

One of the things I am told will assist this is to be out in nature a lot, to commune with the fairies and other elementals. I also am being instructed to continue coming into the closet, and attending these classes. Stand in my truth, no matter what. Be diligent about recognizing in-

terference from the outside trying to derail or sidetrack or distract me away from my mission.

In doing these things, I will be able to maintain this specific mathematical frequency within my Earth body and keep myself healthy and on track with my mission here. I will be attuned to the highest frequency possible in the human body, and so be able to house these energies, these beings.

ETs were designed for this, and there is a biology class designed specifically for them as well, teaching us all how their biological mathematical equation operates.

The ET kids in this class with me are from all kinds of races. I see little mantis kids, some white greys, little blue beings, and hybrid mixtures of different races.

Many of the hybrids have large blue humanoid eyes, but they are more almond shaped. Some have eyelashes even. Some have heads of hair. Their hair is slightly different than human hair and their heads are definitely larger. Some enjoy wearing clothing one might find on Earth. Some wear more galactic style clothing.

I feel very connected to one of the hybrid girls there in class with me. She is cute. She has a bow in her blonde, wavy hair. She is wearing a denim dress with doily-type ruffles along the edges at the bottom. She sits behind me. I feel the closest with her there. I feel she is one of my Sisters. My Earth mother's daughter. Perhaps even my twin, Sulannaya. My mother is not consciously aware of her, but she also sees her on the ships.

The other students and I are referred to as The World Bridgers for our respective planets. We are all there in support of Earth; just some of them do their work from the ships, while others of us do it on the Earth plane. We are all working together on this project though.

I am one of the few human ambassadors to learn in this particular class and play this role. My parents on the ship say to me:

'You are doing good work. We know that it is not easy and we appreciate the great sacrifices you have made. You are doing good work.'

They tell me to remain open, and that the more I can do this and the more I trust myself, the more will be revealed to me, thus the more I will be able to help the planet. They remind me that it's not about "me", and that I know this. That I am here to be of service, and so I must continue to trust my inner knowingness.

'And...You are doing good work.'

I share genetics with both the Mother and Father on this ship. She is from Venus. She has warm blue skin into which I love to nestle. She has no hair and beautiful eyes, almost cat-like and deep purple-black, but so very warm. I am able to see and feel her feelings through her eyes. It's amazing.

I hear her communications with me as English, but what it really is, are high frequency tones that I sense behind the translation that she sends to me telepathically, so I hear both the tone and the translation simultaneously. She sings to me this way as well, and I love this. The tones and frequencies go into me, my body, my cellular structure, and they remain with me when I am back on Earth.

She is also connected to and working with the Pleiadians as well as the benevolent greys who are heading some of the most critical hybridization programs. She herself is part grey, a small fraction, though this is why her eyes are so dark and large. She is a hybrid. A Venusian with the majority of her DNA from the Pleiadians as well as some from the

Greys. Because of this genetic mixture, her head is almost proportionate to her body, and not overly-large like many greys can be.

Her energy is huge, gentle and graceful.

Her hybrid race's purpose is also as World Bridger. It is her job on the ship to be an Embracer. To be a warm, nurturing presence to the hybrid children. She is Love embodied. There are others like her who play this same role for the ones who need it. She also helps the human children who come aboard ship and may be frightened or need extra TLC.

Other beings like her also help seed the hybrid babies, but they all have a choice in this matter, it is not forced upon them. Many do choose to though, as an act of Divine Service. She and I have a strong bond. With our DNA connection, we share an added frequency together. It is unspoken though—she gives the same amount of care and Love to every child she comes into contact with, as she does me.

The Father is "all business," though kind and gentle. He checks in with me when I come visit, he hugs me, but also floats around from meeting to meeting, always busy. He is very tall, lanky. He structures the connections, he is an Architect of Synchronicity, creating and bringing together the Ones who are set up to meet. He helps navigate these timelines, these moments of meeting or experiencing which are Triggers of Activation for the Ones out on missions elsewhere. He is a created being and lives aboard ship.

After my classes finish, I am given free time to explore, play and connect with others aboard the ship. I adore this time and often bounce around feeling very social. Before leaving to go back to Earth, I am sent back into the scanning room, where my field is strengthened and given upgrades before returning to the third-dimensional density. I LOVE this part! I get re-infused with a strong dose of the frequency—the equation—*I need to uphold on Earth to successfully complete my mission there. This is why so many visits occur, as clearing and resetting are essential, and the mission is too important to risk, so we are constantly having our protective shields checked or upgraded if need be.*

Earth experiences naturally lower our frequency, usually vastly, and at the very least marginally, from who we truly are, which is Infinite and Eternal Light and Unconditional Love. This is part of the package deal when saying "yes" to an Earthly incarnation. Believe it or not, it is part of what excites us before we come down and forget everything and wonder how the hell we ended up here in the first place! We require some level of protection when coming here, even though the Law of Free Will is also a mandatory part of the play.

As starseed, we do get some protection, though most of us will return to our galactic quarters with battle scars and wounds quite regularly. The shields are in place to keep us from being destroyed altogether, though unfortunately, they can't save all of us and sadly, many are lost in the crossfires of the downward spiral of the Earth human experience.

In the end, part of the purpose of the human experience on Earth is for us to learn to master our emotions and frequency. Much of this is left up to us to work through on the Earth plane, one of the hardest schools there is. The shields provided for us through our starseed DNA are more like damage control than anything. Protective gear. Proverbial helmets. But a helmet isn't going to do much good when we're shot through the heart with a rifle. A bullet-proof vest is useless when we are targeted between the eyes.

Without proper discernment in place, we may get knocked down through our places of vulnerability, usually our hearts, and if so, we just may bleed to death.

Or perhaps we find the courage and the strength, the discernment and the wisdom, to rise above it all and say, 'You couldn't have me then, and you sure as hell can't have me now!' Dust ourselves off and walk with our heads and hearts held high, knowing without a doubt that ***WE ARE THE PROTECTION*** *and that* ***Our Presence most definitely Has Power****.*

CHAPTER 6

Familial Roots in High Strangeness and Synchronicity

Synchronicity is not new to me.

I grew up with my mother saying things like "There's no such thing as a coincidence, Samantha," and "Everything happens for a reason." She didn't have the terminology to use the word synchronicity but essentially, this is what she was ingraining into my consciousness without even knowing what she was doing.

Unfortunately, when it came down to it, my mother didn't always live her own life by these truisms. If she had, things would have been very different for her, and her children. But she did the best she could with what she knew, and I love her for it and am so grateful for these gems of wisdom she passed on to me.

Our family was well versed in the mystical experience of synchronicity. There are too many to mention here, but being born in Newfoundland to a highly courageous and strong mother, my Nan, Sadie Wareham, and an equally tough yet magical, musical elven-type mischievous sailor for a father, my grandfather, Harold Williams, my mother was bound to carry some deep magic and wisdom in her blood.

Family was always numero uno for my grandparents. They delighted in their grandchildren with such pride and adoration. I would visit my grandparents often as a young adult, several times a week, and I would sit on the couch beside my Gramps with my arm around him, as my Nan sat in her La-Z-Boy, usually knitting a Christmas sweater with her beautiful hands, crippled more and more by arthritis as time went on. She would knit sweaters for each of her 15 grandchildren, then great-grandchildren, every year for Christmas.

Sitting beside me, my Grampa would laugh as he reminisced about some sort of mischievous or slapstick adventure from his youth as my Nan "tisked" from behind her knitting needles. I could have listened to my grandparents' stories for hours on end and not get tired of them. I miss them both so much to this day, but I know they are watching over me and even cheering me on as I step out now.

A true Sagittarian, Harold had a pure heart made of gold and a wildly adventurous spirit. He was one of the most courageous, toughest, sweetest people I'd ever known. He worked on the Atlantic Ocean in some of the scariest conditions, and his job was the most terrifying of all in a storm, of which he encountered many in his time out on the seas. He was the keeper of the "crow's nest," the most vulnerable place to be when winds and rains were high, the ocean wild, and lightning striking the waters all around.

I find it highly synchronistic that he passed from this world on May 21st, 1999, and his celebration of life fell three days later on my birthday, May 24th. It was my 24th birthday too (24 on the 24th), which apparently is supposed to be one of the most significant birthdays in one's lifetime.

I had just moved to Vancouver the previous September of 1998, and my main, and probably only regret I had when moving was that I would miss my grandparents' final years here on the planet. I was very close with both of them. So, I would have rather been nowhere else on my birthday that year than sitting in the chapel, listening to hilarious stories about him, belting out "I's the Biy," one of his favourite sailor songs, which held very fond memories for me and our time together. We cried and laughed and celebrated his zest for life and his beautiful child-like innocence, his silly sense of humour, and his penchant for creating and delighting in mischief wherever he went.

It was a magical birthday for me, even though I already missed him like crazy.

My grandmother, Sadie, was a force to be reckoned with. A mother of five girls, she raised them mostly on her own while my grandfather was at sea. She was a substitute school teacher who lied about her age when she was just a young girl so that she could go to school and become a teacher by the age of 16. She wanted to make something of her life. She didn't give two figs what anyone else thought of it. Sadie played life by her own rules, *always*.

We all miss Nan. She was the perfect mixture of a strict and hardnosed disciplinarian with her daughters while they were growing up, as well as every one of her children's and grandchildren's soft place to fall whenever we needed her. She was a very strong woman, the backbone of our family, and took care of my mother until the day she died at the age of 91 on December 16th, 2004.

Synchronistically again, this happened to be my brother Josh's birthday, and also synchronistically, he just so happened to have flown into St. Catharines from Vancouver that very day, mere hours before her passing. No one knew she was about to go, until that day, so his trip was purely aligned by the powers of the universe.

She had waited to take her final breath until my uncles ran around town to find Josh, and proceeded to whisk him to her bedside as she was about to go. The timing could not have been more aligned.

That same year, one month before my son Noah was born, on September 1, 2004, my mother had moved out to Vancouver to help me out. It was a huge leap of faith for her, and one that shook her entire foundation to the core. But she did it for me and for my then two-month-old son. Probably the most incredible thing my mother has ever done for me, knowing I was a new single mother.

Speaking of synchronicity, Noah decided to be born just at the moment my mother had arrived from St. Catharines for what at the time was just a visit. She had flown out close to my due date to stay for a few weeks and be there for his birth. He was her first grandchild. It was all highly magical that less than one hour after my sister had brought me home to my tiny studio apartment, the night my mother flew in and I'd visited with her, that my waters broke.

But back to my grandmother, Sadie. I believe she waited to pass until after my mother moved away. In a way, she knew it would be too hard for my mother to witness her passing, and she was right. To this day, my mother knows she did this on purpose to help my mother deal with her death easier, if that's even possible.

My mother was the most amazing presence for my grandfather when he was passing in 1999 though. She would stay up all night and sing to him, and whisper to him after he slipped into a coma, making sure he knew that it was okay for him to let go. If that was what he needed, then he should do it. She held him through those final days, and was the most stoic and empowered I had ever seen her. She loved her daddy so much, and idolized him. He made her laugh like nobody else on the planet, and she was his little girl. I was so proud of her for finding the power inside her to be so selfless at one of the hardest times in her life. She was truly incredible.

My mom wrote a poem about him which she read at his funeral that shocked everyone in the family. Her sisters and their significant others were always so used to my mother being the "screw up" and the black sheep in the family, according to her anyway. She was always the emotional one who was usually on the verge of a breakdown, too fragile to deal with reality. This was how they saw her, she thought.

Yet there she was, my mom, standing in front of everyone in the chapel, reciting one of the most beautifully well-written, humourous, heartfelt, and brilliantly recited pieces of poetry they'd ever heard. It was magical.

But my grandmother's passing was another story, and though my mother was saddened that she was not there when it happened, she was also grateful that she hadn't needed to witness it. My grandmother had taken my mother under her protective wing her whole life, like a baby bird, perhaps almost to the point of dysfunction, but it was all done out of love. My mother always knew she could go to her in a pinch, and my Nan always pulled through for her. But it really was one of the sweetest relationships for me to witness growing up, and my mother thought the absolute world of her mama bear, as we all did.

My brother became my mother's representative at my Nan's passing. As soon as he arrived, followed by my aunt and cousin, my grandmother Sadie took her last breath. Josh said it was very powerful, as if in the moment right before she drew her last breath, she saw something magical before her. Her eyes widened as she smiled, bolted upright off the bed to sitting, and then let go. Of course, she went out with a bang. I would have expected nothing less. She was a powerful lady.

My aunts waited for my mother to arrive back home to say their final goodbyes. I always wished I could have been there too. My Nan and I had a very strong connection and it pained me to have to miss her funeral, but it was simply not in the cards.

My mother was the seed of these two incredible and adorable little elven humans. Though they were perfectly flawed like the rest of us, they were also two of the most beautiful, giving human beings that ever walked this Earth. Two of the softest, purest hearts, incredibly witty, with a pair of strange and spectacular senses of humour. They only saw the very best in the ones they loved, and they loved us all equally. There were a lot of us too, after having raised five daughters themselves, all of whom grew to have families of their own.

My grandparents had enough love for us all, all of the time. I miss them both so very much, and thank them for passing on their giant hearts and their natural way with magic.

*

There were more mystical, otherworldly displays of synchronicity in our family earlier on as well. Some of the most notable were through my mother's eldest sister, Shirley's, first husband, Don Rose.

I never had the gift of meeting my Uncle Don, sadly. Though I am sure we would have been close. He passed from leukemia at the age of 38 on July 11th, 1972, synchronistically again, within 24 hours of my sister being born on July 10th in the same hospital.

Uncle Don and my mother were particularly close. He was quite a few years older than her but was the big brother she always wanted. His death was very hard on the whole family, particularly his wife and three children, and also for my mother who thought the absolute world of him.

Thankfully, my mother was very close by as he passed on. When she heard the news, she was obviously devastated. But he'd lived long enough to be told about my older sister Shelby's birth, which everyone knew he was thrilled about.

Uncle Don talked about reincarnation, and the idea that no one ever really "dies"; that we are always born again. He talked of karma and whole-heartedly believed in fairies and elves, "little people" as he called them, and he knew without a doubt that there were worlds that existed beyond this realm.

Of course, my mother soaked up anything he said to her regarding these matters, as I am sure she and he were cut from the same cloth. We all were, and so it was no coincidence he made his way to our family. It was *synchronicity.*

Uncle Don's eldest daughter Lori, my cousin, had been devastated by the loss of her father as a teen, and had never fully recovered from it emotionally. From then on, her life was a series of challenges and devastating events, sprinkled with the joys of having two beautiful children of her own, though ultimately she endured much heartache in this role of hers as well, but would have done anything for her children, she loved them unconditionally and totally.

Shortly after Lori turned thirty-eight, she ended up in the emergency one day, after a bout with a blister she'd endured on her foot from a pair of new sandals. She didn't think much of it, but when her foot swelled and became impossible to put her weight on, and the blister began growing exponentially, filling with fluids that smelled rancid, she was diagnosed with the flesh-eating disease.

This was one of the most devastating and terrifying things I had ever witnessed in my life. Lori almost died many times in the first several weeks she was in the hospital, and we all thought of how eerie it was that she was 38, just like Don had been when he died.

Lori endured about 14 major surgeries in a matter of a couple of months, always with the risk that she might not make it through. It was pins and needles daily, waiting for news of how she was doing, and if the disease was spreading.

The doctors did not amputate her foot and lower leg, though they almost needed to a few times. Lori was their first patient with this insane disease, and the doctors used her as a guinea pig for skin grafting, cutting out the disease as it continued to progressively move through her foot and lower leg, instead of amputating. She was grateful for this at the time, as she had always been an astonishingly attractive woman. Nearly six feet tall, long and lean, with beautiful blonde hair and mystical green eyes. She was a unique being, model-esque, and the thought of losing her leg was more than she could imagine or bear at the time.

But the skin grafting, the major scarring and the fact that she had to walk with a cane afterwards ended up being such a source of emotional pain for her in the years to come. She spent about three or four months in the hospital, then many years in recovery and rehabilitation, both for her physical injuries, and sadly, also for drug abuse. She had developed an addiction from the constant self-administering morphine pump attached to her hospital bed, which she'd had 24-hour access to for months, not to mention the prescriptions she continued to take once finally released just to manage the pain.

This experience changed Lori forever, and though she technically survived the whole ordeal, she never fully got her life back. She lived with her mother most of the time, and in the summer of 2007, she herself passed suddenly after choking on a piece of food. Her teenage daughter was the one who found her. It was all extremely tragic and sad though finally on the bright side, she was set free from her suffering, and was able to fly with the angels again, including her beloved father and our grandparents, I am sure.

When Lori was in the hospital, I would often make trips to Toronto to visit her. One day, I went in and she told me that her father, my Uncle Don, had just been to visit. She said he was "popping" around her room. He had been dead for about 25 years by then. Lori was laughing and seemed so happy to have seen her daddy, and then she looked at me with giddy eyes like a child and said, "He was only *this* tall" as she gestured about a foot high with her hands. She laughed, saying that he kept bouncing and popping around her bed and making her laugh.

When I got back home I told my mother about it. This was when she shared with me that my uncle had believed in elves, leprechauns and fairies. We were certain that he was playing in those realms and having a blast, while checking in on his daughter and doing something outrageous to make her laugh, knowing it would do the trick and help lift her spirits. Lori had a wry and strange sense of humour, so this was the perfect way to help lighten her up.

I knew without a doubt when she was telling me about her father that what she had seen was real. I was so glad when my mother confirmed this for me.

But backtracking again to when my Uncle Don was in the hospital nearing the end of his own life...

He used to listen to the radio in his hospital room, and always called my aunt at 11:00 am each day. This was his routine.

He passed at 11:00 am on July 11th. My family always noted the 11-11, even all those years ago when no one spoke of such metaphysical things, at least not openly. Yet they always knew it somehow held a spiritual significance and was definitely not coincidental that he'd chosen those numbers for his grand exit. In fact, my aunt Shirley, his wife, and my mother were certain he'd done this deliberately.

Remember, this was in 1972.

Sometime shortly after his death, my aunt heard the phone ring late one night. She found this an odd time for anyone to be calling her but answered it anyway. When she picked up the receiver, she heard a radio playing in the background, which sounded exactly like the one my uncle would listen to in his hospital room. There was no voice on the other end, only the radio and silence. She looked over at the clock and it was exactly 11 o'clock.

My mother's other sister, Pat, and her husband, my uncle Brent, also had some high strangeness occur after my uncle Don's death when they were driving together one day. The truck ahead of them was full of dirt, and etched in to the thick dirt, clear as day, both my aunt and uncle noticed something that shook them. Written through the dust and dirt was this message:

"Don Rose was here:

11-11"

There was no denying that this was a demonstration of some sort, and that it had come from the Otherware specifically for them.

My aunt Pat also had a separate encounter while driving with some friends one evening where they all witnessed a UFO in plain sight, up close and personal. It appeared and landed just ahead of them on the road. They all froze, knowing that what they were seeing could not be explained away with logic or rationale of any kind. My aunt apparently remembers nothing else of the incident. My guess is that they experienced a bout of missing time.

My uncle Brent, a successful criminal lawyer, was always very logical, opinionated, and dare I say a touch judgmental, and he made no bones about sharing his thoughts on any subject. Anything pertaining to ETs, UFOs, I am certain would have been beyond his ability to entertain or tolerate as acceptable subject matter for discussion. I'm also quite certain he would have scoffed at or made condescending jokes about almost anything paranormal, especially "aliens." He would have had a logical explanation for debunking anything of that sort.

And yet my aunt's sighting happened, and she and her friends were absolutely certain at what they'd seen. I never heard from her directly about this experience though, so I'm pretty sure she doesn't speak of it very often, if at all. It was my mother who shared this story with me, and only in recent years, since I started writing this book. I couldn't believe there was such a story in our family and no one seemed to ever talk about it.

I think they all agreed to try to forget about what had happened, especially because it appeared to be random and went into the category of truly unexplainable high strangeness.

Here, two of the most unlikely people in our family to have such profound paranormal experiences, yet after these incidences, they must have had to at least quietly ponder the validity of these types of happenings.

Finally, one that perhaps foreshadows my own experiences with high strangeness and messages from the Otherware, concerns my mother and my Earth father.

My mother was a cute, twenty-something, at work as a secretary in a car dealership when one day she glanced at the daily newspaper. In it was a picture of a man she had never seen nor met before. Immediately upon seeing his picture she heard in her head a voice that spoke the words "husband and father." She did not understand what this meant, but always remembered it, as it had been such a strange occurrence the likes of which she had never experienced before that day.

Months later, in walks that same man through the doors of her work place. She was stunned as she remembered this man from the newspaper. And low and behold, before he left, he asked her out on a date!

They dated for a brief few months before deciding to get married. My mother still to this day does not understand why or how it happened, as she always told us that three weeks after they were married, she was crying every day and just wanted to "go home" and live with her mother again. But said she would have felt like a failure if she did this, so she stuck it out for 10 years, and was miserable the entire time. The only thing that kept her going was having her three children. After 10 years though, she had had enough and the rest is history.

I have never seen two people so unlikely to ever have been in love, and don't think this was ever the case. My feeling is that somehow, through what I now believe to be extraterrestrial forces and timing, this event was created by the "Voice of Knowingness". The message she heard and so being curious enough to actually go so far as to marry him, when she was not really in love with him, allowed for an opening of the right genetic match and Earthly experience to be made for this particular experiment, birthing her three children, one of which of course, was me.

I will only talk about my own life and birth in this book, as my sister and brother's lives are for them to talk about, and for them to perceive their own Truth from. Needless to say though, I was not surprised that while writing this book, my mother shared this high strangeness experience she'd had with me.

I most definitely chose my mother well, and I give thanks for this. I am certain that she is intimately connected with at least some of the same genetic experiments as I am, and this is confirmed by a ship experience I would go on to have during the writing of this book, before she shared this information with me.

Let it be known, as Selene says, that "Synchronization is confirmation," and I have learned this first hand through the myriad experiences that I came to have.

CHAPTER 7

The Double Life Revealing

I instinctively knew as a child not to talk about certain things. I knew things that I never dared to speak aloud. I was so young, I may not have had the earthly language for it anyway, but regardless, I had an inner knowing that most of the world was not quite as it seemed, and not yet ready for what I knew.

I say this, but also let me make it clear that I am far from being the only one. When we come here with specific Missions of Service, this may sound grandiose or egotistical in some way, but I assure anyone wearing rose-coloured glasses, oftentimes knowing the deeper inner truths around you sucks, big time. It is hard to digest, and it causes such inner pain, turmoil, and suffering that there are no words for it, and no doctor can help you with this. More often than not, it can feel like a living hell, until you get a grip and learn to move the energies and understand that it isn't personal, most of the time.

Some of us go our whole lives never really figuring this part out, staying caught in that constant state of chaos, confusion and suffering that may or may not even be our own. Many of us never even come close to completing anything we came here to do, though that incessant nagging that we are missing something never ceases. Not exactly glamorous. In fact, it's tragic.

So, I share what I share with great humility and love. It has been a new concept for me to speak my full truth, without shrinking down or making excuses for myself, or hiding what I know, deep down inside. I have spent most of my life hiding: in closets, in rooms, in houses, and metaphorically hiding my true identity not only from everyone around me, but even from myself.

I had all but forgotten who I was.

Part of my journey here was to live through much inner turmoil and pain in order to get back to the core of who I am. Sometimes I thought I would never make it here, to this moment in time and space, alive. There was a time when I even desperately wanted out. I didn't think I could do it anymore. Life. I didn't *want* to do it anymore. It was too painful to keep playing at this game of charades. I was tired.

Most of the time, I thought I would never remember what this nagging feeling was deep within my heart and soul that told me, like a broken record, that there was more to me, and more to life, than I understood or could see in front of me with my third dimensional eyes.

I would often hear the thought roll through my mind, "*There has GOT to be more than this!*"

I knew this truth deep inside, although knowing it didn't make it any easier to navigate through the messy haze that had grown within and around me. In fact, knowing this made it so much harder in a way, because I felt like I was always seeking alone, not knowing where to go, who to turn to, or whom I could possibly call on for support that would have some clue about the answers I was so desperately searching for.

I had experiences as a child that on one hand, especially in the moment, were very simple for me to understand, as they ignited such a sense of truth within my heart and soul that I knew there was nothing wrong about it. And yet, I also knew never to tell anyone about these experiences.

I never told anyone about my "friends" in the garden or the closet, and I never told anyone about the time John Lennon died and I was "transported" to a room where his close family and friends were mourning him. I was to experience it, and then file it away for a later time, when synchronicity and divine timing (often one in the same) would ignite the fires in me to remember, and record this happening, along with many others that would come to follow.

But more on that a little later...

CHAPTER 8

The First Activation: A Stranger in the Room

I never wanted to go to doctors and never wanted to take medications of any kind. I wasn't afraid of doctors. I simply was not fooled by any of it, and knew early on that they didn't possess the entire macrocosmic concept of what health truly is.

I understood from the beginning that our bodies have the ability to heal themselves.

I had one doctor I actually liked, and that was Dr. Samson, my pediatrician. He was the only one I even remotely trusted, but would have rather not had to go see anyone, ever if I could help it. If I'd had to pick one though, it would have been him.

A South African man, gentle of spirit, witty and fun with a good sense of humour, plus he had cool paintings in his office; I liked him. He was also the one who had recognized the congenital hip displacement I'd endured as a result of being a frank breech birth, which was a blessing since, had he not noticed it, I would have ended up with far greater physical issues involving my hip joints, and may have even ended up confined to a wheelchair.

When I was laid out with one chest or throat infection after another, I remember my mother taking me to see a "specialist". They told me that I would need my tonsils and adenoids taken out. Not one specialist asked me or my mother how much secondhand smoke I was exposed to on a daily basis. That might have given them a clue as to why I was constantly sick with throat and lung infections. Not one broached this subject.

I wasn't having any of it! My immediate response regarding the surgery was "No way!" I was eight at the time I began having these appointments and when they booked the procedure.

I was livid that my mother was making me go through with this, and not listening to me; my deep inner knowing told me that I was *not* to have this surgery; that, in fact, it was going to make things worse with my health. No one listened to me.

I had to go through with the doctor visits beforehand, and met the surgeon who would perform the surgery in June of 1984, shortly after my ninth birthday.

I didn't like him. I told my mother repeatedly that I didn't trust him and to not allow him to do the surgery on me.

I think everyone thought I was just afraid. But I knew it was not going to go well. I had a foreboding, which I would later learn to recognize and listen to as intuition and inner guidance. But I was still only a child, with no one consciously teaching me these things, or honouring these gifts of mine.

Now that I am an adult, it is much easier for me to have total dominion over my experiences when it comes to my health and anything else in my life. But a nine-year-old child isn't always granted that sort of sovereignty, unfortunately.

In the end, I'm certain my mother was only doing what she thought was best for me too, so I hold no blame. In hindsight, I was obviously meant to have the experience awaiting me, regardless of my own hesitations and strong feelings against it. Because of this experience, I was able to learn the lesson of how deep my inner knowing runs. It turned out to be a gift, really, and so because of that, I actually thank my mother for not listening to me.

I went into the surgery, after the same surgeon had performed two other tonsillectomies that morning, and had one more after mine. All the others had gone smoothly. Then there was me.

I remember noticing the intensity of the anesthetic entering my bloodstream; it was unlike anything I had ever experienced before. That rush that started at the tips of my toes and vibrated up my body until the buzzing reached my head, and suddenly I was gone, floating away, somewhere else.

I awoke in the recovery room in an immense amount of pain. I had a throbbing in my mid-back that made it impossible for me to lie still comfortably. I was writhing around, like a caged wild animal ready to tear everything in front of me apart. I wasn't complaining about my throat at all. It was my back. The agony of it was unbearable, and I tried to tell the nurses and get their attention, it was so incredibly painful. But I couldn't talk or yell, and I sure as hell couldn't rest.

My conscious recollection of the event is that the nurses pretty much ignored me. At least if they did make an attempt to help me, it was feeble at best from my perspective. No one seemed to question why my back was so sore, which I now find to be irresponsible on their part. At the time though, I wondered if, and even assumed that, I must be being difficult and overly dramatic, so I became embarrassed.

I tried to settle myself down, even though I was incapable of lying still, writhing around and ready to bust out of there if I only could. If there hadn't been bars around my bed holding me in there...who knows what I would have done.

I was finally brought back to my room. No one seemed concerned at all about me, and so I tried to let it go, assuming this must be how it feels after they cut a part of your body out. I know, dramatic, but it's true. And yes, it was very dramatic for me, honestly, having had no one take me seriously and listen to me. What was worse was realizing later that these doctors actually lied to me that I would never get sore throats again. After the surgery, my sore throats would only get worse, and my immune system, increasingly weaker.

So, I was back in my room, not there for too long I don't think. My mother was out in the hallway talking to a nurse. I had been telling her I didn't feel well, and I think she must have been telling the nurse to see if they could do anything to help me, as I still was in pain with my back and could not relax or rest, like I was being told I needed to do.

All of a sudden, I could feel it coming, and I couldn't control it.

I tried to call out to my mother, but my throat was sore and raw, and I could only manage a loud whisper out of my desperation, knowing what was coming and not being able to do anything about it myself.

I called and called as best I could between the violent waves of nausea that were taking me over, when finally, my mother rushed back in and saw from my face that I was about to vomit. She grabbed the closest thing she could, which was a steel bedpan, and I began to vomit huge quantities of thick, black sludge, into it, non-stop.

That filled up quickly, and next was the trashcan next to the bed. My memory is shaky from having been riddled with drugs, but I do remember more things flying at me to project into. I believe one feeble device thrust at me was a brown paper bag, into which, I am certain, I vomited.

It just kept coming, and suddenly, there was a state of emergency in my room. I was hemorrhaging, and it was serious.

The room filled with nurses and other staff, as well as the surgeon himself. They had to throw legal forms at my mother to sign to get her to consent to an emergency anesthetic and a second surgery to pump my stomach and stop the bleeding, and the fine print, no doubt, would have likely included them not being liable if, heaven forbid, I didn't make it.

The room was spinning. I knew it was possible that I could die right now. I could feel death in the room, and I was so angry with everyone for having ignored my plea to forego this stupid surgery altogether in the first place. It was all kind of surreal by this point.

Yet here we were, and there I was. I remember as they were wheeling me out of the room to emergency, I was gripping my teddy bear, and through clenched teeth saying to my mother "See, I *told* you it was *his* fault!" I was gesturing to the surgeon, who no longer had to hazard a guess as to how I felt about him.

Suddenly, out of the corner of my eye, to my right, I saw what appeared to be a man dressed in black robes. I do not remember what this cloaked figure really looked like, but I had assumed it was a man and at the time, I actually assumed he was a priest who had run into the room to read me my last rights. It was that dire in the moment; no one knew what to expect. This was not a usual circumstance after a tonsillectomy; at least I really hope that it wasn't.

I saw this figure standing right beside me, speaking something very quickly. These words felt to be prayers or incantations of some kind though he was speaking so fast I couldn't understand him. I had just finished my first year in a Roman Catholic school, so was now familiar with prayers and priests, but this man was different somehow.

He spoke very quickly, and stood over me making very fast movements with his arms. I can't remember what they were, but remember a few movements over top of me and some kind of chanting or praying. I was whisked out and wheeled down the hall to the emergency room and given another quick anesthetic. I was still coming down off the last dose, and here I was, receiving another.

The tingling in my feet, buzzing up my body happened much more rapidly this time, and I was out. Thank Heavens, I drifted off again.

When I woke up for the second time—I am thankful every day that I had the chance to wake up again at all—I felt so much better. No more back pain. No one knew how it had occurred, but everyone was relieved that I was all right. I'd had to receive emergency blood transfusions, but other than that, all seemed okay.

No one seemed to know who the stranger in the room had been, because no one else saw him but me.

I am quite certain now this was an ET sent in at a critical moment of life or death to see to it that I remain here. A hooded cloaked figure that only I could see.

With what I know now about myself and the way these ET experiments work, I have no doubt in my mind that whoever the cloaked figure was, he was there to assist.

And thus began my interesting relationship with blood, increased high strangeness, the power of resurrection, and some serious activations through ET intervention that would begin to take place in the months, years, and decades that followed.

CHAPTER 9

Sacred Blood Initiation Part I: Learning to Cope

I was in fourth grade now, and all seemed to be going fine. I was still an ordinary kid as far as I or anyone else knew.

Though I began to notice an increase in my ability to pick up on the energies of others, especially the emotions of people in my home. I noticed that every time my parents would have a fight, I would have entertained a thought within 24-48 hours prior about how peaceful things had been and I was always so grateful for that.

These thoughts would come not when my parents were sniping at each other or visibly at odds, but when we all seemed to be having fun together, when we were all laughing and being silly together, everyone seemingly relaxed and at ease.

I would have understood if I had been consciously picking up the vibes of tension between them, but that was never the case, at least not obviously. It always seemed to be a thought I would pick up on when they were enjoying one another's company, sometimes even being a little more affectionate than usual. That's what always made it hard for me to understand as a child when almost immediately after having this thought, all hell would break loose.

A thought would sweep past my conscious awareness like, "*Gee, Mom and Dad haven't fought in a long time,*" and literally within a day, two at most, our home would turn into a war zone. It was brutal. I began to detest these fleeting, uncontrollable thoughts, which didn't happen often, but when they did, it inevitably led to a fight brewing and then exploding between them.

I began to think that it was me who was making them fight. It just had to be. I blamed myself and so every time that nasty thought would sweep in, I would try to cancel it right away. But nothing I did ever helped. It always happened. I felt totally helpless and hated having to know such a thing, as it always left me with a sick feeling inside, just waiting for the inevitable explosion that always followed.

Other than this beginning to happen for me, I had another huge shift take place within months after the dreaded tonsillectomy disaster. I began to menstruate.

I was officially Initiated into Womanhood. I still wore children's underwear for crying out loud, with cute little pictures of fuzzy teddy bears and stuffed animals on them. I had learned to do my own laundry by then, and now held this invisible, yet very present weight on my shoulders from knowing a little too much for a child. Much more than a nine-year-old girl in our culture should know, especially without the conscious care of those around her to offer support during such a critically initiatory time in a young girl's life.

Carrying the weight of the world started to become an everyday reality for me, though on the outside, I was still a child and did enjoy my life immensely. I truly did. I was still able to have fun, odd as I was, and odd as my term for "fun" may have been, I am ever grateful for the resiliency I possessed as a child.

Children truly are miraculous to me. Their superhuman capacity for forgiveness, resilience and unconditional love are astoundingly beautiful.

Yet there was something beneath the surface happening inside of me beyond what I could understand or describe. This nine-year-old journey for me had brought many changes.

I got my first real pet at this age. My dog, Spats. He was our family dog, but I thought of him as my best friend, because truly, he was.

I would talk to Spats in a language I made up on my own, and he responded to me, always knowing what I was saying. I could hear his thoughts and feel his feelings. He was a fun little guy. Everyone loved him; he became the neighbourhood dog. The only ones who didn't like him were the little old Italian Nonas who wore black from head to toe, and would walk alone down the street, their black babushkas tied around their heads.

For some reason, no matter what, Spats would run after these little, harmless ladies, barking and nipping at them until they would resort to hugging a tree, trying desperately and unsuccessfully to access their inner squirrel and climb up to safety.

Spats would come when we called him to give him a scolding, but he never did like those little Nonas dressed in black for some reason. He was a free spirit, and was never leashed up. We later found out that Spats was known all over town. People didn't necessarily know who he belonged to, but as he would wander many blocks over visiting different houses each day, he would snack and nap as he pleased, wherever he pleased. He even hung out inside people's houses. Spats was a bit of a small town celebrity in his own right.

I was devastated when he passed ten years later, when I was 19. It was sudden, and dramatic, and once we brought him in to the vet, he never came home. My step dad and I stayed with him when he was euthanized, and that was one of the most profound experiences of my life, sitting with him, loving him, and helping him through his transition. I watched as his spirit left his body, and I didn't get over this loss for at least two years, if not more. I couldn't watch The Lion King without losing it and breaking down for many, many years. I will still cry when I hear the theme song from it, as it reminds me so much of him and his fierce and free spirit.

Spats started to visit me in my dreams after his death, telling me he was coming back to be with me. I had dreams where he would walk out of his burial plot in our backyard garden, and come in to the house to see me. It was a recurring dream, and always very intense and emotional.

This dream recurred for almost two years, and I always awoke tear-stained with the knowing I'd just been visited by the first and sweetest love of my life. My heart ached from missing him. I would also be left trying to figure out the whole rising from the dead/coming back to me resurrection message, which seemed rather zombie-esque and sort of creepy, but I knew it must mean something, because I received this dream multiple times.

A few years later, we got a cat sort of by accident, and I was certain after getting to know him that he was embodying Spats' soul. It wasn't until finally understanding this one day that I knew what those dreams had been telling me! He came back to me—to *us*—in the form of a cat, and he had been preparing me to understand and recognize it when it happened.

We had named the cat Scamp, after Spats' nickname my grandfather, Harold, had given him. He had always called Spats "Scamp" for some reason. Before we even knew the connection between the two, that Scamp was Spats, we had named him Scamp, simply in honour of Spats' memory. Little did we know then just how connected they were! And little did we know the untimely demise poor Scamp would also face.

But back to my first near death experience. So, there I was, nine years old. Tonsils and adenoids out. Hemorrhage and emergency surgery. Cloaked figure in the room doing "something" to me. New dog = best friend. Starting to know more, becoming more sensitive and empathic, and then to top it off, The Sacred Initiation. My first menses.

I do not say any of this in a negative way. I simply realize that a lot happened in that one year, beneath the surface of it all. A lot of shifting and changing and morphing took place. High stakes for my little soul, to put it mildly.

I was in art class, learning pottery, and I was really loving the sensation of the clay squishing inside my fingers and hands on the spinning wheel, and how smooth and perfectly pliable the clay was; and I was really getting off on it. It was quite a sensual experience for me.

Deeply enjoying this experience, I felt a gush of what I thought must be urine, wetting my pants, and it came out of what seemed like nowhere. I had never had an experience like this before. But I hadn't felt the feeling of a full bladder, so I was confused.

I'd suffered from chronic yeast infections since I was a very young child, years before this, which I later attributed to diet, candida, lack of proper hygiene, and now also realize, my multi-dimensional experiences aboard ship could have contributed to, but I will get in to more of that later on.

So, chronic yeast infections, and then suddenly The Great Initiation. I didn't know what it was until I went to the bathroom. Of course, in true cliché fashion, I happened to be wearing white pants that day. Just my damned luck.

I looked at my little circus panties, and they had a silver dollar-sized puddle of blood in them. At the time, it seemed like the red sea to me. It was big enough to leak through to my white pants and leave a tiny dot visible from the outside. Had

I sat with my legs apart like I usually did, people would have definitely been wise to my "dirty little secret."

Thank heavens it was close to the end of the day, so I didn't have to hide it for too long. I think all recesses were over. I kept my feet and legs close together for the remainder of the day, trying to keep that hunk of uncooperative toilet paper in place, and went straight home after school.

Thank God I'd at least been wise enough to stuff my underpants with that toilet paper to avoid any more accidents or potential embarrassment, as if my bulging pants weren't enough of a giveaway.

I'm somewhat saddened now that I thought of it as something so embarrassing and gross, as I now view this wondrous mystical magic of a woman's body and her moon cycle to be beautiful and highly sacred, but at the time, I must have been one of the only, if not the only girl in my school (which only went up to fifth grade) who was going through this experience.

My friends and I never talked about these things, so I don't know for sure. I am pretty certain though, that of my large handful of girlfriends, it is likely that at nine, I was the only one experiencing this. No one seemed to talk about it, and no one seemed to have changed or had a visibly altered sense of maturity—or the invisible weight that I felt I now carried—on their shoulders. But who knows. Maybe they were just as skilled as I hoped I was at hiding it.

I'd already had an invisible weight that I carried from other issues as well, but this now only added to the growing collection that I would file under "traumatic and confusing, and highly secret." I suppose it's simply "Life," but it felt to me like I had to be different in just one more way now, and for some reason, I felt like I needed to hide it. I now awaited this embarrassing disaster each month, never knowing when the dreaded gush would come, and in the meantime, I would try my best to be a carefree kid, though not feeling much like one anymore.

I was angry, and didn't want to be afraid to wear white or a bathing suit in the summer for fear of leakage. I didn't want to be bogged down by how to manage wearing a thick pad that got sopping wet and made me feel like I was wearing a wet diaper. This time of year was quickly approaching and causing me some major stress. Stress that I didn't notice any of my friends experiencing.

Regardless of what anyone else may have been experiencing, I felt very alone in this.

Perhaps it's because I didn't even tell my mother about it. I was already doing my own laundry, so it would be many months before she even figured it out. I felt too ashamed and embarrassed to even tell her for some reason.

My sister, Shelby, had only just begun her shift around the same time I did, but she was twelve going on thirteen, so I'd heard and seen them talking about menstrual pads, and such. I knew where they were kept, and my mother must have wondered how we were zipping through them so quickly. Maybe that's why she checked my laundry one day and discovered the evidence.

The jig was up. Bloodstained panties full of prints of cute stuffed animals and tightrope-walking teddy bears. Forever tainted, in my mind.

She asked me why I'd never told her, but I really didn't have a good excuse, except that I'd never felt comfortable or emotionally safe to share these kinds of things with her or anyone for that matter. She was a sweet Mama, but anytime one of us became sick, she sort of turned into "crazy mom." We would get scolded, as she asked us "what was wrong," almost like we were being punished and blamed for being sick. I didn't see at the time how this situation would be any different, and so didn't want to be scolded for something I already felt incredibly embarrassed and awful about.

To this day, I struggle with this imprinted way of dealing with issues with my own children, as it was so unconsciously ingrained in me to react negatively. I can usually move through these glitches and catch myself before it happens, but admittedly, I have an unfortunate tendency to get a little too interested in what is happening if my kids aren't feeling well. I have to firmly remind myself to continue to be their soft place to fall, even when the chips are down, sometimes literally, all over the floor.

I really didn't have a good reason to give to my mother for not telling her, but told her that since I already did my own laundry, I'd just been taking care of it myself. I may have even lied and said that I had just got it for the first time. I can't remember but that feels like something I would have said, so that she wouldn't be upset with me or feel hurt that I hadn't come to her for support and guidance during such an important initiation in my life.

I'd moved through this initiation as gracefully as any nine-year old could muster, much like I did most everything else: confused and alone.

CHAPTER 10

Dreaming the Sacred Union of the Goddess with Her God

My moon cycle was an interesting one. I never thought much of it until later on as an adult when I realized that most regular cycles follow a 28-day timeline, typically.

Mine revolved around a number of the month. I noticed that I would always begin menstruating on the second day of every month, like clockwork; even the time of day was predictable. Always in the evening. It didn't matter what month it was, whether it was March, just after our shortest month, whether it was a leap year, whatever. It always arrived on the 2nd day of each month.

When I noticed this pattern, I was thankful, because I always knew when it would come, and it came without fail every single time. With the exception of one summer in my teens, when I was seventeen and didn't bleed all summer, even though there was no earthly way I could have been pregnant. I was not having sex with my boyfriend.

Or was there a way? This happened to be only months after a strange and mysterious activation I'd had through something I'd seen on my television, but that story will come in a little later. It could potentially explain this summer of the missing moon cycle though.

Of course, I didn't know it then, but I did learn many years later that of course these types of mysterious pregnancies were possible, and not only possible, with cases like mine, highly probable.

The number 2, the second of the month, was the time when my uterus lining would begin to shed, reminding me that I was now, officially and anatomically speaking, a Woman. Being a woman whilst still in the single digits of life had been a little much to wrap my brain around at that tender age though.

After being Initiated at age nine, I noticed some other changes. I developed a sudden voracious sexual awareness and what I might refer to as an "appetite," as I found myself being aroused regularly, as well as beginning to experience orgasms, often, and very easily.

AT AGE NINE.

I felt ashamed of this uncontrollable urge I had to experience a man inside of me, and also looking back, oddly enough, I already knew what that felt like. I'd lived many years (before I began to remember my inner Truth) feeling *certain* that because of this, I had been sexually abused. I still don't rule this out, honestly, as there have been too many incidents from my past with a certain member in my family where inappropriate touching and molestation definitely occurred, and other suspect things have arisen, so I know without a doubt that some things most definitely happened in my early childhood.

I have released the weight of this burden from my life though, thankfully, with lots of therapy and clearing and forgiving, but this sensation of "knowing" went far deeper than any sexual molestation or abuse.

I had a deep inner desire and knowing of my own sexuality, my own inner Goddess, right from a very young age, and along with it, the insatiable desire to share these energies in a sacred union with a God who could match me.

At nine years old, I was fully aware of this, and searching for any outlet to understand and experience it; once again, without the proper guidance I needed. But to be fair, how would anyone in my family have known how to guide me on such a path?

CHAPTER 11

Premature Awakenings

I became obsessed with sex, and found the female body to be the most magnificent specimen on the planet. I was attracted to boys sexually, but was really turned on by the idea of one day becoming a fully grown, vivacious, sexy Goddess of a woman, capable of embodying the most magical and beautiful image of the Goddess in my small eyes: carrying a child inside my Sacred Temple, and birthing such a miraculous creation.

After all, I already knew from my visions that this was a major part of my path.

I was still a kid on the outside though, still playing, having fun, cracking jokes and dancing around the kitchen in my bare feet. I was a bit of a tomboy. In contrast to my obsession with the Goddess, a large part of me rejected Her, rejected the idea of becoming a woman; not feeling entirely safe to embrace the feminine form in all its sensual power and glory.

I'd had many past life experiences of being tortured and killed for being a Priestess, a Goddess, a medicine woman, a healer, and a witch, I would later realize. Yet, when I witnessed the sensuality of a woman's body, or when I imagined, quite vividly, a man entering inside of me, I would be brought to orgasm almost instantly.

I longed desperately for this experience and connection with a lover. Besides being a vessel for new life, divine lovemaking had become my greatest fantasy and desire.

I remember when I was ten, a group of friends and I walked over to a park around the corner from my house one day. There were six of us; three boys, three girls. We all happened to be "couples," though of course in those days, we all swapped boyfriends and girlfriends weekly, like a G-rated version of swingers.

I happened to be going out with a boy named John at the time. He was this cute kid with olive-coloured skin, brown eyes, and dark hair. He was a bit mischievous and had an adventurous and daring sort of edge, along with a great sense of humour, which all together was a perfect package in my books. He was always wearing a devilish grin about something or other. John's birthday was December 15th, and he was a perfect Sagittarian trickster.

John had all these wonderful, quirky and attractive qualities, and I was head over heels for him, as much as a ten-year old could be anyway.

At one point, we all lay down behind a log, and started kissing our respective boyfriends and girlfriends. Something came over me. I felt almost like something else took over my body and I started to gyrate on top of him. I was highly aroused, and could not control myself. I was on the verge of orgasm, losing myself in the experience. Here was my moment. I was so into it, I may have tried to have sex with the poor kid had we not been interrupted momentarily. I have no idea. I probably really wouldn't have, but that's what the energy felt like to me, and I'm glad I never had to find out. It would have been a disaster, no matter what. Little did I realize then how disappointing it would have been for me, since I was desiring a man, not a little boy!

Poor John. He didn't know what to do with these intense energies. It was beyond what anyone there knew, I'm quite certain of that. Finally, after a few minutes of us kissing, those disgustingly sloppy ten-year old child kisses, me totally trying to slip my tongue into his mouth and devouring him (pretty sophisticated for ten), that our friend Josephine—a somewhat uppity and outspoken Italian girl, always quick to make judgments and give her opinion, blurted out, "Oh my God, Sam, You are such a slut!"

I was mortified! How could I possibly be a slut?

Sex was absolutely beautiful to me. How did this even happen? I had no idea what was going on, and I suddenly felt so embarrassed and ashamed and even guilty for what I had just done. I think John was in shock, and I believe shortly after this incident we broke up and he never would be my boyfriend again that I can recall. In fact after this, we were hardly even friends. I remember feeling hurt and confused as to why from then on, he always seemed to avoid me. When we were both fourteen and starting high school, he and his family moved away, and that was the end of that.

I never even connected this before right now, but I probably scared the living shit out of the poor kid that day, and he must not have known what to think of me. The other boys there continued to be my friends and knew the kind of girl I really was. I didn't just jump on anyone. I realized then that my sexuality was sacred, so all throughout the rest of middle school and high school, I dated several boys, but while I enjoyed cuddling and foreplay immensely (when I even allowed that to happen, for fear of losing control of myself, I would usually avoid that too), I would not allow any of them to enter my Sacred Temple.

Simply put, I was now very, very confused and conflicted about sex, yet also knew I had to respect these energies and be discerning about what I allowed near me or inside of me.

After having allowed one young man I dated when I was 14 and he 17 to date rape me one night while our parents sat upstairs getting loaded together, our brothers and sisters sleeping on the couches all around us in the same room, it definitely had an adverse effect on me, especially where sex was concerned. He had got on top of me, when all the lights were out and we were all supposedly sleeping, and started kissing. Not ever asking me, he had trapped me underneath him and had sex with me.

It was a complete nightmare. I was trying to stay quiet, which meant I felt like I could not move or talk to tell him no, because I knew my sister would freak out and I was sure she would blame me. Synchronistically, there was that blood connection again as I was menstruating, and was even more ashamed to say anything to him about it, besides which I was in shock at what was happening. I became even more shocked and ashamed that my voice, this girl who had always been so outspoken and always known how to stand up for herself so well, was frozen here, trapped, unable to say a word, and allowing something to happen to me that I absolutely did not want or consent to.

I don't even want to think about what the couch may have looked like the next morning.

After that brief nightmare of a relationship, I dated another sweet boy, with the same name, and to add to the synchronicity, he was also three years older than me—seventeen. I dated him for about a year. The first boyfriend was an extremely gifted musician, and this one, a total fitness junkie. I did end up trying to have sex with him, since all my friends had boyfriends by that point, and they were all sexually active with them, but it just did not feel right to me. I knew that I was not ready for this, and that these boys were not the way it was meant to be for me.

Regardless, in my attempts to be normal like other people, I tried with him twice, and both times were met with dismal failure on my part. I simply could not do it, though he was very sweet and never once pressured me to try if I didn't want to, and understood the both times we tried and I stopped it.

After this, I had two different, both very sweet, long-term boyfriends spanning throughout my remaining four years in high school. In Ontario at the time, we had a grade 13 we were required to receive credits in, with a high enough GPA before being able to apply to universities. I would not ever have sex with either of these boyfriends.

I learned from my experiences with those older boys that I was not prepared for everything it meant to be engaging in sexual intercourse with boys who weren't in their mastery yet, and of course, I was still a child myself and was not willing to take on a responsibility of such magnitude, or to give myself to anyone.

I realized that I could very easily get pregnant. To this day I am still extremely fertile. I also realized I was not willing to put chemicals into my body via a pill just to be able to have sex with a boy, which I knew would inevitably end up being dissatisfying anyway. I wasn't willing to do any of this tedious or health-altering nonsense merely to have mediocre sexual encounters.

I had a deep, unshakable yearning in my soul to be a mother though. Yet I knew I was far too young still. I wanted my freedom and I wanted to explore life much more than I had. I wanted to be ready so that I could be the best mother I could be. You see, I also knew I was meant to have children in order to break the generational cycles of pain, dysfunction and abuse. I knew I was to help with our ancestral healing through my becoming a mother. Don't ask me how I knew this, but I did, and I was serious about it.

I was always a "good kid," always the responsible one. The one in the family who would hold it all together behind the scenes, helping everyone through their tough times.

I realize now that since becoming sexually active, even mildly with my boyfriends, my strong desires and my sensual, pleasurable side still existed in a very intense way. It took all of my reserves to hold those energies in and keep them as safe as I could; I knew it was not "time" for this.

Then something else began around this time in high school. *I started to feel like I was being watched.*

CHAPTER 12

The Invisible Eye

I didn't know what this feeling of being watched was all about. At times though, it was highly unsettling to me, though most of the time, it didn't seem to bother me. Even now, I think about recurring dreams I would have growing up, all the way through high school, and on into my adulthood, and the themes are interesting to me now, with the wisdom and knowing through experience I have gained since then.

I had three types of recurring dreams:

1. Dreams where I was being followed by someone, a man, who was attempting to take my life, via knife or gun or through strangulation or asphyxiation. He would almost always "get" me, but in every single dream, his attempts to kill me or inflict pain on me never worked. It was as if I was super human and could survive anything. I would usually end up overpowering him in the end. Once he could not get to me, he often would go after the people I loved, and attempt to take their lives. Again, I was always able to stop this from happening, thank heavens, and ultimately defeat him.
2. Dreams where I was being chased by a car driven by large men in black suits. They were dark figures, and did not

seem fully human. They were more robotic than anything. I was almost always with my two brothers, whose birthdays both happen to be December 16th, and who were born in the same hospital on the same day, even the same year, but by different mothers. We always referred to them as the "twins" even though they have no known blood relation. They became step brothers by marriage when they were just two. From what I know now about the military, the CIA and the all-too-real versions of "the men in black," I can see how these recurring dreams or experiences I'd had as a child probably had more truth to them than I realized. I had this particular dream scenario so regularly that I even created with my mind a controlled dream that I would insert consciously whenever this bad dream occurred, because it was just so real and disturbing to me. The controlled dream was a simple fabricated dream I titled "The Ball." I would even see the title written as such to begin it, in cursive in front of red theatre curtains on a screen, like an old, classic movie. The dream consisted solely of me bouncing a ball, throwing a ball, catching a ball, etcetera, and I would insert this into my dream state whenever the large men in black were chasing me and my brothers, in an attempt to make them go away.

3. The third kind of dream, the most disturbing of them all to me, involved me being pregnant, and having babies that I was unaware I had been carrying. These dreams are KEY to what I am about to share in the following pag-

es. They were awful dreams, as I always, without fail, awoke from them with a soaking wet pillow, eyes crusted shut from crying so much, and a broken heart I could feel just as real as if it were happening to me right then and there. These were, by far, the worst of them all. I put the word "dreams" in quotes now, because I have become privy to a great amount of information in the past few years which has helped me realize the subtle yet very real truth within these experiences, which I now refer to them as, instead of merely dreams. They were so much more than that. In many of these experiences, I would birth babies that were small, greyish and wrinkly, and often looked like tiny little monsters or old men, but they were precious to me all the same. Some were so tiny, only the size of my hand. In some of these experiences, I gave birth to beautiful, plump humanoid babies with large blue eyes, and yet still, I would not have known at all that I was even pregnant until they slid out of me spontaneously and surprisingly. Then I would somehow forget I'd birthed them. I would later find these babies, among others I had birthed without any knowing, and experience the utter devastation of a mother having forgotten about them, having abandoned them. Oftentimes, I would discover these babies in a strange room by themselves, starved for love and affection, some nearly dying from not being held, fed or loved properly, ever. When I would finally find my babies, I often ran to them, picked them up, hugged them, and apologized profusely, while crying my eyes out, always waking with a tear-stained face, wet pillow, and a *very* heavy heart. These dreams broke my heart into a million pieces, and I never did understand them, until only recently. In most of these experiences, even though with some I'd had no recollection of having given actual birth to my babies, I still somehow knew without a doubt, that they were, indeed, mine. This is why the utter devastation of not knowing they even existed, or worse, having had forgotten about birthing them, having forgotten them altogether, was so confusing, and agonizingly hard for me to accept. This dream scenario I experienced over and over and over again as a young girl, and in to my young adulthood.

Because of the very real post-traumatic stress I experienced as a result of these dreams, I had developed a severe phobia and fear of having babies and giving birth physically. This newfound fear and terror started to grip me like a vice, because I felt unsure about myself, and if I would even be able to carry a healthy, normal baby to term. I was not even sure if I could trust myself to be a good mother—would I just abandon my "real" babies? And what if, heaven forbid, I actually did give birth to an alien "monster" baby? What then?

These questions plagued me, and though they may sound unreasonable and like the workings of an overactive imagination, they were real concerns for me, and thankfully, I would later come to understand them from a whole new perspective—from a *galactic* perspective. But this would take years, decades even, for me to come to understand.

I would have these birthing dreams more often than any of the other recurring dreams in my dismal repertoire. I know now it is because they were not actually dreams but rather, as I already stated earlier, *experiences*—cosmic experiences and the beginnings of my galactic training, showing me a very important piece of my own cosmic puzzle I would receive confirmation about many, many years later.

Never in a million years could I have predicted the direction this information would take me in. If I'd have known, I cannot say for certain if I would have been able to hold my sanity intact. So for this, now, I am grateful I did not understand them, as painful as it was at the time. I needed to hang on to my sanity in order to complete my assignments. Admittedly though, even without the knowing throughout the years I teetered that fine line between the two, living on the edge. One foot in both worlds, yet completely and utterly in the dark.

CHAPTER 13

The Second Activation: A Soul Recognized

I was seventeen, and from all appearances, I was a typical 17-year old girl. I was bright, happy, a friend to all. I was an excellent student, a dedicated competitive dancer and assistant teacher to the younger children in the dance studio I trained in, whom I adored with all my heart. I had a very kind boyfriend, and we were the best of friends. Going to a small high school, I had lots of friends I'd known since we were in elementary school, though I didn't spend much time with them outside of class anymore, since my evenings and weekends were filled with teaching, physical training, homework, often until the wee hours of the night. In whatever spare time I had, I was with my boyfriend and his family, who had embraced me as a natural extension of their little posse. It was beautiful, and I was grateful.

This was my life, and I loved it.

When I was at home, things were just like normal there too. My parents were both busy working full time, always the mad rush after work to get dinner on the table, which I often helped with if I was around, and then either driving me to my work or classes at the studio or taking my brother to his hockey practices and games. He was on a traveling team as well, so they did a lot of hockey travel to different cities as well as to tournaments some weekends in the winter and spring.

My sister was the quiet Cancerian homebody, who was finished with high school, and at this time she may have even recently finished her first year of university, I can't remember.

I do remember her often sitting in the basement, watching music videos, which was something she enjoyed doing a lot of.

I wasn't much of a television or music video girl. I was always juggling so much that TV seemed like a waste of time to me. But it was also a great chance to bond with my big sister, and so occasionally I would sit and watch simply to get to hang out with her. Usually if she wasn't watching TV, she was holed up in her room, reading Stephen King novels, and in those moments she was not to be disturbed. So, I would opt for watching TV with her, which often proved to be entertaining at least, since we'd crack jokes together about whatever was on the screen.

This one day, I was sitting with her while she watched music videos. I wasn't paying very close attention, I never did unless it was a song I really liked. Shelby and I were joking around as usual.

My sister's a funny one. She has a quirky sense of humour that I have always adored about her. I'm sure I was especially fond of it since she's my big sister and I always looked up to her.

I have a special affinity for Shelby. After all, she was the one who played "airplane" with me in order to coax me into eating my Kraft Dinner and bologna sandwiches when I was only a toddler. She was also the one who eventually figured out my stealthy game of dumping my food behind the sofa and television, then tricking me back by telling our mother.

She was always the one who would comfort me if I was upset about anything. She was the one who lent me $2,000 for my kitten's ear surgery when I thought all hope was lost and he would die. She let me pay her back with monthly payments for the next year and a half. Shelby always felt like a second mother to me while I was growing up, and was my soft place to fall as a young adult as well. So naturally, spending any time with her whenever I could when we were kids was golden.

We were sitting together that afternoon, probably making each other laugh about something stupid, when a music video came on, by a band I had never really made a point of giving any attention to.

The last boyfriend I'd had liked this band, and little did I know that my current boyfriend, whom I would stay with for the next four years, and who happened to be a brilliantly gifted self-taught drummer and also an incredible singer, would go on to play this exact song in a Battle of the Bands event about six months down the road.

In this moment, though I had definitely heard the song before randomly, either on the radio or through friends, I had never paid close attention to it, and had never seen the music video prior to this day.

Shelby and I were talking, yet I kept finding my eyes being drawn in to the screen, almost hypnotically, watching the vocalist with a deep unconscious kind of attraction, which I could not figure out logically.

Being a Gemini with a Virgo Ascendant, I am naturally curious and logical, and have always had an insatiable urge to try and figure things out, especially if they perplex me in any way, which this strange attraction did. So, I sat there, attempting to have a conversation with my sister, while feeling this unusual, overwhelming compulsion to watch this man on the television set.

I really didn't understand it. I kept saying ridiculous things inside my mind like, '*He's not even hot, Sam. He thinks he is, but he's not that hot. Come on! Look away! You're not attracted to him, so why are you looking at him like this?*' And on and on.

This silly inner banter with myself continued throughout the duration of the video. I was probably most resistant because this band had become very popular, and usually anything too mainstream irritated me and I would immediately judge it and not give it the time of day. This band, though their obvious rebelliousness was intriguing, they didn't really appeal to me, because my ego told me they were "getting too popular."

Silly, I know. Embarrassing now too, but the truth is this was how I felt, and I feel this point is important to sharing this story. I was never content to follow the crowd with anything, and wasn't about to start now.

It seemed to me like all they sang about were sex and drugs, so this helped me justify my resistance, since those topics were not exactly appealing musical content in my arrogant opinion. In my attempts to thwart my own sexuality, plus growing up around the uglier side of booze and drugs, I was becoming a bit of a prude.

But this song had a very different energy. It felt much more personal and tender. I could feel the life blood pumping inside every word and note simultaneously. Yet I had a stubborn resistance gurgling inside of me, and didn't want to buy into any of it. The life force I was feeling through this music though was so palpable, and undeniable. What started as outright resistance quickly turned in to an obsessively forced resistance the more I watched, as I attempted to convince myself that "*I wasn't interested*" in whatever this strange connection was that I was experiencing, as if I'd needed to justify this to anyone but my own ridiculous monkey mind.

I was the only one hearing my crazy thoughts anyway. *Or was I?*

There was this uncontrollable and overwhelming feeling of somehow being connected with this man that I didn't understand, and though it was impossible to deny, I didn't want to admit it to myself, because that wouldn't have made any logical sense whatsoever, of course.

So, I continued on with the inner struggle of fighting the urge to watch him; to *feel into him*. I tried desperately to avert my eyes toward something else in the room or on the screen. Nope. It was that "thing," that strange invisible cord that wouldn't allow me to look away from him, which I was desperately fighting to break free of the whole time.

And then the end of the song came; the bridge to the end. In the video, he is running toward the camera, in slow motion. He is running from the disaster of a nuclear explosion behind him, and this is where I became emotionally overwhelmed.

I noticed this Voice quietly telling me "*He's running to you. He's trying to find you.*"

What????

I was overcome with emotion, as I could feel the blood begin to course through my veins, pumping wildly, like nothing I'd ever felt before. It was so intense, and truly, otherworldly. I definitely could not look away any longer. I stopped fighting myself, and I most definitely stopped superficially judging this man.

The walls surrounding my heart instantly collapsed, and it was no longer about if I thought he was "hot" or not, or whatever other ridiculous judgments I feebly decided to project onto him. It is somewhat embarrassing now to admit what my mind chatter was saying, but to cut myself a bit of slack, I was a confused kid who didn't understand what the hell was happening to her.

But I remember at this point in the video, all of the ridiculous mind-chatter dropped as my heart walls crumbled to a million pieces, and all I could feel was an indescribable love for this man's soul. Like I knew him, like we had known each other before—*many, many times before*.

There I sat, all childish earthly judgments dissolved, against him as well as myself, as I felt this man's innermost being, the beating of his heart and soul, running toward me, and I could do nothing to stop it or the emotion that accompanied such soul recognition. Nor in this brief moment of deep recognition, did I even want to stop it.

This was to date one of the most profound experiences of my life. And I had no idea what was happening. I was seventeen but basically still a child. Although I was most obviously an old soul, I still could not understand what this was all about. I had no earthly frame of reference for such an otherworldly experience.

I truly didn't care about this band. I wasn't even a fan. Yet somehow, there was something about him that ignited something within me that I did not have words for; that I did not have any earthly understanding of.

I remember feeling moved to tears, locked in my gaze with him, and was honestly quite relieved when the video finally ended, as it had caught me so completely off my guard with its intensity. It felt as if the invisible cord that connected us so strongly when I first saw him was able to dissipate and release as soon as his image was off the screen.

Relief. I could breathe again.

I am not sure if my sister even noticed the intensity of what had happened for me, but I am pretty certain I said nothing about it, and am even more certain she never asked me about it if she had suspected anything.

Still to this day, the things my family finds strange about me for the most part stay left unsaid, like the huge pink elephant in the room. God Bless them, I love them and they love me anyway.

The video was over, and that was that. I chalked it up to a very bizarre experience I would never figure out. Back to life as usual, right? If only it were that simple.

CHAPTER 14

Beyond Awake

I'd had other strange and paranormal experiences throughout the rest of my adolescence, including waking up one morning as I was re-entering my physical vessel.

This was a very odd experience that actually frightened me at first.

During the same time frame as the DNA activation I'd experienced seeing the music video, I awoke one morning to the top half of my physical body being hoisted up off the bed as I literally saw a bright light descend down into me very quickly. I could feel it enter me with a thud as a weight fell upon me, and I collapsed back onto the bed. All of this was involuntary. I gasped for breath as it happened, it was so intense.

I remember lying there, motionless for a few minutes wondering what the hell had just happened to me. I was about seventeen or eighteen. I had taken to sleeping upside down in my bed, with my head at the foot of the bed instead of the way I was "supposed" to sleep. Always a rebel, always doing things "backwards."

As I lied there and my head took over, a fear began to descend on me. I took note of my regular nightmares and disturbing recurring dream themes, which always involved either having babies I didn't know I had, or being stalked, chased or having attempts taken on my life. I realized that I had nightmares more nights than I didn't have them. As I had already been a horror movie addict for about 10 years by then, always seeming to flirt with fear and how far I could take it, a terrifying thought kicked in.

"What if I've just been possessed?"

This thought was way too much to handle, and I didn't know what to do about it. The wheels began to spin, now out of desperation. How would one go about removing a demon from their body if they've been accessed by it? I was only a kid really, and had no idea what to do. I had seen one too many scary movies, and the paranormal thrillers were always my favourite. I have since realized that watching things like this can affect us in many ways, and not positively. Perhaps more detail on that another time.

I was unaware of this at that time though, and the best solution I could come up with was to wait it out. After all, who could I go to with this kind of question that would take me seriously? I decided to wait and see if my behaviour changed, if my thoughts changed, if *I* changed, and then I would know if I had to tell someone or do something more about it. I was certain I could find an exorcist in a Catholic community if I truly needed it. But until then, I'd just be Sam and hope to hell I stayed that way.

And I was Sam. Thank the Goddesses. Nothing changed. I remember one day, about two weeks after this experience, thinking to myself, '*Has anything changed? Are you different?*' And

I realized I hadn't, and I wasn't. It was in this moment that I was blessed with a vision and an instant knowing that what I had experienced was literally my own Self coming back "in" after my nightly adventures and work in other dimensions. This could also have been me being dropped back in from the ship, but that notion did not occur to me at that time.

The simple notion of my Self coming back "in" to my physical body though, I understood, and recognized very strongly as the Truth in this case.

What a great relief it was that I didn't have to start looking up how to perform exorcisms on myself, or worse, find a priest who would perform one. Being in a small community in a Roman Catholic school, afterwards having to go to regular confession among the few priests in town, would have literally been hell. They used to send the young girls out of their dark "confession" rooms in tears. It always left me wondering what in the world these poor girls could have done that was so awful to have the priests telling them they were going to 'burn in hell.' Because they literally did tell them this. I heard this from more than one of my girl friends in high school. It was traumatizing for these young girls. Talk about abuse.

And there I was, a teenage kid, confessing to teasing my brother and playing pranks on my dog, and I was beside myself with grief over the guilt of such "sins." Those sacraments are set up to embed the debilitating programs of guilt and shame, fear and punishment, and we're supposed to accept it like it's the moral high ground to submit to such abuse. It's sickening. Imagine I'd had to confess that I thought I may have been possessed by a spirit or a demon? It wouldn't have gone over well, I'm guessing, and I was more than relieved to realize I'd never have to tell anyone about this experience if I didn't want to. I certainly didn't feel like burning in hell for it.

It's amazing the hold religion can have over people even when they don't think that it does. I was always a rebel, yet was also always striving to be the best person I could be, to do the "right" thing when it came down to it. I have never intentionally hurt anyone in my life, and the thought of the hurts I may have caused in the past or in my life still, always choke me up and weigh heavily on my soul.

My intention has always been to love. So to think of being overtaken by a "demon" when I was but a young lady was frightening indeed. I'd seen *The Exorcist* when I was ten, and the memories of Reagan's possession experience was more than I could bear to think of. That was the only movie that ever truly frightened me.

So, demon possession was averted, thank my lucky stars.

I continued to be able to feel or sense others' emotions more strongly than ever. My empathic and psychic abilities had been upgraded once again by this experience.

CHAPTER 15

Messages from the Otherware: The Cosmic Celebrity Connection & Extraterrestrial Genetic Experiments

If I were to attempt to conjure up a subtitle for this chapter, it might sound something like, "How Galactic Forces Pair Low-Profile starseeds with those of High-Profile Status for Cosmic Assignments Created to Reach the Planetary Masses Thus Grounding these Galactic Messages for the Upliftment of All." Quite a mouthful, I know, but one that quite accurately describes my, and many others' experiences.

For someone who has always had an aversion to the whole "fame game," who admittedly has even judged it in the past, as well as those who appear to be playing it with such finesse, I have also experienced some extremely intense and soul-altering connections with a small handful of people viewed as celebrities by the mainstream.

For the record, all connections were ignited 20 plus years ago from the time of this writing, long before I'd come to peace with the whole idea of celebrities and the role they undoubtedly play here on the planet on the great galactic chess board.

It all started with my bizarre connections with John Lennon and Yoko Ono at the tender age of five, having experienced an unexplainable devastation over his death on December 8th, 1980, which I'm certain a part of that was my extreme empathic sense of my mother's intense grief around it, admittedly. Regardless of the source of the pain I experienced, it hit me like a ton of bricks nonetheless.

I remember that day vividly. I had an experience with teleportation, remote viewing, or something along those lines at this time. I am not exactly sure what it was, but what I know for certain is that I was brought somehow to a place where loved ones of John's were mourning him. I remember feeling confused slightly, knowing that I had shown up alone, without my parents, *instantaneously*, truly not knowing how I had actually gotten there. All I knew was that I was, undoubtedly, there.

No one could see me though. It was as if I were an invisible ghost or a fly on the wall. I only remember people's legs and feet, as I was only five when this experience happened, so my memories of it are from the perspective of a small child.

I wasn't really sure why I was there at all. My mother had been in agony over his assassination, as were millions upon millions of others. I remember feeling this agony so deeply.

Watching my mother mourn the loss of someone she had never met before was astonishing to me, yet at the same time, I understood what she was going through wholeheartedly, as I too was deeply mourning the loss of this Soul somehow.

Elton John wrote the song "Empty Garden" for John after his death. This was a song I couldn't even bare to listen to. I would sob my little heart out and relive the grief of his loss all over again, no matter how many years went by.

And then there was Yoko.

I had never even really listened to The Beatles up to that point, and at this time, Double Fantasy was only just being released to the public. I remember feeling much more drawn to Yoko's music and her strong, mysterious energy than I was to John's. In fact, I used to put that album on by myself and skip most of John's songs, bee-lining straight to Yoko's.

I was immediately transfixed, and developed a mysterious connection with her through her music which seemed to touch my soul on a very deep and profound level, so much so that I became obsessed with listening to her constantly, as her music transported me to other dimensions and worlds, and times of knowingness that somehow seemed more familiar to me in many ways than this one.

I loved that album, and even though I did like most of John's songs too, it was Yoko who magnetically drew me in to a sort of spell that I became enthralled with.

I was obsessed with the song "Kiss Kiss Kiss." At the end, Yoko goes into what I now undoubtedly recognize as an orgasm. When I was a kid though, I was absolutely certain that she was simulating giving birth, and thought it was the most beautiful thing I'd ever heard. Interesting connection between birthing babies and orgasms. This reality would go on to be a running theme in my own life, which is probably why I was so drawn to her music, and particularly, this song. It's my Scorpio Moon to blame, I know it.

I also now hear the ending of this song as a death, which likewise, holds great power of alchemy, from a spiritual perspective. We need to die in order to be reborn. We need to allow parts of ourselves to die in order to birth newer, truer versions of ourselves, each moment of every day.

I used to play this song over and over again, and I know my parents thought I was weird. Here I was, a five-year-old child, listening to this "crazy woman" having orgasms, dying, birthing, on repeat. Those were the days of LPs and this wasn't a CD. I would have to manually go and pick the needle up off the record ever so gently, so as not to scratch it (my step dad would have made me regret it if I did), and get the needle back to the start again. I had to use finesse and it took great concentration and reserve, but I did it in order to enter another state of being within myself, hearing, experiencing, this beautiful, magical moment of climax at the end. Waiting for it, I would melt into the sounds of her pain and ecstasy, and dream of becoming the living embodiment of this experience myself, at five years old. It was truly magical and out of this world.

Around this same time, the visions began. I would see very clear visions of myself as a Mother, a Goddess, Birthing a Divine Being into this world. Only there was a catch, which didn't really feel like a "catch" actually, but rather, a *Truth*. A very deep-seeded truth that would remain as a knowing, even now to this day. The difference is that now I have the tools and understanding in some form of earthly language to be able to speak about it and write it down, like I am doing now.

The truth that accompanied this very romantic vision for me was the clear knowing that:

"I was going to have babies in a very different way than other women on Earth have babies."

I really didn't know what this meant exactly, at least in words, but I felt the deep, ancient truth of this knowing, and saw it as a vision in my mind's eye of being implanted with a Divine Seed into my womb, and growing a baby this way. It felt like God was giving me babies to grow and birth for Him, and that I would not necessarily need to have an earthly man in my physical presence to do this. I have no idea how I knew this so deeply as a child, but I did. It was simply the way things were. I knew it and accepted it, and was even, dare I say, excited about it.

I didn't realize in my conscious mind that had I spoken this to anyone aloud, I may have been sent to have my head examined. Or worse, now noting that I have always lived within miles of a US military base, still to this day, and knowing what I know now about the very real possibility of interference on their part within these particular circumstances and experiences, they may have been inclined to examine a little more than just my head.

I knew I had to use discernment and needed to keep this Truth of Knowingness about my place here on Earth to myself. So, I did. It never felt like a big deal to me either, or that I was hiding some big secret. It simply was what it was, and I knew I was not to talk about it with anyone.

I didn't attend church or take religion classes; I merely understood that some of us, me in particular, were meant to conceive babies differently than most other women; without the need for a human male sperm to join with a human female egg, usually through the course of third dimensional physical intercourse, to make it happen. So, by five years old, I somehow knew my path was a bit different than the ordinary one. No big deal, right?

Kindergarten had *nothing* on me!

My affinity for and connection with Yoko remained silently with me throughout all those early childhood years.

The next phase began when I started to have recurring dreams in my adolescent and early adult years that I knew in my heart were messages from the Otherware. They were not merely "dreams" though. I had no clue what they were attempting to convey to me.

In every dream, Yoko and I would meet synchronistically at some sort of celebrity event or gathering, and it was as if we were magnetically drawn to one another. We would meet, our eyes would lock, and an instant knowing would occur. We shared a soul recognition of one another, accompanied by the urgent feeling of a certain mission or assignment we were to work on and accomplish together that was ignited from that first moment of eye contact. Without fail, we were both instantly committed to fulfilling this mission together.

I always awoke certain that at some point in my life, this event would take place, as I knew Yoko and I had a shared assignment together, even though I didn't know what that could possibly be.

These dreams began shortly after the activation of remembrance where I experienced myself coming back into my physical body after my nightly sojourns aboard ship.

These strong "celebrity assignment" dreams with Yoko were very interesting for a young girl of nineteen or so to repeatedly have, awake in many ways, yet still totally unaware at that point in my life what the hell I was really doing here. But there it was. This same recurring dream. Over and over again, reminding me, to remember.

Also, when I was nineteen, I had taken the year after high school to audition and work to save money for university. I had no clue what I wanted to study, and was mentally burnt out after the intense combination of earning honours in high school with two scholarships, while dancing competitively, training five days a week and teaching dance to children under ten years of age three days a week for the last three years of school.

I was ready for a break, to have a chance to breathe, to have some fun, and to audition for things that came up, just for the hell of it. I lived only an hour and a half from Toronto, where auditions were aplenty. I had an aunt and uncle who lived in

Don Mills, a suburb of Toronto, and if need be, I could always stay with them for a night here and there.

This was the same uncle who interestingly had a connection with Natalie Wood. He had grown up with her as a child, and I remember him one day going on and on about her drowning to me, probably shortly after she had died. At the time, I had no idea who she was, and in my mind, I always pictured her as a young child, drowning in a pool accidentally. I could not understand why my uncle was telling me any of this, but I could feel his sadness over the loss of his childhood friend, that much was clear.

Natalie Wood, of all people. Synchronicity would later reveal to me that Selene had a very important galactic assignment to complete with her, though her time here sadly ended too soon due to a grave error in her ability to discern, and so their work together was not able to be realized on this plane.

Back to my auditioning though. On the bus back from Toronto after an audition one day, I was struck by a profound feeling of "Oneness," of "Brother/Sisterhood," with a particular celebrity who was making his way into the hearts and homes of people around the world. Again, I never watched him on television, but my sister did, so I'd heard all about this new young rising star through her.

I finally got to witness and experience his true comedic genius after he released his first feature film, and I was totally taken by the familiarity of his energy to me. Jim Carrey.

This experience on the bus happened circa 1994, when *Ace Ventura* was newly released and Jim skyrocketed to fame beyond being the hilarious elastic white guy playing extreme burn victim Fire Marshall Bill and other brilliant characters on *In Living Color*. I later found out that he grew up only a 45-minute drive away from St. Catharines, my hometown.

I remember riding the Greyhound back home after another audition. I was exhausted from a long day, looking out the window of the bus. Funnily enough, this happened just as we were passing the area where Jim himself grew up. I did not know this at the time though, I didn't yet know he was Canadian.

It had only been days since I'd finished reading *The Celestine Prophecy*, and my consciousness had received a major upgrade from the contents of this book. Besides seeing auras quite clearly, mostly around plants and trees, in this very distinctive moment on the bus, I was overcome with a vision of Jim in my mind's eye, and in this image, I saw and felt us merged together, and our energies became One.

I had never experienced anything quite like this before and was not sure what to make of it. I remember while having this experience simultaneously having a thought wash over me like a gentle, yet powerful wave. I heard it so clearly that I remember the goosebumps it gave me to this day.

The thought was: "*We are One and the Same. We are the same energy. He is my Brother. I am the female version, and he is the male version, of the same energetic frequency. We are two parts of One Whole Energy.*"

It was such a calming, beautiful realization, and tears streamed down my face as I absorbed the truth of this knowing. Whatever in the world it meant exactly, I did not know, and I felt no desire to figure it out either, which was unusual for my inquisitive Gemini mind. In that same moment, a powerful knowing told me that there would come a time when he and I would meet face to face, and when we did, our souls would recognize one another instantly upon eye contact.

There was the eye contact signal again.

I sat with this unusual, yet powerfully mystical experience, breathing deeply, allowing it to simply "be" whatever it was. All there was to do was to sit there and embrace this experience, pondering the outlandish possibility of this revelation actually being realized someday. Yet I had no doubt that it would.

Only time would tell the how, when, where, and why of it; and I was okay with that. I had a lot of time, and I had zero expectations and no stars in my eyes. I had no need to be attached to this vision or message, or any celebrity for that matter.

Even this experience did not change how I felt. I was okay if it came to pass someday, and okay if it didn't. Nothing's changed.

I do take note and find Jim's more recent delve into visibly and publicly living a life more in alignment with a mystic and spiritual leader than a celebrity very interesting. Back in 1994, how was I to have a clue who he really was given what I was shown (and minimally at that, since I did not pay attention for the most part) through the eyes of the media? All I knew of him personally was his zany portrayal of *Ace Ventura* and a couple short clips my sister had shown me of *In Living Color*.

Yet, this entire experience makes all the sense in the world to me now, and Jim's beautifully eloquent, courageous, intelligent, and quirky ways of coming out of the cosmic closet, so to speak, about this side of him only confirms for me how real and true the experience was that I had about him more than two decades ago.

He has been a pioneer in the celebrity spiritual and cosmic awareness movement, as were John and Yoko, which again, I did not know about at the time I'd begun having mystical experiences connected with them. Five-years old is much too young to pay attention to these kinds of things. You really can't make this stuff up.

And then, finally, and most intensely, there was the mystery man from the music video on my television who would activate me like no other when I was seventeen, who many years later, I would go on to have so many experiences connected with this man. I would not even learn his name, Anthony, until 14 years after the initial activation. Even later still, I would come to realize that Anthony, too, has extremely strong cosmic ties to dimensions and realities beyond this Earthly realm.

I was aware of none of these things all those many decades ago, when the energies and imprints of every one of these cosmic celebrity souls began working with and through me, oftentimes on profoundly deep levels. I have no doubts now that there have been distinct galactic forces initiating and overseeing these activations and assignments between us, many of which still hang in the balance. I feel no need to direct these happenings myself, though admittedly, I have faced moments of wanting to control these connections, thinking my small and limited human mind knew what was best and what "they" wanted. I realize now that any such silly assumption is just that, and now flow with whatever is presented to me, in each moment. Beyond that, I allow to be revealed in "their" timing, as I do my best to stay in my own alignment, poised and ready to make my move when the cosmic signal is given.

Knowing what I have learned now about galactic tracking thanks to Selene's 30+ years of experience working with and tracking these energies, Jim Carrey's birthdate is January 17, 1962. The sun was at galactic degree in Capricorn when Jim was born. This is the mark of the Crystal Grid, indicating crystal mastership, which is indeed a major star marking. Jim is without a doubt a "starseed." And, as synchronicity would have it, this happens to be the same year Anthony was born—whatever *that* means, if anything.

To take it a step further, Yoko Ono's birthdate is February 18, 1933. According to Selene's discovery of star markings, the sun was at galactic degree in Aquarius when Yoko was born, which is the mark of Atlantis, and also indicates crystal mastership on a another level. Another starseed I was connected with long before I ever knew what a starseed was. And I know without a doubt that both John and Anthony were, and are also starseed.

Perhaps someday I will garner all the pieces and confirmation to this intriguing little celebrity connections puzzle and be able to decipher the full meaning of it all. For now though, I remain standing inside the mystery of it, in which I am more than comfortable. Are my connections with each of these beings interwoven as part of one major assignment, or are they separate assignments?

Or, are they merely demonstrations I was presented with as part of my galactic training in order to awaken me to the greater cosmic web that connects us all? Or is it perhaps a combination of all of these, and maybe more? I will continue to connect all the cosmic dots as they present themselves to me, and perhaps I will see clearly the full galactic picture someday.

Perhaps...perhaps...perhaps.

CHAPTER 16

Two Hours Lost

It happened in November of 1996. Mid-November to be precise, in my small, thickly bedazzled Italian hometown in Southern Ontario. It was after 10 pm and wintertime had come in full swing. The sky was dark, the roads were snowy and it was crisp cold outside.

I had just returned home from a play rehearsal at Brock University, where I was a theatre student in the first term of my second year. I was living at home with my parents, only a five-minute drive from the university. I was a full-time student, and was still teaching dance to young children three days a week. I was now twenty-one.

I had been dating a young fellow, Darrell, from the theatre program who was a bit of an anomaly to me. He was an odd duck to put it mildly. I had started hanging out with him after talking extensively one day about weight lifting, and he told me that he would help me learn to lift weights in the university gym on our breaks.

I had stopped training in dance that year, since I was spending most of my time and energy in the theatre, and I really missed it. I missed feeling fit and missed the physical outlet to release energy, as dance had been such a huge part of my life since I was four and had become one of my greatest loves, with the added perk of helping me stay in shape. Not to mention it was the greatest creative and emotional healing outlet I had, and it had gotten me through a lot of rough times growing up.

I missed it so much, yet did not have the time to commit to my training, and besides which, the girls I had danced with for many years, my "sisters," had all retired and moved on to university and careers themselves. I had been the only one still dancing and training for the pure love of it, and now the only kids left for me to dance with were many years younger than me, which didn't work when it came to competition teams.

Though I always loved performing, I was never big on competing. But the competitive training classes were the way to get the best and most juicy physical training, the most fun and challenging routines, and they pushed me to my limits, which I loved. Don't get me wrong. I would have danced with anyone, and did, but the rigorous training was what I was missing, and my body was definitely feeling it.

So, I turned to working out instead, which in the end turned out to be a mistake in hindsight. Well, the way I did it anyway. I had always been such a "go hard or go home" type of person, and overdid the weight training a bit. I looked great then, but now after more than 15 years, hitting my 40s, being a mother, and not having been nearly as active as I want to be or used to be, those nice, muscular legs I'd developed doing countless hours of pointe work, and which I buffed up further working out like a maniac, my legs and butt are where I now carry any excess weight I might gain. But so long as I eat well and at least moderately exercise, do yoga, and hike occasionally, my body maintains a pretty decent size and weight. When I'm flying high, totally inspired by life and am eating really cleanly and well, my body always feels and looks great.

I give great gratitude for this.

So, after finishing rehearsal and having come home to drop off my books and get changed before heading over to Darrell's for a later dinner and most likely some Star Trek episodes I would be expected to endure, it felt like any ordinary night.

Darrell was a *Star Trek* junkie. He also loved *The X-Files* (like most of the kids at that time) and, of course, *Star Wars* was a given. I was into none of these really, and couldn't have given a rat's ass about any of them.

I was never much into TV, magazines, the radio or the media in any way, which I've already stated repeatedly. I saw celebrities as real people, and didn't put any of them on pedestals and it always bothered me when people did.

I could see through the deception of the cameras, the airbrushing, the makeup and perfect hair, the perfect bodies. Even as a child, I saw right through it. Growing up, it made me sad that my best friend was always talking about Christy Brinkley, and yet seemed endlessly unhappy with how she felt about herself, always wanting to be skinnier or prettier or whatever.

I thought my friend was one of the most beautiful, funny, intelligent, and perfect people I'd ever met, so her interest in this model, in my opinion, made her too focused on what was on the outside, and I never understood how she couldn't just look in the mirror and see herself that way too. To me, she was the most beautiful girl I knew.

My sister was also very interested in celebrities, but barely ever left the house or her room. She was a genius with an incredibly high IQ and could read a Stephen King novel in a day if she wanted to. She could read the newspaper front to back by the time she was four, before ever going to school, without being taught. And yet, she would obsess about celebrities and watched television and *Much Music* (Canada's equivalent of MTV) every single day. I loved her, but I just didn't get it.

Darrell, coincidentally, loved anything having to do with extraterrestrials and outer space. I never even put that together until years after what I will share next. At the time, I was so enmeshed in the intensity of it all, I could not see it clearly until many years later. That whole adage about not being able to see the forest for the trees would become one of the main themes of my life, running in circles, never knowing where I was really going. Thank Heavens those days are over.

I had this odd, inexplicable aversion to, or anything seemingly related to, science fiction. I think it probably hit too close to home for me, and I didn't want to ever have to go there.

But Darrell forced me to watch *Star Trek*, along with *The X-Files* and even the original *Star Wars* Trilogy, though I'd already seen them all as a kid. We had a very odd relationship. It's strange to sit here and write about these things I used to allow; ways I allowed myself to be controlled by other people, especially men. All part of a giant learning curve, I suppose.

So, I called Darrell and told him I was on my way over. I lived about a 5-minute drive from him, maybe even less. It was somewhere between 10 and 11pm as I headed out the door.

Darrell told me that he had just started on making dinner, and that it would be ready soon. I was so hungry after a long day of classes and rehearsals for a very physical play we were on the verge of opening in a couple of weeks.

For some reason, that night I had parked on the road in front of our neighbours' house as I stopped quickly at home to change, pack my bag for the evening, and call Darrell. This parking choice in itself was unusual, as I had never parked there, and I can't remember what my reason was for doing so, since we had two large driveways in front of our home, plus a parking spot on the road in front as well.

It was snowy and icy outside as I walked to my car and continued to open the door and get in, when the entire sky began to light up above me.

The light came from behind our house and slowly moved across, and over top of me, lighting up the entire street, and on over to the other side of the streets' homes, including the Setacci's household. This light was so enormous, I could not see where it began and where it ended once it was directly over me. This "thing," whatever it was, was massive.

From there, it seemed about 15 seconds of watching this gigantic vibrant white light travel directly over me, at a distance of only about 50-100 feet above me.

After it appeared to be gone, I remember my response being somewhat odd as I said aloud to myself, "*Wow! That was incredible!*"

And that was it.

There was no moment of puzzlement, no wondering what it was, perhaps because I'd had a "mind swipe" or because I had no doubts about what it was. The fact that I had no fear or reservations about such an enormous object hovering directly over me strikes me as interesting now that I look back on it, though I am glad I was not afraid, and grateful that I was able to embrace the experience, because it truly was magnificent.

As far as I knew, it was roughly 15 seconds of sheer delight and awe, and then it was over. As far as I was concerned, I'd hopped right into my car, somewhat high from the enormity of it all, and headed on over to Darrell's for dinner.

The interesting thing is that I never remembered actually seeing the light leave. It was simply there, moving over top of me, and then suddenly it was gone, and I was getting into my car.

From the time I'd called Darrell from my parents' kitchen, to walking out to my car, seeing the starship, getting in and driving to Darrell's, none of that would have taken any longer than ten minutes tops, and that was if I were moving casually and taking my time.

I arrived at his door and went to hug and kiss him like I always did, but he was cold and seemed very upset with me about something. He was often getting into little snits about things, but not usually with me. I had no idea what I'd done. I could feel his anger, and so I asked him what was wrong.

He looked at me as though he were offended I even needed to ask. I was dumbfounded and had not a single clue as to what was going on. I must have still been in an altered state because for me to not tell him right away what had happened was also highly unusual, especially since I was well aware of his great interest, verging on obsession, with UFOs and aliens—an obsession I did not share with him at the time.

I said, "What is *wrong* with you? What did I do?" I was so confused. According to my memory, we had only just spoken and he had seemed excited to make me dinner and see me.

"What do you *think* is wrong?" he implored.

"I really don't know!" I was starting to get frustrated here.

"You're two hours late! What were you doing? You call me and tell me you're coming over, and then you don't show up until after *midnight*? Why would you do that to me?"

He was hurt, I could see that clearly underneath the upset he was displaying. He had prepared a really nice dinner for us, and I hadn't shown up, even though I'd said I would. He hadn't even eaten yet himself, choosing to wait for me, and he was obviously very hungry and agitated, as unbeknownst to me, it was now after midnight.

"What are you talking about 'I'm late?' I called you and came right over! I have no idea what you're talking about!" I was the one getting agitated now.

And then my tone shifted, and I blurted out in excitement, "I saw a huge light in the sky right above me as I was getting into my car. It lit up the entire sky for blocks beyond what I could see. It was as light as the brightest, clearest summer sky. It moved over me, and was so close I could almost touch it."

I wasn't sure what this had to do with me being late but in that moment of remembering it, I felt like he would want to know what I had seen, and besides which, in all the tension, it was all I had to say for myself, feeble as it seemed.

All of a sudden, Darrell's face changed. His eyes popped slightly, and his jaw hung open in true Darrell fashion, and he stared at me for a moment, knowing I was not one to tell stories or make things up. I was about as real as you could get, for better or worse. My sister Shelby used to lovingly refer to me as "The Queen of Tact" due to my penchant for telling it like it is, no holds barred.

I blurted this out so matter-of-factly that he had to take a moment to let it sink in, and then he looked at me with such intensity and said, "Oh my GOD, you have missing time!"

He had a slight smile on his face that I could see beneath his shock as he began to process what I had said. He looked like a kid who'd just found a buried treasure filled with candy or something.

I had absolutely no clue what he was talking about.

"What? What the hell is 'missing time'?" I really had no idea what that meant or what it had to do with me seeing a light in the sky.

"Missing time! It's when you get abducted by aliens and then they bring you back. You don't remember going, you think you just saw a UFO. You can't remember what happened besides seeing the spaceship, but when you come back, hours have passed and you don't know where you were!"

Darrell was starting to look at me like I was the anomaly now. Like I was somehow the buried treasure he had just discovered, or some fascinating animal on display in a zoo. It made me feel really exposed and uneasy.

I started wondering then what the fuck had happened to me. This whole thing started out as an incredible, awe-inspiring light in the sky, and now I had 'missing time?' It was too much to wrap my brain around. I don't know what we did after that, probably ate the cold dinner and tried to process the reality of the situation.

Of course, I couldn't. I didn't know what to think or how to feel about it all. I had been enamored with it at first, but now I wasn't so sure. Why do people *lose* time and how come we can't remember where we were or what we were doing? What could "they" be hiding, I wondered?

The more I thought about it, the more I didn't like not knowing what had happened to me. So, I decided not to think about it or talk about it. I decided it was only an isolated incident, that I was obviously a random "pick" and that that would be the great UFO experience for my life. Done. Whew. Could have been way worse, I reasoned with myself, even if I had no idea what I'd experienced during those lost two hours of my life.

At least I wasn't traumatized. I'd heard horror stories from Darrell about what can go down in a so-called abduction. I was still viewing experiences as abductions and still bought into the whole victim/perpetrator mentality, which is disempowering and not in alignment with the truth at all when it comes to most authentic experiences, which I now know.

Authentic experiences are almost always pre-destined, and certainly not random. Sure, these beings may lack the grace of handling us humans with care and sensitivity, but we certainly don't need to be victims to anything or anyone. I know this now.

So that was it. I'd seen a light, had missing time, and was back, seemingly exactly the same as when I'd left. I didn't feel any different inside really, so I concluded that it wasn't so bad. I decided to be grateful for my easy encounter with whoever was aboard that ship and took me and did God-knows-what with me.

It was over now. Finito. I sure lucked out, I thought.

Little did I know that this encounter was only just the beginning of what was to become a growing list of high strangeness and various ET activity over many years to come.

CHAPTER 17

The Meeting Room Part I: Implanted

My relationship with Darrell started to rapidly decline from this experience onward. I am not certain why exactly, as the events of my everyday life at that time are more blurred than the clear experiences that awaited me (much to my ignorance).

About two weeks after seeing the light in the sky, I had my first ever recollected dream—or semi-conscious experience with extraterrestrials.

It took place while I was in a lucid dreaming state, and began with me and Darrell driving on a road at night in a car together. We looked up ahead and saw a round silver ship with white lights lowering toward the middle of the road, and we knew we were going to be driving directly underneath it. I was more than aware that they were there for me.

I felt afraid and uneasy and said to Darrell, "Stop! Drive the other way! Don't go near it!" but he kept driving toward it, as if he himself were a vacant shell, not really there, just an empty vessel, which was also highly strange. Because in truth, he *wasn't* really there, so he couldn't hear me, and I sure as hell couldn't stop him.

We drove directly underneath the ship, and in a flash, I was no longer inside the car, and Darrell was nowhere in sight. I was alone in a round room with what appeared to be metal furniture—tables and chairs and other structures. It was all metallic blue and silver. I can still see it in my minds' eye, and this experience happened 19 years ago at the time of this writing.

There were two beings there with me. They appeared to be dressed in navy-coloured metallic suits. They looked almost like business suits, but were skin tight fitted and had a slight shine to them.

There appeared to be a male figure and a female figure. The female figure had wavy blonde hair. I believe the male figure was bald, but am not certain of this detail.

These beings were not threatening at all, although I was admittedly quite scared. I didn't fear for my life, but had no idea what they were doing with me. Why was I alone there with them? Where was Darrell? Where was I?

They spoke telepathically with me, and asked me to sit down on the chair. I did so. They asked me to hold out my left hand for them, which I also did. There was no reason fighting any of this, I knew I was outnumbered as well as out-powered here. Besides which, I don't think I could have said "no" and gone on my merry way anyway. They were only being courteous to ask first, as they don't really want a struggle either. And I knew through the niceties, I didn't really have a choice here.

I gave one of them my left hand, palm up. The being took my hand and suddenly I saw a device in his other hand. This device looked like a thick pen or something similar in size and shape, only it appeared to have a small laser at the tip.

The being placed the device in the middle of my left palm, and I felt something shoot into my hand. It was quick and painless, yet I still screamed from the shock of it. I retreated my hand away instantly but noticed there was no mark on it anywhere. Nothing. It was as if the skin had not even been punctured at all.

What was going on here?

I sat there in silence, observing my hand and wondering what the hell had just happened. Then the beings invited me to come with them. I say invited, because there was no force involved. I still said no because there was a part of me that was afraid that going with them meant that I might never come back to Earth.

The next thing I knew, I was in the corridor of a ship, walking somewhere. I could feel these beings, or some other beings perhaps, I'm not exactly sure. Whoever they were, it felt like they were leading me. Though I also felt oddly like I already knew where I was going, so it is entirely possible no one was leading me at all. Of this detail though, I am just not certain.

I looked to my right at one point as I walked, and saw a room filled with earthly things, possibly for examination purposes. Within this room though, I also saw a lot of earthlings, and amongst them, I saw someone I knew. It was my Uncle Will. Interesting to note, his birthday is August 17th. Galactic Sun in Leo. Total starseed.

At that time though, I hadn't seen my Uncle Will in years. He was my stepdad's cousin, so technically he wasn't really my blood uncle. But growing up I had spent a lot of time with him and his children, staying many a weekend with them in Toronto, where he lived at the time.

I adored my Uncle Will as a child. He was a big teddy bear of a man, and I know he had a soft spot for me, and I for him. We always did share an interesting connection, so it is doubly interesting to me now to note that not only was he aboard this ship with me that night, but from all of Selene's tracking of starseed codes, he is also one of "us." At the time though, not being aware of any of this, it all seemed entirely random.

So, there was Uncle Will in this room amongst all of these other people, probably also starseeds, amongst samples of our earthly "Muggle things." The room was packed with junk, but I still managed to catch a glimpse of him as I passed. From what I remember, he seemed sort of out of it, most likely drugged with a special ET forget-me concoction. Who knows though? Certainly not me.

I remember nothing that transpired after this. What I would come to know as the imminent ET "blackout."

Sadly, my Uncle Will passed on from this world suddenly on June 26, 2016. I can't help but wonder if he's up there, aboard ship, reading this beside me as I write.

CHAPTER 18

A Cosmic Pain in the Ass

I awoke the following morning after this first experience, chalking it up to being no more than just a very vivid dream. The energy of it remained with me though, lingering around me like a little cloud of mist. I didn't feel anything in particular about it by way of emotion, and I certainly didn't feel upset about it.

After all, it was only a dream, right?

Admittedly though, I felt odd. But I wasn't relating any of it to the strange dream I'd had, even though it kept popping up in my mind periodically, just as vividly as if I had been there moments ago. In truth, I was clearly in denial.

I went on with my day as usual, keeping myself busy and occupied. I woke up, ate breakfast, and got ready for the day ahead.

At one point that morning, I began to notice a sort of dull aching sensation deep inside my anus. I noticed it, but it was dull, and it wasn't disturbing my day all that much, so I decided to not think about it. It felt like a kind of presence in there, not having felt anything like it before, but I assumed it would pass. I was still heavily in denial, big time.

As the early afternoon wore on though, that dull sensation turned into an aching, which started to get more and more pronounced, that by the time I had to go open up the dance studio at 4 pm to teach for the evening, I would describe what I was feeling inside my anus as a deep, aching, pointed, throbbing pain.

It was affecting the way I was walking as well as sitting. Basically, however I moved now, I was feeling this pain and it had become extremely uncomfortable to the point of becoming unmanageable.

Having gone into complete denial by this point, I racked my brain, trying to figure out what on earth was causing this outrageous pain. Shockingly, nothing came to mind, which, in hindsight, is very telling of the depth of delusion I was actually in, because the cause of this pain was definitely not "of Earth."

Still, I tried to justify and explain it away to myself, trying to recall perhaps an odd bowel movement I may have had, and even that couldn't explain this sensation away. I'd had issues with constipation my entire life, but even being in the hospital and passing masses the size of baseballs as a child had never amounted to such deep, internal pain like I was experiencing now.

Nothing added up here.

The students of the first class all arrived, ready for their tap lesson. These children were roughly ten to twelve years of age, and had all been taking lessons for several years already.

They knew the warm-up and the class routine. They were used to getting down to business as soon as class began, and were standing ready at the barre, waiting for the music to begin their ankle and foot exercises.

I stood in the front at the mirror, as the teacher often did, put my hand on the mirror (at this point, to hold myself up) and began to circle my foot and ankle. I could feel an inner wincing happening, but I was able to mask it. And then I began toe tapping exercises.

As I called out the exercises, I went to demonstrate the rapid toe tapping, when suddenly a sharp electrical pain shot through my entire body, beginning at the exact point where the pain inside my anus now overwhelmed me, and I gasped for breath, rather dramatically I assume, because the kids all stopped dead, staring at me and asking me if I was alright. They could tell something was definitely wrong.

"Miss Sam, are you okay?" a few of them asked, with looks of genuine concern and even panic.

"Oh yeah, sweeties. I'm fine." I tried my best to assure them (and myself) that there was nothing to worry about. And then it simply poured out of my mouth without a single thought: "It must just be that alien abduction dream I had last night."

I heard myself blurt this out beyond any ability to control it, and for the first time that day, it actually hit me.

'Oh my GOD,' I thought to myself. What had I just said? My own mind was reeling now, and I suddenly remembered where I was. I looked around the room, and all of the girls were standing, staring at me, eyes wide in disbelief and shock, not

knowing how to respond to what I'd said. Some even looked frightened.

Though I realized what I had just said was in fact true, I couldn't let on to the kids that it actually was true. But believe me, I was freaking out inside.

"Just kidding!" I heard myself say with forced laughter. "It isn't that, obviously. But I don't know what it is, and I can't really move right now, so you'll just have to listen to me call out the exercises and do them on your own."

I was sort of dancing between worlds by this point. I was in a haze, seeing stars, partly because of the excruciating pain I was now in, and partly because of the truth and weight of what I had suddenly realized. I was attempting to wrap my mind around how this could possibly be true. Yet I knew without a doubt that it was; it must have been if I was experiencing such an intense physical symptom one would assume to typically be related with such an encounter, especially a symptom this unmistakably strong and odd.

It seemed like a cliché to me —the infamous "anal probe"— so much so that I didn't want to believe it could really be happening, though I couldn't deny it either as I was most definitely not imagining this unbelievable pain I was in.

I went to sit down in a chair beside the sound system, and as I sat, there was another zing of pain that shot through my anus, and my entire body tensed up completely. I couldn't even sit now, and I couldn't walk or move without extreme discomfort either. So, I sat on one side of my ass and taught the rest of the evening's classes in this very strange and uncomfortable sitting position. It was the best option of any by this point, so that's what I did.

I was incredibly uncomfortable, and it was a real challenge for me to stay present with the children, as I ran over and over non-stop, almost obsessively in my mind, any memory I could recall from the dream sequence of the previous night which had landed me here, in pain, and utterly confused. My whole inner foundation had been seriously rocked.

I could remember nothing more about it, nothing that would account for this incredible pain I was feeling. I went home that night and rested, hoping it would feel better the next day, and that I could write it off as 'nothing.' Just a strange co-incidence. Clearly still hanging on to every last ounce of denial I could muster.

The pain lasted, though. It lessened a bit each day, but still was an ever-present aching deep inside for about a month. I knew enough not to go see a doctor though. What would I say to them? That aliens abducted me and put something inside my ass? That wasn't going to happen.

After about a month, the sensation turned from pain to mild discomfort, then literally it became only a sensation of a small physical presence inside my anus, like a device, or a lump or something that never used to be there, but now was. I knew it was inorganic. If I thought about it too much it might have scared me, so most of the time, I did my best to ignore it.

It graduated to only feeling this mysterious presence if I was sitting in a straddled leg stretch on the floor, which was highly uncomfortable but I took that over agonizing pain. I could handle it, even though all in all, this sensation, this presence, remained for the better part of the entire next year, and was always a somewhat unwelcome reminder of those dreaded experiences. Never allowing me to slip into my blissful denial again. But at least I could pretend on the outside like life was trekking along as usual. I could easily pretend that nothing out of the ordinary was happening to me, and no one had to be the wiser.

Except me.

Within about a week after having this initial experience, while I was still experiencing quite a significant amount of pain, though manageable (I somehow managed to go about my daily life, dancing, teaching, acting classes in school, sitting in a chair, etcetera, now), I started feeling that this nagging presence inside my body, was also now in my womb. I didn't know what it was, yet I took serious note that my menses, which always commenced on the 2nd day of every month without fail, had not yet come.

I most definitely took notice, as this had never happened before, with the exception of that one summer when I was seventeen and it didn't come at all for two months. I'm pretty certain now that my work with these beings was already in full swing, even back then. I was only now beginning my conscious training with these beings.

And it all started in the womb.

Yet here I was, still taking university classes, getting ready for final exams that following week, and then the Christmas holidays. It was December 1996 and I didn't know it then, but my life was about to take a turn that I would have never seen coming in a million years.

CHAPTER 19

The Big Lady Jesus

I had been asked by my acting teacher to take a one-day job on a Saturday in December 1996 with my friend, Dawn, and travel the new city bus line system that was being launched in St. Catharines. We would travel in town for the day bus-hopping, performing little improvisational sketches wearing our red clown noses, in character as clowns.

Dawn and I both loved physical theatre and we'd both been thoroughly enjoying the clowning block in our acting class. I suppose this was why Glenys had asked us to be the ones to take this particular gig. She loved me too, because I was a dancer and she had trained intensively with Jacques Lacoq in Europe. She also was responsible for introducing us to one of her favourite dance and physical theatre companies, Pilobolus, as well as Gilles Maheu's company out of Quebec, Carbone 14. Glenys took an instant liking to me with my dance background and because I was so willing to be way out there in my work and fearlessly go for it, no holds barred.

That's always been my way. Somewhat fearless in exploring creativity when given an open floor to connect within and let my inner freak out. I'd lay it all out without a second thought—

guts, scar tissue and all, of which I had plenty in my personal repertoire.

So of course, Dawn and I said yes to this gig. We were flattered that Glenys didn't send some of the upper year students out on this gig and instead entrusted us second year kids with the task as representatives of the acting program. Or perhaps we were the only ones crazy enough to take the job. Who knows?

Dawn and I showed up, ready for some wacky, light-hearted fun that day. We rode the bus together and made complete asses of ourselves, all in the name of theatre and silliness. We had a blast. Some people riding the bus didn't know what to make of us, as they were simply trying to go about their day and get to work on time, yet here Dawn and I were, red-nosed and acting like a couple of idiots. That was our job, after all.

We had been riding the buses for hours by this point, when we stepped off of one at the terminal, which was our headquarters for the day. We were in full character still, when something extremely bizarre happened.

As soon as we got off the bus, a woman, who appeared to be dressed in rags—one might have assumed she was homeless or mentally ill to the extreme, or both—cornered us. I don't even know how it happened. One minute we were stepping off the bus, the next, Dawn and I were standing enclosed in the corner with this heavy-set and wide-eyed woman. It felt like we were inside of some invisible bubble, and she was ready to rip into us about something.

And rip into us, she did.

She started in with proclaiming to be Jesus Christ, and she meant it. This woman was talking all up in our faces, practically spitting on us as she spoke. She was talking with such intensity and conviction; we had no choice but to hear her out. Besides, we couldn't escape that bubble she had us in.

First, she directed her message to Dawn. Then she went on and on about what, to me, sounded precisely, clearly, and obviously targeting a very sensitive and serious health issue Dawn had been struggling very much in silence with, and that from the outside, no one would have been able to tell. The woman didn't come out and say exactly what it was in literal terms. In fact, I don't even remember the words that were coming out of her mouth exactly, but I do remember thinking to myself in a bit of a panic, '*Oh my God, she is talking about Dawn's health! How does she even know about this?*'

The whole thing was tripping me out, because it really was not at all obvious from an outside perspective what Dawn was even going through. Unless she confided in you, which she had done with me, and I knew I was one of the only people who knew about it. There was no way this woman could have known this very secret information.

So, I literally was tripping out inside my own head over how on Earth this woman could have known what Dawn was going through, unless somehow, amidst the apparent craziness she displayed, she was actually psychic. Perhaps she was. Stranger things have been known to happen.

Regardless, I felt awful for Dawn, and was becoming seriously concerned about this woman triggering Dawn's situation and causing her to spin more deeply into a downward spiral with her health. I panicked inside a little bit, trying to figure out how I was going to help my friend once this bizarre ordeal was finally over.

And then, it happened. The wide-eyed Mystical Maniac in the form of a bag lady turned her attention, just as intensely, if not more so, to me.

"And *YOU!*" she yelled, her finger in my face, her eyes seeming even wider now, if that was possible.

'Oh shit. What is she going to dish about me now? What can she see?'

"THE ANSWER IS IN YOUR BELLY!"

She was baring her teeth by this point, almost gritting, and whatever sense of personal space she had (which wasn't much) seemed to lessen significantly, as it felt like we were almost nose-to-nose. I am sure this part of my memory is exaggerated somewhat, and that it was more me feeling her energy penetrating my own so deeply, but at the time, I felt like she was almost standing on top of me, nearly pushing me over, and I was beginning to suffocate with an inner panic at what she was saying to me.

As soon as these words spilled from her mouth, I knew exactly what she was talking about, but had no idea how it could possibly be with my logical mind. I was still completely unaware of my part in this very real, ET/human experiment. I had not yet received the memo describing my work aboard the ships inter-dimensionally at night, which I had been a part of for years, if not millennium, by this damn point.

In that moment though, I knew I was pregnant, but didn't know why or how that could be.

Somehow, I just knew. I knew this had something to do with my ovaries and my womb, and assumed I must be carrying a physical being inside of me, and that would explain what had been fluttering in there for the past week or so. I had thought it was a new kind of indigestion that I'd never had before.

'*Holy shit.*' The weight of this realization sunk in and my mind went totally blank, almost comatose.

Finally, after an extremely intense moment that lasted who knows how long, the mysterious woman claiming to be Jesus Christ released Dawn and I from the corner and disappeared.

We realized then that we still had our clown noses on. The joke was entirely on us.

This went far beyond bizarre now. This wasn't just a dream that I could poo-poo away now. It wasn't something I had to decide for myself actually happened or didn't happen. I even had a witness to attest to it happening now.

This was high strangeness to the nth degree.

Dawn and I were both shaken. We attempted to continue our work for the day, and boarded another bus line. But, for the most part, we sat there, forcing the clowning and silliness to come as best we could muster. It felt so contrived though, and from what I gather, it probably was not funny at all. We finally realized this and let it fizzle out.

The adage about clowns being the most fucked up and tragic characters of all, hiding beneath a false smile, had suddenly become my own personal truth.

We decided halfway through the ride that we were done. We just sat there, noses still on, not giving a flying fig what we looked like, silently riding the bus, side by side.

The best theatre is always the most honest depiction of life, so I suppose that pathetic scene in and of itself could have been a performance, but it really wasn't one to us. It was definitely more authentic than the shit we'd been trying to force right before it though. We were both stunned into silence and stillness by what had occurred, and there was nothing else left to do or say.

Finally, what felt like the never-ending bus ride ended and we returned to the terminal. Thankfully it was the end of the day, or close enough at least, and Dawn and I decided it was time to clock out. We were so done.

We went into our changing room, took off our noses, put our costumes in our bags, and walked back to her apartment downtown where I had left my car.

I looked at her at one point during our walk, and without explaining anything, as calmly as I could muster, said, "I need to take a pregnancy test."

CHAPTER 20

A Positive Negative

Dawn and I bought the pregnancy test on our walk home. She didn't ask questions, though I sensed she knew how crucial this was for me. She knew I was dating Darrell still, so must have assumed I thought he may have impregnated me. I didn't tell her differently that I can remember, but I knew there was no way Darrell had impregnated me. I knew that if I were pregnant, it was going to flip my world upside down, because then I would have to really face that fated night, only weeks earlier, where I had lost two hours of my time...of my life.

We got back to Dawn's apartment, and though I was terrified to take this test, I did it anyway. Thank God I have the capacity to face issues I may not want to, even in the face of utter fear. I would rather know than not know and pretend I do.

I took a deep breath as I sat on the toilet to pee on the little stick I had grasped tightly in my hand. I knew that within minutes, I would know the truth.

I peed on the stick.

I sat for the longest two minutes of my life before I looked at it, all the while, breathing deeply into my belly, feeling like I might be sick.

And then I looked over. A huge sigh of relief washed over me. Somehow, someway, it was negative. Supposedly, I was not pregnant. Not anymore.

CHAPTER 21

The Death of Samantha

I still could not shake these experiences though. I told no one about them, and went about my days, thankfully busy with school and work, so I definitely had enough distractions.

I barely remember my time with Darrell after all of this high strangeness started happening, even though I didn't officially break up with him until the summer of 1997. So, he was indeed a part of this journey with me somehow, for whatever reason, I still am not sure. Possibly to be a catalyst for me, and to be a source of information for me when things would happen. I never told him everything, though there sometimes were things he found out by default because I had become such a live wire; anxious, nervous and afraid, especially at night. I was starting to develop some mild paranoia, so I suppose my experiences did end up seeping into our relationship, which quickly unraveled under the pressure of it all.

There was one night in particular where we had spent the evening together, and then Darrell dropped me off at home. It was later, probably after 11 pm, and everyone in my family was already asleep. The house was eerily quiet, and honestly, though it was late, it seemed to be a bit early for my grown brother and my parents to all be this quiet.

But it was. And they were.

It was quiet and dark throughout the house. I walked in the door, and felt it right away. I will add that on the drive to bring me home, I had looked up in the sky and saw lights zigzagging above us. I had never really seen something so noticeable before that I could recall, and they seemed to be following us. Following me.

I kept it to myself for a few minutes, watching them, but then finally, when the realization that they really were following me hit, I said to Darrell, "Do You see that? Look! It's like they're following us!"

Darrell looked out the window for a minute and he saw it too, and said "Holy shit! I think they *are* following us!" He started driving in different directions, to test it out, and every time he changed direction, so did the lights in the sky. It was eerie. He seemed to be enjoying it, but I sure wasn't. I knew this meant that I was in for more experiences and I definitely wasn't looking forward to it.

Finally, he got me home, and I got out of the car, thinking '*At least they're way up there, and not right here,*' and I went inside. But when the house was so dark and quiet, I began to feel very strange.

Every move I made, I could feel something, a presence, behind me. It felt as though there were mere inches between us, and that was it. I swore I could feel its breath on the back of my neck and it made my hairs stand on end. I picked up the phone and felt it. I went to brush my teeth, and it was right there. It was when I went to change that I really felt it, and that was the last straw. That was when I lost it. I started to shake, and whisper-yelled desperately, in great fear by this point, "*WHAT* do you *WANT* from me?!"

I really thought I was going to snap. It had only been about ten minutes since Darrell had dropped me off, but I called him, knowing he would be home already.

"I need you to come back and get me please. Something is here and it's following me around, and I am scared and I have to get out of here!" I was frantic by this point, in tears, and my heart felt like it was about to jump out of my chest.

Darrell came right over, thankfully, hearing the desperation and panic in my voice. I was waiting outside for him to show up. I'd just had to get out of that house.

Those car headlights coming down the street and up into my driveway were the most welcome sight I had ever seen in that moment. I ran over to the car, got in, slammed the door, and locked it.

He was probably thinking I was losing my mind. I was losing my mind. I felt like I was teetering on the edge of insanity and it was terrifying me. It felt like the ground was dropping out from underneath me and I was losing my grip on reality.

I thought I was going to die.

I didn't think any of this could end well.

What is interesting to me now that I am writing this is, I had always carried a thought-form my entire life up to then: *that I would die when I was twenty-one*. I had never actually put the potential significance of that together until right now, as I write these words.

All of these experiences started to happen, and as a result of them, a part of me did die.

The me I was pretending to be for so long, the lost me, started to die the moment I saw that ship, the moment I experienced missing time. The moment I met those beings for the first time, consciously. The moment my grip on reality started to alter in such a drastic way, making me question everything about myself I had ever known.

The Samantha who had been everyone's support, everyone's "go to," everyone's rock, everyone's soft place to fall, always placing the needs of others before her own, the one who had her shit together, had started to crumble away and die. She was now entering a new phase of activation and initiation in preparation to eventually give birth to her true essence, which is Who She Is Now.

And yes, this "death" did occur for me, *within* me, when I was, indeed, twenty-one.

CHAPTER 22

The Paper Pants Rebel

The next experience in the form of a dream came almost, if not exactly, a month after the first dream experience. Thankfully this time, they took it easy on me, and I didn't encounter any pain as a result of it. Though, I was still nursing the previous anal encounter, which as I said, lasted the entire year of 1997, lessening in sensation with time, until eventually, the sensation disappeared completely, synchronistically when the experiences seemed to end.

So, this next experience graced me with merely memories, which were more than enough in my opinion at the time.

It started much the same way as the first one, but this time, I was with my sister, Shelby. We were also driving in a car, and I can't remember who was at the wheel. For some reason, I feel like this time I may have been, but can't recall for certain.

Again, I saw the lights. This time, I knew that there was no stopping the experience and although I wished with all my might that I could, I was also aware that in some way, it was destined to take place and no amount of wishing would change the outcome.

Next thing I knew, we were underneath the lights, Shelby was gone, and I was transported, this time to a desert land. I had no idea at the time what the Four Corners of the United States looked like (being an untraveled Canadian girl), where Area 51 was or what it looked like, nor the amount of activity and high strangeness that takes place in those areas. Living in Arizona now for the past eight years, and having traveled to New Mexico and Utah since this dream, the land I found myself on was most definitely identical to one of these places.

I was in an open vast land, dry and dusty. There were rocks and cacti and tumble weeds interspersed, but mostly it was rocky and dusty.

And I was not alone.

There was a landed space craft to my left, and in front of me stood three beings. These beings telepathically spoke to me, telling me to look down and put on the clothing that lay there on the ground in front of me.

I looked down and saw a pair of white pants that appeared to be made out of paper. It was the strangest thing, and I had no idea why they were asking me to do this.

With great defiance, I said, "No!"

They insisted that I wear these pants. I kept refusing. I was being verbally combative, and was doing my best to fight going anywhere with them. After the pain of the first experience, I wasn't so sure I trusted these beings.

"No!" I kept yelling at them. They seemed to be getting a bit agitated with me by this point. I mean to them, it was simple. Cut and dry. *'Put the pants on and let's get on with this. We have work to do!'* But my thought was more like, *'Get on with WHAT exactly?'* I didn't want to play.

Next thing I knew, a window-like screen appeared and opened up in the ground. It was actually very interesting, and unlike anything I'd ever seen before. There was the face of a being displayed in it. This being appeared to be female, as she had long, reddish-brown wavy hair. She was quite beautiful actually.

In all of these experiences, I never could remember their faces, which has always frustrated me, and I am not exactly sure why. Others whom I have shared these stories with sometimes get the look of "*Oh....*" on their faces, with a general feeling of alarm or concern, which perhaps they have reason to feel, but to me, these beings were interesting and still beautiful in their own right, even though I was terrified of them in the moment. A very multi-layered experience to be sure.

The being on the screen that had appeared in the dusty floor of the desert was talking to me, telepathically. She assured me everything was all right, and to please put on the pants. A rebel at heart (with a large dose of stubborn), I was surely not about to give in to their demands, and I still refused.

The agitation of the beings standing there with me grew, and I began to feel frightened, as if I may be in danger if I didn't comply. I am quite certain now that this was my own projection due to a fear of what would come next. I do not feel now that these beings were actually threatening me in any way. They never did harm me. They were simply there to get their job done and I was getting in the way of that by whining and throwing a tantrum about those ghastly paper pants (which seemed to me to have legs a ten-foot tall person would fit into).

I remember nothing after this last moment of defiance, though I awoke the next morning with a strong knowing that I had indeed gone aboard ship with these beings, wearing the paper pants, and yet again, I couldn't remember any of it. Yet I was absolutely certain I had experienced contact.

This was all starting to take a serious toll on me. My relationship was becoming more strained as I realized I didn't want to be in it anymore. School and work were great distractions, but still, that sensation in my anus proceeded to nag at me; that ever-present physical reminder that I was not alone and not in control of my body or my life; that I was being watched, and that at least some nights, I was indeed being taken somewhere aboard a space craft or facility of some sort, and what was worse, I had no idea what was happening to me when I was there.

CHAPTER 23

An Unlikely Confidante

I was sitting one day in the Green Room where all the theatre students went to eat and chat on our breaks. This day, I sat in the back part where the kitchen was, where it was usually quieter and darker. I was getting some much needed solitude when Al, the technical director of the theatre—not one of my teachers, but an employee of the university theatre—came in to eat with me.

Al used to sit and chat with the students on his breaks. He was a guy who appeared at the time to be in his early forties (which seemed way older than me, yet a club of which I am now an honorary member).

Al was an interesting man. He had one of the highest-pitched voices for a man I had ever heard, which made him sort of odd and intriguing to me. I sometimes thought he was flirting with me which made me a tad uncomfortable since I didn't find him to be the least bit attractive, but who knows. I was so fucked up then; I was probably misreading signals left, right and center.

What I feel now is that there was perhaps something in common we may have shared, which is most likely why the events of our lunch together unfolded as they did that day.

Al sat down to eat with me. All of our interactions previously, surprisingly, had never seemed this intimate. Making chitchat at first, he quickly realized I was not really in the mood for idle talk. It was unlike me to be so obviously disinterested, as I was usually bubbly and friendly with people and never intentionally rude, so I'm sure Al sensed this as he said to me, "What's wrong, Sam?"

I looked at him. "I don't know," I said, feeling defeated, and something in me, beyond me, started telling him everything that had been happening with me in the past two months or so. I was lost, confused, and desperately needed someone to talk to, and for some reason in this moment, which thankfully I now understand, I chose Al.

I dished out every detail of what had been happening, from seeing the light over my street, to the first dream, the anal pain afterward (which, of course, was still all too present), the woman cornering me at the bus terminal, thinking I was pregnant, thankfully the test came back negative, feeling like I was being followed and watched, and finally, this last dream in the desert with the paper pants.

Al sat there, staring at me, mouth open, listening intently. After I finished spewing all of this information to a mere acquaintance of mine, a stranger really, Al stared at me for a moment, then said, "Wait right here. I have to go get something."

He ran out the door, and was only gone for a minute or two, when he returned with a book in his hands.

"Have you seen this book before?" he asked me. I hadn't.

"No," I said. He proceeded to open it up to pages that had been ear marked. He displayed them, one page at a time, for me to read segments from, upon his direction.

The book was called *Communion* and it was written by a man named Whitley Strieber. I had never heard of this book nor had I heard of the author. And, honestly, I wasn't much of a reader then, but Al told me that it was a true story written by a man who'd had similar experiences as me.

As I read the pages he was showing me, tears began streaming down my face, uncontrollably. Every single segment I read, I understood and could visualize perfectly, because they had all been, almost to the letter, exactly what I had experienced and described to Al.

"What do they want from me?" I pleaded aloud as I wept. I didn't expect a reply. It was more like I was begging the Universe to please tell me why this was all happening to me. I felt completely out of control of my own life.

I was overcome with emotion at the realization that I was not cracking up after all (a part of me had actually hoped I was, so that I would be able to fix it by getting help, which I was millimeters away from doing by this point). At least if I was losing my mind and cracking up, that would make logical sense, and there would be something to do to correct it. People go crazy all the time.

Or do they?

I suppose sometimes they do. I don't know. But some people, like me, think they are, yet learn eventually (hopefully anyway, unless someone else gets to them before they realize the truth for themselves) that they are fully in their right mind, and it is simply being challenged and altered—even tested.

Sadly, some people who have these kinds of experiences end up being medicated or worse, locked up, for accidentally telling the wrong person the wrong thing at the wrong time. This truly breaks my heart whenever I think about it, but it makes me more determined to do what I came here to do, and to be a voice for those who could not give voice to their experiences themselves.

These are only my personal experiences, but my intention behind sharing so deeply the experiences I thought I would hide from the world forever, not thinking they had any significance to the world around me, is because I now know that these things do happen, and in fact, these experiences are much more common than we might think, and this awakening to the truth of these experiences is what I actually came to this planet at this particular time to share.

I can no longer run from my destiny, and I have embraced the truth, that I am here to share my personal story.

CHAPTER 24

First Love + Sex = Dysfunction

My life was never the same after 1997. I teetered on the fine line between sanity and insanity, and for a while I got myself into some really messy situations, especially with men and intimacy.

Always remaining incredibly sexual and sensual by nature, I chose to keep that part of me for me, mostly. I had protected my sexuality for so long, and shared it with only two men, by choice, the first of which occurred exactly 20 months before I encountered the light ship and missing time, with a man I was certain I was supposed to marry and be with forever.

We'd met when I was twelve and he was fourteen while both of our families were vacationing in Florida. We were staying at the same hotel in St. Petersburg, and once we met, we spent every minute we could together, talking, kissing, walking on the beach, and swimming in the ocean. It was heaven, and I fell in love with him instantly.

We managed to stay in touch, him living in Ohio, me in Southern Ontario. My sister and I somehow talked our father into taking us to Ohio to visit him and his friends two years later. I was sure I was going to marry this boy one day, at least I really wanted to. He was my first true love.

His name was Geoff. I loved the American drawl he spoke with, and he would send me the sweetest love letters filled with pictures he'd drawn with poems he'd written for me. One letter he sent me when I was about thirteen had a picture of a ring he had drawn. He said he was going to give it to me one day, and that he was surely going to marry me as soon as I turned eighteen.

We went to visit him for the Fourth of July when I was fourteen and he was sixteen. Of course our parents were there, but we still managed to sneak kisses together during fireworks at his high school, with lots of hugs and cuddles. We had so much fun together that trip too.

Then years passed, and though we attempted to stay in touch, life happened. Even though we were getting older, we were still too young to travel by ourselves, so we just didn't see each other. He had girlfriends, and of course, I had my boyfriends too. I kept my "seed" to myself though, and would not willingly give my whole self to any of these boyfriends after the mistakes I'd made with the two other older boys I'd dated when I was fourteen and fifteen.

I knew, especially after the traumatic sexual experiences I'd had with them that my sexuality was sacred, and I needed to protect it, and myself.

Geoff and I went back and forth for about eight years, in and out of contact, going long periods of time without speaking, and then one day, one of us would call the other out of the blue, and we'd be head over heels again, making romantic plans for a fantastical reunion.

When he contacted me one day in early 1995, I was almost twenty, and Shelby was twenty-two going on twenty-three, we decided we wanted to go to Ohio over spring break, which also happened to be Geoff's birthday, March 15th.

We went, and I was certain it would be a glorious reunion, filled with love and passion, and I was ready for anything. I was ready to make love with this man I had met almost ten years earlier and whom I was sure was the man for me, since we'd managed to never really lose our connection.

I think I just wanted it to be true so badly. I'd never received any sort of message or vision about me and him, I just really believed in "us," since we'd managed to never lose touch after all those years. I thought, and hoped, that was sign enough.

Boy, was I wrong!

The trip ended up being disastrous, especially after I made love with him, and realized he was in love with someone else, a woman who had just broken his heart, and I was completely crushed. It was beyond devastating for me. I'd felt like I was "saving myself" for this man, and yet, here we were, in a dysfunctional mess, not quite the ecstatic realms of magic and bliss I had anticipated and so desperately wanted.

It was awkward staying with him and his friends after that, as he kept avoiding me, not coming home from work until late at night, etcetera. I kept getting drunk and high to deal with the pain. Or rather, to avoid the pain. Even on his birthday we attempted to all go out and have fun with my sister and his friends, but it felt contrived and utterly painful for me to be pretending we were having a good time together. We were missing the mark with each other all over the place; meanwhile, I was crumbling to pieces inside.

He had led me to believe he wanted to see me and be with me, never telling me about his heartache over this other girl, and so I thought we wanted the same thing: to fall into blissful dimensions of altered states of consciousness and love together, which is what I had dreamed about with a partner all my life, thinking he was The One. I knew it was possible and thought I was about to experience this with him. Instead it was icky, messy, entangled cobwebs of old dusty memories of what once was, which was nothing more than a fantasy we both shared—to be together forever one day—but it ended up to be just that, a fantasy.

Perhaps he was hoping that seeing me would shift him out of his pain and he too would be able to go there with me, and let her go, but I didn't know that and obviously, it was not meant to be the way we thought it was.

So, I came home with a heavy heart and a very different feeling about it all. The magic was gone forever for me. No more fantasizing. Time to forge ahead and move on.

It was so hard.

But I did it.

And then, eight months later exactly, I saw the ship, and that whole story unfolded.

And from that experience I was left so open, raw and confused from these other-worldly encounters that I sort of "fell off" myself. I started getting very angry and aggressive. I would be out at Gord's Place, the local punk bar, with my eight holes on, getting high and drinking way more than my petite body should have ever allowed, taking up the entire dance floor with my furious energy. I was trying to dance it out and break free from this insanity, trying desperately to figure out who I was and what exactly my purpose was here on this planet, because I hadn't a fucking clue.

I remember often thinking to myself, '*There has got to be more to life than this. I just know there does.*' Dancing was always how I moved my energy, how I worked things out for myself, and I swear it has definitely saved my life more than once.

Of course, I didn't know what I was doing at the time, which was simply put, trying to solve the riddle of "me" and who I was, exactly. At the time, I was simply drinking a lot, doing more and more drugs, having strange sexual encounters with nearly complete strangers, basically trying to run away from myself, all while desperately needing to and trying to find myself at the same time.

I was in such a state after my experiences in '97, I seemed to be looking for trouble everywhere I went.

It was brutal, and I was self-destructive. I just couldn't seem to help myself. I was losing all control of my life, quickly spiraling downward, and in a way, flirting with the idea of death. I was pushing myself to see how far I could go to the edge before falling over it. It was a dangerous game I was playing at for a while there.

I got myself enmeshed in the most dysfunctional relationships in that one year following my experiences than I had my entire life up to now. A guy who'd already had a nervous breakdown and was like a shaking leaf hidden behind the mask of a smile, for one example. Completely unstable. He lived in Ottawa and showed up one day on my doorstep to stay with me "indefinitely." St. Catharines is an 8-hour drive from Ottawa, and we had only just met each other, so this threw me off, *big time*. It was a tad too needy and desperately presumptuous, I thought. Not to mention creepy.

He would smother me, and was a large man, over six-feet tall, and heavy in comparison to my petite 5' 2," 115-pound frame. He would literally trap me underneath his body while he had sex with me repeatedly all night long. I would be unconscious and he would penetrate me until I was bleeding and raw and bruised all over my body. I won't get into all the gross details, but it was a very brief relationship that really messed me up for a long time.

And after that, I dated a couple of different skateboarders. The first one was a nice guy, but not at all seeking a relationship. We had sex on his bedroom floor. He slept on a small camping mat amongst piles and messes strewn everywhere. Not exactly sexy, but I managed. He was an incredible skater. A raw, unrefined street boarder who could do some of the craziest shit. He would try almost anything. He actually broke his leg one day when he and his buddies were shooting some videos, and within about a week or two of going crazy not being able to skate, he cut the cast off himself with a chainsaw and hopped back on his board. Insane. I loved that about him, he was so hardcore.

I think I was too needy for him at the time though, which was very unlike me. I was really messed up then, and didn't know what I was doing. I had never been the needy girlfriend before, and somehow now, I was like some pathetic groupie hanging out with these skaters whose lives revolved around skating, smoking pot, drinking, playing video games all day, and often harder drugs. Most of them were on welfare, and most of them had more serious drug habits.

Then I dated his friend, Mark, and had incredible sex with him. He used me though. I think there was a part of him that genuinely liked me and cared about me, but he was too into his cocaine and booze and of course, his board. He was already a professionally-sponsored skater, on covers of skating magazines, sporting new gear every time I saw him. This guy just wanted to skate, drink, smoke, and get high. I was a great thing to have on the side, because I had a car and we had a lot of sex. I would give him my car while I was in classes or rehearsals, and he would take my car, no license, and use up all my gas, drive the shit out of it, and bring it back on empty with no intention of helping me out with gas, yet expecting to take it the next day again to do some more filming with his buddies. I was the idiot that let him.

It was brutal, and this relationship was a testament to how fucked up over my experiences I had become. I was out of control. I almost didn't give a shit about myself, or my life, anymore. It was devastating actually, and I'm shocked at how lost and careless I had become when I look back now. Sometimes I can't believe I am still alive today.

Mark would disappear for periods of time and I wouldn't hear from him for days on end. Even his mother wouldn't hear from him, and he lived with her. She would be worried sick, calling me asking me where he was. Last I'd heard he was in Hamilton or Toronto, I'd tell her. At one point, he got "stranded" in Toronto for about a week supposedly and finally called me and begged me to wire him money or buy him a bus ticket back to St. Catharines. Once again, I was the idiot that did it.

That pretty much about sums that relationship up. And that was the one I was in the entire spring of 1998, before moving out to Vancouver after touring a show I'd created with three other women in my theatre program, one of which was my clown-nosed bus-riding compadre, Dawn.

We toured our "Fringe" show across the country, during which I met a man who I was about to have some of the best and craziest times of my life with. I believe now that this relationship saved my life. It wasn't always easy, but it was all so very worth it. The amount of inner growth I would experience in that relationship was monumental.

It was time to leave it all behind, leave my old life, time to leave my otherworldly, unexplainable experiences and the near insanity it had ignited in me, behind in the dust. It was time to start to live a whole new life. Time to save myself before it was too late. It was time to live a "normal" life.

Or so I thought.

***Sadly, I discovered Mark took his own life in September 2014, interestingly, during my first trip to meet with Selene. He did it only days after his son's birthday (September 17th, a starseed with galactic Virgo Sun), and days before his own birthday, September 28th. My heart broke for his children and his family when I found out. It broke not because of my wonderful memories of him, because there honestly weren't many, but it broke because I always knew he was incredibly sensitive, lost and lonely, just searching for himself, confused about how to be here, even when he was surrounded by all the love in the world. I tried so hard to love him, but he couldn't accept it. He had such a hard time on this planet, and I hope and pray that he is finally at Peace.

CHAPTER 25

Attempts at a New Life

I was madly in love with Paul. Although we had a roller coaster of a relationship that was filled with me releasing the last bits of "crazy" that my ET experiences had left me with. I began forging ahead however, learning how to truly just be me.

I wasn't so successful in the beginning, though. I started off trying to be perfect, always trying to please Paul. I was basically trying to hold my shit together because I really wanted this relationship to work out. After all, we'd met on tour and had connected instantly.

When my tour was finished and I headed back to St. Catharines, I remember one night feeling and hearing a voice call to me from up in the sky, which was unusually filled with stars that night.

I could hear and feel Paul calling out to me, trying to find me. I could feel him communicating with me and it moved me to tears. I didn't know how it was possible, but I could hear him calling to me through the stars. That was the first time anything like this had ever happened to me that I could recall, at least so clearly and compellingly.

Paul was a brilliant artist who created his own rhythm to life wherever he went. Always pushing the envelope, he was always at least a bit outside the box, usually extremely so, in every aspect of his life. A rebellious punk rock performance artist slash actor slash anarchist all rolled up into one beautiful and intriguing package. He was the most original person I had ever met and he was always true to himself, no matter the cost. It was breathtakingly beautiful. I so admired his strength of character and his unwavering commitment to himself. I was smitten, in love almost instantly.

Paul was also the first vegan I had ever met, and at the time, I was still eating entirely unconsciously, filling my body with one toxin after another, unknowingly. When I look back now on what I used to fuel this beautiful vessel with, it saddens me, but also makes me grateful for all of the growth I have consequently experienced as a result.

One of our first times hanging out at the Saskatoon Fringe Festival (he later named his propane-fueled RV that we would travel across the country in "Saskatchewan" because of how and where we met), Paul showed up with an organic lemon and some organic grapes. I had never heard the term organic pertaining to food before then. I had never touched an avocado in my life. I didn't even know how to cook rice and beans. I was really lost when it came to food! This guy had his work cut out for himself with me, and later, I found I had mine cut out with him too. We taught each other so much.

I will never forget eating the grapes, which tasted a million times better than conventional grapes. I'd never even known that I had an alternate choice before that moment. Then Paul shoved a cut up lemon wedge into my mouth and told me to eat it, and enjoy it.

Who *was* this man?

It was profound for me, this connection, and instantly, I knew there was much to learn from this beautiful, crazy man who was so thoughtful and sweet in all the right moments, and yet was also entirely capable of taking a shit in an empty Slurpie cup and presenting it to a room full of near strangers, straw inserted and all, asking if there were any takers. He was endlessly crazy, disgusting, fun and fascinating to me in his unpredictability and his unconventional sense of adventure. I loved it.

That was pretty much our four-year relationship, with a ton of love, laughter, adventure and tears all mish mashed in there together. It was some of the most fun I think I've ever had in my life, and huge personal growth happened for me within the time of this relationship. Whenever I was going through something painful, he never once ran away and was never afraid of me, or my darkness. He could, and would, remain present through it all. Can't say that about too many people.

Paul always encouraged me to discover my inner light that he always said he knew was hidden in there, somewhere. He would say to me, many times, "I see your light, Sammy. It's *huge*, and I can't wait to see it all come out one day, and to really see you shine. You're going to be *amazing*." And he meant it, always in the most sincere way.

Now, that's not to say we didn't have our problems. Paul loved me more and more all the time, I knew that, but he was still commitment phobic and thought that being in a truly committed relationship would mean losing himself and not being able to do what he came here to do. He had a compulsion to create art non-stop in various forms, to be out exploring art most of the time, and he didn't ever want anything stopping him from creating and exploring, because it would literally have killed him.

Though oddly, I never, ever tried to hold him back from anything, and always honoured his process and loved him even more because of his unwavering commitment to be true to himself. He was an artist and he inspired me so much to be the artist that I knew I was too. He would leave for days at a time sometimes, always letting me know he was leaving, but never having to "check in" with me.

There were also many times where he would experiment being with other women, unable to truly embrace being only with one. I never made him feel he had to. I hoped with all my heart that one day he might feel ready to only be with me, but when I knew he'd been with another woman (I always knew, too), he would dance around it until finally he would come around and admit to it, knowing that he couldn't really pull the wool over my eyes, so why even try?

I finally tired of this game, and moved in with a friend one time temporarily in order to allow him to explore a relationship with a woman he'd been secretly seeing. I didn't want him to feel he had to hide it for fear of hurting me, so I moved out of his way so that he could do what he needed to do and experience whatever healing or lesson he needed to before I would come back.

It was not easy, but I also realized during this time how unbelievably strong I was, as never once in these situations did I ever doubt myself or feel that it was because I wasn't good enough. I had finally realized my own self-worth, though that may sound strange considering what I appeared to be putting up with.

The truth is, I didn't need him to be any certain way for me other than exactly as he was. And the benefits and joy I got out of the relationship, and the amount of growth, love and support I had experienced within it, far outweighed the times that were painful.

In the end though, in an attempt to give him the gift of space and freedom after he'd asked me to marry him, I offered him up a summer of "sowing his oats" in 2002, no questions asked because after he'd asked me and I accepted, he began to spiral into denial and fear. It seemed the most loving offer for me to do this for him, so I moved in with a girlfriend of mine, only intending it to be a short time—just a "summer of sowing the last of our oats."

Sadly for both of us, we never did make it through that summer together. It was all fine and dandy while he was dating a few girls with no attachments or any self-imposed guilt, but as soon as I was attracted to someone and decided this was a great time for me to explore other men as well, the game shifted and everything changed.

Paul had a very hard time with it, and though I was strictly only attracted to this other man physically, it was not something that Paul seemed prepared to handle.

This other lover was Jon. I was in desperate need of some major sexual healing, as I had never felt entirely free with another man, even Paul. Here I'd finally met someone whom I was having the best sex of my life with where it was easy, passionate and electrified, especially in the subtlest of touches. It was otherworldly. This was the only man who had ever known exactly how to touch me in a way that my whole body and soul responded to.

Jon's birthday is October 19th, another starseed, with his sun at galactic degree in Libra, so not much of a surprise to me now, how connected in a cosmic sense we were.

As it turned out, Jon is the man I would be dating when I eventually became pregnant with my first born Earth son, Noah, in middle-late November 2003. It was what I would later come to know through Selene as "Pleiadian Lineup." Most definitely the work of synchronicity at play there.

CHAPTER 26

Galactic Training 101: This Plane Can Fly!

It was 2001. I was still deep in my relationship with Paul. I had opened up so many vulnerable, unhealed wounds from my past via this relationship as well as through my acting training at Studio 58. On September 8, 2001, I received a "knowing" to take a train out immediately and travel to New Mexico to a place called The Light Institute for a series of multi-incarnational sessions that coming winter. I had been planning to go the following summer when the school year was over, but the message was so clear, having come to me during a shiatsu massage on my living room floor as the healer dug deep into the guts of my core.

I knew I had to take heed of this sudden knowing and follow through with this drastic new change of plans. As it turns out, I had planned to go in to talk with my teachers that following Tuesday to let them know. That turned out to be an experience all on its own, as I woke up that morning, Tuesday September 11, 2001, in a state of inner panic and tears. I couldn't for the life of me breathe properly, I felt such a feeling of inner panic, fear and state of arrest wash over me, and I just couldn't shake it. It didn't make sense to me, and as I wondered why I kept bursting in to tears and having panic attacks (which I was never prone to, and had never experienced before), my friend Anthony (yes, his real name!) called me from the Green Room at school. He was also in tears, and told me about the Twin Towers and what was happening in New York.

I remember being glued to the television that day with Paul, as we both cried the tears of the collective consciousness. I remember seeing the horrific footage of people jumping out of the buildings, and hearing the Voice say to me, "The world will never be the same after this. No one will be the same, and in the end, that will prove to be a good thing."

I had no real idea what this meant, but knew with everything in my soul that it was true somehow.

Paul and I decided to channel this overwhelming energy into something creative. He went to the paint shop in our neighbourhood that morning and we proceeded to spend the rest of the day painting our beloved little kitchen bright orange. It had suddenly become even clearer to us that *we* had to be the creators of our world. We had to be the creators of our own Destiny. So we started with our home, where our hearts dwelled.

The experiences I would go on to have at The Light Institute changed my life. Yet, I was also given an opportunity to demonstrate my own powers of intentional manifestation, as well as my ability to create miracles and perform magic.

After working day and night for two and a half months in order to make the money I would need to travel to The Light

Institute from Vançouver, the plane nearly didn't go up in the air that day—November 30, 2001.

All of the passengers on our flight to Albuquerque were being told we were going to need to exit the plane. This was after we had taxied onto the runway, revved there for a while making a very strange sound, with no movement. Eventually the pilot turned the plane around, and taxied back to the gate. We then proceeded to sit there for nearly two hours while we waited as the plane was being serviced, to no avail. Finally, the pilot came on the intercom and told us they were going to have to reschedule our flights and were already working on it. He was apologizing for any inconvenience it may cause.

Inconvenience?!

I remember almost panicking, thinking *'I didn't work this fucking hard for the past two and half months, making twice the amount of money I thought I'd need* (because of 9-11 the exchange rate on the dollar from Canada had doubled) *to do this work that I know will change my life forever, only to have someone take it away from me because this plane can't fucking fly!'*

And it was then that it hit me. I was the only one standing in the way of this plane going up. My fears of the Unknown were so powerful, powerful enough to short out a plane! As soon as I realized this, and recognized the deep inner truth of this thought, I immediately began focusing on reversing it.

I started meditating like I had never meditated before. I started visualizing that plane getting up in the air and flying me, and everyone else on it, to wherever we had to go, safely and on time. I visualized making my connecting flight and arriving in Albuquerque in perfect time for my hired ride to pick me up, without him having to wait for hours for me to get there.

It was truly miraculous!

I had visualized this image so clearly and with such powerful intent, that within minutes, as everyone else was gathering their belongings and preparing to exit the plane, the pilot came on again, and in a surprised and relieved tone, he announced that they were now able to use this plane. The problem had been fixed and we would be taxiing and taking off within minutes!

That was one of the most incredible demonstrations of my own power I had ever witnessed and experienced. And I was fully and absolutely conscious of having done it which was the best part of it all for me. I couldn't deny my power any longer, after having mastered a grounded, broken plane.

I wasn't aware of galactic beings at the time. I always took it as an obvious and unspoken truth that we were not alone in this vast and wondrous universe. How could we be? But even then, even after my series of sessions was complete, after how many lifetimes not of this Earth I experienced in them, I really didn't grasp how much this otherworldly reality would become my reality one day; how much it already was my reality, try as I might have to run away from it all those years.

I met a man during that first trip to The Light Institute in a Sexuality workshop I took part in. He kept talking about being a "galactic seed." I had no clue what he was referring to. He talked about it like it was some huge burden, a most painful existence really, so it didn't sound very appealing or interesting to me, especially after the miraculous healings and releasing of my own pain I experienced in my private sessions leading up to this workshop. I was on a personal high, and this guy seemed to be treading water just trying to stay afloat.

If anything, I was nervous around this guy; I felt very uneasy around him. I didn't know quite what to make of him. He was odd, and obviously, not of this world, that was for sure. Let him be the seed, I thought. Sure! Have it all you want, buddy, I'm fine over here being a regular old boring human. How silly I was.

I was obviously not ready to know the whole truth yet. It probably would have derailed me even more than he seemed to be.

Little did I know, this man was planting a seed for me that weekend which would many years later become one of the memories and experiences I would piece together in my own journey, and which would aid me in understanding my own mission here, on this planet, now. I am grateful for his presence then, even though, back then, to me he was just some really sad guy who was lost in this strange and broken world, straddling that ever so fine line of his own fragile and teetering sense of sanity. How blissfully unaware I was of my deeper connection with him.

CHAPTER 27

The Quest Begins

When I was on my first healing journey to The Light Institute in December 2001, I recall going in to a multi-dimensional state of awareness during the Sexuality workshop, and being asked to "see" my first sexual experience in this incarnation.

I was shocked at the time with what I witnessed.

What I witnessed was me, as a baby. I remember seeing this green monster standing over me, and inserting something in to my vagina. I also remember it feeling pleasurable, not painful. But regardless, I was a baby, and this being did not appear to be human, at least from the perspective of my young, innocent eyes.

At the time, I assumed this meant it had been an adult male in my life, and perhaps it was. But my curiosity can't help but wonder now if it was, perhaps, something even more than this. Given all I have learned about myself in recent years, it does not seem merely coincidental that my first sexual experience was so odd and out of the norm in comparison to all the rest of the experiences of the other workshop attendees. One, because mine happened as a baby, and two, because "the other" involved in my experience was, at least according to my memory, embodying an otherworldly form.

This could mean any number of things, I realize. But the fact remains, it was a very young and out of the ordinary sexual experience.

After I was Initiated into the beginnings of womanhood at age nine, it was as if a switch had been turned on, and I knew exactly what it was like to make love, and how to create babies. I started to look at myself in the mirror every time I took a bath or got changed, and I would become aroused as I protruded my belly to make it appear as though I were about four or five months pregnant. I thought it was the most beautiful sight in the world. I was proud of my body, and the fact that I could carry babies inside me was fascinating beyond belief, even though I didn't consciously make the connection between my moon cycle and the consequent capability for impregnation.

I also loved to belly dance, even though I had never learned or even seen anyone belly dance before. Somehow, I knew from deep within the core of my being how to roll my stomach in both directions, easily, as if I were already a pro. I used to make my parents laugh, because here was this skinny beanpole of a kid, no womanly curves to me in sight, and yet I would belly dance and shake it like the most Holy and Sacred of the Ancient Egyptian Goddesses. At least that's how I felt. It was a very powerful feeling.

The main message here though is that I was already a very sexually and sensually aware being as a child. I'm sure my Scorpio Moon has helped with this and most definitely I planned it this way.

I truly feel that the experience leading into beginning my menses, the tonsillectomy near death experience, prepared me and activated me for the next phase of my Galactic Mission: Hybrid Babies 101.

CHAPTER 28

A Journey into the Light

This is a chronicle of my experiences in December 2001 at The Light Institute.

Multi-Incarnational Sessions December 2001

December 1, 2001: Light Institute Cranial

During my first set of sessions at The Light Institute, I went into the experience ready to clear and heal as much as I possibly could. I knew there was much for me to clear in order to open up my path in this current dimensional reality. I was more than ready.

I had worked so hard to create this opportunity for myself, and I had already witnessed miracles happening both within me and all around me. I knew that I was the one solely responsible for creating these miracles. It was an exciting time for me. I felt like I was finally able to get past all the pain and confusion that had been covering up my magnificence for so long, and I was diving in and getting the work done, enjoying every blessed moment of it.

That's not to say that the sessions were a walk in the park. Some of them were absolutely vicious, brutal, and incredibly painful to witness and experience. But I was fearless and did a lot of deep work, peering into every corner and crevice of my own hidden worlds of shame and guilt and suffering that I could find. I was relentless in my search to clear whatever I could.

It was a miracle in itself that I even made it there, and I acknowledged the power I'd discovered within myself to make it happen, not allowing anything to deter me or get in my way—not even at the risk of losing my relationship, or the irritating setback of a broken airplane!

I had set myself up to begin my time there with an opening and clearing cranial session with Carlo Castiglione. This session, however, blew my mind beyond words, so I will do my best to share the essence of this experience.

The cranial sessions at The Light Institute are similar to cranial sacral therapy, which in and of itself I find to be a powerful healing modality. Chris Griscom developed a specific cranial treatment designed to support the deep, multi-dimensional work that takes place at the Institute.

I was so ready for this entire experience, I am sure I brought my own kind of magic into this session, but I have to say that it blew the roof off of any kind of healing session I had ever experienced up to that point, and quite possibly, since.

The treatment is incredibly gentle and subtle, and one might lay there thinking not much of anything is happening, especially if they are not fully ready to open up to the infinite possibilities just waiting at our fingertips. I was beyond ready.

I moved through emotions, tears came, deep breaths, moving through the subtle yet huge waves of energies activated through Carlo's touch.

And then he got to my ears.

He placed his fingers in my ears, essentially plugging them, then began tapping them repeatedly, with a muffled "thump" that ignited some sort of soul or cellular memory that became larger than life in the blink of an eye, and I began to scream and shout with a power so deep, I am pretty sure I nearly blew the roof off the adobe building.

It was primal. It was deep. It held the experiences of lifetime upon lifetime. A portal opened through my mouth, and I began to release some very powerful memories that had been trapped inside of me, "plugging" my own ability to hear, to express myself clearly and safely.

At first, the shouting had much anger in it, but the more I shouted, it shifted into this power that felt simply amazing.

I clearly remember during that first session levitating about two inches off the table. I could feel my energetic body levitating above my physical body. It was unlike anything I'd known before, and it was incredible.

Carlo and I were both moved deeply by this session. So much so that he requested we have another session before I leave, as he wanted to work more with me.

It was then that he gifted me with two sacred gifts to take back home with me. One was a stone he told me he'd had for 20 years. He didn't tell me the story behind it, just that it was very meaningful for him and he would like me to have it.

The next gift he gave me was exquisite. It was the breast feathers of a spotted owl—the entire breast, not just a few feathers. I didn't know at the time how connected I was to owls, and that in fact, Owl is my main animal totem. I only knew it was powerful when he gave it to me, and I was humbled by how much this man believed in me, having only just met me.

At the end of our first session, he'd said to me, "You are a very special woman, and you have something very important to do here in this life." He told me that the first time we spoke over the phone, he knew there was something about me.

I had gone back to my room at the Galisteo Inn where I was staying. I could still feel every single cell in my body vibrating at such a high frequency. I was sure this is how I had been able to levitate. I was amazed at what I had already done, and I had only been there less than 24 hours at this point!

I played a game with myself in the sauna. I wanted to lay in the sauna for exactly 10 minutes at a time, and then take a 10-minute break in my room, which was perfectly placed right beside it. I didn't wear a watch and I didn't set a timer. I wanted to explore what I was capable of.

I went into the sauna and lay down, breathing. I asked my Higher Self to please let me know when exactly 10 minutes had passed. I closed my eyes, and simply breathed, and trusted.

When I felt something inside me nudge me to get up, I listened and immediately looked at the little clock just outside. It had been exactly 10 minutes. I laughed to myself thinking,

'Okay, maybe I got lucky. Let's try this again.' I went into my room and looked at the clock and asked again for my Higher Self to please let me know when it was 10 minutes, and time to go back into the sauna.

There was a mirror in my room on one of the walls, and I felt drawn to look at myself, up close, and stare into my eyes. What a powerful experience!

First of all, I looked like a completely different person. It was so wild. My eyes were different than I'd ever seen them. And then I noticed the rest of my face. I could literally *see* the cells in my face and neck and shoulders *moving—vibrating—* and in between the millions of cells, there was a bright liquid light pulsating and moving as well! I could actually *see,* with my own eyes, that I was not a solid piece of matter, but in fact, a magnificent, divine spark of light.

Time ceased for me as I reveled in this most spectacular experience. It was not just a concept or an idea or even a fact from science that I was reading about. I was seeing first-hand the Light Being that I am. I would never be the same again.

December 2-4, 2001: Days 1--3 of Multi-Incarnational Sessions

When one does a set of sessions at The Light Institute, it occurs over the course of four consecutive days. Each session is three hours in length, totaling 12 hours of multi-incarnational exploration and clearing for each set. It was amazing to me how time ceased and three hours would fly by, with so much happening during that time. It was fascinating!

The first three days of sessions cleared the more traumatic and painful experiences around love. The first day we focused on the present lifetime, and day two and three were spent on other lifetimes.

The fourth day is always about exploring and clearing the lifetimes where we experienced great love. We clear those too, because what is most important is the life that we are living now. In the sessions, we take the lessons and the gifts with us, and clear all of the experience—"the story." It is truly a remarkable process.

I had my sessions with Susan Hemmerle, and I adored her and her energy. I felt completely safe with her, and something in our connection just clicked, of course. Everything about this journey was pure perfection! I had manifested it to be that way.

On our second day, when I went into other lifetimes of painful experiences, I went right to it. It's important to mention that the mind does not control or guide these sessions. There is no way for this to even happen with the state of multi-dimensional consciousness one enters into, through the activation and opening of certain multi-dimensional portals or windows by way of specific acupuncture points in the head being ignited.

Chris first learned this technique of seeing across dimensions when she was studying acupuncture in the Peace Corps. Her class had a guest teacher come in from Asia and teach them about a specific form of acupuncture he called "The Windows to the Sky." She learned how to use high vibrational acupuncture needles made of gold, placed in certain acupuncture points in the body which specifically open up these windows to seeing through multiple dimensions at once.

Chris facilitated sessions using the actual needles for years, which is how I read about them in Shirley MacLaine's book, *Dancing in the Light*. Over the years, Chris developed a way to use points of consciousness brought to the person's attention by the facilitator, and breathing light into those points to open them up in the same way the needles would. It is incredible what we can do simply with our consciousness. The facilitator takes you through a specific series of breathing exercises, with a focus on multiple acupuncture points they indicate with their fingers on the skull, and the person having the session breathes light from the cosmos into each point, essentially bringing them into the exact same state that the needles would. Truly incredible!

Once one is in this altered state of awareness, lifetimes needing to be cleared at that time are seen and experienced as if watching them on a movie screen, while having a total sensory experience at the same time. It's as if you live it and witness it simultaneously. You are also still fully aware of being on the table, of the facilitator guiding the experience, all of it. You become truly and consciously multi-dimensional.

The first three days were painful, yet liberating. The first lifetime I witnessed was me as murderer, rapist, basically what many here judge as monstrous. If people actually knew what they were capable of, perhaps not in this lifetime, but in others, we might stop judging everyone around us.

I was witness to myself doing the unspeakable, and yet I also experienced the pain and confusion and sorrow that accompanied these despicable choices and actions. It was mind-altering and humbling, to say the very least. Suddenly, my whole way of viewing the world of right and wrong and good and evil was destroyed. Even when I witnessed myself mutilating another human being, there was a sense of utter helplessness, complete numbness. There was always a balancing of karma that was occurring, which I could relate to in my current life, and which was where the true healing came in.

I saw myself abusing people who have abused me in this lifetime, and suddenly, instead of seeing them as the enemy or with judgment or a desire to punish them, I understood that they were simply playing a divine part for me to help balance my own karma in this lifetime. They were giving me a gift.

I realize this might sound crazy to some. I would have thought it was crazy too, before actually experiencing it. No university or school could teach me this most valuable life and spiritual lesson.

From these experiences, I was able to encounter deep healing in some of the closest relationships in my life. It healed many of the multiple layers, but those top layers were the toughest. I no longer felt the resentment and anger towards people in my life who I had perceived had wronged me in some way. Instead, I began to take responsibility for myself. It was one of the most empowering things I've ever done for myself.

I was able to understand things I had done, people with whom I felt unsafe with for no apparent reason, you name it.

These sessions completely changed how I viewed the closest relationships in my life. I am eternally grateful to have given myself the permission to gain this wisdom, as I would need to draw on it in the years to come.

December 5, 2001: Day 4 of Multi-Incarnational Sessions

This was my last day of sessions. My world was already altered and so much inside of me was healed and cleared, just in those three powerful days.

The fourth day arrived, and I was looking forward to this one, because I wouldn't have to see or witness or re-experience any more pain or trauma. This was the day I would get to witness and re-experience lifetimes where I was living in my highest version of myself. I had no idea what to expect, but I knew I could handle whatever came up for clearing and integration into this lifetime. I'd moved through and cleared the unspeakable already, now it was time to witness the beauty, empowerment and magic.

I had already experienced at least one other lifetime in the previous days which appeared to be otherworldly, but what I was to witness in this final day would be more brilliant than I could have even dreamed.

At the time, I was still unaware of my deep connection with ETs beyond the experiences I'd had in this lifetime, which so far had terrified me and to which I'd felt victim. By this point in the sessions, I no longer felt victim to anything in my life. I was beyond empowered; yet I was also not thinking of ETs, my experiences, or potential lives having taken place elsewhere in these ever-expanding universes.

I had assumed everything I would experience in my sessions would be "earthly." I didn't even entertain the idea that I had lived on other planets or heaven forbid, that I was not actually human. I knew, without ever consciously thinking about it all my life, that Earth certainly was not the only planet in the multitude of galaxies and universes out there that could sustain life. I just didn't think about any of that enough to explore it or spend any time caring that much about it. It just "was" to me, and that was enough for me.

Until one lifetime after another began to surface. These experiences and lives, these times and places where, not only was I not on Earth (at least not the earth that we are all living on today) during my session but, in some lifetimes, I wasn't even fully human. It was such a trip, and one I was not expecting.

I witnessed myself as an ageless being, switching from a child form to a feminine adult form, within moments. I was speaking telepathically with another apparent boy, and we were teaching one another through light transmissions via the Third Eye. I had never even considered this before!

Excerpt from session:

"The boy and I are spirits. I don't feel like I'm on this planet. I stay in this form and experience everything at once—there is no sense of time here. I take my fingers into my Third Eye, and I open my flesh. I am peeling it away.

Immediately I witness a brilliant golden light bursting out of the hole at my Third Eye, and as we peeled away the suit (the boy also peeled his away at the same time), that's all we were.

"I am a transparent, glowing being. No sex. I am not male or female. I am a humming vibration. I am standing there in this transparent light. There is a white outline around me—I am not human. There is a sense of nothingness. I am simply here, existing."

As with each lifetime, the facilitator took me to the moment of transition—of *death*—yet what I witnessed in this particular lifetime was not death. It was merely a change of form, without the experience of any pain or suffering of any kind.

Light Institute Session Notes: December 5, 2001

(Begin transmission) *The first lifetime on this last day that Susan and I had explored, I found myself in an open field full of yellow flowers, blue skies, lots of bees, and so much light. There is a small brown hill, and I approach it and sit there. I am dressed all in white. I sit in the middle of the hill, legs crossed in full lotus, meditating. There are children all around me; they are also in white; all but one, who is dressed in red.*

I appear to be female; radiant and peaceful, enveloped in a bright aura. I am sharing my light with the children, teaching them. I am smiling.

A boy with blue eyes is there. We share a deep connection. We communicate exclusively through our eyes. Beams from my Third Eye travel to his, and a circular flow between us begins; from my Third Eye into his, down to his belly button and out to mine, then back up to my Third Eye, etc. He and I are old friends. We are teaching one another.

He has brown hair. A bird emerges out of his left ear. It is blue. The bird flies to me and sits on my right shoulder. This bird is a Gift of Peace.

I give the boy a gift through my mouth. A red scarf with a ladybug on it floats towards the boy, and covers his face, slides down into his hands. This is a gift of Love.

There is an older man here as well. He smiles at us. He has grey hair and wrinkles. He touches me, and then puts his right hand on my Third Eye.

He is teaching me about Light. From his hands comes light. It goes in through my Third Eye and fills my body.

Suddenly, I appear to be only five or six years old, though when he touches me I still feel like an old soul. I am walking through the body of a woman. I am a teacher, and I will now teach about the Light.

We all take turns teaching. It is my turn now.

We are not on Earth. I am living all realities at once. There is no sense of time.

I take my fingers and hands into my Third Eye. I begin opening the flesh, peeling it away.

I emerge as a transparent, glowing being. I have no gender. I am a glowing humming luminescent presence surrounded in a white outline. It is powerful. I am not human.

There is a strong sense of nothingness to me. I simply am.

I release this life by releasing the light. I strip away the white outer layer containing my light. There is no pain in this release. All that is left is a grey transparent light. I have transcended out of this form. (End transmission)

I was then asked to try to focus on a human lifetime where I really loved myself. This was after several galactic incarnations/parallel realities had presented themselves.

(Begin transmission) *I am a young boy, about twelve or thirteen years old. I play the flute every day, and many small animals come visit me as I play. One small squirrel in particular comes every day, runs around, plays and laughs with me.*

I have a younger brother who also enjoys playing in this energy. I pick him up. We are playing, holding hands, walking together. I show him leaves and flowers, and the light in the sky.

He asks me what the sun is. I tell him that it's the Light that he carries in his own body. He is full of wonder and awe and amazement. I know he knows what I am saying is true.

I too am filled with this light of the sun. I also know how to fly. I am a teacher, and my purpose is to help others realize that everything is possible.

I discovered this on my own when I was a young child by talking to the sky and the sun, and inviting them inside of me. I experienced a sense of Being Everything. I would then tell myself "I am going to fly," and I did. I would float above the ground and would play these kinds of games with myself all the time. It was fun!

And now that I have a little brother, I help him discover this truth for himself. When I ask the Sun what I am, I hear "You are a Teacher," and I know that is my Purpose.

My parents love one another, and they love my brother and me very much as well. They allow me to be who I am. They allow me to go off and play as I need to in this way.

I begin to go into hospitals and work with sick children. I help them discover their own light, and so help them to heal. I can heal them through the use of my hands as I hold them up as an offering to the Sun. I would use my hands to help heal them but always focused on empowering them to access the healing powers of the sun and the sky for themselves.

The sun cures them instantaneously. I kiss each one on the forehead, their Third Eye. I bless them with everlasting Light, and witness any trace of dis-ease leave their body. I see it as a dark cloud rising out of them, and once it is fully out, I know the healing is complete.

In essence, I help heal them through love and through light. As I heal them, they in turn learn to heal themselves because now they know it is possible.

There is a woman, pregnant with my child. She is all in white. I am blessing this child with my hand on her ripe belly, communicating with our child.

The birth is painless. She is born like a beam of light emerging from this beautiful mother's loins. There are no tears. She is fully awake and smiling even. I feel incredibly grateful, and there is so much love shared between the three of us.

I hold this child up as an offering to the sun, stating aloud that she is a Child of the Light. My wife is hugging me from behind, her head on my shoulder. We are all being blessed by the sun.

My wife is the image of my Higher Self, which is interesting.

I build a round shelter where people come to transition back into the light, into Source. This is a peaceful place for them to make their transition. The roof and ceiling is one large window, so the rays of the Sun always come inside.

There is no mourning, no sadness. There is not even sickness anymore. This is simply a place where people come to transition into the next reality for themselves. For those who choose to transition back into pure Light with full consciousness, I am here to facilitate this transi-

tion. My wife provides water, blankets and warmth through her loving presence.

My Mission is such that I felt it was important for people to understand and be able to choose when and how to transition out of their physical bodies. I know that it is a celebration, and that there is nothing bad about it, and nothing to fear in it.

I have a feminine energy, so am balanced in my masculine and feminine energies. It is sometimes difficult to tell whether I am male or female, but this does not matter. This is what we are all striving for.

I live until a very old age. My transition is peaceful, joyous and ecstatic. I simply make the choice to transition when I feel my mission has been fully accomplished and I am ready for my next assignment.

It is like a surge, a pulsing from within. It is a surge of white light which almost takes my breath away. It swoops me up quickly, ascending me at lightning speed up into the Light.

I ascend with my arms wide open, and I am dancing, moving, floating, smiling, rejoicing, and laughing all the way "up." I dance all the way into the sun, where I become a beam of light, which I in turn radiate out into the universe. As the beam of light, I continued to live consciously, sending my light back out into the universe. I am a being of the sun.

This is who I am. (End transmission)

I remember taking note that I had never heard of anything remotely like this before.

Then, the final lifetime I was able to witness in this remarkable series is the one that stands out in my memory as the most powerful of all for me. This was a lifetime where I used my powers well.

(Begin transmission) *I am a woman, climbing a mountainside. Going to the top to get something. It is a crystal. I am gathering crystals and herbs and bringing them back as healing tools.*

The herb is lavender, and the crystal is a ruby. I bless the crops with the ruby. The crystal sprinkles like a fine dust over the crops and the crops are enriched and healed instantaneously.

I grow and harvest these crops for healing purposes. I am a healer. I help heal people's hearts, minds and bodies. I help them cast away and let go of demons and negative forces that are making them sick.

I alchemize specific tinctures and special blends for each person depending on their needs. There is one woman who I help and she carries a tremendous amount of sadness. I lay my right hand on her forehead, her Third Eye, and I place my left hand over her solar plexus. I channel light into her body, and feel into where she is holding the frequency of dis-ease.

I feel blockages in her intestines and her heart. I prepare a special blend for her of lavender, dandelion, orange, and fennel. I place some drops of the tincture under her tongue. I assist the first time it is administered with everyone I see. I tell her to breathe in the Light, and exhale the darkness. I instruct her to look into her body, to see where the tincture moves from her tongue, through her body, and to visualize it healing and clearing her completely. I give her tea to drink made of these same medicines, and tell her to drink the tea.

In this particular lifetime, I had endured hardships and the pain of losing my mother at a young age. And my father, through his grieving, had become an alcoholic and was killing himself slowly through his disease. I had reminded him too much of my mother and the pain of losing her was something he just never got over. Being an empathic, his actions began to make me sick as well.

As a young woman, I wanted to help my father. I looked after him, and tried to help him, but finally realized it was of no use. Nothing I could do would save him if he didn't want to save himself. I had to let this go and heal myself, as his drinking had started taking its toll on me.

I made the choice to take care of myself, and embarked on a Vision Quest. My father eventually died of his disease while I set off with Spirit leading me, to Egypt, at the age of nineteen.

Spirit guided me the entire journey. It was as if God were leading me to my destination. I felt magnetized, sometimes by a thought, sometimes by my heart or by a feeling, as these sensations physically moved my body for me, by way of walking my feet in a certain direction. I just "knew" what to do and where to go in the moment, and I trusted this guidance.

I was alone in Egypt, a young woman. I was led directly to a woman, who had been waiting for me. She was a healer, an herbalist and a crystal master. I went to her to be healed and to learn from her.

She was a Master Healer who utilized herbs and crystals. She told me that she recognized a power and strength within me, and said she was going to teach me how to heal myself and others. She taught me to grow medicine plants and food. She taught me about crystals and their use in healing the body. She taught where we store our emotions and experiences and how to heal them in many different ways. I learned through experience. Through being healed, I learned to heal.

People began to be led to me in the same way I'd been led to my teacher. They would be drawn there by Spirit, at the perfect, Divine Time, and they would learn to heal and be healed.

People would in turn show up to me in a very similar way as I was led to my Teacher. They would be led by a Divine Guide beyond their own comprehension. Those who would come to me would stay with me until they were healed. I had a space to house them, and I would feed them healing foods and medicines. I would use crystals and teach them the energetics of healing their body. I also used music and sacred sound and frequency to heal. There are vibrational frequencies that each one needs for healing, and this is part of my alchemy.

I hold a very strong Mother energy ~ each one who comes to me is like my Child. I am a Mother of the Universe, this is my Gift. (Pause transmission)

The transition of this lifetime was the most magical I'd experienced. I was not privy (at least consciously) to the concept of "ascension" when I experienced these sessions, so I had nothing to draw any of these experiences from.

(Continue transmission) *I chose when to transition, when I felt my purpose had been filled and my mission completed. I create a ritualistic ceremony to invoke the elements for an ecstatic and powerful transition.*

I set out a large white round silk cloth on the ground in the middle of a beautiful field. I place white candles all around the edges, and light them like a ring of fire. I stand in the center of the silk, and summon a huge energy vortex within this space. It is almost like a tornado but is filled with Light and is sparkling. It is magnificent!

I open my arms wide in an embrace of All That Is, and I allow myself to be swept up into the spinning vortex! I spin quickly, so quickly that I literally "spin off" the dense aspects of my body until they are dissolved into trillions of particles of light, set free.

The white clothing I'd been wearing drop to the center of the silk on the Earthly ground, surrounded by the ring of fire, and my body is released and has moved into the higher realms, all by way of my own creation. The fire is out, and I am now ascended into the Light in a wave of pure Ecstasy, Knowing my Mission has been completed.

I Am Now an Ascended Priestess of the Light! I Am Divine Ecstasy! (End transmission)

Experiencing such empowering incarnations, even before I'd had a living clue that this kind of life experience was even within the realms of possibility, yet giving myself the incredible gift of witnessing them so intimately and totally in these sessions, was a serious game changer for me.

For the record, back in 2001 my knowledge of health and healing herbs was basically nothing. There was no way for me know that these herbs and foods I was naming in my session were all actually the exact herbs and foods a true herbalist or healer would give someone with the conditions mentioned in the transmission. For example, the woman with heart and intestinal blockages, "I" gave her a combination of lavender, dandelion (I had no idea what a medicinal powerhouse this plant was at the time of this transmission, or that it was even used in health and healing at all!), orange and fennel. In my research, all four of these foods are used for exactly these conditions. Heart health and digestive health. I did not know this at the time of my sessions. I didn't even know what fennel was, and I clearly remember wondering why, of all the foods and herbs in the world, I was naming those four at the time. I remember questioning this while lying on the table as my consciousness spoke out loud what it knew, as I witnessed the entire event.

I also "saw" my teacher in that lifetime, and recognize her today as Selene. I have since shared this with Selene, and she confirmed she felt the same recognition as she read this part of my story. She and I have been working together for many, many lifetimes, this was simply one of them.

When I got back to my "normal" life after this life-altering healing journey to the Light Institute in 2001, no longer did I see life as limited, or myself as victim to other people's choices. Sure, I have created scenarios in my life since that have rocked my entire foundation. Not only did they test my Knowing, but they also gave me ample amounts of life experience to continue growing and continue deepening my experiences, eventually bringing me closer to the Light again, Here and Now.

Admittedly, over the past 14 years since these experiences, I have had many periods where I forgot who I was again, and allowed myself to be ruled by my surroundings rather than be the ultimate creator of my reality.

I have experienced excruciating pain. I have endured more suffering than I care to admit in my last-ditch attempts to put these teachings to the final test.

I had to see just how much I was willing to step up and take the reins of my own life. I had to *prove* to myself that if, when it came down to it, I was faced with the choice of *life or death*, would I be *willing* to step out *beyond* the limb, *Knowing—truly* Knowing, beyond a shadow of a doubt - that the moment I step off that branch, the only direction worthy of going is *up*?

And in Knowing this, would I still choose "up"?

CHAPTER 29

Synchronistic Demonstrations of the Flow of Abundance

Mid-April, 2003, it had been nearly a year and a half since my initial life-changing journey to Galisteo, New Mexico at The Light Institute where I'd submerged myself in one of the most epic healing journeys I would ever embark on. My life had never been the same after that trip, which was froth with galactic demonstrations, *keys* which I would come to recognize and unlock doors with nearly a decade later. Yet at the time, I simply experienced it all as miracle after miracle, magic happening all around and through me.

All I knew for certain was that I was forever changed by this experience.

So many things occurred in the year and a half following this trip, and by the time April 2003 came around, suddenly finding myself dealing with some deeper, darker layers of my past, I knew I had to make another trip to New Mexico for further exploration and clearing.

This trip was much more spontaneous, occurring within weeks of deciding on it. I asked my father to help fund this healing retreat for me, as much of what I felt I had to go clear was connected with him, and I knew he had the means to help me, and I was desperate. I knew if I were not careful, based on some information that had just come to light, if I didn't find a way to deal with and clear these issues immediately, I would slip into a downward spiral, again, and what if I wasn't able to get myself out of this one? The stakes were much too high...

I am so grateful my father heard me, and understood how crucial this trip was for me. That it wasn't about traipsing across the border for shits and giggles. I was going to do deep inner healing work that ultimately I *knew* would save my life.

I also knew that I was capable of digging deep enough to save myself, and I was eternally grateful to have the means to be able to do it. If nothing else, I am fearless of my own darkness.

I had decided to leave my acting training at Studio 58 in April 2002, after only one term following my first sojourn to New Mexico, but I was still closely connected with my teachers as well as my classmates there.

It was April 2003, and I was leaving for New Mexico the following day. My friends still in the program had their singing and tap performance finals, and I wanted to be there to support them and see their work. I was looking forward to it; singing and tap finals were always a lot of fun.

I had to stop in at the bank machine to withdraw the rest of the cash I would need for my trip. I had no credit card, and debits were limited to a few hundred dollars per day, especially during international travel.

I was on my bike, riding up to the college, and was passing by my credit union branch on the way. I had already withdrawn most of the cash I would need, but still had a few hundred dollars left to withdraw before leaving town.

I entered the ATM area of the bank, which wasn't open for business for the day yet. I walked in and saw a homeless man, asleep underneath one of the two ATM machines. He was out cold, and it was obvious he'd been there all night. I was glad he'd had a relatively warm place to rest, and my heart ached as I thought that he was someone's child....and how did he get here?.....In all my 10 years of living in Vancouver, I never became desensitized to or cynical about the tragedy of drug addiction and homelessness littering that beautiful city...it truly is tragic, and touched my heart and soul daily.

I sent this man a silent blessing, and a wish for a brighter day for him. After all, I was on a schedule and I needed to withdraw this money and get up to the theatre.

As I went to walk out of the bank, being *extremely* empathic, I heard a Voice whisper to me that I was to give this man some of my money.

I desperately wanted to comply, yet I knew that I needed every single penny of this money for my trip! There were a handful of people I was going to have to hand this money over to as soon as my plane landed in Albuquerque, so *how* on *Earth* was I to give this man *anything*? The money wasn't even *mine* to keep! If it had been, it would have been a no-brainer for me. But it wasn't...

All this panic and reasoning occurred within a matter of milliseconds, when I suddenly found myself walking next door to the convenience store. I never go into convenience stores unless it is absolutely dire and necessary to. There was nothing there I could eat or drink, I already knew that. *So what was I going to do there?*

I knew I had to give this man $10, but the bank machine only dispensed 20 dollar bills. I had to find something, so that I could get change.

I bought a small bottle of Minute Maid orange juice for $1. I got my change back, with a $10 bill as part of it. I walked back next door into the bank where the man was still fast asleep. I tucked the $10 bill under his hand so that no one would steal it from him, and left the orange juice beside him, unopened, so he would have a drink waiting for him when he awoke.

I needed nothing from this man. I was merely following orders from The Voice Within, and it was a euphoric feeling to do this for him, especially without him knowing. The thought of him waking and being surprised, feeling that someone out there cared about him busted my heart open in that moment.

Admittedly, only moments into my euphoric bliss-fest, a quiet panic began to set in as I mounted my sweet electric-green banana seat bike with cruiser handlebars, a bell and basket. I loved that bike. And in this moment, I was mounting it in a state of panic about being "short" $10 for my trip. Then,

The Voice came back into my ear and in the most soothing tone, said to me:

"You need not worry, dear One. The money will come back to you, this is how it works. You will have all that you need, when you need it. Be calm, and continue to Trust."

It was as if this "Voice" was beyond me. It wasn't exactly "me," so who was it?

All I knew was that it soothed me completely. I felt any sense of panic immediately leave my field, Knowing that of course, there is nothing else I would have rather done with that $10. Of course, I wanted to give it to someone in greater need than I. So I decided to relax about it, trust in the Voice, trust in my*self,* and focus on getting to the college to see my friends rock their finals.

The credit union where this demonstration took place was located at the corner of Main Street and 26th Avenue. I rode straight up Main to get to the college, which was a block away from where it intersects with 49th Avenue. When I arrived at the intersection of Main and 41st, I was stopped by the traffic light. I put my foot down on the curb to hold my balance while waiting, when I heard The Voice again, gently, in my right ear. *This* time it tugged gently at my body and said:

"Look down, and to your right."

I felt my eyes be "pulled" with the rest of my body, very slightly and gently, but directly enough to realize it was not exactly me leading my own movements. I was not afraid though. I could sense Divinity all around me.

As I looked down to where my body and eyes had been drawn, I gasped in shock, then in realization, and then in utter amazement, amusement, joy, and relief, for at my feet, *right there* in between my foot and the curb, lay a perfect $10 bill, *literally waiting for me!*

In that moment, something in me changed. I had received a *very* clear demonstration of the flow of abundance, and how money is simply a form of energy, nothing more, nothing less. Without a "story" or any sort of anxiety or negative attachment, it is free to flow like the waves in the ocean. The tides move out, then they move back in. It is a dance, in constant motion. The money went out, and then within *five minutes,* it flowed right back in.

'*What a miracle*', I thought!

Synchronicity showed up to confirm for me what I was finally beginning to understand. I was beginning to "get" that I was powerful beyond my ability to entirely comprehend. That I could manifest instantaneously whenever I choose to. ***That some unseen forces were working alongside me....teaching me.... about myself....about the world....about the universe.***

These forces had provided very clear demonstrations of my power as well as my ability to perform "magic and miracles" right before *both* of my trips to The Light Institute. The first trip was the plane ~ a demonstration of "mind over matter" as well as the notion of calling on cosmic assistance for help ~ and *this* time, it was a lesson on manifesting abundance, and the flow of giving and receiving through the energetic form of "money," by way of compassion and Love.

Whatever this force was, whether it was me, or something *beyond* me, it was definitely starting to prick up my ears. I was listening now.

CHAPTER 30

"And How Many Pregnancies Have You Had?"

One of the reasons enjoying anything of a sexual nature for me had been so stressful, was that I started to have this feeling like whenever I became aroused, especially in connection with a man, that I was being watched. I would see and feel invisible eyes on me, and it was extremely creepy, not to mention that it started to make me feel *very* paranoid.

It felt like there was a camera on me and I was "on screen" somewhere. Little did I know then, but that was *entirely* possible, even *probable*. At the time though, it messed with my head, and I hated it.

I was always a sensual, sexual being by nature, so suppressing this instinct was the hardest thing for me to do, which is why after everything that occurred in '97 as a result of my experiences, I tipped off the other end of the teeter totter and started going crazy searching for men. The problem with this was that I was finding men that were not seeing me or treating me like the Goddess that I AM, which is why it hurt so much in the end, and why I eventually had to stop.

In reality, the deeper Truth is that *I* was not treating *myself* like the Goddess that I Am, so there was no chance in hell anyone else would.

It had got *so* bad at one point, I'd actually managed to get myself into a situation where a police sergeant kidnapped me and attempted to assault me one night after I shot my drunken mouth off and laid into him about being a "hypocritical asshole" when I noticed he had snuck his open beer bottle into his undercover police vehicle, and was drinking and driving.

I lost it on him and his work partner, mouthing off to them all night about it, I was so disgusted by their hypocrisy. As my friend and I went to get out of their car (she was friends with his partner), he locked me in just as my friend and his partner got out, and drove away with me.

I won't get into all the details of what happened here. Lucky for me, not much, after he spontaneously had a meltdown about his daughter, crying on my shoulder immediately after he had just assaulted me but I'd put up a good fight, and beat him off of me. I don't think he counted on me being as strong as I was, since I looked so small. I think it shocked him, and he finally gave up. Thank God it didn't end worse than that.

He finally drove me back to my friend after 2AM, and let me go, nearly two hours after he'd left with me. That whole night was terrifying and insane. Someone was *definitely* watching over me, though after that incident, I really went off the deep end and lost all control of myself, and things got much worse before they got better.

Being with Paul really helped me with my self-esteem in a lot of ways. And mostly because of mistakes we'd both made, and the hard times we went through together. I finally realized my self-worth through all of it. Both he and I grew so much in our four years together, it bonded us so deeply (no doubt he is one of my closest and most significant soul mates in this lifetime) that we are still very dear friends to this day.

He and I will always share an understanding and great love that goes beyond the Earthly realms for one another through our friendship, because of how much we went through together, and the depths of one another's soul we both witnessed and embraced in that time we shared.

I'll never forget him saying to me, "If I don't hate you already, Sammy, there's no way I ever will!" And we would both laugh at that, because for both of us, it was so incredibly true. You can't go through that much soul exposure and vulnerability with someone, all the while loving them with all your heart, and end up hating them. It just doesn't work that way.

Paul was the one I chose to be with me when my son, Noah, was born. He was unwavering in his support throughout a very long and intense labour, which eventually resulted in a hospital Cesarean birth, the polar opposite from what I'd "planned." Paul was the first person to ever hold Noah after he was born, even before me. He was the first to look into Noah's bright little eyes. To this day, the two of them share a unique and special bond.

I am so grateful for my journeys with Paul; I sum up my journey with him like a fantastic day at my favourite amusement park. It was a wild, fun and crazy ride, with some really sweet, easy, slow rides, taking in the scenery and enjoying the views, and in contrast, some really fast rides that sometimes made me feel queasy and sick to my stomach. But overall, it was all purely magical in how much we both loved one another and were able to grow from our experiences together.

Though I'd thought I was no longer receiving visitors from the other realms during this time, I remember often thinking and feeling like I was pregnant. I had never experienced this sensation to such an extent before. Paul and I were very careful about this most all the time because he really was *not ready* for that kind of commitment and major life event yet, and in hindsight, neither was I.

I learned the rhythm method and the precise stages of my cycle, which after my original ET experiences, were never the same again. Never again did my cycle begin on the predictable second day of the month anymore. So, I charted and learned how to navigate the positioning of my cervix, how to read my mucus levels and textures and the correct body temperature for optimal protection. It was all very romantic. In all seriousness though, it was empowering as a woman to do this, and I actually loved it.

We were in our early to mid-twenties, and Paul had a promising acting and film career in front of him, as well as a strong desire for freedom and he didn't want to ever be tied down to a responsibility as enormous as raising a child. A committed relationship was hard enough for him to accept much of the time.

I remember feeling like I was pregnant *so* often, that I started learning little tricks to make certain I never had to give Paul that kind of news. I became a master at making parsley infusion teas and learned the power of high doses of vitamin C in bringing on my menses. My inner witch was definitely seeing the light of day more and more.

It was quite the dance, but never once did I consider in all these times I'd thought I *may* have been pregnant, that I might actually *have been*, and perhaps not by the means one might *assume*? I suppose it happened so often that when I actually *did* become pregnant with Noah several years later, and suspected I might be, when I told my friend Jandy, she just laughed at me and said, "Oh Sammy, you *always* think you're pregnant!"

Jandy was a good friend of mine, and she sloughed it off like it was old news from a tabloid or something. I couldn't blame her. I understood what she meant. I *did* always think I was pregnant, especially during those years with Paul.

I will always remember that moment, especially *now*, knowing what I know about these ET experiments I am involved in—having been Awakened and Aware of my greater role here on this planet...

Now, whenever health practitioners asks me "how many pregnancies I've had," I laugh to myself, and wonder if I actually answered with, "Oh, about a hundred or so," what their response might be.

I could always bring a punch line percussionist with me sometime and report back with the results. I can hazard a guess though that I might be the only one who finds it funny.

*

In my youth, my menses were timed so perfectly in order that my ovulation and such were entirely predictable, I am quite certain of this now. I was on a schedule, and it would not surprise me if I'd been impregnated tens of multiples of times, starting right from age nine.

My *Knowing* Now is that the roles of "victim" and "perpetrator" are no longer viable. I see the world and all experiences now as soul choices. Sometimes the choices can be painful or challenging if we do not acknowledge them, accept our responsibility in creating such challenges from a higher perspective and for the purpose of soul growth, and then *move forward* from them a more evolved being.

Ignorance is not always bliss. In Truth, it is one of the greatest roads to pain and suffering in the end. I had to learn this the hard way.

It is our ignorance and lack of personal responsibility, combined with leaving emotional traumas unresolved, which ultimately is the root cause of all physical dis-ease in the body. *This* is the true cause of our pain and suffering.

As I grew and tried to fit in and be like other people around me, I forgot who I was, Who I *Am*, and I became blinded to the truth. Deep down though, unconsciously, *I knew*, which is why I would soak through my pillows and hair on those disturbing nights when I would see my forgotten babies.

I knew the truth, but my conscious mind could not accept this and so could not have wrapped itself around the fact that these experiences were real.

I simply was not ready. You're only ready to know when you're ready to know, and not a moment earlier.

I had to prepare myself for many years to become *ready* for something as life-altering and consciousness-bending as this.

I was seeding babies, seeding *life,* and was not aware of it consciously in the least. I was ignorant to this fact, and in turn, it was hurting me. Especially because my original plan coming into this life was to remember and help others to remember also. I would not be allowed to forget indefinitely.

Throughout those confusing years, I often thought to myself, *'I'm pregnant. I know I am. But I can't be. There's no possible way.'*

I would have this inner battle going on with what I knew to be true, and what was logical in the Earthly realms. I would feel flutters of movement inside my stomach, which would often be accompanied by a slight protrusion, like a very early pregnant belly. Before having babies physically, I was gifted with a flat stomach, so this belly protrusion which would happen every so often, accompanied by the feeling of an unknown "presence" inside of it, made things even stranger for me.

I never knew anything like these genetic experiments existed in any realm, never mind the realms of probability for me, and many other women (and men—men are not exempt from this!) on our planet. Right now for that matter.

Well it is. And it's happening whether we realize it or not. Whether we want to accept it or not. I didn't want to accept it, but eventually, for my own health as well as my sanity, I had to.

The truth is that many extraterrestrial races have lost their ability to feel emotions, at least in the ways in which we are able to here on Earth. This is actually one of the many reasons these types of experiments are taking place for their benefit. We are mutually helping one another. We are sharing and combining our DNA in order to create a hybrid species of advanced humans where we can all thrive together.

This is actually a very beautiful thing. It is truly a Divine Experiment when we are working with the Benevolent Ones who are here to lift us up and evolve and expand our consciousness as a planet. Many incredible and highly gifted, intelligent beings have been and *are being* created as a result of these experiments *now*.

Perhaps taking a look at our own children will show us this.

CHAPTER 31

The Cosmic Mating Ritual

In the end, Paul and I decided to simply be friends, and I began my whirlwind relationship with Jon, which mostly consisted of us having mind-altering sex. It was so easy and yet so profound, by far the easiest I had ever had–I was multi-orgasmic. This went on for a year and a half, intensified, and then interestingly, it all fizzled out as soon as I became pregnant in November of 2003 (though I didn't know yet that I was pregnant). It was like I was suddenly with a different man.

Throughout the year and a half that we were sleeping together though, it was like we couldn't be in the same room and *not* end up in bed together. I was permanently aroused and ready to go with him. This was unusual for me, and it wasn't ever contrived or forced either; in fact, it was *so* natural, that we were both blown away at our inability to control ourselves when we were together. I know I sure as hell didn't understand it. We were incompatible in just about every other way.

One day, I stopped by to visit Jon while he was working, making music on his computer in his bedroom. He was almost always doing this at that time, and in the course of our relationship, he wrote me two beautiful songs, one in which he used all Yoko Ono track samples spliced together with lyrics he wrote about me. The base track was from her song "Let Me Count the Ways." It was so sweet it made me cry when I first heard it. I sat on his lap, and knew exactly what that was going to lead to, yet I just couldn't help myself.

We started kissing and feeling into one another, our bodies more than ready for this, knowing where "this" was all leading, when he whispered in my ear, "What is this? It's like we're a part of some primal cosmic mating ritual that we're not in control of."

We went on to make mad and passionate love, and lay together afterwards talking about quantum physics and God, the stars, Christ Consciousness and the universal energies all around us. I had never had a lover I could talk to like this before him. Jon only opened up this deeply right after making love and, in the end, we were too incompatible outside of the bedroom. This incredible sense of consciousness did not usually filter into our interactions outside of the bedroom. I was in love with the God I made love with. I didn't really know who he was outside of that space and time; the connection was just not there. It was such an anomaly to me.

To his credit though, Jon had learned and mastered the ways of stepping outside of his own ego enough to know how to make love to a woman and make her feel like a goddess. I didn't know it as this at the time, but I sure see it clearly now.

As soon as I was finished with the relationship—after I'd attempted to have him live with me to try out what a "real" relationship together would be like, within a matter of *weeks* he changed—and it was quickly over for me. The dream of "what if" was over. He suddenly became possessive and jealous, and instantly, this man I'd experienced such sexual freedom with up to that point was trying to control me and box me in to the category of belonging to him and only him. He would try to stop me from even talking with another man. It was crazy and I put an end to it immediately. No way, no how was I going to stand for that garbage.

But he wouldn't leave my home, so in December of 2003 I went to house sit for Jandy while she was traveling in India. I looked after her cats and plants for her, so it was a win-win. While there, I began feeling an even bigger surge of sexual energy coursing through me, more than I'd ever felt before, which was saying something.

I started desiring all sorts of wild sexual experiences, day and night. I even called Jon over one night because I couldn't take it anymore and needed to be with a man, and badly. That's exactly what it felt like. I felt like an animal. It was that overpowering for me.

I was ravenously hungry all the time too, and craving odd things I'd never craved before, spices I'd never cared about, suddenly I needed. Fresh organic strawberries, for the first time in my life, were an absolute must. And lots *of sex.*

I realized within a month of this beautiful insanity, of non-stop obsessions with orgasms and food that I was, indeed, *pregnant*.

CHAPTER 32

Prophecy Fulfilled: Could There Be Two?

I'd had visions of this moment, and knew it was going to happen since I was a young child. Even being alone as a single mother was a part of the vision, so I accepted this wholeheartedly and allowed it to be exactly as it was.

I enjoyed a beautiful pregnancy in which I connected with the soul of my baby every single day. Not a day passed the entire pregnancy that I did not meditate with this baby before laying my head on my pillow at night, sharing my love with this Divine Being, letting them know how much I loved them, how much they were wanted, and that I was so excited to meet them one day very soon.

I spent the majority of the pregnancy feeling that there may be twins inside of me—specifically a boy and a girl. The most prominent energy I could feel was a female energy, though I would always tell people that if it wasn't twins I was either having A) a girl, B) a boy with very balanced masculine and feminine energies, or that C) a boy who perhaps may be gay. I really felt like any of those options may have been possible and I was okay with all of them, however the dice landed would be perfect. I knew I wasn't in control, nor did I want to be. I loved this baby, these babies, with all my heart already, and that was all that mattered to me.

What is interesting to note is that in both of my pregnancies I was "given" girls' names, and yet both times I ended up birthing solely boys. Now, with Noah, I knew about two weeks before he was born that he would most likely be a boy after I'd had a dream of birthing a little old man. He was beautiful and cute as can be, but very obviously an odd looking old man. It's funny that when he came out, he acted and looked much like that baby in my dream, though he was absolutely beautiful, and much larger at 8 ½ pounds in the flesh, than the tiny little "man" in my dream.

Interesting that also in that dream, he much resembled the tiny grey babies that would be born in my dreams while I was growing up.

In utero, Noah's female name was Satya. Rubin's was Maya. Both names came to me, and yet both times, I birthed boys. I know now that I was given the names of their female twin counterparts so that their presence of existence would remain in the back of my consciousness for when I would be ready to remember them and know them.

I will get into my odd pregnancy story with Rubin later on, but let's just say that I thought I had been in the clear from having experiences with other dimensional beings. Much to my chagrin at the time, those experiences made a very unlikely and visible comeback during my pregnancy with Rubin, and ultimately, became a huge Activation and instigating force on the path of my ultimate Awakening to this Divine Mission I am now consciously walking.

CHAPTER 33

Tiny Healer

Noah was born, and as a baby, he was such a welcome gift in my life, and the life of everyone he touched. And he touched so many. He was a light and a joy to be around for anyone.

It seemed that he would seek out the most down and out person he could find, and would proceed to attempt to get their attention with his baby babble. Then he would continue to talk away to them, babbling on in gibberish with such a sense of animation, even the most strung out drug addict on the bus would usually at least notice him, and often he would make them smile, perhaps even reminding many of them about their own children they'd undoubtedly lost or had taken away from them, or simply lost contact with along their path of addiction.

Noah was naturally a healing soul. I remember one day when he was about one; he could only just walk and didn't talk yet. I was crying about something on our bed while he played. I was really having a good solid cry, when suddenly, he walked right up to me, took my face in his hands as if Christ would have done, looked me deeply in the eyes, and then kissed the very middle of my forehead so gently and yet with such grace and intention, I was blown away.

After he held the kiss there for a few seconds, he pulled away and looked me in the eyes again, still holding my face with his tiny hands. He looked deep in to my Soul, smiled, and then bounced off with his big, adorable diaper bum, and continued playing.

I was instantly healed of whatever heartache I had been experiencing, because I knew this wee soul had truly seen me, witnessed my pain, and had transmuted it with his deep, profound, unconditional love for me. I will always remember that experience.

These kinds of things were second nature to Noah, and although he was a regular toddler and baby in many ways, he would grow to do and say the most incredibly profound things sometimes. I was certain this child was a gift sent to me from the Heavens.

CHAPTER 34

"Is This Water, Mommy, Or Is It Pee?"

When Noah was one and a half, he and I moved into a government housing cooperative, which was a godsend to me. I was supporting us without any financial assistance from Jon. It was interesting to me that even though he is present with all his other children he has to date, he never once really made an effort to be a part of Noah's life. I truly feel it was meant to be this way, and hold nothing against him. He is playing the role he agreed to before ever coming here, and I am grateful for this, and for his wisdom in not standing in my way when it comes to raising him.

My rent was set to 30% of my income, which was peanuts, I realize, and I was grateful for this gift. I'd chosen to be a mother to Noah, to be present with him, especially for those first couple of years, so I sucked up my pride and went on government assistance after my hard-earned year of maternity leave expired.

My rent was about $250 a month, which was outrageously low, and included utilities. I simply paid my phone and internet bill, and we always had money left over to eat fairly healthily as well as some extra to "play" with, whether it was a trip to the Granville Island kids' arcade, play zone and water park, or a day at Grandview Park on Commercial Drive for an epic park session and fresh samosas, kitcheree and a slice of vegan carrot cake, or some vegetarian sushi and miso soup, which was one of Noah's favourites then. We had the money to have fun and still easily pay our bills. We had a lot of sweet times together in those days.

We had moved in to the co-op in March of 2006, just weeks before my nephew Mason was born. I'd had a bit of hesitation, as there were two buildings that this cooperative operated. The one I had actually applied to for us to live in was in Chinatown and had nice big apartments, and floors with outdoor playgrounds in the community gardens. I had a good friend who was living there. He was a single dad with two children and their live-in nanny. He had a huge three bedroom/two bathroom apartment, in suite laundry. His rent was only $300 a month, and it was actually nice!

But this building had a massive waiting list, which was understandable. So when I put in my application, and after waiting about five months for a call, they got me in for my interview, and accepted my application that day after meeting Noah and me. They told me it was for a two bedroom, but the catch was that the suite was in their other building.

The problem with the other building was what I thought at the time to be a deal-breaker for me, especially living with a young, innocent and sensitive toddler, not even two years old yet. It happened to be smack dab in the middle of the downtown eastside, otherwise known as the heroin district of Vancouver; in fact, one of the biggest heroin and drug communities in North America. We lived right next door to The Portland Hotel Society, the non-profit housing project for the homeless (most of whom were drug addicts) which is where the wonderful and beautiful man, Gabor Maté, is one of the resident physicians. Many of my friends and acquaintances have worked there over the years, most of whom got to work directly with him, including my dear friends, Jandy and Dawn, as well as my brother, Josh.

Needless to say though, because of my situation, I was still hesitant. I expressed this hesitation and my reasoning for it over the phone with them, along with my gratitude for having been accepted so quickly. The response from the administrator on the other end was that I had better say yes if I really wanted a spot in the co-op, because if not, my application would get placed back at the bottom of the pile for rejecting an offer. As it was, they had placed mine at the top of the list because of my needs, being a single mother on government assistance.

I heard her loud and clear, and said yes even though I still had reservations about living in a building with multiple drug addicts and people living with severe mental illness, including violent outbursts. Hepatitis and AIDS ran rampant in this neighbourhood and building as well. I have absolutely zero judgment against anyone living with either of these dis-eases, in fact, my heart regularly aches for them. I simply wasn't sure it would be the healthiest environment to raise my baby in. After all, people were regularly found dead in their apartments, or overdosed and rushed to the emergency. There was even a swat team there once because of someone who'd pulled a gun on another member and threatened to murder him. And this was in Canada where it is still very rare to see anyone with a gun, ever.

The streets just outside our door were littered with makeshift tents, sleeping bags, cardboard boxes, and the sight and stench of feces and urine all over the sidewalks. Noah got so used to asking before he jumped in "puddles," which was eye-opening when we moved to Sedona and one day, a beautiful monsoon rolled in and blessed the parched Earth with her moisture. Out on our walk, Noah looked up, almost four years old then, and said to me, "Is this water, Mommy, or is it pee?" I admit, that day I breathed a sigh of relief and fresh air, feeling so grateful for this cleansing, pure rain, and clean sidewalks. He splashed away to his heart's delight, which made my heart sing.

But back in 2006, deciding whether or not this choice would be a good one for us, amidst my humming and hawing over having said yes to this apartment, I heard the Voice inside very calmly say to me, "*Do not worry, dear. Embrace the mystery. You are exactly where you need to be, and there is a very important opportunity awaiting you by embracing this environment. It involves Your Destiny, and you will know what this means once you are there and are able to receive what it is offering you. Open your heart, and listen to its Voice."*

I trusted this message instantly, and never looked back. I am so glad now that I listened.

CHAPTER 35

Someone's Child

It was the summer of 2006. Life was sweet and appeared to be moving along much more easily now that Noah and I were living in an apartment that I could easily afford, and we were even getting used to our colourful and intense surroundings.

There were so many kind and lovely souls in our building and around the streets where we lived. Even if some were lost, they were still beautiful. Yes, many were drug addicts, some not, but most everyone there had some sort of addiction or at least had lived a life of hard knocks and were getting by with the grace of this offering we were all being gifted.

We were a small community. Dysfunctional, yes, but still a community of people doing their best in the moment with where they were at and with the hands they were dealt. Noah and I would walk the streets and he would smile at our homeless brothers and sisters as we strolled and explored; the life of a toddler.

Often walking right up to them, smiling from ear to ear, Noah would seek out the most intense and lost souls, it seemed. Some noticed him, most didn't and would walk right past him, hungry and crazed for their next fix. Noah didn't seem to mind. He smiled and bounced all the same.

He would walk up to the trees along the sidewalk and hug them warmly as he passed. We would go play together in the Sun Yat Sen Gardens' bamboo faerie "forest" as he called it, and sit and watch the koi fish and turtles swim in the large pond there. We found magic in our little syringe-infested neighbourhood, and we loved it and called it our home.

I had already renounced all drugs and alcohol from my own life about five years prior to us moving to this neighbourhood, when one day it dawned on me that anytime I drank, smoked or ingested any sort of drug, I didn't like who I would become, nor how it made me feel. I detested the "coming down" shitty spiral into my own personal hell, and whether it was a hangover from a few drinks that would turn me into a combative asshole, picking fights with anyone who looked at me the wrong way, or the month of paranoia and depression I would have to endure after getting high, either way I sliced it, it fucking sucked, and I hated what it did to me and who it turned me into.

For me, drugs and alcohol would be something I could easily let go of, knowing how much it was damaging me when I indulged in either. I had that capacity to make this decision and stick with it, thank the Goddesses. But these other beautiful souls I was surrounded by were sinking into the abyss, and there was nothing anyone could do about it except themselves. We had to witness this desperation and loneliness all around us, day in and day out.

It broke my heart, because I always looked at every single one of them as "someone's child," and wondered how on Earth we could ever let our children hurt so much. I wondered how we as a species were able to sit back and watch our dearest, most sensitive hearts ultimately spin in to such a vicious downward spiral of unspeakable pain and self-destruction. It made no sense to me, and ripped my heart out daily.

I wanted to be everyone's Mother and help heal their broken and lost hearts, as if it would make any bit of difference.

Yet in those moments, I witnessed the purity of Noah's soul embracing these beings without any pity or sadness, and only unconditional love and compassion. I learned a huge lesson. I learned, through the innocence of my one-and-a-half-year old son, that we are all perfectly on our own paths. We are all where we are meant to be, whether it is living a life thriving and having fun, or whether we're two steps from the grave and searching desperately for our next hit. And that it is all Divine Perfection in its own way, sad as that sounds.

We can love one another no matter what the circumstances, and honour the Divine Path in each of us. Sometimes we are just not meant to interfere, no matter how much our hearts may wish we could take everyone's pain away for them.

I felt an immense sense of love for these sweet souls, and I would still do whatever I could to make even a small difference in their lives. A smile of recognition is often all it took. I would talk with the ones who were coherent enough to have a conversation with, and I would listen to them for as long as they wanted to talk. I would hug them if I felt they were open to it and able to handle it.

Most stories I heard would be about their own children, which obviously saddened me, but I also found it touching that

Noah's presence could help bring back that feeling of love and joy they were able to experience remembering their own loved ones in his presence. I am certain some of them felt the pain of their loss afterwards like a fresh open wound, and maybe it even drove them to their next hit, but hopefully they also experienced the healing innocence Noah exuded, and that might have helped balance it all out.

I don't know though. I am not an addict, so I cannot speak from this perspective. I can only speak from my heart's wishes for these precious souls.

There were ones who would peg me from a mile away, knowing I was "the one" who would throw my money at them, without judgment of what they may or may not do with it. Admittedly, I seriously prayed they would get themselves a warm meal for crying out loud. I even brought hot food for some whenever I could, and most were grateful for this.

I felt a real sense of responsibility in this community, not as an enabler, but as a sister. A friend. A fellow Earthling who understands a little bit about pain, suffering and loneliness.

I often found myself wondering, that if we are truly all interconnected, all "ONE," then what was my part in this devastating creation, and how could I assist in the healing of this pain that was manifest in the form of addiction everywhere I turned?

Also, and just as important, if not more, was '*Why me, why here, and why now?*' There was a much greater purpose for all of this. I simply didn't know yet what that was. But I would come to know, and it would rock my world inside out.

CHAPTER 36

The Third Activation: Who Are You?

It happened one night in mid-July 2006, while on the toilet having a pee before going to bed. I wasn't feeling any sort of emotion about anything; in fact, I was quite contented with my life at the time.

Why wouldn't I have been? I was able to be at home with my babe each day, to be his Mama. We got to spend our days doing sweet, fun things together. At night, I would meditate, read books, and occasionally flip on the television, since it was one of the free perks in our building.

I had been gifted a used TV from a friend when Noah was born, and my mother, who had moved to Vancouver from Niagara Falls after his birth, had just moved in to the co-op herself as well. She watched a lot of TV, especially in the evenings, and we would bond over ridiculous shows like *Desperate Housewives*, which she would come over and watch with me. I never would have watched these things on my own, but it was a way for us to have fun together and connect, so I enjoyed it.

On evenings when I was alone though, I most often read or meditated or both.

This one night, as I was on the toilet, my bathroom, which was only lit by a small night light, suddenly began to fill with a bright, majestic white light. I remember feeling the most immense wave of unconditional love wash over me, and I breathed it in, grateful for its presence. Besides Noah and his pure-hearted love, I had never experienced this sensation throughout my entire body before. It was like waves of the most Divine Love splashing over me, overpowering me, and my eyes started to run like flowing rivers.

I was not crying though; it was more like I was melting, softening, opening. Like a flowering bud after it's been watered, petals unfolding, and the juicy, vibrant colours and unique essences of the flower blossom. It felt much like that, only in the moment, I was not certain what was happening, though I did know it was most definitely some form of Divine Intervention.

As I breathed deeply, soaking it all in, experiencing this immense wave of love unlike anything I had ever encountered before, an understanding deep within my heart and soul washed over me, and I was finally certain somehow that I was living in the right place, even though the "why" was still very much a mystery to me.

I didn't care though. In that moment, I let go of all concerns about when it might be time to leave, how long we needed to live there, and I surrendered into the unknown, happily. The "when" part of the equation was no longer important to me. What *was* important was the experiences, the mysteries, that I knew awaited me

I trusted this message with my entire being, and continued to enjoy my life, watching my beautiful baby boy slowly learn to talk, us living our simple, sweet life together.

Then one night, shortly after the incident in my bathroom, something strange happened. As I was flipping through the channels mindlessly on the TV, deciding whether or not to go to bed, my hand stopped clicking the remote when I got to the music station, which curiously, I never went to. Yet now, I found myself there, and that's when it hit me like a ton of bricks.

There "he" was again.

It had been about 14 years since my last "encounter" with this man, as far as I knew. The mysterious music video experience when I was a ripe seventeen years of age. Now I was thirty-one, and completely shocked that this band was actually still making music, quite frankly! I knew absolutely nothing about them, nor "*him,*" still, except that here he was again, in front of me, on my screen.

What was this? And who was *this man?*

Once again, there was that overwhelming feeling of being uncontrollably drawn into him, and again, I could not look away. The DNA crystals in my blood began to activate and pulse wildly.

I still didn't even know his name—even after all these years.

I had a computer, but didn't think to do any sort of search to find out. I simply sat in the energies, so potent, so strong; unable to take my eyes off of him. That hauntingly familiar, otherworldly sensation of my blood taking on a life of its own, pumping wildly as it had done when I was a young girl upon seeing him for the first time.

He was so familiar to me.

I felt as though I knew this man, but could not for the life of me justify to myself how this could possibly be. I couldn't even tell anyone his name if they'd asked me. But I knew his soul. How?

And then he was gone. I sat there, in the stillness of the silence, the television now turned off. I went to bed that night, breathing deeply into the mysterious and vast unknown.

In the morning, I was still thinking about him. I couldn't shake his energetic signature from my cells. I wrote my friend Angela an email, telling her the name of the band, saying, "What is up with this guy? This same thing happened to me with him when I was seventeen, and now suddenly here he is again! I felt sort of foolish, but if I could say this to anyone, it was Angela.

It had honestly been a rhetorical question; more of a '*what the fuck?*' email than anything, but Angela responded almost immediately. What was so strange to me was that Angela, who was the very last person on the planet I'd have expected to have an actual answer for me, was all over it.

"Oh him," she wrote. "His name is Anthony _____, and he's actually written an autobiography; they have it at Chapters." Angela is kind of a book fiend, and she used to work at Chapters, so she knew that store inside and out.

Immediately that day, I went out and bought his book. I knew in my blood and bones that I needed to read it. The Voice told me as much, and I knew it never steered me wrong.

As soon as it was in my hands, the energy that poured forth from this book was almost too much for me to handle. I couldn't even start to read it right then, I had to keep it sealed in the bag for a while and not so much as even look at the cover. I simply had to sit with it for the day before looking at it or opening it up, the energy was that potent and strong for me.

Right after buying the book, I headed over to Jandy's house for a visit. We had scheduled this visit days before, and even amidst the current insanity, I went. Anything to keep me grounded in this reality was a welcome distraction.

When I arrived, her brother, David was there. David is a lover of literature, and has since written and published his own children's book. He saw I had a Chapters bag in my hand, and asked me what the book inside it was. Doing my best to mask my nervousness, I pulled it out. I was a little embarrassed, because I really wasn't a fan of this man's music and knew absolutely nothing about him or why I'd felt so compelled to buy—and read—his book. I wasn't sure how to explain that if he'd asked. Thank God he didn't.

"Oh cool. Genesta (his wife) read that book and said it was one of the best books she's ever read," was his response to seeing it. And then he said, "Do you have their new album?"

Again, I felt somewhat foolish because I really didn't know that they had a new album, but that would make sense as to why I was suddenly seeing him all over the place.

All those years since I was seventeen, not once had I seen him again, and yet all this time, they were still making music. Who knew? Now, suddenly, he seemed to be popping up everywhere around me, and suddenly everyone around me was talking about him and they all knew who he was! I felt like I was being swept into some sort of other dimensional whirlwind, unsure where the hell I was going to end up.

"No," I responded, honestly.

"It's amazing. I have it here with me. I'll put it on so you can hear it. I can even burn you some of the songs off it," he offered.

My head was sort of spinning by now, trying to figure out what was going on here, but I sat back and witnessed it all happening around me. I accepted his offer to take the music, as the Voice inside me was nudging a resounding "*Yes*" to it.

I could not have predicted the turn of events that would take place in the days, months, and years that followed this day. Those 24 hours came to be one of the most significantly powerful and Divine Activations of my life.

CHAPTER 37

The Law of One: Revisited

I couldn't bring myself to listen to the CD David had burned me for quite some time. Merely having it in my possession felt like enough.

I did, however, open the book and begin reading it that night after Noah was in bed. I had been awaiting this quiet opportunity to delve into it without distraction, as something inside was telling me that this was one of the most important books I would ever read.

I was "in" from the very first line. He had me right along on his journey with him. I have since heard others talk about this book, and always hear the same thing. This man certainly does have a natural gift for writing. His descriptions are detailed and uniquely expressed, and it's as if I were seeing the world through his eyes. For me, it also helped that his sense of humour and unabashed fearlessness in sharing his gritty, raw sense of honesty and his version of the truth was something I connected with instantly.

An interesting thing began to happen to me as I got more involved in this book. It felt as though I was somehow merged with this man's spirit, and was literally experiencing "us" as part of the same whole. Whatever that meant I didn't know, but it was honestly how it felt. At the time, I didn't understand what was happening to me in the least. Shocker, right?

Of course, we are all part of The One; the Universal and Infinite Oneness of all. I get that. But at the time, I hadn't even heard of The Law of One, or the RA material. I had no clue I had ties to Thoth, or for that matter, who Thoth, or Tatos, Tahuti, Hermes, whatever we want to refer to him as, really was. I would later be introduced to him, and he would work with me as I began writing this book. Suffice to say, I was completely unaware of the teachings of this material at the time.

I had run from my earlier life experiences, especially those pertaining to extraterrestrials, inter-dimensional beings or anything too wildly metaphysical of any kind, even though in my core, I knew these Divine Truths already. I actually embodied them. I suppose that's why I didn't really seek them outside of myself. They were already a part of me, and in a deeper way, how I existed in this world at the core was shaped by these truths.

Growing up, I was totally fine with angels and their presence among me. For some reason, angels seemed acceptable, yet anything along the lines of ETs just weren't. I knew they existed. How can our universe be so vast and these beings not exist? As far as me personally being in contact with them? Other than the adorable character of E.T. from the movie, my only cultural connection with extraterrestrials was that they were to be feared, or just debunked altogether. Anyone who believed in them was a quack.

Probably because of the positive connotations that go along with angels and their pristine sense of purity, as opposed to how ETs are presented in the media around us as dangerous and villainous. Who could blame a kid?

I have since discovered though, that while angels can truly be benevolent and pure, and powerfully so, they also, as with everything in existence, including ourselves, have a potential dark or shadow side. This is simply the natural order of things. It doesn't mean I'm saying angels are bad because they too have a shadow aspect, just as it doesn't mean *we* are bad for the darkness that dwells within each one of us. It simply means that when we are willing to see and embrace the darkness, and learn to be discerning of it—for instance, discerning when a being is not in contact with the Highest Intent—then nothing is good or bad, it simply *is*. Is-ness.

I hadn't arrived at this realization in my life just yet, though. It would be a few years and several hard knocks before I did. Enough of that digression though.

Reading the book was somewhat of a transcendental experience for me. I had picked it up to learn more about who this man really was, and why *on Earth* he kept showing up in my life, over a span of decades, in unmistakably powerful ways beyond my logical mind's ability to compartmentalize and rationalize. I wanted to learn a little bit about him. What better way to do this than to go as directly to the source as I could: to read his own story, written in his own words.

I couldn't have prepared myself for what I was in for on this journey, but I sure as hell was not disappointed in the least. In fact, while reading it and learning that Anthony had experienced some extremely dark times spanning decades with a very serious addiction to heroin and cocaine, I received yet another jolt of lightning zapping through my body. My blood was awakened again, as somehow, this bit of information confirmed for me in a sense the location I had recently been placed in by Spirit, the ETs, what have you, and the cryptic messages I'd received through the Otherware, solidifying my "Knowing" that indeed, there was a deeper spiritual purpose behind me and Noah living and witnessing this reality daily for a year and a half, which went way beyond the physical realm.

I was suddenly receiving hits on how connected my son and I were with this mysterious man's personal experience and journey.

WOW. But how exactly? I would only receive bits of the puzzle at a time. Whatever I was prepared to handle and remain with my sanity intact was all I was given. And even then, it was questionable at times.

Why though, did any of this make any difference to me? This piece of the puzzle was what the Voice had been referring to when it had told me that it was important to my Destined Path for me and my son to live in this particular area. But how in the world was it connecting me and Anthony? That part, I couldn't make sense of.

Yet flash after overwhelming flash while reading the book kept barreling me over, and I often encountered uncontrollable waves of emotion flooding through me, or I would lose my breath completely just reading one simple sentence which would speak such deep, ancient truths to the core of my very soul. All encoded between the lines.

As I read Anthony's book, so many times I found myself thinking, '*Oh my gosh, this sounds just like me...*" Accompanied by a strong, even nagging, feeling that he and I were intimately, *Divinely*, connected in some mysterious, cosmic way, and that it only made sense that one day we would be able to meet in this dimension.

I felt pretty embarrassed about this, wondering if this was what being "star struck" was like, and if so, could I simply cancel it out? But this recurring thought wouldn't leave me alone. It nagged at me, tugged at the core of my soul, and was extremely persistent much of the time, try as I did to push it away.

Annoyingly to me, I had learned to trust my intuition by this point. So finally, I had to take note of the persistence of these powerful thoughts and feelings, frustrating and confusing as they could be.

With every encoded connection, I was left with yet more questions. It was as if this never-ending puzzle I was being asked to solve kept presenting itself to me, from beyond the veil, and I was lost in the abyss, trying to piece it all together in a way that made sense to me, the Great Cosmic Idiot.

CHAPTER 38

One Hundred Feet

Within weeks of receiving, reading, and completing his book—experiencing this cosmic "Knowingness" of some connection I shared with this man—my friend Angela informed me that his band was coming to Vancouver in a couple of weeks. September 14, 2006 to be exact.

There was synchronicity after synchronicity happening in my world all of a sudden, and it was all connected with Anthony. I was simply riding the waves, seeing where they would lead me, which honestly at times felt like crazy-land, but I was willing to take my chances, the inner knowing was just that strong.

No way though was I going to buy a ticket to this show. I only knew a few of their songs, and they were all from almost two decades earlier. Besides which, I had been scheduled to work that night, and so there was no way I would be going, and that was that.

Except, the concert just so happened to be at the stadium which was located two blocks from my home, and also synchronistically that evening, I was asked to leave work early because we were slow and had too many servers on deck. *Hm...*

I remember finding this interesting, as I had been well aware of the date and that Anthony was in town, mere blocks away from me. I had felt him the entire 24 hours leading up to the show, which was in itself a tad overwhelming energetically. And tonight, I was tired, relieved I was let off early, and wasn't the least bit interested in being a stalker Thank-You-Very-Much, plus I knew my mother would be happy if I were home early for a change, as opposed to our regular crazy 2 am nights. I had every intention of going straight home.

Riding home from work that night, as the bus pulled up to the stop at the sky train station, I heard the voice inside me tell me to get up and off, and to head to the stadium, which was the next stop, and would take all of two minutes to get to.

I complied. Reluctantly, but I complied all the same. I got up with a sigh and headed off the bus, not wanting to do this at all, though curious as to why it was necessary.

Mid-September in Vancouver can get a bit chilly at night. I was dressed for working in a busy jazz club, so I only had a wee sweater on over my tank top; not enough to keep me warm outside for very long, and anyone who knows me knows I am not a fan of the cold. But I listened. Dammit, I listened to that pesky, asshole of a voice, which were my honest sentiments about it at the time.

When I arrived at the stadium, I could hear the concert winding down, and as I heard his voice, my entire body started to shake and vibrate as the blood in my veins began to do its thing. It was different this time though. This time, I didn't have the safety of the television screen between us. His energies were within hundreds of feet from mine. My entire being could sense this.

I got very present, and breathed deeply as this full body vibration was totally rocking me. Instead of trying to name it or control it, intuitively, I stood outside the stadium doors, held out my arms, and I became a conduit, embracing and running these enormous energies, pulsating through my veins, through my entire being. I opened myself up fully, allowing these energies to move freely throughout my body, assimilating them, transmuting them, doing whatever they were asking for and needing. I wasn't even fully aware of what I was doing, but I knew it was powerful. I could feel that, no doubt about it. This wasn't "me." This wasn't even about "me." This was beyond time and space as I knew it.

I embraced the mystery of this experience wholeheartedly. It was so incredibly magical and empowering. I truly felt like I could have held up the entire building if I'd had to. Without thinking, I followed the movements of my body, channeling an intelligence all on its own. I allowed it to lead me, and reciprocated, by consciously helping hold the space, the container, of this enormous magical energy, whatever it was.

The entire experience was astoundingly powerful, and I was so grateful in that moment for having dropped my ego to begin listening to the Voice. Who could have known? Maybe this voice wasn't such a pesky asshole after all!

I was more than content to call it a night after this, I was so high on these energies. The concert ended in about two or three songs from my arrival there, and the timing felt perfect for me. I would come down off of this strange and wonderful experience with a nice walk home. I only lived two blocks away so I could get there in a matter of minutes, still early enough to relieve my mother from another late night, I thought. Then the Voice popped in again and told me to go down the steps, to the left and to keep walking around the building.

Already beginning to come down a bit off this high, people started to file out of the stadium and I became agitated again. I felt done. And besides which, I was starting to get cold and wanted to be able to give my mother the night off. But again, I listened. This voice is never wrong, and I knew it. So to my own chagrin, I listened.

I walked down the steps, to the left and around the building, just as I had been instructed.

I saw a bench and sat down, not exactly sure what I was doing there. So I began to write. I was getting back into the habit of bringing a journal with me everywhere I went, as I felt that recording all of these synchronicities as well as my dreams associated with them was going to be important someday. Funny enough, never once did writing a book about any of this come to mind at the time, if you can believe it.

I am truly grateful for listening to that calling now though, especially at that particular time in my life, because those journals have helped me fill in many of the smaller details of this book, and possibly others to come.

Sitting on the bench, I was writing stream of consciousness, when all of a sudden, I looked up and noticed that there were two big black buses parked about a hundred feet away from me. '*Those must be the tour buses,*' I thought.

And no sooner was I sitting with that thought, when out walks the band. There were about ten or so people, not many, standing around, waiting to talk with them. Maybe they'd heard "the Voice" too. Joke. But hey, maybe they did.

Yet there I sat, alone on a bench a mere one hundred feet or so away from Anthony, writing the whisperings of the cosmic stream that poured down the back of my head, through my spine, and out my arms to my fingertips.

I remember popping out of this altered state when the realization hit me: '*He's right there, Sam! You could go introduce yourself right now and get this all over with already.*' You see, by this point, I knew without any doubt whatsoever, that I was going to meet this man one day.

It's true. I could have done so in that very moment, and very easily. If I'd have let my ego into the driver's seat I would have walked right over there, introduced myself, and expected him to recognize me. If it's one thing I am not, it is patient. I am learning through this experience as well as motherhood though, that patience and timing can be everything. But in that moment, it took everything I had to restrain myself from walking over and introducing myself to him.

But I wasn't really a fan though, and such a meeting would have been out of place. I realized that the energies of the circumstances just did not match up in frequency, even though I continued to have this inner debate with myself to ignore this fact. After all, he was *right there*. How could this possibly go wrong? Isn't he waiting to meet me too? Don't we have work to do together?

Then the voice came in and very clearly said to me, '*Not now, dear One. It is not yet Your Time. Sit here. Meditate. Share in the energies from here, this way. Trust that this is enough for now. Be patient. The time is coming. You will know when it arrives, without doubt. Introducing yourself now will not serve anyone. It is not the correct timeline for this. Simply be here now. For this is the work required at this time. That is all.*'

The message was unmistakably clear, so I heeded the advice of my trusty Voice, and sat in meditation for the next fifteen to twenty minutes or so and simply sat in the energies. I breathed deeply and ran the energies through my body. I was grateful to be a part of this mystical creation, even from afar. Thank Heavens, I was not being asked to present myself like a groupie or a fan. Indeed, I was much, much more than that. I was something I didn't even have words for yet.

I finally walked home. By this time my teeth were chattering, and I was ready to rip my work clothes off, melt into my comfy, warm jammies, and lay down to rest next to my precious child, and hopefully process what the hell had just happened back there.

As I lay there, settling myself to slip into dreamland, the reality hit me like a wave. This mysterious man and I had only moments earlier literally stood mere feet away from one another. I drifted off to sleep, wondering what this must all be about, and why it had been so important that I be there, almost close enough to touch him. Almost, yet not quite.

CHAPTER 39

Dream Encounters, Parallel Realities and Karmic Clearing

I soon began to see Anthony consciously during my meditations as well as in my dream state, and often. I realized immediately that we had met in the dream state, in the Otherware, many times before.

These dreams were not sexual encounters by nature either. I wasn't having "lonely single mom" sexual fantasies about this man, yet at times, I would encounter us in a scenario that involved being together in a room with a bed, wearing only white underwear, or nothing at all. Then we would lay together in the bed, and hold one another as if we'd been there and done that a million times before. I will not lie, there was always the sense of a deep, ancient love present between us. It was a soulful and otherworldly kind of love; one of having known the other since the beginning of time.

There was always a gentle, caring quality to our embrace that felt like home to me, and I knew we'd been holding each other this way forever, without a doubt. No words were needed; there was a telepathic recognition, a knowing between us. There was also an unspoken vulnerable, simple yet beautiful truth connected with what we were creating together that I always remembered as the main message of these dream sequences upon awakening. Even though I didn't know what that truth really was, I could feel its presence permeating me as I would go about my day after such a dream encounter.

I went on to have many encounters with Anthony, as if we were always coming home to one another. We would meet up through some kind of synchronicity, lock eyes, and a Knowing would happen for both of us, activating the blood in our DNA. Tears would begin to stream down both of our faces. We would hold each other, crying or laughing or both, in a great sense of relief to have found one another again, and that was all I could remember. I had this dream sequence many, many times; different situations, always the same conclusion.

Early morning at the beginning of November 2006, which synchronistically happened to be the morning of his 44th birthday, which I realized later on in the day, I'd had an intense encounter with him, almost as if it were a regressive healing or clearing we had needed to do together.

I refer to these as "encounters" because I have since seen Anthony a multitude of times in the dream state. Though some I tend to think of as perhaps merely dreams (me working through fears around our connection or working through some other issue in my life), the ones that are authentic experiences, or true encounters, have a different energy than any regular dream. Much the same as when I have ET encounter dreams, the difference is obvious. These encounters tend to penetrate my entire being and remain in my consciousness upon waking, every single detail recalled with great clarity, no matter how much time goes by.

This particular encounter I experienced with Anthony on his birthday in 2006 was actually quite intense, and involved him standing on the wing of a blue and yellow plane, threatening to jump off. There was something he was yelling about 'giving up', and he was very upset and had a lot of anger.

He was actually attempting to risk it all, everything he was, everything he had, to see whether or not he would make it through.

Interestingly, in this sequence, he looked as he did back in the '90s when his drug addiction was overtaking him, consuming his life force, and he appeared to be embodying this same state as he teetered on the wing's edge.

There were many of us watching him with bated breath as he screamed about giving up and basically losing his mind. He was sick, and rife with the inner pain and turmoil of what he was experiencing. It hurt me deep inside to see him like this. I could feel my own heart breaking as I watched him—as I *felt him* - waiting to see what he was going to choose.

There was nothing I, or anyone, could do for him in this moment. It was all up to him, and it pierced my heart to the core.

I sat and watched, as the others there who also loved him did—his family, his friends and his band mates. We were all sending our love, some were yelling at him to come down, most of us just cried, breathed and waited to see what he would choose. I felt nothing but an overwhelming abundance of love for this man, who felt, painfully in this moment, like a part of me.

Finally, the wait was over. He took action and began to pour gasoline all over himself, and then he struck a match, seemingly to light a smoke, and set himself on fire. It was horrific. I can still feel myself gasping as if I too were about to catch fire and die a horribly painful death.

All of a sudden, he jumped from the wing of the plane, in a desperate attempt to put the fire out. He realized in this moment that he did not actually want to die. He rolled around, and I ran to him among some of the others, and helped him put the fire out.

He was burned quite badly. His long hair, which had always been a feature people seemed to know him by, was gone. He had burns all over his body, and did not look like the same man. All of a sudden, the "looks" that the world had always worshiped and known him by were no more. He was burned, scarred, and his hair would never grow back. He would *never* be the same.

At first, he cried. He was angry, upset, and embarrassed. He sat down, would not speak to anyone, and cowered away, curling himself into a ball on the ground. He was also in a great deal of physical pain.

I went to his side, and sat with him. At first, he pushed me away. He did not want anyone there, and the sense was that he felt as though he did not deserve anyone's love or affection. I didn't care. I stayed by his side. I allowed him the time he needed to feel his anger and upset, and when he continued to push away any attempt at support and love from anyone, I finally started yelling at him, in order to get through to him, because I knew that if someone didn't, it would only be a matter of time before he would succeed in another attempt. I yelled:

"You need to accept that you are loved here, Anthony! Look around you, asshole! Don't you realize you could have that love you are searching for, if you just allowed yourself to? The money, the cars, the houses don't mean a damn thing, don't you get it? All of that isn't even real! None of it matters if you don't have love in your life! THIS is what matters! Look around you! Look at all these people who care about and Love you! These people are here right now because they LOVE YOU! WE LOVE YOU! You need to realize this and accept it dammit! We care about you! And none of it will mean a damn thing until you start loving your SELF! Look what you're doing to yourself..."

By now, I was weeping.

He finally stopped his temper tantrum and looked deep into my eyes for the first time.

"I love you, and I don't care if you hate me for it. I won't stop loving you, even if you never want me to come near you again. That is all right. That doesn't matter to me. I can love you from wherever I am. But if you can accept my love, I will be by your side, for eternity."

Tears started to stream down his face. He said nothing. His eyes had turned to waterfalls, like mine. This man had never looked more beautiful to me than in this moment, no matter what that fire had done to his body. We cried together, and held one another for a very long time. His physical pain seemed to cease completely, and miraculously. It were as if he was healed instantly by this exchange.

When I next looked at him, he was his Now Self. Completely healed and regenerated. We sat together, holding one another, in peaceful silence, and the dream encounter was complete.

When I awoke from this experience, my pillow was soaked with tears, my face and hair were sopping wet, and I was still crying. To me, this was so much more than a dream. These are the experiences I am talking about with "dream" versus "experience" or "encounter." They are unmistakably different. Typical dreams often show us our subconscious fears or anxieties. Other Dimensional Encounters penetrate deeply into our Soul, and involve a very real Healing or an Awakening to the ultimate Knowingness of Truth.

In this particular dream experience, I felt as though we were working to heal a part of his Soul, together. That is a very different experience than a dream. Ain't no mistaking the two.

This was nearly nine years ago at the time of this writing, and I still remember every single detail of it as if I'd awoken from the experience this morning.

CHAPTER 40

"Daddy!" Another Soul Recognizes...

These types of dream encounters, synchronicities and signs became a regular occurrence for me. Way too many to include here, and yet, I did not talk about them with anyone, except occasionally Angela. Even then, most things involving this evolving connection with Anthony, I kept to myself.

How does one explain something to anyone that they don't fully comprehend themselves? As more and more started happening, I continued to struggle to understand what the root of this connection with this man really was, because it was an ever-growing mystery to me. It stretched beyond what my mind could comprehend, as my heart strangely and uncomfortably continued to crack open more and more. It stretched beyond Time and Space.

With my Gemini Sun and Virgo Ascendant, and so much Mercurial energy in my natal chart and blood, I wanted to understand things with my mind. I was searching to understand with my head just who this soul was and how we were really connected, or if somehow, I was only imagining it.

Little did I know that I should have been leaving this entire quest up to my Higher Self and my heart. I probably could have avoided a whole lot of inner turmoil if I had. My intense Scorpio Moon, digging into the hidden aspects and shadows, wanting to uncover anything hidden or unknown, wouldn't allow me to leave it alone though. I could feel a deep, mysterious resonance here, and try as I might, my subconscious mind was searching for answers even when on the surface I wasn't.

This whole dance with myself drove me crazy and made me furious much of the time. We had, obviously, never met in this dimension or lifetime, and this minor glitch in the equation made me feel confused about having such a strong connection with someone I'd never even met, especially a damn celebrity. Even the word made me cringe.

I was still cynical about fame and fortune then, and admittedly, I judged it. Fake personas and fancy falsities, all hidden behind a mask of perfection is how I saw it, and it bothered me so much that the world tended to put these people up on pedestals, when in reality, they were just regular ordinary folks trying to make their own way in this crazy world, like the rest of us. Of course, they didn't have the luxury to do this in private, and for this, I always felt empathetic.

But I didn't agree with worshiping someone like a God just because they make great movies or music. What about the amazing mothers and fathers out there who make a huge difference in the world daily by raising incredible human beings who will one day go out into the world and actually be this change we are all so desperately seeking? I'll worship that first, to be honest.

And yes, there are those who are using their status to help bring change to the world through their voice, through their creations, as well as through their personal lives. I applaud this, and am grateful there seem to be more and more who are taking this stand now. I do have huge respect for the ones doing this. It seems Anthony has come to be one of them.

In fact, I have since come to learn that all of the celebrities I have ever known had an otherworldly or psychic connection with do fall into this category, which is just further confirmation for me, and has helped me accept the validity of these connections. At the time they were Initiated though, I'd had no concept of these aspects of these people. No signs displaying these sides of them, which I find fascinating.

Somehow with Anthony, whether I liked it or not, whether I attempted to deny it or run away from it, I had to come to terms with the fact that, in some way I was connected multidimensionally with the soul of this man in a deep and personal way, more so than I had been with anyone in my waking "real" life. I suppose that is sort of a sad statement, but the truth.

This difficult discovery was a bit jarring to face, and really challenged my own core beliefs, not to mention the grip on my sanity at times. Not knowing which world was more real—my waking, third dimensional world, or my dreamtime and alternate states of consciousness world, which seemed to begin bleeding into my waking life more and more. They were melting together, yet I had no idea how to live them out loud, simultaneously. I knew, from the outside I would look batshit crazy.

It wasn't until one day, when I'd placed a photo of Anthony up on my computer screen that something completely shifted for me.

Angela had insisted that I do this for one day only (that's how she got me to agree to it). She knew a little bit of what I was experiencing in regards to Anthony, and she also knew how resistant I was to all of it. She strongly suggested that I needed to have him "physically in my space" on this one particular day to move things along for me.

Her reasoning was probably something to do with the Mayan calendar, the current wave spell or something like that, which we were heavily following at that time. I look now and see all the galactic and cosmic references in Mayan Astrology, and laugh to myself at how much in denial I really was then.

Angela told me that I needed to have Anthony's picture up on my computer, just for the day, and I was to do this to support a deeper, subtler integration of the multi-dimensional work he and I were doing together in order to help ground it in this dimension. Whatever that meant.

Needless to say, I hated this idea. It actually made me want to punch a hole in the wall. Truly, I detested it. I still struggled with my ego and didn't want to feel like some silly fan, of which I was certain he had tens of thousands of those already without needing to add the likes of this freak to the mix. If anyone were to walk into my apartment (chances were slim, but it still could have happened, I thought) and caught a glimpse of this madness, they may have seriously thought I had a celebrity crush. The egomaniac in me did not want to go there.

The embarrassment at the thought of this kind of scenario made me want to scream. My ego resisted and I fought it as long as I could, but in the end, I listened to Angela. I took the first picture I found of him online and hastily made it my desktop image. *'Just for the day,'* I assured myself, then walked away from the computer, not wanting to have to stare at it a second longer, as the whole situation was making me uncomfortable, big time.

I remember playing with Noah, who was freshly two. He was a little bouncy bean, always popping around the furniture, flying, jumping, playing and rarely ever sitting still. We were dancing around, having fun together, when all of a sudden he walked over to the computer, which I had stuck in the corner of our very tiny living room, angling the screen with Anthony's face plastered on it right into the corner so it was at least partially concealed, just in case.

Noah had to walk right into that corner in order to look at the screen, which was odd. But for some reason, that's exactly what he did. He never usually did this or paid any attention to the computer at all, so I definitely took note.

All of a sudden, he pointed to the screen and said with great conviction and delight in his tiny voice, "*Daddy!*"

My breath stopped. *What did he just say?*

"Pardon me, honey? *Who* is that? Who did you say he is?" I asked him, thinking I must have heard him incorrectly, as he'd never even seen a picture of Anthony before this that I knew of, other than perhaps his book cover, but that had been put away and shelved for some time.

Noah looked at me almost as if to say *'Are you an idiot Mom? Who do you think he is?'* but instead he said, with greater conviction and a little bit of force now, probably to knock it through my own thick skull, "*DADDY!! DADDY!! Me want...*" And he reached out to the screen, touching his face, trying to grab him out of the computer and hold him.

This floored me, especially because he had once seen a picture of Jon holding him in the hospital a few days after his birth, and had asked me who he was, and when I'd said, "That's your Daddy," he looked at me and said, "*No* he *not!*"

Noah was still not yet forming full sentences, but I knew enough by looking in his innocent little eyes that he definitely recognized Anthony somehow.

But HOW?

To make it very clear: Yes, I was a single Mother, but Noah had never until this very moment, given any hint that he wanted, or was searching for, a 'Daddy.' Not once.

He had seen and met men often as we had a little social life. But never once did he seem the least bit interested in having a 'Daddy' before now. Not even with Paul, and he was closest with him than any other man.

I'd even attempted dating a couple of men before renouncing dating altogether when Noah was only one, not wanting to be introducing my child to different men constantly throughout his childhood. I was resigned to dash—and more than happy and prepared to—be a single mother until he was eighteen. Raising my child meant way more to me than any man on this planet.

So, when, seemingly "out of the blue," as if being prompted by an invisible force, my two-year old walked right up to the picture of him, that alone surprised me. Noah not only never looked to any man to be his Daddy, not from a picture or anyone in the flesh, he had actually developed a sort of aversion to most men, with the exception of Paul and my brother, Josh. So, this definitely struck a chord in me, and hard.

Now suddenly, I had my child here, with such unwavering conviction, telling me that this *man on my screen—Anthony* of all people for heaven's sake—was his "*Daddy*"?! I didn't know what to do with myself. It made no logical sense whatsoever that Anthony could be his 'Daddy.' *Absolutely none,* as far as I could tell.

Noah finally dropped it, as if the inner prompting he appeared to be led by dissolved. I was having a hard time wrapping my brain around his persistent proclamations and sat, dumbfounded. He walked away just as quickly and simply as he'd approached it, and continued to play joyfully like nothing had happened. But to me, something had indeed "just happened."

I am so glad I took notes in my journal at this time, because I was floored again when recently I discovered that the date this happened was on August 20, 2006. This may seem like just an ordinary date to most, but thanks to Selene's tracking expertise of dates and natal chart markings, this date is extremely significant.

It is connected with the Harmonic Convergence of 1987 which, when I'd had a "star marking chart" done for Noah back in April 2012, is one of the events and energies that shows up in Noah's natal chart as being very important to note throughout his life.

Arielle (Selene's best friend, colleague, and the woman who did his reading for me) specifically told me that though Noah wasn't technically born yet during the time of the Harmonic Convergence, that he is connected with it, and because of this, he should always pay attention to significant events that occur between the 15th and 20th of August each year throughout the duration of his life. For instance, messages that come in to him via his dreams, conversations he happens to overhear, ***people that show up in his life***, people that leave his life, basically anything significant that takes place, happens deliberately on a soul level, and nothing is coincidental or accidental. Synchronicity will be working overtime during these dates each year for him.

When I saw this confirmation in my journal, confirmation to something I'd already known in my heart as "Truth," it took my breath away. Here, even at two years of age, Noah was right on track, right on Time, and not only that, he was helping keep me on Time too, whether I realized it or not. I was amazed by this, and the power that this small being held in my life.

Yes, it was a very strange interlude in our day when Noah came out with this bizarre proclamation, and it always stuck with me because it was so shockingly odd. Thankfully, I now have an understanding of what happened, at least in part, and what my young child was attempting to convey to me through this moment of high strangeness.

At the time though, and for many years afterward, it continued to elude me. I had simply added this incident to the growing pile of '*What the hell just happened?*' experiences, without the slightest hope of ever figuring it out.

Thanks to Selene and her mastership in galactic tracking, the pieces to this strange puzzle finally started to fit together, and what I was to discover later on would add a whole new level to the meaning of "Daddy" for me.

CHAPTER 41

That Song Again

Noah continued to show signs of a deep connection with Anthony, and it would show up in the most shocking of ways sometimes.

Like the day we were in the department store across the street from our apartment building. We often would go there and play on rainy days, since going to the park or playing outside for too long wasn't as fun an option.

In the basement of the store was their outdoor gear section, which was sprinkled with inflated rafters, pitched tents, flashlights, fishing poles and other fun stuff for a two-year-old boy to enjoy. Noah loved that section of the store, and it would entertain him for hours sometimes.

So, we were in there one dreary day to get out of our tiny apartment for a while. The store always had a radio playing with background music, to varying degrees of volume depending on the day, and probably who was in charge of the music.

This particular day, the music was very low. So low, it was almost impossible to make out what we were hearing. I never really listened closely to it though, since it was usually Top 40 pop music.

Noah and I were running around, playing and being silly together as usual. The music was barely audible, more like a whisper in the background, especially beneath Noah's boisterous squeals of delight from me finding him in a game of hide-and-seek and chasing him around the store.

All of a sudden, Noah's mood completely shifted. He was in the backpacks section by this point, trying to hide from me or pretend he was "in jail" with the bars that were now separating me and him. A game he also loved to play.

I didn't know what was happening with him, as one second he was giggling and running, and the next, he had stopped dead in his tracks, and actually sat down on the shelf with the backpacks, held his face in his hands, and started to weep.

My child had never done anything like this before. He was still two, he was always ready for the action and fun to begin as soon as his eyes opened in the mornings, and he really wasn't a child who cried or threw tantrums at all.

So, I was taken aback, and not sure what was happening. I thought he must have hurt himself, which was also very rare. Maybe he'd been so excited, he'd jabbed his hip into the corner of the shelf or something, I thought. I was quickly trying to figure out why he was sobbing into his hands, seemingly out of thin air.

I ran to him and asked him if he was all right. I asked him why he was crying, expecting to see some sort of "owie" on him.

"It this song Mommy. It just so sad." He continued to weep into his hands, as I now held him in my arms.

I strained my ears to listen to what song he was hearing, as I still couldn't make it out, it was playing so low. When I finally tuned in, my stomach dropped, and I thought I was going to be sick right there in the backpacks.

It was "the song." The same song I'd heard and seen the video to when I was seventeen that Anthony wrote, all about his loneliness and drug addiction. It was, indeed, a very sad song, for anyone who could really feel and hear the energy of his heart in it, which very clearly, Noah had tuned in to, even when the song was barely audible.

I had never played this song in our home. I didn't have a copy of it to do so. I had never played any of this band's music in my home. I didn't own any of it, except for the burned CD David had given me, which I hadn't ever listened to. I truly never listened to the band's music, and the only times I'd heard any of it was during my attempts to learn more about Anthony, and this I would do in the evenings after Noah was in bed. Even then, only occasionally if I was experiencing something in particular and was looking for any sign of synchronization to help me sort it out.

So Noah had zero reference for this song, and had surely never heard it before. The fact that he could even hear it was almost a miracle, and that he could hear the words and feel the energy encoded in it was even more incredible to me.

"Yes, it is a very sad song," I gave in (what else could I do?), and I held him in my arms. He wept even harder at my validation of this, and the fact that I was hearing him and understood his pain.

Tears began to stream down my face too, as it started to sink in for me that perhaps this connection I had with this man went even deeper somehow than I might ever know, and perhaps it involved my sweet child in some mysterious, unknown way.

I wept at the truth of how this felt, and I wept at the fact that I might never know what any of it meant. I wept at the fact that now this connection was touching my precious child in a way that I didn't understand or know how to deal with. I wept at my baby son's pain which, in this moment, was indeed very deep and real.

We went home after this, both of us emotionally exhausted and finished there for the day. We needed to shift the energy and let whatever this was go, and move on. I especially needed to do this for my child. I had never seen him in such emotional pain before this moment and though I was entirely perplexed as to what had ignited such a wave of emotion for him, there was also a deeper part of my unconscious soul that in some way, somehow, though my conscious mind could still not grasp it, understood it completely.

CHAPTER 42

Spontaneous "Drop-By" Activation

Channeled Transmission ~ December 20, 2006 *out of the blue* at 2:22pm in Vancouver, British Columbia:

"Somewhere in the galaxy, there is a planet that I call Home. It is FEMUS.

I left this star planet long ago in order to experience Earth. This was 50,000 years ago in Earth time.

I traveled to Earth by means of a transport called Starship Light. This spacecraft appears to Earth Humans as a beam of white light.

My reason for coming to Earth was to learn about and transcend duality through the frequency of LOVE, teaching others through my actions and Mastery of this frequency. Since that time, I have incarnated on the Earth plane 5,300 times.

My original plan was to remain on Earth as long as I was needed. My feelings about the current situation on planet Earth lead me to believe that this Mission is still very much in need of fulfillment.

Back on my home planet, I work as an Ambassador in charge of the Messengers of Love who are stationed on Earth and other planets in need of this Service.

My gender is non-existent ~ I Am Pure Light.

People on our planet live up to hundreds, even thousands, of years, equivalent to Earth timelines. There is no sickness or death. The "body" is simply transcended when it is time to move on.

Our planet looks like water ~ fluid, and light ~ illuminated.

Our language, when translated audibly, is similar to what Earthlings refer to as "Druid."

Our homes are open space, and are transparent. Our family life consists of sharing pure Unconditional Love through the essence of our hearts and souls.

My family consists of other beings of pure white light. We are all equals. There are no hierarchy structures in place."

**I recently looked up "Femus"/ "Phemus," only finding fictional planets from media sources, specifically Avatar and Star Trek. The only sources even coming remotely close to this name, neither of which I had seen or heard about before this transmission, was scribed in 2006. This is the definition I received as a result of my research:

"Phemus, also known as femus, is a noun, or an adjective, used to name or describe someone or something that is just so indescribable."

So I suppose if the shoe fits... For what though?

CHAPTER 43

Mystical Messages & The Execution of a Dark Lord

I still remember when the Gulf War broke out in the early '90s. I was about sixteen or seventeen—around the same age as when I'd first seen Anthony. I was horrified by the news my sister always had on the television. I never paid too close attention to anything in the media, thankfully, but I do remember feeling very saddened and hurt by this war, which was apparently over oil, something I just couldn't wrap my youthfully naivety around.

Why would people kill each other for oil? My brain simply did not understand this concept. I hadn't a clue how the people on this planet were thinking or operating. After all, I lived in a country that was abundant in oil naturally, so why on Earth were "we" even taking part in this insanity on the other side of the world? Then I heard the name Saddam Hussein.

The barflies in my father's pub were a rowdy and rascally crowd, always taking the piss out of each other, including my father. He played along too, it was just good business. He was a very good business man, with a usually great sense of humour, and his clientele were loyal to him until the very end.

I'll never forget walking into the bar on our usual Sunday with our dad, and seeing the display a few of the guys from the bar had put together. There was a picture of my father next to a picture of Saddam Hussein, with a caption something along the lines of "*Who done it?*" It was then that I noticed how oddly alike these two men looked. It was uncanny actually, and became a running joke at the bar for the duration of the war.

My father looked like he and Saddam Hussein could be brothers, some might even go so far as to say *twins*. It was very odd.

Here Saddam was Iranian, and my father, some poor supposedly white country bumpkin of a kid from the east coast of Canada. And yet, they could almost pose as clones of one another. *Almost.*

I never really did give it much more thought throughout the years. The war ended, Saddam was apparently "crazy" according to the media and the world, and that was that. I was still nestled safely in my own little bubble, a young small town gypsy artist Canadian girl.

Life happened. And along with it many more synchronistic and experiences of high strangeness continued. Fast forward to the year 2006. Nearly exactly 10 years after my initial UFO contact. 2006 was a huge year for me. This was the year I really started to listen to my own intuitive guidance, following synchronicity consciously. I admit though, oftentimes begrudgingly or hesitantly. Even so, it became such a strong force in my life that I could no longer ignore it, even if I tried. Even if I whined about it while I followed, I followed it nonetheless with a strong sense of commitment and duty, often through gritted teeth.

I remember in the summer of 2006, I started to become plagued by an awful, dreadful feeling in my gut. Whenever this feeling occurred, it was always accompanied by the thought, '*My father is going to die before the end of the year.*'

It was a rather unsettling, eerie intuitive feeling, and it always upset me. Who wants to be hearing over and over again that their father is going to die, and so soon? I would always try to put it out of my mind, but this was not easy to do, especially since I received the message more than once.

My father had had a series of heart attacks and close calls the two years leading up to this, so of course, this was an added concern for me. I would call him, or anytime I spoke with him, I would tirelessly ask him how he was feeling, "*really* feeling" as I always put it, assuming, due to the ever-nagging feeling in my gut, that he must not be telling me everything, as he always tended to downplay any kind of unwell feeling he might have.

The end of the year was approaching, and thank the heavens, my dad was still alive. But there were still a few days left in the year, so we weren't out of the woods just yet. I was riding the bus on my way to work at the jazz club the evening of December 29, 2006. It was just like any other night. I had a book I was reading on the bus, knowing the ride would take about 40 minutes, and being a single mother with a toddler at the time, I would use any chance I got to nestle in with a good book. It was usually something esoteric, metaphysical or spiritual in nature. I'd dive on in, getting lost in the pages before I would be run off my feet for the evening.

We were heading over the Granville Bridge in Vancouver when, out of nowhere, I couldn't breathe. It was as if something was tightly wrapped around my neck, strangling me, and I was gasping for air, panic-stricken, sweating profusely and totally confused as to what was happening to me. I felt like I was going to die if this lasted much longer. Everyone else on the bus was acting "normal." This was all on me.

I lost all sense of composure and was gasping for air, holding my neck. I almost jumped off the bus, but there were no stops on the bridge. I wasn't thinking entirely clearly, as one part of me was ready to bust through the people on the bus and push my way out the back door while we were moving. But thankfully, there was another part of me watching this entire scene play out, as if from a bird's eye view, knowing I was going to be okay, and that it would pass somehow, and soon.

And then it stopped, just as quickly as it had started. We made it over the bridge, and I could breathe again. My neck was no longer seized up, and air was able to pass in and out, unhindered. '*What the hell was that about?*' I thought to myself.

By this time, high strangeness and unexplained physical symptoms and bizarre happenings were nothing new to me. So, I wrote it off as some strange planetary energy I must have been clearing for God Knows Who, and I left it alone. I went back to reading my book.

I arrived at work, walking in through the back alley entrance into the kitchen where the chefs were prepping food for the evening. They had the radio on as they often did, but were not listening to music as usual. They were listening to a live news broadcast.

Almost as soon as I walked in, one of them said to me, "Did You hear, they just executed Saddam Hussein! They hanged him!"

WHOA. *What?*

My mind was reeling. It honestly took me about 24 hours to assimilate the synchronicity of what had happened, and I still do not fully understand my connection with this man, but somehow, in some way, there is a soul connection that I can't explain, and for some reason, it is being asked of me to include this experience in this book.

Here it was, December 29th for me, but actually December 30th where Saddam was when he was hanged. It was literally "the end of the year," and a man who could almost be considered a clone of my own father was dead, after me receiving repeated messages leading up to it that my father would be dead before the end of that year. Another odd thing I noted many months after this experience was his name: Saddam. If one were to rearrange the letters of his name, you get "Sam dad." When I was "shown" this one day through tele-thought-form, I was floored.

What did any of this mean? I hadn't a clue, but the very real fact that I had somehow physically experienced this man's death at the precise time he was actually dying, as if it were happening *to* me, was unsettling and extremely mysterious and curious to me.

Thank God it did not need to be my own father, who is still alive today, thankfully. But what was this mysterious connection between the three of us? After all, this man wasn't exactly liked on the planet for his great acts of kindness and Divine Service. It always made me wonder, and always bothered me a little, and I often wonder if I will ever really know the full extent of this connection, and why on Earth I needed to become aware of it in the first place?

I am quite certain these events were some sort of display of one of many thousands of ET experiments on the planet. One thing I have come to learn on my own galactic journey here is that sometimes, we just never get to know, and that's okay.

Very curiously, in the past couple of years, I have become aware through Selene's discovery of star markings that Saddam had them in his natal chart, which directly connects him with Galactic Knowing in his soul. He was technically a starseed, albeit one running some serious Dark Lord programming.

I have also since heard of a theory that he knew about a specific star gate, and supposedly he had planned to open it and access it. Supposedly, this was the true purpose for the wars he was waging. And supposedly the Powers That Were didn't want him to do this. Apparently, the fear was that he would use this power for acts of malevolence and planetary domination rather than benevolence and service, which I can certainly understand given his track record this incarnation.

But what do I know? And still, I can't help but occasionally wonder, what did any of this have to do with me? A little small town Canadian girl? How was he connected with my Earth father? How was I connected with this man? Were we connected via the same cloning experiments? Was I carrying some of the same genetic codes, and if so, was it because I am supposed to help clear and transmute these genetic frequencies on the planet? I shudder to think on the possibilities, though with the path I have been asked to walk thus far in my life, nothing would shock me at this point.

I do find it interesting though, that my family, and I in particular, had such a strong awareness of, and mysterious connection with, this powerful Dark Lord in his final years and moments on the planet. And only to discover there he was, holding a great and hefty galactic secret, whilst I was still running away from and denying my own. To this day, I still wonder who this man truly was.

CHAPTER 44

Ceremonial Rights of Passage

I have to go from memory while putting these next pieces together, because I didn't write in my journals about the witch energies that were beginning to channel through me spontaneously in 2006. But from what I recall, they were triggered by me finding a spell card deck, and a sudden pull I felt towards learning more about Wiccan and other white witchcraft ceremonies. I know now I was tapping into my own memories and times as a Druid priestess witch.

Looking back even further, exactly 10 years before beginning to channel these energies, I remembered a book on Wiccan candle ceremonies I'd bought myself during my year of ET encounters in 1997. Synchronicity presenting itself again in 10-year cycles, taking one decade to come full circle with its energies, and nearly two decades to achieve full understanding!

At the time of receiving this message at the end of 2006, I hadn't performed any conscious ceremonies in my life. But I had always, even as a child, been fascinated by the occult and particularly by real magic. I felt that, somewhere deep within me, I understood this Rite of Passage. I also felt that sometime, somewhere, I had been a witch myself. More than once.

As I said, I now know this to be absolutely true. Yet at the time, I was merely dipping my toes into my own multi-dimensionality. I was honestly still not willing to own my full power and potential, so I treaded lightly and cautiously. I'm sure a big part of this caution was from the awful cellular memories of being tortured and killed for being who I was, as I have heard about similar feelings from everyone I know who holds these records. What I didn't know then, was that I was part of the Cathars, back in the times of Jesus and Mary Magdalene. But more on this in another book.

And so, during the 26th anniversary of John Lennon's assassination, at 11:11 pm on December 8, 2006, I tapped into my higher consciousness, and asked myself: *"Is this witch energy I am sensing coming in for me to work with now?"*

Immediately after the first question, I asked another question, still at 11:11, and received this answer, which thankfully, I wrote down:

"The prophecy will be fulfilled. You are AT THE RIGHT MOMENT. The stillness of your heart will always Know the Truth."

I have no idea if this part was a telepathic message or a reading from a card deck, but this was the answer in quotes after my question, all written in my journal. I find it rather synchronistic that it was December 2006 when the witch energies began reigniting in me, because it was February 6, 2007 when Yoko Ono released her LP "Yes, I'm a Witch." This means she would have very likely been recording this album during that time.

I remember really taking note of this, because as soon as January 1, 2007 came along, I was feeling guided to perform rituals and ceremonies daily. To practice. To prepare. I never missed a night, and couldn't for the life of me explain why suddenly this meant so much to me. The inner drive to make *absolutely certain* I stayed on track with these ceremonies was so strong.

For what purpose, though? I would soon find out.

CHAPTER 45

My Intimate Meeting with John

Amidst all of this training I was suddenly undergoing, partly consciously, partly unconsciously, and *quickly*, I had an encounter one night, in dreamtime, with John Lennon. The depth of which I had not experienced with him since my childhood. I went full on multi-dimensional, and knew that familiar feeling I had come to recognize so well, when the dreamer is fully conscious and "awake," while having an experience in an alternate dimension of time and space.

I found myself in a circular room that had the feeling of a movie theatre. Beside me sat John. I remember seeing him, and knowing that this was not an accidental meeting, but rather it had been scheduled. By whom, and the reasons for which, I didn't know, which was par for the course with the way these situations usually occurred for me.

We sat in a sort of knowing silence, with a comfort that one would feel with a family member or a very close, intimate friend. We were definitely familiar, whatever the status of our connection, and I knew I was there specifically to sit with him, and that he had information for me.

I noticed there was a movie playing on a very large screen in front of us. John was fixated on this screen with a sense of calm focus, as if he were living the scene along with the players in it. Yet, there was a sort of inner sadness I could feel aching deep within his heart. He was okay, but the sadness was surely present. He accepted this, yet still allowed himself to experience and feel it.

The movie playing was his family on Earth, in third-dimensional time, or, "present" time. He was watching Yoko and Sean as they were experiencing life and time in the third dimension, and a piece of his soul ached that he was no longer there experiencing the Earth plane with them.

The other side of this, the *Galactic Knowing* side, was that he had no regrets as he knew and understood the bigger cosmic picture. However, even with this knowing, John simply missed two of his closest soul family members whom he was momentarily having to be separated from in many senses. And for some reason, I was to bear witness to this experience of his, perhaps as a demonstration of sorts that I was to record and track for later purposes.

I sat with John in this sacred silence, as he telempathically (wordless communication through the heart chakra and pineal gland) shared with me that sometimes he comes into the "viewing room" and watches in an attempt to feel closer to them, like he is there. And though he experiences sadness, it is also something he enjoys doing, as it helps him feel like he is back on Earth with the ones he loves most, even for a short time. When he passed, it was such a shock to him, and he was not yet ready to leave his family behind. In this dream encounter, his heart was so palpable that I awoke with both a heaviness of emotion as well as an expanded sense of the power of love in my own heart.

I realized it doesn't matter how advanced or "enlightened" a Soul may be. We are all still sentient beings, and John was no exception.

I did not know where this "circular room" was exactly, though I knew strongly that it was somewhere "up in the sky." At the time I'd had this encounter, I had no frame of reference for the exact location of our meeting in order for that aspect of it to make any sort of sense to me. I only knew for certain that it was "up" somewhere. *But where?*

With my expanded sense of awareness now, and having since learned about John's experiences with UFOs and how, after seeing a ship outside of his apartment in New York City in the 1970s, he had intensely desired to "go with them," this piece of information helped me make a little more sense of it all.

I wouldn't receive this piece of the puzzle for almost 10 years following this particular "dream" encounter, yet I am fully aware now that John and I were aboard the Pleiadian ship The Star of Bethlehem, in one of their "viewing rooms" (the circular structure should have given it away for me then but it didn't!), and for some reason it was important that I see this and be privy to how this piece of the cosmic puzzle works.

I woke up the next morning with absolute certainty I had shared an intimate encounter with John Lennon. It was that real. There was no denying it. Each moment shared was etched into every living cell of my body, vibrating with Truth and Knowing. I also knew, without a doubt, that one day, I would be asked to relay this message to his family, only when the timing was aligned: that he is still with them, that he watches over them, and that he lives as closely as he can their days with them from aboard the ship. That he loves them more than anything, and that he misses them there, as much as they miss him here. And that one day, though they all already know this somewhere deep in their hearts, he assures them they will all be reunited.

As for whatever information John had for me personally during that encounter, this is still being revealed to me, as there are aspects of our encounter I have not been allowed to remember just yet. I know that in Divine Time, through the waves of synchronicity, I will receive full remembrance of this. That a certain sequence of events must take place before the full revelation occurs. And that I will be ready when it does.

CHAPTER 46

Request from an Angel

Life continued on in a predictable way for me. I was still pretending to be living a regular life. Meanwhile the high strangeness, otherworldly and psychic experiences continued to mount up. And the more I opened myself up through meditation, prayer, and the nightly ceremonies I would perform after Noah was in bed; lighting candles, setting out what I now know as "crystal grids" with various crystals I had suddenly started to collect, playing my Tibetan singing bowl I had recently acquired, which was attuned to the heart chakra; the more activity and experiences I continued to have.

My evenings were no longer polluted with anything having to do with television or mindless escapism. I had developed a discipline for meditation and ceremony every night, oftentimes incorporating sacred dance, yoga and the occasional Osho Dynamic, Kundalini or Nadabrahma meditation, in order to gain a deeper connection with my own Soul, and to begin to align with whatever my True Soul Purpose here on the planet was. I still had no idea, and this bothered me on a daily basis more and more. Of course, admittedly, I was also hoping I might begin to understand what this connection with Anthony was that both my young child and I were experiencing.

It was now January of 2007, and my evening ceremonies had grown to including prayers and setting intentions for the healing of the planet back to a place of global Peace, Unconditional Love and Sacred Divine Harmony amongst all of Her inhabitants. I would consciously send out this vibration through the use of my Tibetan singing bowl, as well as chanting. I would create a vortex of sound and energy, holding the vision of Unconditional Love and Peace in the form of an earth grid connection, Uniting us All as One around the planet.

I started noticing different sounds and languages coming from me that I'd had no prior access to; "words" I had never heard myself speak before would resound from such a place of power and knowing inside of me during these improvised ceremonies. I always let Spirit lead them, and would get out of the way, happy to be a vessel for Healing, Love and Light for this beautiful planet.

The sounds and chanting, if not playing the singing bowl, would be accompanied by arm and hand gestures as well. These felt very sacred and oftentimes ancient to me. I didn't know what I was doing, but I trusted I was an instrument for the Divine, and that I was On Purpose, because it always felt so incredible, and I felt complete, whole, empowered and divine. I knew that what I was doing was always done with the purest intent of being in service to the greater good and healing of the planet. I truly felt this within my heart and soul, so these ceremonies were very moving for me.

It was early one night whilst in this state of openness and service, feeling a deep sense of peace and unconditional love within myself that something unique happened that I had not experienced before in all of my meditations or ceremonies up to then.

Things were moving as they usually did in the evening, and I had begun my nightly ceremony when an angelic light presence entered the room. I can still see in my mind's eye where this entity had emerged from. I was deep in ceremony, in an altered state of consciousness (with full conscious awareness of the room and my surroundings), when suddenly, this beautiful light-being was beside me.

This being had the energy of a child, yet was a very angelic, wise, and knowing child. A very advanced soul, in the form of a beautiful, angelic light-being. I could feel the energy of this being as male though his energies were extremely balanced, and so a very gentle feminine essence was also strongly present around and within him.

He was so beautiful he brought tears to my eyes. I was also not used to being physically visited by inter-dimensional beings while I was fully conscious, though I had zero fear of this gentle being. There was actually a deep sense of knowing who this soul was, and being very strongly connected with him, almost as a mother.

I embraced him, and he I, and I heard him speak to me, though now I am not sure he ever spoke aloud, but rather, most probably he spoke telepathically. He told me that he was being called to embody here on Earth, and needed my assistance. He needed me to help him descend into a body, *as Anthony's Earth child*.

Again, my breath was gone, yet there was also this very familiar feeling I was experiencing, and I heard myself saying, "*Of course I will help you.*" This beautiful being embraced me with such gratitude and love that I was moved to tears, weeping in the purity of it all. Of course I had to do this for him. He was so pure, and such a bright angelic source of love, there was no way I could refuse his request.

In that moment, I was certain of what I needed to do, didn't doubt it at all, and proceeded to complete the ceremony. He thanked me, said, "*I love you so much*," and was gone.

I sat there, in the candlelit room, my crystals in front of me, some placed on different parts of my body, as I often did, and I continued to breathe deeply, tears streaming down my face. I knew now what I would be doing the following evening.

CHAPTER 47

Ceremony for a Sacred Seed Incarnate

I went to bed and slept very deeply that night, but the next day, anxiety kicked in.

All day, this task I knew I needed to complete consumed my thoughts and my energies. *How was I going to do this? Would I be messing with Anthony's Free Will by doing what this Soul was asking me to do?* I definitely did not want to enter into that kind of karmic mess, and I definitely did not want to play with cosmic fire in that way or any other way for that matter. Somehow, I was deeply aware of the consequences of messing with another's Free Will, and I wasn't interested in venturing into those dangerous realms.

I tried to find any loophole, any out I could to justify to myself why I would not or could not do this. After all, I was potentially getting into some seriously sticky territory, as this could end up affecting Anthony's physical, personal life if this mission were successful. But did I even have that capacity? Was this egotistical to even consider that I did? Of course, I doubted my own power. Sadly, I was so used to giving it away that I rarely thought of myself in a truly positive, empowered way.

It also felt wrong when I tried to justify to myself that perhaps this otherworldly and odd request made to me by this angelic soul was somehow ill-intentioned, or even worse, I completely made it up. But that simply didn't feel right to me in the least. I had felt him, he was *REAL* and I knew it. I also knew that his request was *pure*. Anytime I breathed deeply into it, and felt into my heart about this request, I knew exactly what I had to do. Like it or lump it, I was being asked to perform this ceremony, and for some reason, I was the one to have to do it.

It is incredibly interesting to me now to connect the answer to the question I'd asked my higher consciousness back in December when I'd inquired about the witch energies it was prompting me to begin working with, especially the part where it says "*The prophecy will be fulfilled.*" That part gives me chills when I see it written in my journal. I truly had no idea the magnitude of what that message would come to mean for me, and perhaps all involved in this particular assignment.

At the time, I simply wondered, is this child some sort of a prophecy? Did he need me specifically to work with him and Anthony in this way because it was somehow a part of his, perhaps all of our, Destiny? I don't claim this as the truth or even outright knowingness. These are merely questions I have as I see everything laid out in front of me in sequence through my journals and can't deny the synchronistic connections, even if I don't always have a name for them or full understanding of why this great task was being asked of me.

I took Noah on a little journey that day to a metaphysical store on Commercial Drive. In fact, the address had a 777 in it, and to me, that felt like a confirmation that I should follow through and at least go there to see if I could receive any guidance as to what tools or special gems or crystals I may need to carry out this ceremony I was to invoke that evening. As soon as I entered through the door, the experience was otherworldly.

Abraham, a tall, fully bald, black man who owned the store, came up to me. His eyes were dark and piercing, yet very kind. He looked at Noah, who was already exploring, holding crystals, looking at figures of dragons, touching swords and wands...basically in heaven. Abraham smiled and thanked me for bringing him in, saying that the children now were so important, and exposing them to these things was a beautiful thing, and what they truly needed.

I smiled, only half understanding what he was talking about, and yet knowing inside that he was right. I was grateful he was welcoming of my two-year-old, rather than the usual response I would get in crystal shops from the staff concerned and worried that such a young child might break something. I knew Noah though, and knew he would not break a thing. He was always so caring and conscious as he held and touched such sacred objects. Abraham asked me if I had any questions or if I needed assistance with anything.

"Well, I've had sort of an odd request, and it involves two lovers, and the ultimate creation of love. I have been asked to assist with this. I don't know how to do this and I don't want to create karma either. But I feel I am to honour this request somehow and was looking for some assistance or at the very least, some ideas. And please feel free to tell me I'm out of my mind, and to not dabble in this sort of thing."

Abraham stared into my eyes for a brief moment, smiling. I wanted desperately to look away, but I couldn't. I was locked in to them. There was a certain kind of warmth, as well as a level of amusement dancing around inside of those deep, dark windows to his soul.

"If you have been asked, and your intent is pure, then trust that. This (he pointed to a red pouch that said "Love Spell" on it) is a little kit I put together myself." He saw my face wince, I'm sure. I have a very expressive face that isn't capable of lying, especially when caught off guard.

"Don't let the word 'spell' frighten you," he laughed. "I have placed quartz crystals, dried rose petals, sea shells, some candles and other goodies inside. There are clear and simple instructions, and this is sweet, pure magic if you approach it with a pure heart. It will hold the energy of your intentions. So long as your intentions are pure, you will do no harm." He had a twinkle in his eye, looking at me for a moment, and then walked toward Noah..

"If it feels right for you, listen to that," he called back to me as he smiled at Noah entertaining himself, being very gentle and caring with the crystals he was playing with and holding.

I walked around—more like paced around—the store for what seemed like a long time. I really wanted to do the right thing. I really wanted to be certain that I was not breaking any kind of universal or cosmic laws by adhering to this unusual request.

I felt anxiety bubble up inside, and had to breathe deeply, then finally decided it was time, and I was to bring that little kit home and figure out what to do with it later. And if I decided not to use it, at least I could return it. I couldn't decide not to buy it and then wish I had later that night. It was settled then. I would intend on performing the ceremony that night, and have the kit there just in case.

Once I got out of the way, it was easy.

I purchased the little red pouch, as well as a Native American Medicine Woman Tarot deck that seemed to be calling out to me (I didn't know how to read tarot, and still don't, yet still have these cards), and also purchased a little handmade holly wood wand with a little leather tassel on the end you hold, and a white feather with a pearl attached to it at the tip. It was simple and sweet and felt like it wanted to come home with me too. I spent the remainder of the day being a mom, doing mom stuff, enjoying Noah, and every so often, thoughts of this task I had to perform that night made my stomach turn. I still had no idea what I was going to do. I still had not opened the pouch.

I decided to give it all up to Great Spirit, and allow myself to be led through whatever it was that I was being asked to do, and trusted that when the time came, I would just know what to do.

Evening came, and I got Noah settled and sweetly nestled in our bed for the night. I came out into the living room, took a few deep breaths, and went into meditation. I sat there, an open vessel, allowing whatever was meant to come in to do so.

I began with setting my intention on being of divine service with the highest intent, asking only for the purest, highest guidance and possible outcome for all.

That was all I could do, then it was time to step out of the way.

I opened the little red pouch and very gently removed its contents. They were tiny, and felt sacred. I could feel a powerfully charged energy in these tiny dried roses, the tiny stones, seashells and crystals. It was incredible. There was a little paper folded up with step-by-step instructions on how to perform the ceremony "for best results." It seemed simple enough.

One thing it asked though, was that I write out my intention—what I was intending to manifest—onto a small piece of paper to be included in the ceremony. I had a sudden wave of panic set in, but breathed my way through it, and moved back into that deep sense of inner trust where I was certain my intentions were pure, and that this being who had come to me, this angel I had encountered the night before, had felt very authentic, and seemed to be of a very pure intent also. So, what was there to be afraid of?

I took out the only paper I could find; a small sticky note pad, white with a red design around the border, and a pen. I had no idea what I was going to write, but trusted, and hoped, that the pen would write it for me.

Shockingly, and thankfully, I actually kept the red pouch with the message in it and only recently since writing this book did I synchronistically come across it. Up to then, I had forgotten all about it, consciously. I didn't remember keeping it.

Once I came across it, there was something in me that kept nudging me to open it up and look inside, and it was only then that I recalled the paper with the message I'd written with my manifestation hopes on it. I opened it and read my earlier wishful intention for this sweet being.

Not knowing at all then, back in January 2007, what I know now, the choice of wording I used in my descriptive manifestation intent is interesting, to put it mildly.

More than 6 years later, reading this intention was a bit of a trip actually. Here's what I wrote, word-for-word:

"May this child of Anthony and ______ be conceived, germinated and birthed into this world through the beautiful energies of Unconditional Sacred Love. And So It Is. <3"

I can see this statement now with a new awareness, and in hindsight, I feel I am now able to grasp what it was I had been asked to do, and what my role in this manifestation was, at least partially.

After performing this ceremony, which was so very powerful and profound for me, it ended with the same angelic child present in the room with me, wrapping his arms around my shoulders from behind and whispering in my ear the sweetest, *"Thank you. I love you"* I could have ever hoped for. I could feel the completion of this request. And then he was gone, and I never saw him or heard from him again.

I sat there, in the fully charged, magical energy of what had just been created, not knowing if it would make any difference whatsoever on the physical plane. I didn't know if anything would manifest as a result of it, or if Anthony would go on to have a child after this.

Of course, a big part of me was assuming, even hoping, that it was all a fluke. If nothing happened, it would be proof for me that I was a fraud making all of this up once and for all, and to be honest, I would have been totally fine with that! I questioned my own sanity enough from day to day, especially then.

And yet still, there was a part of me that couldn't help but be curious. This experience had been so powerfully moving for me, it had felt so far beyond me, so otherworldly, that I couldn't help but wonder that if it had been some divine intervention that had guided me on this particular mission, that it was quite possible that I would see something manifest physically as a result of it one day.

The wondering drove me crazy, and I still had a physical life of my own to live. I had a beautiful child of my own right in front of me. I had to let it go, for everyone's sake.

It wasn't until the summer of 2007 when I finally received the confirmation, and naturally, it came to me seemingly out of the blue through the magical hand of synchronicity.

I must have been having one of those days where I was feeling the pull to find answers, to learn more about my connection with Anthony, because the dream state experiences had been going strong still, never ceasing, as well as synchronistic events that continued to bring him into my conscious awareness on an almost daily basis.

It was maddening.

It truly was not easy trying to juggle having one foot in both worlds, whilst attempting to appear like I had my life all figured out. The more I experienced, the more I realized I didn't know.

On the outside, I was a working mother, holding it down with lots of love, taking care of my son, enjoying life. Yes, all of these things I was definitely doing. And yet, I had this secret life at the same time. What felt to me like a double-life. This life that involved meeting with a familiar soul in my dream time and working together, sometimes it was delightful, sometimes it was challenging, but it was always profound, and it was always beyond any regular dreaming.

I have learned from my childhood when to know that I am working in a multi-dimensional state, and when (and if ever) I am merely dreaming. I always know that I am working or taking part in multi-dimensional experiences when I am simultaneously living the dream, while at the same time, hovering above it, witnessing the events, whilst fully conscious that another part of me is lying in bed sleeping as these other aspects of me are having these experiences in the moment. It is truly multi-dimensional.

And for the record, any dream state experience I am sharing for the purposes of this book are ones in which I was consciously multi-dimensional—watching myself sleep and watching myself experience, as well as *LIVING* the experience, all rolled up into one.

I have many other dream experiences, many involving Anthony, many not, that I am not sharing at this time. Only the most pertinent ones that feel appropriate and supportive of this particular aspect of my story that I am sharing here.

When they are enriched with intricate detail, especially when I later receive confirmation of its synchronistic accuracy to this timeline and reality, this is when it is very appropriate to take note and realize that one is recalling a multi-dimensional experience. *What is it telling me? What is it showing me? Who is involved? What is the feeling of it? What are we doing in this experience? What is the lesson? Am I able to remember Who I Am, without question or doubt?* And, as Selene likes to say, "*Is it real, or is it Memorex?*"

We all do this, by the way. Work and travel to other dimensions when we sleep. It's just that some of us are more aware and remember our experiences and ask these pertinent questions. We are consciously working with these energies. Others are too, just still unconsciously. Yet we are, in truth, all doing it to some degree. We can always become more aware and work more consciously if we choose to. The choice is always ours. So, let's remember to ask ourselves, "Is it real, or is it Memorex?"

CHAPTER 48

The Goddess Gift Exchange

March 13, 2007, about one and a half to two months after performing this ceremony, I had another experience in dream-time. Synchronistically, I notice this is exactly 10 years after the Phoenix Lights incident, for whatever that is worth.

I had put the angel child and the ceremony mostly out of my mind, assuming I must have made it all up or that nothing tangible would come to pass from it. It was much too mystical and grandiose. At the very least, I had been unsuccessful in my attempts to assist this angelic soul. After all, I didn't possess that kind of mystical power now, did I?

Then I had a dream.

I recalled this dream in full detail as soon as I found it in my journal archives. I didn't understand it when I had it, and have only begun to understand it more in recent years, while doing some research on the symbolic references that appeared in this dream experience.

This is my recording of the dream the morning after receiving it:

I am walking down a sidewalk on a residential road. There are flowers and trees everywhere, and it smells vibrant and fresh. The atmosphere is quiet and peaceful. I am unfamiliar with the street. I am "new" here, yet I also live here.

I am wearing what I remember very vividly as a Galactic Suit. At the time, I didn't think of it that way. I describe it in my journal as a "copper-coloured outfit" and I remember it as shiny and metallic-looking. The pants are straight-legged bell bottoms, and on top, a fitted jacket/shirt. If that doesn't scream "straight from the ships" I don't know what does! My hair is huge and wavy, and I remember it vividly now as being almost identical to the ETs I would see in my dream sequences back in 1996/1997—again, exactly 10 years earlier. Also interesting.

As I am walking down the street, a copper cruiser car suddenly drives up behind me. It is Anthony and the young woman he is currently dating in his physical third dimensional reality at the time.

I am looking for a street called "FARFALLA STREET."

All these years I have wondered what that word meant, only to find out now that it means "Butterfly."

As a reference for this book, I researched what the significance of a Galactic Butterfly might be since the galactic energies were so apparent. When I looked up "Galactic Butterfly," immediately I found information on the Hunab Ku, and how Hunab Ku's symbol is a Galactic Butterfly, and not only *that*, but that it is symbolic of the Yin Yang energies, which was a symbol I had received in my work and connection with Anthony back in 2006, before ever understanding the true metaphysical energies it also holds.

I found this particular description of Hunab Ku synchronistic, especially for what was happening, unbeknownst to me, at the time I received this dream, and how much it connects to the path I know I am on now. The following excerpt is borrowed from the Evolving Now website (http://mayanprophecy2012.blogspot.com/2009/07/hunab-ku-galactic-butterfly-mayan.html).

"The Mayans knew where in the sky the exact center of the galaxy was located and they even had a glyph representing it which is now named Hunab Ku; it was known to the Mayans as The Galactic Butterfly...Hunab Ku was, to the Mayans, the supreme God and ultimate Creator...Hunab Ku, according to the Mayans, is also the consciousness which organized all matter from a ***whirling disk*** *- into stars, planets and solar systems.* ***Hunab Ku is the Mother Womb which is constantly giving birth to new stars*** *and it gave birth to our own Sun and planet Earth as well as the other planets found in our solar system."*

The "whirling disk," the "Mother Womb." All connected with my own place in the galactic picture. This synchronistic discovery of the deeper meaning of this dream I'd had seven years prior to doing this research gave me goosebumps.

Within this dream encounter, Anthony and his girlfriend ask me to come with them in their car, so I jump in and we arrive at a place that has the feeling of an outdoor marketplace. There are pieces of art creations on tables all around us, and we walk through, glancing at each table and the creations each one displays.

I don't remember every single piece that was there, just that there was a large variety. My eyes were only meant to take in what was most important for me to remember.

The next thing I know, Anthony's girlfriend approaches me, with a very peaceful and loving look in her eyes, and pure intention in her gesture. She has the most exquisitely gorgeous rose quartz crystal house in her hands. It is about the size of a shoe box, but two times the height. It is quite large, but not awkwardly so. She hands this very powerful piece to me, and smiles. I remember feeling as though she were handing me "home"; the most precious and generous gift she could have given me, as it felt as if she were handing me a piece of her home. I was so touched, and remember we both understood what this meant, without any need for words.

I also remember as the dreamer witnessing this, wondering what this gesture meant. Because surely it meant something, the energies were so strong in our interaction and her gift-giving. It felt sacred and beautiful, that much I knew, whatever the literal translation might be.

I also sensed a small bit of sadness present within her, and that made me very sad also. Here was this beautiful young woman, giving me such a precious, sacred gift, as if we had both exchanged it somehow, but it ended up in my arms, so I really wanted to give her a gift that she could hold on to for herself, to help her heal this sadness within her own heart.

I walked through the marketplace, feeling into where and what her gift would be. I knew something was waiting for her, waiting to help her with her healing.

And then I saw it.

I looked down at a table filled with Native American animal totems. The only one I saw clearly, thus knowing it was the one that was meant for this beautiful young woman, was a fish totem.

I held this totem, infusing it with my loving Intentions to help bring her the healing she was needing, and I brought it to her. I held her hand as I placed it in her palm, looking deeply into her eyes. We shared a knowing, an understanding, that both of us recognized. I smiled, and so did she, and we embraced.

This experience was so powerful for me. Again, I awoke with a tear-filled pillow, and soaking wet face, ears and hair.

I didn't really understand the meaning of this dream at the time I had it, but knew from the energy of it that I'd unmistakably had a multi-dimensional experience and a loving exchange with the woman that Anthony had been dating in his waking life. Who knew and who cared what it meant. It was so intimate, it made no difference to me, because in my soul I had the answer—I already knew—even if I wasn't aware of it yet, and that was enough for me.

The specific details of this experience always stayed with me; they had felt very important, though I didn't quite understand what made them so. I was so used to not knowing what anything I experienced meant.

But since I had awoken so moved by the experience, I immediately researched rose quartz crystal houses and fish totems to see if the symbolism of either could be clarified for me.

I couldn't find any solid information specifically on crystal houses, but felt like I had a pretty decent grasp on the rose quartz house from the dream. Rose quartz is the crystal connected with the heart chakra and unconditional love. The fact that it was in the shape of a home felt like it had to do with gifting me with one of the closest most intimate parts of her life. Her foundation. That could be connected with a baby, I thought, especially if it were the angelic soul who had come to me asking for my help.

But who knew? I hadn't heard anything about a baby by this point, and frankly, was over trying to find out.

With fish totem, I found that often in dreams, fish are connected with fertility, and often women who are pregnant will have dreams of fish. They also are connected with swimming the currents of life, and riding the tides of new adventures. Further, they can be connected with using our intuition to navigate the waters of our experiences and emotions, the subconscious, "other-worlds," as well as heightened senses, including visions and psychic abilities. *

I also found this, quoted directly from http://ladyguinevere.hubpages.com/hub/Totem-Animals-and-Their-Symbols:

"Fish symbolize love, fertility, victory over death, healing, prophesy, abundance, wealth, harmony, regeneration, children, pregnancy and bringing love into your life. They are connected to the Moon, to Water, Atargatis, Ishtar, Derceto, Isis, Aphrodite, Freyja, Venus, Dagon, Poseidon and Kuan Yin."

I didn't know it then, but now see several connections with me gifting this beautiful Goddess a fish, and I find it all fascinating, indeed. My main hope was that this gift would be embraced with the same love I felt in giving it to her, in Divine Gratitude for her own precious and sacred gift to me.

Though I had no clue when I had this dream in March 2007 that Anthony and his then-girlfriend were indeed expecting a baby, and I certainly didn't understand half of the symbolism in it until now, which is almost exactly seven years later to the date as I write this in 2014, I realize how incredibly significant this dream sequence was.

I was being shown clues that I would not understand for years to come, but that would help me track the energies when it was time to, when I was ready. For all it would reveal to me, for the purposes of this book, and this Galactic Mission.

*reference from http://www.starstuffs.com/animal_totems/dictionary_of_wateranimals.html)

Two nights after this dream encounter, on the 15th of March, 2007, I received a flying dream sequence with Anthony and one of his bandmates. I had a few dreams where I was teaching him how to fly, or where we would fly together. I was used to flying dreams as I'd had those all my life, so this was not new to me. What was new to me was that in these experiences with Anthony, I was usually helping him remember his own power, and these dream sequences often did involve flying in some way.

Reading the dream sequence as I recorded it fresh from the experience in my journal archives, it was also extremely galactic in nature. I believe now we were all aboard ship to start, as I described where we were as having "*very high, maybe no ceilings, and there are beautiful fabrics draped up, and it looks like a set of some sort.*" We also start our adventure off with me handing us all water and pills or supplements that are made up of organic fruits and vegetables that heal and energize the body. No need for large physical meals. Sounds suspiciously like ship cuisine to me.

From here, after taking our "supplements," we begin to fly.

Except for Anthony. In this particular sequence, he was being extremely resistant. I didn't push him, but was reminding him that he already knew how to fly, just as I did. He was experiencing doubts about himself, and I was kindly showing him how I moved my arms to take flight; I can still feel the physical sensation of this flying pulsing through the cells of my body as I think of it.

I noticed all of his bandmates there also. A rarity, but occasionally this happened. One of them was flying next to me, having the time of his life, so enjoying the experience. I have since learned that this particular man's intimate connection with Source, his awareness of his own multi-dimensional aspects of Self and existence, is very strong. At the time of this dream though, I didn't know this.

So, this other man and I flew together and had quite a joyous experience. He felt like my brother. Even Noah joined in, flying on my back with me.

We all ascended higher and higher, until we broke through to the "nothingness," the "nowhere." We both became a bit anxious about it, and came back down a bit. Noah and I kept flying, faster and faster, until suddenly we were flying at the speed of light, dodging military helicopters and buildings with no lights.

At the end of the dream sequence, Anthony was still there on the ground, in somewhat of a huff. I wasn't sure why, but left it alone, knowing he would fly when he was ready to.

As Noah and I skidded into a very intense landing, he woke me up in our bed. At the time I had this dream, Noah was two-and-a-half years old.

There are so many dream sequences and visions I recorded then, that all make sense to me now, but at the time they all seemed rather random, cryptic, and encoded in a way I wasn't quite yet equipped to decode.

Interesting how we don't know until we are ready, and it is *time to know.*

CHAPTER 49

Synchronization Is Confirmation: Truth Knows Its Own Source" ~ Selene

Fast-forward another few months, after these dream experiences.

I was on the YouTube channel for some reason, searching interviews with Anthony. Perhaps I'd received an inner nudge to do so, as there was indeed something awaiting me there.

Believe me, over the years as I've stated repeatedly, I have attempted to run away from this connection. I have attempted to justify it by making fun of myself or putting myself down in any attempt to discover that I have imagined the entire thing.

I have tried it all. I have attempted to live a normal life, moving away from Vancouver, away from my experiences with Anthony, to Sedona. Got married, and expanded my family. I have run my own business. All of these things I have embraced wholeheartedly, and yet, this connection with Anthony has continued, time and again, to find me.

I have learned, and finally accepted, that it is beyond my control. And now, finally embracing it with all my heart and soul, I am releasing the details of this journey after being proven time and again through synchronicity that I can attempt to run away from it, but when something is a part of your destiny, it will keep knocking on your door until you eventually give in, answer the call, embrace the experience and allow it into your heart, fully and completely. Or else, it'll take you out.

I have finally reached this place of acceptance in my life, after living through some of my darkest hours while attempting to ignore and run away from this cosmic connection. I have come to a place where I have surrendered my own human will to that of Divine Will and I embrace it wholeheartedly; this mysterious and powerful "*Unknown,*" without attachment to what it "should look like on the Earth plane.

A few months after my heartfelt multi-dimensional Goddess gift exchange with Anthony's girlfriend, I found myself in the midst of some sort of internet search when, quite effortlessly, I came across a video that had been posted on my birthday, May 24th, of that year—2007.

I realized immediately this was what I had been pulled to do this search for, and opened the video. The date was uncanny, and the still image of the link was peculiar to me. It was an image of Anthony and his girlfriend sitting at what looked like a coffee shop. In it, his hand was placed lovingly on her belly, which appeared to have a small bump.

My veins rushed with blood, that familiar DNA activation jolt I was getting used to, and my body heated up and started to sweat. I was becoming old hat at this bodily response to these synchronicities with this man. I had to consciously take deep breaths because otherwise I would have stopped breathing altogether.

It was now July of 2007, roughly two months after this video had originally been posted. I hope this proves that I wasn't sitting there stalking this man all the time, like a crazed fan. Sure, sometimes admittedly I felt like one, assuming that is what it might look like from the outside, but deep down, I knew that was the furthest thing from the truth.

It was only when something significant had been shown to me, either in my waking life or in the dream state, that I would wear my Sherlock Holmes hat. I usually felt like I only had a few puzzle pieces in my conscious awareness, and still had most of the puzzle left to solve. Yet, I was being constantly prodded and nudged by Spirit to solve it.

This journey could be disheartening most of the time, to be honest. But every little piece I discovered led me that much closer to understanding and solving what felt like the most important mystery puzzle of my life, though I didn't understand at all what the theme of it was. I had given up attempting to know and understand that a long time ago.

So, I saw this video, and indeed, it confirmed my suspicions: **that Anthony and his girlfriend were, without a doubt, expecting a baby.**

The thing that got me the most was that here was this man, known for having slept with literally hundreds of women, if not more, in the span of a few decades, and not once did he ever have a physical child with any of them. He'd had relationships, according to his own autobiography, where he'd wanted to spend his life with some of these women, and whom he'd wanted to have babies with, and yet never had it manifested into his life as a physical child.

The timing of this pregnancy was uncanny to me. I later found out when this child was due to be born and did the math. That was the last confirmation I'd needed in order to realize that whatever that ceremony had done, whatever the significance of my part in it—why the being chose *ME* of all people to assist him in coming into his physical body—this was not something I made up in my own mind. It was not something I could logically comprehend, but it appeared with all of the synchronistic evidence that in some way, to some strange capacity, I had indeed been involved.

And not with any ego-driven intent either. I have never wanted to go public with this information. Who would? It can be a tad controversial, to put it mildly. I realize I am putting myself in the line of fire by coming out with this story. But it is not meant to stay hidden, and no matter what my own personal wishes might have been, I agreed to do this long before coming here to the planet.

The fact is that these types of multi-dimensional connections and mystical experiences are much more common than many of us consciously realize.

As Selene says, "*Truth knows its own source.*" When you hear or see something and there is a resonance within that vibrates throughout your entire being, you can be certain that there is a deep truth present in whatever it is you are experiencing.

This was most definitely my experience upon seeing the evidence that indeed, a seed had been planted, and would be gracing Anthony's life in the form of his child in a very real way. I was incredibly happy for him, as I was starting to take these little nudges, messages, and requests from "the beyond" a lot more seriously.

What else would be asked of me, I wondered? If only I'd have known.

CHAPTER 50

Sacred Blood Initiation Part II: Embody 'The Seed'

After having also had visions and received Divine Guidance back in 2007 as to the next step on my path, I was given the message both in the dream state and with signs and messages in my waking life that I was going to be moving to the U.S. within the next year.

Of course, I did not really believe this, nor did I want to believe this. I was content where I was at, and honestly, never anticipated giving up my health care benefits or parental benefits to move to a country where it was legal to carry firearms and who declared war on the most impoverished and innocent countries in the name of greed. This was not my idea of freedom nor was it a dream I'd held in my conscious heart space. Thanks, but no thanks. The Land of the Free never seemed truly free to me. I was happy sticking with my own country. Flawed as my country may have been, at least in 2007, I still felt safe and secure there.

Yet, throughout that year, I continually received phone calls from toll numbers in Arizona, which for some reason, piqued my curiosity, as there felt to be some sort of connection for me there. I knew it was a sign of some sort.

In my mind's eye, Arizona was a dry desert, I had no idea there were parts of it that ever received snow or the harsh winter conditions that I came to discover later on that year.

I had once during this period almost booked an impromptu vacation for me and Noah to Phoenix, after receiving a surprising lump sum of money through a life insurance policy I'd taken out at eighteen. I was searching for places to go and things to do for fun, just he and I, and seriously considered heading to Phoenix for a few days together, during which Anthony's band was scheduled to play on tour.

I was still trying to figure out this connection, thinking it was within my control to make it happen, and yet anytime I would see an opportunity present itself, and I would feel into it, it was never right, and never timely. That voice again, telling me so. I knew when to let things go, and never pushed any of it from an ego standpoint, tempted as I might have been at times, mostly just to get answers and to make logical sense of my confusing inner life.

Instead of booking the trip on a whim, I patiently awaited the Voice to let me know when to make my moves, and what those moves would be.

In April 2007, after being led by seeing an image of a jewelry pendant online one day, I realized I *just had* to get my third tattoo. It had been more than ten years since I'd got a tattoo, and never really knew if I'd get another one. There was a resounding "*YES*" within when I saw this pendant though, and realized that I didn't just want, but rather *NEEDED* to receive this tattoo on my body, and *soon*.

I received the tattoo April 4, 2007.

At the time, I thought the symbol looked like a flower. Angela later saw the picture and told me it was the sacred geometric symbol for The Flower of Life. So, we referred to it as my "flower" tattoo. I went for a couple of years calling it and thinking of it as simply a flower.

This tattoo has the colours of the rainbow, plus pink, for LOVE. When I was "told" I needed to have this symbol placed on my physical body, I was also shown where it would be placed. Just like a pendant, over my heart. But not my physical heart, my Higher Heart, or rather, my Sacred Heart.

This part of the download, I was not too thrilled about. Firstly, I knew I was going to have to deal with my mother and her judgments of me getting another tattoo, especially one so visible, and for spending my "hard-earned money" on it—being a single mother and all.

I was a very responsible mother and provider for me and my son, yet I knew this would bring up things for her, which I honestly didn't feel like dealing with at the time. I'd had so much going on internally, in the midst of my connection with Anthony that, by this point, it was in my daily awareness, no matter how much I tried to push it away.

I listened to my guidance, as I always tried to do, no matter how much I might resist what it asked of me at first. I received the tattoo.

I woke up that morning knowing that this was going to be a pretty significant day for me. Of course, Noah was there with me, but stayed with Angela while I was in my appointment.

The artist's name was Christopher, and he was a really kind fellow. Gently-spoken, he had a really nice energy. I lay on his table and he started imprinting this symbol onto my skin, and encoding its energetic frequency into my bloodstream by way of the ink through the needle.

He said nothing to me during the tattoo imprinting other than checking in with me occasionally to make sure I was doing all right, which of course, I was.

I'd had a pretty incredible experience where, as I lay there as he got started, I felt a wave of love wash over me, and then felt something, someone, lying next to me, holding my hand.

This being next to me was with me during what felt like a Sacred Initiation, which I wasn't entirely sure I understood cerebrally, but understood it in the language of the heart, exactly where it was being imprinted into my being, which is why I went through with it at all in the first place.

I really didn't feel like having to talk about this new tattoo to anyone, as it felt so very personal to me in a truly cosmic way. I didn't want to have to explain *anything to anyone* about it, yet I knew I would have to, and would have many people noticing it.

Ironically, this was one of the main reasons I had to get it, which honestly didn't thrill me. It was not only an Initiation and Activation for *me*, but for any who took notice of it. It was meant to serve anyone who saw it, in whatever way they may need.

It was a beacon of light and love, that was all I knew. And it had what I called a "triple infinity" symbol inside it, with the six petals of the "flower" making three infinity symbols. Three was a significant number for me as well. In fact, three 3s, which also equal 9 when added together, were numbers I'd attributed to my work and connection with Anthony. Mainly because his life path number according to numerology is 3, and mine is 33. And the triple infinity, or 888—a symbol of The Goddess—was also one we worked with "together" in the higher dimensions, and which I was preparing to share with the world around me via this tattoo, putting me a little more "out there" yet still entirely in an encoded and private way, which I was grateful for at least.

There have been other numbers involved in our connection and work over the years, but I will stick to mentioning these ones, which are the most prominent for this book and have been the strongest of them all.

So, Christopher was the facilitator in activating me with this symbol on my skin, and which was now beginning to course through the blood in my veins for good, and here I was, this seemingly ordinary girl receiving this seemingly ordinary tattoo. Meanwhile I had this energetic presence lying next to me the whole time, even holding my hand, which gave me great comfort.

All of a sudden, Christopher starts making small talk with me, and decides to tell me a story. Very random, had nothing to do with anything happening in the room. Supposedly.

I was being polite and listening, while melting together with this invisible being, whom I could physically feel next to me. As he's telling me the story of his friend, he finally says this friend's name.

Anthony.

Of all the names, and of all the moments. *Anthony.* He continues to talk about '*Anthony this, Anthony that...*' Right then, I knew that somehow, this tattoo was a significant activation in my connection with Anthony.

I will also mention here, Noah's middle name is Anthony. He was born in 2004, *two years before* I was even aware of Anthony or his name. And Noah had no first name for nearly two months after his birth. The only name I knew without a doubt that he needed to carry vibrationally in this lifetime was 'Anthony.' I felt strongly that it was not meant to be his first name, but *knew* it had to be his middle name.

It all started as an homage to Paul, since he was so present and such an amazing support during Noah's birth, and of course, Paul's last name is Anthony.

Paul was the one I had chosen to be at Noah's birth, even though we had been quite disconnected during most of my pregnancy. But in the end, I'd felt a very strong sense to ask him to be there with me, and in honour of him, I didn't give Noah the name Paul but rather, truer to Noah's heart's wish, I chose Anthony.

We would even refer to and Noah as "Little Anthony" before he let me know his first name finally. And then two years later, for Noah to be referring to this soul, Anthony, as '*Daddy*', and all that has transpired since—Noah is now eleven- years old as I write this—is astonishing.

The Initiation of the tattoo kicked in instantly too. Within two weeks after receiving it, Noah and I were walking across the street in our neighbourhood, holding hands. He was two-and-a-half then. It was the middle to end of April 2007. We were halfway through the crosswalk when my head was pulled down and to the right, by an unseen force, and my eyes were instantly fixated on the numbers 919 on the license plate in front of me. I remember hearing the voice inside say '*September* nineteenth," and I knew right then and there that this was going to be a date to remember. That something significant in my life would happen that day, which at the time was still five long months away.

Of course, that would turn out to be the day that I met Jeff, whom I ended up moving to Arizona to be with, and for immigration purposes, ended up marrying within a year of our first contact. I didn't realize it at the time, but after reminiscing back a few months after the start of our relationship—which I was thrilled to be exploring as it made me feel like I might just have a chance at living a normal life after all—it hit me one day to run and search my emails. I saw that indeed, our first interaction had occurred on September 19^{th,} or 919.

I was really beginning to trust more deeply in my intuitive and psychic gifts. How could I not? I was constantly being shown evidence supporting the facts. Especially when I looked back in the journal I had been keeping from 2006 (after Anthony coming into my conscious awareness again after the initial Activation I had received 14 years prior, through the music video incident) to then, September 2007. I was so grateful I had started to record my experiences, dreams and visions, even though they didn't make sense to me.

During that same year, only months before receiving the tattoo and the "919" message on the car, I'd had another dream experience, in which I was shown myself walking hand-in-hand with a man I did not recognize. As far as I can recall, I was not actually shown his face, but who knows? I only know I did not know this man I was walking so intimately with; he was a stranger to me.

As we walked down the street together, a white moving truck drove past us. On the truck, in red-orange writing (these are the colours of the earth and rocks here in Sedona), though at the time I didn't even know Sedona was something other than a meditation technique or a New Age magazine, were the words "Phoenix, Arizona." The word Phoenix was transparent, almost see-through, and Arizona was solid and very readable.

There was a phone number on the truck underneath the words that included the numbers 777. Anyone who is familiar with angel numbers knows that 777 is a sign of listening to Divine Guidance and putting the wisdom learned into use in the present moment. It also signifies a time to reap the rewards of hard work and efforts, sort of as a pat on the back for a job well done for providing inspiration and assistance to others in the process; for teaching by example.

I wouldn't have thought of this then, but I feel perhaps the 777 may have been a foreshadowing for the work I would come into alignment with once I made the move to Arizona, specifically to Sedona.

Also significant about this dream was that, while having this multi-dimensional experience, being shown this vision, I was in the dream state with my physical body in bed, holding a jade gemstone in one of my hands. This is significant, because when Jeff and I first met and were getting to know one another, he and I both shared a very special "Jade" connection, in the form of a plant he had, and a vision of mine, both involving a child we would each one day bring in to this world and become parent to.

My vision had come to me one summer when I was spending time on the native reservation in Red Bank, New Brunswick when I was twelve and visiting with cousins. After this visit, I left with a knowing that, one day when I was grown, I would give birth to a child named Jade. There is much more to this story, perhaps for a later time, but Jeff's story involved him and his former wife placing the energetic intention of having a baby together one day into a small jade plant. He still had that jade plant when we met, during his divorce from her. So when I became pregnant as soon as I moved to Sedona, we both knew instantly that the child I was carrying would hold the name frequency of Jade in some way.

Both of my children's destined names have become their middle names, which I only connected while writing this book.

Jeff and I were definitely led divinely to be together. I had been shown through the 919 license plate, and he had been shown by way of a feeling that he needed to search for a woman in Vancouver, even though he lived in Flagstaff, Arizona at the time.

It was confirmation for me through all of these synchronicities that we were supposed to be exploring a relationship together at the very least. For what precise reason, I didn't know. But I had learned to trust my Guidance and intuition by then.

Our union was able to bring forth our little Jade boy, Rubin, to whom I will forever feel grateful.

CHAPTER 51

Clues Unnoticed by the Clueless

I went through a phase of having many readings and sessions with different people; I had no idea how many I'd had in 2007 alone until I started gathering the data for that time frame. It must have been because I was trying so desperately to figure out what to do with all of these synchronistic experiences I was having, but *wow* is all I can say after looking at some of the notes I took after them.

On May 13, 2007, I had a reading with a woman named Liza, and it was here that she started telling me that I was going to write a book one day, and that I was going to be working with symbols and shapes and I was to record them. I never did remember this until I saw it written down while writing this book! Funny that, in my initial reading with Selene on September 26, 2011, she told me the exact same thing.

Liza also emphasized that I was going to be working with children, and that this work was to be HUGE. I'd had no idea what this meant, but from where I'm at now and the path I'm on, I get it. She meant the hybrid children, even if she didn't realize it herself. She was picking up on the enormity of this work, and how I would be coming out with this information on these ET experiments, long before I ever knew they existed. *WOW.*

Liza also mentioned that Noah in particular was a big part of this work, and that I was to record things he said, as they were going to be important in this work. She hit the nail on the head, I'd say!

At the time though, the whole writing a book thing freaked me out. I didn't understand at all what I could *ever* write about that other people would be interested in or needing to read, especially having to do with children. I had no credentials that I knew of to write about this topic, or so I thought.

I did wonder if this might be The Book I'd been seeing in multiple visions for months pertaining to my connection with Anthony, which I will go into more detail about a little later. At the time though, I was definitely not ready for this information or the enormity of what it actually meant, so I forgot all about this part of the reading until now, during the recording of these experiences, when I was always meant to make the connections.

In 2007, on my birthday, May 24, I had another reading from a woman named Leanda who studied with Doreen Virtue as an Angel Therapy Practitioner and Medium. I wasn't expecting her to start off with saying "You've got a different name. There's a different name for you. I'm surprised you don't know it yet!"

She went on to tell me that I was not using my gifts, and that I was meant to. And at one point she even said, "You're a space person." I only recently saw that in my notes, but also find it interesting how many clear clues I was receiving but not picking up on, even when someone was basically hitting me over the head with them. I suppose I had been so traumatized back in 1997—again, the year of the Phoenix Lights which, according to Bashar, is the ship which houses many species of the hybrid children. With all of my encounters and high strangeness phenomena, I wanted to believe that I never had to deal with anything alien ever again.

I had conveniently forgotten about channeling my origin to a place called "Phemus/Femus," where apparently I had "really" come from, that previous fall. I must have written the whole Phemus channel in an altered state of consciousness, because, though when I saw it in my journal looking back I totally remembered it, if I wasn't actually looking at the transcription, I couldn't ever remember transcribing it.

Very strange.

Sort of like how I often wouldn't remember how I'd got from point A to B while driving. I would be "gone" somewhere else, and not remember looking at the road once, stunned that I'd somehow managed to get where I was going, alive, but with zero memory of the drive or anything I'd seen on the way. I could feel that my hands had not been steering the car before coming to and this always freaked me out. Because if not my hands, then whose? My memory would always be a blank slate.

I have a photographic memory, so this was always disturbing to me. I would have zero recollection in my mind's eye of streets I'd been on, turns I'd made, things I'd seen, yet somehow, I would end up safely where I was going. I suppose this could also be considered missing time. If this does count as such, then I've had a lot of missing time in my life.

Zoning out for three to four hours was normal for me before having children. × I would put on music, and literally disappear, to who knows where. But next thing I'd know, I would be coming to and it would be hours later. Perhaps I'd experienced missing time much more than I ever realized.

My hunch is that perhaps I was shifting dimensions, going aboard ship, or taking care of my galactic duties that my earthly mind was unaware of still. Though I didn't have a clue what was going on, I did always take notice of how odd it was that these things occurred on a daily basis for me, but seemingly for no one else around me.

CHAPTER 52

"Jimmy"

This chapter was written on top of Fisher Mountain in Mount Ida, Arkansas as a direct transmission of Remembrance from the Pleiadian ship The Star of Bethlehem on May 17, 2016.

This particular encounter was full of high strangeness at a time when I had no clue what high strangeness was. I was used to unusual things happening to me, I was very used to strange metaphysical experiences, but at the time this one happened, I could not recognize it for what it was: a galactic discernment test.

It was September 2, 2007, in the midst of my metaphysical training with Anthony. Noah had turned three the day before, and unbeknown to any of us, Anthony's son would be born exactly one month after this incident.

I wasn't really making it my business to follow anything having to do with Anthony, unless it presented itself to me by way of synchronicity. I was working to live my life in the physical realm. I was a single working mother, and my son was my focus. I was going deeper in my meditation practice and had taken to doing nightly Osho active meditations, to align my energies and keep them moving in an upward spiral, positive direction.

I was working as a hostess in a fine dining restaurant in a hotel on the west side of Vancouver. I had become tired of working nights at the jazz club I'd been at almost a year; too tired to take care of my son during the days, and so I changed my schedule to working the breakfast and lunch shifts.

This particular morning, one of the hotel guests who apparently was in town for a "friend of a friend's" wedding, came into the lounge where I stood welcoming guests. He seated himself next to my post and said his name was Jimmy.

Right away, Jimmy noticed my Seed of Life tattoo, the activator over my sacred heart I'd received the previous April. The seed is the centerpiece of the sacred geometric design of the Flower of Life. He began to speak to me with great interest, saying he knew that he was there to meet me and that my tattoo had been his sign for this.

He spoke to me about the metaphysical meaning of this symbol, but I was busy and distracted with my job, and besides which, I didn't yet know myself what the symbol truly meant. At the time, I still simply referred to it as my "flower tattoo," and had no idea the galactic power it held or the sacred codes it carried. I do now, but then, I was clueless. I understood that it was meant to be a type of activator for others, but it took my moving to Sedona a year later to even begin truly figuring that one out.

So, when Jimmy talked about the metaphysics behind this symbol, I could hear him talking, but it was almost like in The Peanuts cartoon when the adults talk to the kids. None of it was sinking in, and I was too busy working to figure it out. Maybe that's a good thing. Who knows what he really said to me that day? I wonder now, was this a display of mind control, and even if I didn't understand it, was it somehow permeating my psyche unconsciously? I certainly do wonder about this now.

I say this, because I actually experienced a total mind swipe of our entire interaction that day by the time I woke up the next morning, and didn't even remember meeting this strange man until years later, in 2016, when I was finishing the last edits for this book.

That's nine years.

This experience with "Jimmy," or whoever he really was, was to be a test for me. You see, I was very deep in my galactic training, but didn't know it, and this test would be the one that determined what the next move would be from the ships.

Jimmy created a huge distraction from my work that day. I found myself challenged to stay focused on my job, like I had a magnet drawing me to him. I felt very pulled to stand next to him, in his energy field, the tug was so strong, but in an oddly mysterious way that I didn't understand.

I was thirty-two at the time, but I looked to be in my twenties. I was petite, cute, and wearing a low cut little black dress and knee high black heeled boots. This man was easily in his fifties, and I would say pushing sixty. Yet I felt a subtle seduction happening with him, unlike any I'd ever experienced with a man before, and I've experienced some weird shit. Somehow, this Jimmy character did not feel like a regular person.

At the time, I was so deep in denial about my work and connection with ETs, there's no way I would have guessed this man might not even be from this planet, or that he and I might be players in a larger galactic experiment. I still don't know for absolute sure. I'd certainly always known life exists out there in the ethers beyond this planet, and that ETs are very real, as I'd already had my own personal saga with them 10 years earlier, and naively thought that was all over and done with.

So, even though Jimmy had a very distinct otherworldly energy about him, he walked in the body of an apparent human, and since my perception then was that aliens were mainly little green men and the like, well, Jimmy simply appeared to be a plain old regular human being to me. From the galactic perspective that I hold now, I see Jimmy and my interactions with him that day as something of a high strangeness training experiment, possibly with some trickster and seduction energies designed to attempt to throw me off the strong galactic course of tracking cosmic energies and stepping into my own metaphysical powers.

Before I continue this story, I feel it's important to mention that, up until the past few months, I had completely forgotten about this day of my life, and my encounters with this man. It's as if I wasn't allowed to remember until I was ready to understand the energies at play and write about them for the purpose of this book.

Jimmy spent the majority of my shift that day sitting next to my welcoming post, telling me he'd never met another woman like me, and telling me how my tattoo was part of this symbol he'd been working with. He told me he was only in town until the next morning. That he was here to go to his friend's wedding that night, but now that he'd met me, he was considering skipping it altogether and spending time with me instead. He hadn't even asked if I wanted this!

I told him that wouldn't be possible, as I was a single mother and did not have a babysitter. Jimmy seemed unfazed by this and left the lounge for a while to "rest," asking me beforehand what time I would be off shift. Like an idiot, I told him two o'clock, so at two o'clock, he showed up and offered me a ride home.

I have no idea what possessed me to accept. I want to kick myself hard when I look back at this embarrassing display of poor discernment. Here I was, making a careless and potentially dangerous decision on the fly (under mind control, no doubt, which is the only way I'd ever agree to something like this). Even I knew better than this. Yet I felt strangely incapable of saying no to this man, even when I immediately experienced a split moment of severe conflict over it.

That powerful moment of knowing was quickly shifted to '*You can trust this man,*' even though I knew absolutely nothing about him. Now where did that thought come from? What does that sound like? Mind control? But from where, and from whom? These questions did not even enter my mind then, though they certainly do now. All I know is that my discernment had up and left me high and dry.

So, I let this man drive me home. He now knew where I lived. As I was getting out of his car, he told me that he just had to see me that night before he never had the chance to again. What was his obsession with me? Like an idiot again, and wondering to myself what in the world I was doing, I found myself handing this man my buzzer code into the building and elevator, along with my apartment number, complete with detailed instructions on how to get up to my apartment successfully through the highly secured building. I gave him the paper, and before I knew it, he was gone.

I did not dare tell my mother what I had just done. I didn't even know myself. I knew that if I told her that some strange older man I had just met was going to come over that night while Noah was asleep, she would have knocked me up the side of the head and told me not to let him in, under any circumstances. I knew this. I even would have agreed with her. Yet I said nothing.

She lived in the same building as me though, and usually knew what I was up to, as she could see inside my apartment window from hers. I would have to draw all my blinds shut that evening if this man actually showed. Why was I even thinking like this, I wondered? It sounded crazy. But I knew it was always a possibility that she might pop over in the evening to see me for a bit. I had to put that thought out of my head, hoping to holy hell I wouldn't have to go there. I felt nervous, like a teenage kid who'd made plans with an older boy to come over when her parents weren't home, knowing she would be punished if they found out. The whole situation was crazy, and here I was, a thirty-two-year old woman!

All I knew was that I was scared of getting "caught" by my mother with this man in my home, yet some strange force inside of me kept wondering about him, if he would even show up, and what he was really all about. Curiosity killed the cat, right? I didn't necessarily even trust this man, which makes such poor decision-making all the more reckless and embarrassing.

To this day, I still can't believe myself. As much as I've struggled with discernment over the years and made some embarrassingly poor decisions, even this was a move I never would have been stupid enough to make under normal circumstances. The protection and care of my children always trumps everything. The moment I found out I was pregnant for the first time, the mama bear in me was activated, big time. If anything, I will tend to become overly-protective of my children, so this move was completely off the charts suspicious. I would never knowingly put my children in the potential of harm's way, even a smidge, and I've become way less daring with my own life and choices since motherhood became my reality and top priority.

So what was it that made me do this? And I say "made" because I truly do question now what sort of hand was overseeing this entire situation.

For what it's worth, I didn't feel Jimmy posed any sort of real threat to Noah, or myself, but that is neither here nor there. No one thought Paul Bernardo and Karla Homolka posed a threat either, and they did the unthinkable, even to their family. So I am not making excuses for myself for this very poor display of judgment and safety. Shame on me. My personal control over what I allowed in this situation was definitely askew, no doubt about that.

Part of me hoped to hell Jimmy would decide not to come, so I wouldn't do something I might regret. I hoped he would lose track of time, whatever, even though I knew this was wishful thinking. As the evening wore on, a strong knowing came through my psychic pipeline that I was going to have to reject whatever it was Jimmy was really coming here for, which was still a mystery.

I could feel his energies though, and was taken aback by a sort of sexual tension building. I was not attracted to this man physically, though I did feel something attempting to push me in that direction. He could have been my father which made it all the more appalling to me.

What I did have was an unexplainable attraction to something in his energetic field. No doubt about it, there was an electrical charge I think we both felt between us. I put Noah to bed, and prayed that this man stay at his function and leave me alone so I never even had to find out. And then the buzzer rang.

I looked at the security camera, and there he was. Goddammit.

My irrational, uncontrollable urge to see him and figure out what this mysterious connection was took over, and I buzzed him up, and waited. My heart pounded with fear and excitement all at once, but I pushed all that aside and suited up as best I could. I stood strong in myself, shielded and ready to potentially stand in the line of fire. Why did I feel so compelled to do this?

I had no idea what, or whom, I was dealing with here. And I sure as hell didn't understand how the galactic chess board works, or that I was even playing on it. I was standing there, blind and naked, with only my inner strength, courage and trust in myself to see me through whatever I was inviting in.

Talk about dumb. But if I knew only one thing about myself, it was that in a crisis, if challenged by the darkness, I had the ability to dismantle it, to destroy it. I had no idea how I would, but knew in that moment that if this man tried anything, I would somehow be protected. I was used to playing Russian roulette with my life. What I wasn't thinking about was, what if this was the time the gun landed aimed at my temple? Or worse, my child? I am quite certain now that the Galactic Secret Service must have been watching my ass that night, probably saying, "What in the world are we going to do with her?"

I took a few deep breaths as I heard him get off the elevator and walk to my door. I poised myself, inner alignment intact as much as I could muster, and opened the door. Who said I ever had to open it? Who on Earth was I really obeying here anyway? He walked in to my tiny sanctuary, my sacred space that I shared with my little boy. This was bound to get interesting.

We sat on the couch and talked for a while, about 3D type of things. Work, parenting, etcetera. I remember thinking '*I wonder what the point is of him being here? He seems harmless enough. What does he want from me? Why did I even invite him?*' My evenings were sacred to me, being a working single mother, and I secretly kicked myself for giving that up.

And that's when things took a strange turn.

It felt as though he could hear these thoughts I was having. He became very intense all of a sudden, telling me that he needed me. What on earth did that mean anyway? I'd just met this man! What could he possibly need from me?

He said he was leaving the next day, I can't remember where to, but I think that was because it was all very vague. I do remember there being more than one destination, and them being somewhat cryptic, as I remember having no clue where these places even were. It was like I could not locate them anywhere on my mental GPS.

He said he was not going alone either. He told me that he was traveling with a "friend," a "female companion." He began almost begging me to go with them. He said something along the lines of it being destined, and that I wouldn't regret it.

This is when I snapped out of whatever spell or mind control I'd been placed under, and it happened in a matter of a nanosecond. Why was this man acting so desperate to convince me to go with him? Who in their right mind would try to convince a complete stranger, a single mother, to leave her toddler behind on a whim to go to God knows where with a stranger and his "companion"? I wondered what in the hell was really going on here.

He used a sort of sexual seductive energy to try to ensnare me. Though it was subtle, it was undoubtedly there. Nothing physically intimate happened between us, but the energetics were in place, and I could feel the hooks going in, trying to grab me. It was a powerful energy, and I shuddered at the image in my mind of what it might look like if I actually said yes, though there was no way in hell I was going to do that. I realized right then I was playing in a field I had no business playing in. I had to get this man out of my house, and fast.

In that moment of snapping-to, I became instantly horrified and shocked that I had allowed this at all, and wondered how it had been possible for me to exercise such a precarious and dangerous level of discernment.

Exactly who was I playing with here? This man was attempting to seduce me into abandoning my child, saying life would be so easy and wonderful where we would go. Who in the world does this, especially with someone they have only just met?

There was most definitely something very off and scary about this situation, even masked in the suspicious stench of love and light. I did not yet have the galactic training or proper knowing to navigate this with full awareness, and I certainly had no clue how serious a violation this situation really was.

I was playing in the realms of Galactic 404 as Selene calls it, and had no clue I'd even graduated out of Spiritual 101, or that there even were such "classes." I certainly had no idea what was happening, but my galactic ass was on the line here, as well as my future assignments.

Nothing on the surface would have given anyone from the outside any idea that there was something wrong here. This man appeared to be a non-threat. But my inner knowing that kicked in o high gear told me to get him the hell out of there as quickly as possible.

I had to play this very smart though. If I'd have flipped out right there on the spot and started 20-questioning him, who knows what would have happened? Maybe nothing, but maybe something. I wasn't about to find out. After all, I didn't know this man, and had no idea what he might be capable of. Was he even a "man"? *Human?* I certainly question this now.

But in the moment, I played my role. I worked through an exit strategy in my mind to get him out of my apartment. He could see or feel the switch go off inside of me, and asked if I was alright. I told him I was just tired from a long day of work and needed some rest, and apologized. I tried to sound as sincere as I could, and told him I'd enjoyed his company and getting to meet him, but that I now needed my rest.

I also told him that I could never leave my son. Then he started in with the seduction that maybe Noah could come too. I told him I was not prepared to up and leave my life, to uproot myself and my child with him, and so even if Noah was "welcome" to come that it would probably still not be possible. I did my very best to keep calm and composed and not let on that I was freaking out inside. I had to stay strong in my knowing and in my alignment because this man's powers of persuasion and seduction were off the charts.

Things amped up even more.

He became rushed in his attempts to get me to reconsider his offer, as I must have had said "no" about 20 more times. I stood strong, in my alignment, with grace and courage, meanwhile maintaining an air that I was not suspicious or upset by any of this. I did not want to provoke an attack or leave an opening for him to swoop in on my vulnerability. I had to "fake it till I made it."

He finally appeared to hear me, and got up to leave realizing I was a lost cause. But he asked me for one "dance" with him before he left.

Remember, I had no clue about galactic energetics, and didn't realize what I was dealing with, and just wanted this man out of my apartment, and if dancing with him helped move things along, then that was what I would do. I had no idea about the very real aspect or potential consequences of energetic transference of galactic information through physical touch.

We stood up, and he took both of my hands in his. He turned my palms facing upward, which was unusual, but I allowed it, thinking maybe he was going to read my palms. Why else would someone do this?

He proceeded to trace a spiral pattern on both of my palms. Also unusual. I wondered what he was doing. He then raised his hands up in front of him, palms out in my direction, and I did the same, involuntarily. I was watching this happen, watching my arms move by themselves, and my heart raced. What was happening here?

We stood for a moment together, looking in to each other's eyes. I look back now and wonder what exactly this man's true intention was with me? Was it benign or was it sinister? I was so naïve at the time, I couldn't see it for what it was. DNA upgrades and activations can occur through eye contact and physical touch, as well as the passing of genetic codes. The same can also be true for DNA hijacking.

All I knew in that moment was, that whatever was happening between us was beyond comprehension for me. I felt an enormous energetic exchange, a sort of transference, and I remember feeling, and even seeing, a bright green light moving in between us, emanating directly from and through the symbols he'd traced on my hands moments before.

What in the world was this, and what did any of it mean? It was definitely not of this world, I was quite certain of this.

Then, Jimmy put one palm over my seed tattoo, and one over my solar plexus, which I allowed, as I was frozen and stun-gunned by everything that had taken place already. By this point, I had fallen under his spell momentarily again. Something else was in charge of my body other than myself.

I felt something happening but could not decipher what in the world it was. There was no earthly experience or explanation for it.

Now I realize it could have been all manner of things that he did to me. Jimmy could have been taking galactic information or codes from me, or perhaps he was taking, putting or transferring something into or out of me, by way of my womb (eggs, babies, implants, etc.), and my heart, by way of the portal of my tattoo. Perhaps it was some of both.

After this was complete, Jimmy pulled me into a long embrace. He was much taller than I was, so my solar plexus and womb were pressed right against his genitals, and my chest and heart, against his solar plexus.

He held me tightly, and I was finally able to disconnect us by pulling away gently, breaking the link and the hold he had on me, back to my senses, meanwhile trying to keep my cool with this strange being.

Jimmy locked in a gaze with me again, and looked deeply into my eyes once more. It felt like a laser beam, burning in to my soul. He told me to have a nice life; that he "loved me," would miss me; that he was sorry I could not come with him, and then he left the building. He told me I would never see him again.

I never did hear from Jimmy again. He literally disappeared, and all I thought to myself in that moment was, '*What in the living fuck just happened here?*'

I woke up the next morning and my mind had been swiped of this entire encounter. Two and a half weeks later, I met Jeff.

CHAPTER 53

When Destiny Calls and Knocks You Flat on Your Ass

Fast forward to the end of 2007 and early 2008. I was about to move to Arizona indefinitely with Noah, who was now a three-year-old. I was going to see if my new relationship was going to work out, and the only way to find out was to cut the long-distance "bliss visits" and see what life was really like when we were living in the same town, together.

I would be unable to work legally, literally becoming an "*illegal alien*" which I find so funny now, and indicative of the massive journey of awakening I was in for. But Jeff had a decent job, which could support the three of us, at least for a while, so I'd have time to figure all that out. I would also continue receiving my monthly government child tax, since I still technically lived in Canada, as I would still have a home in my name there. I didn't feel like I was totally reliant on this new love of mine, which was nice, and I wanted to see where it could go.

I remember, just before leaving Vancouver, I went to see yet another psychic medium in a town called Maple Ridge, about

45 minutes outside of Vancouver. I had seen this woman once before, and had had a great reading from her. She was more raw and gritty and told it like it was, without the flowery language and tip toeing around issues some psychics use in order to make their clients happy.

Her name was Debbie Hayler, and I enjoyed her vibe a lot. Something about my energy and hers just clicked. I remember Debbie telling me months before moving out to Sedona that it was a critical time for me to step into my own power, to stand in my truth, and to figure out who I was. I remember it as a very profound, almost terrifying, message when she literally said:

"You have until the end of 2008 to step into your power, to take charge of your life and begin living being of service in the ways in which you came here to. If you do not do this by year's end, the rug will be pulled out from under you, and it will be much harder to get back up. But you will be able to do it if you really want to. If you don't find the courage to do this though, it will be a very hard path. You can't run from your Destiny, it will just keep knocking on your door. If you do not listen, you may be sorry."

Of course, I instantly felt the pressure. Here she was in one breath telling me my life could be flipped upside down if I didn't step into my power and get my shit together, but in the next breath, she spoke in a way that was absolutely certain that I would, eventually anyway, and that she believed in me wholly.

Also interesting to note is when I asked Debbie about studying Angel Therapy with Doreen Virtue, she told me I "could" do this, but that in truth, the beings I actually "worked" with were not "fluffy angelic beings" and that "fluffy" was not meant to be my path. I know now that this woman was privy to my intimate ties with ETs and my work with them, yet she also knew I was not yet prepared to handle this information. Deep down, I am certain I also knew this already, but was still wading in the shallow waters of self-denial.

So, after a roller coaster of the first half of 2008, living part of the time in Flagstaff, then Sedona, Arizona, and spending the spring and summer in Vancouver after border troubles, Noah and I finally got back in to the U.S., and back in Sedona with Jeff in mid-August, 2008.

On September 8t, 2008, exactly seven years from the day I was told by my higher guidance that I needed to go to the Light Institute for the first time, I received confirmation during my immigration physical that I had become impregnated with Rubin, literally within days of getting back to Sedona. I had no idea the ride that was in store for me. If I had, I probably would have run back to Canada. In hindsight, I'm glad I didn't.

Looking back though, it doesn't surprise me in the least that nearly as soon as my feet touched the Sedona soil, I was impregnated, knowing what I know now about Sedona, especially in connection with my particular mission with hybrid babies. We may try and run away from our destiny, but our destiny will always find us.

Nevertheless, I was pregnant, and it turned out to be a very difficult time for me, between moving to a new country (often it felt like a completely different world!—it's still amazing to me the culture shock I experienced moving from Canada to the

U.S.), becoming pregnant and all that ensued during those very interesting, often challenging months while I was carrying my second child.

Thinking back to what Debbie had told me about stepping into my power before the end of the year, and having been "knocked out" in many ways by this pregnancy, needless to say I felt huge anxiety around this prediction, knowing that there was no way in hell I was figuring anything out about my life by the end of 2008, except maybe how to get through the pregnancy, how to navigate my new life as a married woman. How I was ever going to find anyone willing to deliver my baby the way this warrior mama wanted, which was a natural homebirth without medical intervention. My first pregnancy had ended as a hospital Cesarean birth. I was not about to let any "official" anyone tell me how this baby had to be born, and homebirth VBACs (vaginal birth after Cesarean) were, and still are, illegal in the state of Arizona.

The wild ride had only just begun. I had to buckle my bootstraps, because Sedona was about to dish me out a major dose of "get your shit cleared, or else." The following three years were the craziest, most challenging, and most terrifying ride of my life.

CHAPTER 54

Alien Unrecognized

It was a very charged time for me. I was sick nearly the entire pregnancy, and it was quite stressful because I was now living in Arizona, technically an "alien" in a foreign land. How ironic.

I'd had no idea when I moved here to Sedona the stigma it carries, and how it is very popularly known for its high-strangeness, both in the form of miraculous healings, and in particular, by way of UFO activity and extraterrestrial encounters.

I knew upon first driving in to Sedona with Jeff though that I'd seen this place before, and in fact, had been told in a dream about ten years earlier that I needed to come to the land of the red earth and rocks. I cried the first time I ever saw this land, as I had remembered it so vividly from my dreams all those years earlier. I knew Sedona held some significance for me, but could not have fathomed then exactly what that would come to mean.

I wanted desperately to have a natural home birth, and not end up in a hospital this time, especially after my experience with Noah where I was forced into having a Cesarean birth just because my waters had been broken for 24 hours. Of course, perfect for what we both needed to experience on a soul level, I know this well now, so the healing I needed around that experience is thankfully complete, but the whole thing was unnecessary and I knew in my heart I could have eventually birthed my baby myself.

We all "come in" and give birth in the way that will best serve our soul's journey, even if it is painful. But still, I was determined to keep my rights as a birthing woman this time and bring my baby earthside the way I saw fit: naturally. I was going to empower myself this time!

Jeff wanted desperately for me to find a midwife who would take insurance, since he had a supposedly "great" insurance policy through his work. And I was not willing to bend or to give up my rights as a birthing woman. We were stuck between a rock and a hard place.

I was unusually ill during the majority of the pregnancy, breaking out into full body rashes which scared the living shit out of me in the first trimester, not having a midwife or anyone to follow my pregnancy yet. I even had three different nights within a month before Rubin was born where I was up all night, puking and with diarrhea, my abdomen in a constant state of contraction. It was beyond intense. I now see that my body was preparing and clearing itself in order to be able to hold the frequency he needed me to sustain in order to be birthed.

But when I went back to Vancouver for the Christmas holidays during the second trimester to visit my family, I called up my GP there, and asked her if she wouldn't mind me coming in and having a prenatal checkup. I was now five months pregnant, and still hadn't found a midwife that would legally help me in Arizona. I was looking forward to seeing my GP and at least having the basics looked after, including blood work and, I was hoping, an ultrasound. She was more than happy to do this with me.

I had really wanted an ultrasound because I'd felt something was very different about this baby. Besides which, I had been sick almost the entire five months leading up to our trip, so I wanted to make sure my baby was healthy. I even strongly suspected again that I might be carrying twins.

Dr. Anita Lee had seen me through some of my darkest times when I was going through many shifts and awakenings in my mid-twenties, all in preparation for where I'm at now no doubt. I had started seeing her while in acting school at Studio 58 back in 2000 for eating disorder issues and health challenges I was experiencing as a result of them. She was such a sweet, empathetic and non-judgmental woman. The added bonus was that she used to be an ob-gyn, so I knew that she would help me any way she could.

Anita gave me my PAP test, and gave me the forms I needed to get my blood work done. I heard the baby's heartbeat for the first time. She also said she would try her best to get me an ultrasound, but that it didn't look too promising, considering I was only in town for a week and they were not easy to come by in the best of times.

I was grateful for anything she could do, but did admittedly really want the ultrasound. Something in me kept nagging at me that there was something very different about this baby, or "babies." I couldn't shake this feeling, and I assumed it must mean that something was wrong, considering how sick I'd been. Having an ultrasound would either help ease my mind, or prepare me for perhaps some unpleasant or challenging circumstances ahead. Either way, I wanted, and needed, to know.

Miraculously, Anita got me an ultrasound, much to her surprise and delight, as well as mine. It was scheduled for the same morning that Jeff would be leaving Vancouver to fly back to the U.S. on his own, since he was required back at work two days later. Noah and I were staying in Vancouver a little longer since I was now married and free to travel in and out of the country again. We were going to milk this visit as much as we could, as Noah was missing our home there, and my mother.

We'd been attempting to drive our car from Sedona to Vancouver that trip instead of flying, but Noah, who rarely ever got sick to his stomach, spiked a fever and was throwing up constantly. We only made it as far as Salt Lake City in two and a half days of driving. The first time Noah ever got sick like that was exactly a year earlier, right after we'd moved to Arizona, interestingly enough.

Aside from all of this messy drama, we were snowed in by a blizzard in Salt Lake, and the highway we'd needed to take, our only route forward to Vancouver, was closed. Definitely a sign.

Instead of just accepting this fate though, and driving back to Sedona to spend our Christmas there, we spent nearly $2000 we didn't have on last minute plane tickets and flew out to Vancouver the very next day—the day before Christmas Eve, 2008. Of course, Noah was completely fine by then.

I look back now and truly feel that something was trying to keep me from doing this drive. Or else there were forces working overtime in order to keep me in the dark about what was going on inside my womb. Or both. Either way, it was all very strange, and once in Vancouver, things would continue to become increasingly much, much stranger.

CHAPTER 55

A Close Encounter of the Strangest Kind

It was the morning of January 2, 2009 and my ultrasound was scheduled for 8 am. Noah, Jeff and I were all sleeping in the huge king size bed in my Vancouver apartment, which my brother, Josh, was now living in. He had stayed elsewhere while we were in town to let us have the space and to allow Noah the comforts of a familiar place to sleep.

I don't know what time it was because I was lying on my side with my back to the clock, but dawn was definitely breaking, when all of a sudden, my eyes popped open, and I was completely paralyzed.

'*Oh shit*', I thought, '*not this again!*'

It had been nearly 12 years since my previous conscious experiences in 1997, when I had begged these beings to stop doing things to me. And here I was, five months pregnant, *paralyzed*, and this time, I was not alone. Wide awake, I was unable to do a damn thing about any of it.

I panicked. I had always physically been alone during my experiences; they had so far for the most part taken place in the dream state, with the exception of the light ship, missing time,

UFOs following me, and invisible beings in my home. Right now, though, I was fully conscious and could feel something—*someone*—very distinctly in physical form, standing behind me, though I could not move to see who or what it was.

I felt a large device being placed across my lower back, and then what I can only describe as a sucking motion began. Though by no means painful, this was not a gentle sucking; it was very powerful, something akin to the strength of a Shop-Vac had been attached to my body. There was no mistaking it for anything else. I had a vacuum-type device across my lower back, and it was *sucking something out of me*.

At first, I had been more concerned because Noah was there sleeping next to me. I didn't want "them" doing anything to him. Then once the sucking started, I realized it was my baby I should be thinking about. They wanted something to do with my baby!

It took all the mental strength I had to telepathically say, '*Please don't hurt my baby! Please! Please don't hurt either of my babies!*'

I was pleading with them. If I could have moved and cried, kicked and screamed, I certainly would have. If I could have attacked whoever this was in my room doing this to me and my baby, I would have. Which is probably why they had paralyzed me in the first place. I am definitely a protective mama bear when it comes to the safety of my children.

Then just as suddenly as I'd been awoken, a wave of calm fell over me, and I heard, '*Relaaaax, everything is aaaalriiiiight.*

We are not hurting your baby. We are not hurting anyone. Just relax, everything is going to be aaaalriiiight...'

With that, it was as if a "relax serum" had been injected into me, and I totally surrendered, feeling half drugged, even euphoric, as I slipped into a lucid dream-like state, all while remaining completely conscious. I was still not able to open my eyes as the paralysis had taken away the ability to use any of my physical muscles, including my eyelids. It felt like being on some trippy psychedelic drug while simultaneously remaining totally sober.

During this entire procedure, the vacuum-type apparatus was making a very loud droning sound and vibration that shook the entire bed. It penetrated to the core of every cell in my body—blood and bones. It was all I could feel, all I could hear, like it was somehow inside the center of my skull, coming from the inside out. Very, very strange.

When it finally stopped, which was abruptly, there was an eerie quiet in the room, a silence so charged, so magnetically thick, it made my hairs stand on end. I could now open my eyes, but still could not move any other muscle for several moments. At least I could see that Noah was all right, thank God. He and Jeff were fast asleep still, which was utterly shocking to me. I didn't know how this was even possible, after we had just been so rocked, the movement and vibration in the bed so physically intense.

Noah looked incredibly peaceful. I could feel the being(s) behind me still, yet I was still unable to move. Then, suddenly,

I regained all muscular movement, bolted upright and turned to look behind me.

Nothing. No one was there. *They were gone. What the hell had just happened to me?*

I was in total shock, disbelief, and sheer panic that this something I thought had ended years ago, was back for me.

WHY??? And why my baby???

I shook Jeff and woke him up. He was acting very strange, like he had been drugged or something. That is the only way I can describe it. I know now that this is indeed how these beings can make certain that others in the room don't witness what they are doing—so that they don't panic (like me).

How many times had this happened to me before, where they had me drugged too, so that I was never the wiser to their tinkering inside my person? I seriously began to wonder.

This time, though, was different. I had been allowed to be fully conscious of the experience. But why? Perhaps so that one day, I would be able to explain it in detail and tell the story.

Knowing what I know now, I am certain this has happened to me a multitude of times throughout my life. But at the time this experience took place, I was so in the moment, and so unaware of the truth of who I was, who I AM, that again, I went into victim mode, thinking it was all random that "they," to my misfortune, happened to pick me, and that I had no say in the matter. And dammit, what the hell did they want from me anyway?

Jeff finally came to out of his hazy fog, and when I got in his face, all intense, asking him if he'd felt it too, he had no idea what I was talking about. *'Great!'* I thought. *'I have to experience this again and STILL have no one to talk about it with! No one else who understands me!'*

To say I was a tad upset, not to mention completely bewildered—I mean how could he have not felt it?—would be an understatement.

I then became a bit crazed, and admittedly, worried. I mean, the timing was impeccable really. I was scheduled to see this baby for myself in just a couple of hours. I was also suddenly very grateful for this, as more and more, I began to question all of the experiences leading up to this one in relation to this pregnancy. Not having been able to see or hear the baby until now, was highly unusual. Was there a bigger reason why it had been this way? Were invisible forces trying to keep me from seeing something inside my own womb about this baby?

This experience was the icing on the cake of high strangeness where this pregnancy was concerned, and so help me God, if they had done anything to my baby.

I didn't know what I would have done exactly, but I was making these sorts of inner threats anyway, like somehow, it would make one iota of a difference. I was more relieved than ever to have this appointment and to be going to get some answers for heaven's sake.

The timing for this mysterious visitation was uncanny though, no doubt about that. Mere hours before seeing this baby for myself for the very first time. So many different obstacles trying to keep us from getting to Vancouver in the first place, where all along, I was determined to find a way see this baby and receive answers about how my little seed was doing.

I am now very aware of my role in these ET hybridization programs, and I look back on that pregnancy with newly awakened eyes. I had always said that it felt like the whole having no midwife or caregiver following the pregnancy was set up that way somehow by forces greater than me, specifically so that I would not have access to knowing what was going on with this baby I was carrying. I always took note of that intuitive hit, as it always felt this way to me. I now understand a deeper aspect of this truth.

Writing this story has also made me realize that even Noah's mysterious vomiting and fever, the "indefinite" highway closure we faced, reads so very clearly on paper that of course an unseen force was setting the stage, trying to keep us from driving to Vancouver, or at least trying to get my attention as to what I was about to face in the days ahead, giving me the option to bail on these experiences that awaited me there.

But why?

Perhaps, because if had we driven, I would not have had the time for the ultrasound because we would have been driving back to Sedona in a rush after the holidays to get Jeff back to work on time. Perhaps the forces at play were creating a situation where we *had* to fly, so that I would have the time for the appointment, and so that I would have this conscious experience in order that I may recall it and thus share this truth with others in the name of Divine Service at this time.

Or perhaps something was trying to stop me from knowing anything.

Or maybe it was simply all an entirely random sequence of events that had nothing to do with anything...which is almost laughable and *highly unlikely*.

CHAPTER 56

The Lone Shot

Jeff and I got ready and woke up Noah , who was also extremely groggy; not typical for him as he awoke every other morning of his life with a smile and a sweet "Good Morning, Mama!" Not this morning though.

As he struggled to open his eyes, I was on autopilot, still in a bit of a haze, but on a serious mission for some answers. We finally got him moving and gave him his banana, and were off to see what was going on inside of my womb. In a haze, Noah ate his banana with us needing to feed it to him (very unusual) and went through the motions, but was really struggling to wake up. I had never seen him like this before.

The experience overall of this ultrasound left a very bizarre taste in my mouth, and even Jeff had to finally admit it was all very unusual. We got there, the first and only people in the waiting room, which is unusual in and of itself. We were in this strange basement inside the back of a building, which also had an unusual feel to it. Of course, everything probably seemed highly suspicious to me by now, considering the morning I was having.

I was called in to the examination room, and proceeded in with Jeff and Noah in tow. The ultrasound technician, an older

Asian woman with a very curt bedside manner, ordered Jeff and Noah out of the room. I was feeling vulnerable still, and wasn't too thrilled with this, but they did as they were instructed.

I lay there, alone with this odd woman, as she put the cold blue jelly on my protruding abdomen. It's always a strange sensation, as anyone who's had an ultrasound can attest to, but with the mysterious "procedure" I'd already been through with my bedroom "visitors," the blue jelly might as well have been alien goo. My senses were in overdrive.

She started in with the examination, and I, still so shaken, in an attempt to reassure myself and calm myself down, started talking with her and asking her questions about the baby, trying to find out anything about it that I possibly could. I wanted to make sure my baby was okay, and of course, normal. I was simply asking her what she was seeing, measuring, and noticing, if it seemed that baby was on track, but she didn't appreciate my obvious concerns, and instead of reassuring me, she became agitated with me.

"*SHH!! DON'T* TALK TO ME WHEN I AM DOING THIS!!! I need *ALL* of my concentration for this! You can ask me questions later! When I am done."

Wow. This woman was really a piece of work, I thought. I started looking more closely at her, and again, probably still being overly sensitive, I started to notice that she looked sort of non-human to me.

I have no idea if that assessment was accurate or even appropriate, but given her shitty attitude, along with her unusual physical appearance combined with the dingy, dirty room we were in, I was highly suspicious of what was happening here. Not to mention what the outside streets had felt like driving in for the appointment. It felt as though the rest of the city was still asleep; all except us. We were in the middle of Vancouver, and it felt like a ghost town. Talk about high strangeness.

When we'd arrived at the address, the rest of the office and the entire plaza were completely empty. It was so very quiet. Of course, due to what had transpired only two hours before this, I had become a tad paranoid, and a hell of a lot suspicious. Who could blame me?

Finally robot lady finished with her silent assessments, and said only that the baby looked "good." She gave me the due date; beginning of May 2009, and Jeff and Noah were invited back into the room, thank the heavens.

Jeff could tell I was a bit rattled, but I was also very grateful that my baby seemed normal and that I could now see the loving sweet smiles of Noah, witnessing his baby sibling for the first time, and Jeff, also his first experience seeing a new baby, his baby, for the first time.

The world sweetened a little bit for a few short moments. *Was I being paranoid? Was I blowing everything out of proportion? Should I just relax now that I could see for myself that my baby was healthy and growing like any baby should?* I decided to relax and breathe a sigh of relief. Maybe things would be okay after all.

I got up and we went to the front desk to wait for the pictures of our baby, having a tender family moment all together, after sharing in the sweetness of witnessing our precious new addition.

I have always known women to be given a series of shots from different angles of their babies after having an ultrasound, which is what turned this high strangeness morning even stranger. Even when I was pregnant with Noah, I had received three different shots of him, not to mention that my sister had been allowed to be present with me the entire time.

The envelope arrived from the back room and the woman behind the desk handed it to me with a smile, and no words. Strange, but I decided to let it go. I was excited to show Noah the pictures inside.

When I opened the envelope, it was like the elevator in my stomach dropped to a bottomless pit in a matter of a split second.

One lone picture. One single shot. Just one. One angle of our baby.

A frontal view of only the baby's skull. No body, no cute little sideways profile shots, no sweet little arms or tootsies, like most people receive. Nope. One shot only for us. Just a skull, facing dead straight ahead like it was looking right at us.

And it looked identical to a fucking alien head.

This was when Jeff also started to have an overwhelming sense of "something is not quite right here." Up to that point, I think he was a bit confused by my behavior that morning, maybe even humouring me. But after that highly strange ultrasound experience which ended with the cherry on top, this unusual lone "alien baby" shot, even he had to admit something felt very strange and even eerie about the whole thing.

And to take it one step further, when I showed the picture to Angela after I saw her later that day, she immediately grabbed the crystal fluorite skull I had been carrying around with me in my pocket day and night for months leading up to this and said, "It is identical to your crystal skull, Sammy! Look at this!"

She placed the crystal next to the picture, and true enough, same shape, same size, same proportions. *EXACTLY*. Two twin skulls sitting there, staring at us. It was creepy. We both dropped our jaws and sat there, not knowing what the hell was happening, what any of this even meant, as of course, I had already told her the whole story leading up to it.

Angela and I were both so used to high strangeness and crazy shit by this point, yet this one sort of took the cake, and neither of us had a witty comeback about it. No joke or laughter here. It was simply all too strange.

*

About a month later, Angela came to visit me in Sedona and we took a girls' trip to the Grand Canyon together, knowing we had some important work to do together there, though we didn't exactly know what that would be.

It ended up being a pretty short trip and not really that exciting, adventurous or even enlightening, considering I was now almost seven months pregnant. I was totally laid out mentally from the previous month's experiences, not knowing what in the hell was going on with me, with this baby, or anything. I was feeling even more in the dark about this baby now than I had before going to Vancouver, if that was even possible.

While at the Grand Canyon, I was "asked" by Spirit to offer my fluorite crystal skull to the canyon. So, as much as I'd hated to part with it, over the ledge he flew, and ended up exactly where it needed to be, I assured myself. In the end, as much as I did hate to part with it, there was also a sense of relief accompanied with releasing it into the abyss of the massive canyon. The ET energies inside that tiny crystal skull only added to the intensity of what my life had become since the morning of January 2nd.

I wondered though about the skull's landing; did he split, shatter, or stay in one piece? I wished I could have known. The thought of him possibly cracking or shattering for some reason gives me goose bumps even to this day.

CHAPTER 57

High Strangeness, Baby Heads, And Puzzle Pieces

Even Jeff started noticing unusual happenings in our home back in Sedona after that very strange ultrasound appointment that even he couldn't deny or explain away with logic or reasoning.

He and I would hear "someone" in the kitchen at night sometimes. We'd even heard the pitter patter of feet one night, and cupboard doors opening and closing. I was highly suspicious, so Jeff ran out to see if it was Noah or one of our three black cats, but all four were sound asleep, and it was clear from their imprinted pillows and cozy-warm blankets that none of them had moved even an inch for some time.

These kinds of things continued to happen around me, now 12 years after I'd thought I had taken care of the "problem." I became re-obsessed with what these "aliens" wanted from me, and now, also—and more importantly—from my baby. Though I didn't have another conscious experience after this, I knew things were still happening. I simply had no idea what those "things" might be, which only made it worse.

Rubin's birth was fast and furious. Only four hours of labour, as opposed to my first birth which was 24 hours and counting. I had back labour again, which was devastating for me since I had done everything I could think of to make certain this time the baby was positioned "perfectly" so that he could ease his way gently through the birth canal.

Instead, it was excruciatingly painful on my back and spine during each surge of energy, and I was screaming and writhing in agony during each one, sure that my back was about to snap in half and certain the experience was going to kill me this time. All logic is thrown out the window in the throes of labour.

I took in zero medications besides a homeopathic remedy here and there, but that was it. When I heard my baby's heart rate drop and the midwife say, "Call the paramedics" to the doula; that was it for me. I went into mama bear warrior mode, and within three surges, he was out.

Was that all it took? Sheesh!

A plump, beautiful, nearly 9-pound baby boy! He was perfectly chubby and round, calm and sweet. Noah adored him instantly, we all did. And I was at home in my own bed, snuggling with this precious babe and loving him up. *I did it.* And "it" was no small feat, to be sure.

We noticed he had an odd-shaped head, but chalked it up to the fact that he had kept turning his head at a weird angle in the birth canal, which the midwife spent hours manually (read:

both hands up past her wrists inside me at once) attempting to turn it. Absolutely excruciating.

By the time his birth came, we had managed to put the strange experiences of the pregnancy out of our conscious minds (I have no idea how, but I never thought about it again until almost two years later.) and were focusing on this baby and the new big brother in the house.

Noah was a doting big brother, totally enamored with his new baby brother, lying next to him holding his hand, staring into his eyes, constantly wanting to be near him, and Rubin was so round and sweet, taking in every ounce of love from his big brother. He was so easy for the first few days of his earth-side journey, we thought we'd hit the jackpot as far as easy babies went. And then five days after his birth, he transitioned into an increasingly intense, although still equally as sweet, handful at the same time.

Rubin was unlike Noah this way. He had his "witching hour" which he kept up for the first year and a half of his life. This consisted of screaming and crying, no matter what was happening, sometime between 11 pm and 2 am. It was like clockwork, and had nothing to do with the day he'd just had as far as we could tell.

Though we grew to find it endearing in moments, it was also, honestly, quite a test of our patience and ability to stay Unconditionally Loving amidst the piercing chaos and inconsolable screams that would go on sometimes for hours. Most of the time it was heartbreaking, as we hadn't a clue what was troubling him.

Early on, these episodes would last literally from 11 pm until 2 am or later. Thankfully the older he got, he'd finally settle around 11:30 or 12 for the night after kicking and screaming for an hour or so. We came to consider this "easy."

We always held him as he had his screaming fits. We could feel something within his soul that was deeply needing to release these tears and anger. This was obviously an adjustment that was not an easy one for him, bless his precious little heart.

When my brother Josh first saw him at almost five months old, he kept laughing and cracking jokes about the protrusion on the back of Rubin's head, asking me if he was "holding extra brains back there." This was the same protrusion we'd noticed at his birth, but figured it was a result of his head turning in the canal, in which case, the swelling would have eventually subsided. The protrusion, however, was still very much there, and was definitely the shape of his skull.

I laughed off Josh's harmless jokes, still in complete denial. To this day, Rubin still has that protrusion at the back of his skull that angles outward and upward at a strange angle. His hair hides it now though.

In December 2012, when Rubin was three and a half, he told us he wanted his head shaved, so we did it for him. We were at our friend Larry's house for a holiday party, and when another friend of ours first saw him with his new hairstyle, he was mesmerized by Rubin's head.

After watching him for a bit, this friend looked at me and said, *"Do you know who David Wilcock is? He talks about people hav-*

ing heads shaped just like that. He has one too. Wow, look at Rubin's head!"

I might mention that as far as I knew, this friend did not know anything about my experiences with extraterrestrial beings, he was really more of a social acquaintance. He did not even know then that I was writing a book about this very subject.

David Wilcock is one of the leading researchers and speakers on quantum physics, ancient civilizations, and especially any type of research connected with extraterrestrial existence.

I was in shock at hearing this unexpected, and yet what I felt to be a very accurate observation. I smiled, as it was nice to have someone other than me notice this unusual quality in my son, and to comment on it to boot.

I hadn't expected this type of awareness from that particular man either, as he is a well-respected acupuncturist and doctor of Chinese medicine here in Sedona. Before this interaction with him, I had never heard him talk about anything even remotely like this before; never even heard him utter the word or allude to the existence of ETs.

More than one person in this community has surprised me over the years. I suppose it's no wonder we were all drawn to Sedona at some point. Sedona itself feels like an ET experiment, sometimes going right, and sometimes not. But always interesting nonetheless.

CHAPTER 58

Reuniting Lost Aspects of Self

When Rubin was one, I went through one of the most challenging times of my life. I was having a major health crisis and didn't know what to do. My entire life was turned upside down, not to mention the past year postpartum had been a really hard adjustment on our whole family. None of us were happy or thriving.

I had been denying who I am for two years and counting, and it was beginning to take a major toll on my entire well-being.

Upon this diagnosis, I decided to take my life into my own hands, knowing that the best way to heal would be through self-empowerment and a major shift in my outlook on life; my attitude going back in to an up spiral motion, as I dove deeper into learning about healthy eating, healthy thinking, and healing the body naturally in these ways.

I had been ignoring my connection with Anthony the two years leading up to this crisis, especially during my pregnancy, after the ultrasound incident, and throughout the first year of Rubin's life. During this time, I was merely doing my best to stay afloat and survive.

What had Debbie Hayler said to me back in 2007? That I had "until the end of 2008 to step in to my power, or the rug would be pulled out from under me." Boy, was she not kidding.

It wasn't until my diagnosis, and the fact that my life was crumbling all around me, that on my way to my first yoga class in nearly two years, of course, I heard one of Anthony's songs, and it totally uplifted my spirits.

It was as though I could feel him sending this message to me that everything was going to be all right, that he was going to help me, through his presence in my life via his music, and that I could heal myself. From then on his presence has remained with me, stronger and stronger all the time, now nearly six life-altering years later at the time of this writing.

At the time of my diagnosis in July 2010, I had already been vegan for 12 years, but I eventually took health and eating to a whole new dimensional level by cutting out processed foods and sugars, and anything that was not in its whole food state and 100% certified organic.

The majority of my new diet consisted of raw foods, and eventually, after much cleansing and approaching health and healing from many different angles, I regained my health, the process of which I will share in another book in the near future. I had become self-empowered and regained my will to live back in full swing.

I started the process of writing this book in May of 2011. It was Mother's Day weekend. Paul had raised money for me and my healing journey during one of the live tapings of his Vancouver-based televised Variety Show, "Paul Anthony's Talent Time," during which he raised 400 US dollars and sent it to me.

I was so grateful for this unexpected gift and wanted to use it in the most healing way possible. I decided I wanted a weekend to myself, at a holistic spa, being nourished and treated through massage, saunas, steams, morning yoga, nourishing healthy raw organic food and some down time to simply be with Me, Myself and I.

No mama duties, no "wife" duties, only me. I had never had that before.

Jeff booked it all through our friend Sharon, who was working as a massage therapist at one of the local resorts in Sedona at the time. He even threw in a couple hundred dollars of our own and so with Sharon's "friends and family" discount, I was able to enjoy three days and two nights there, meanwhile receiving two incredibly healing massages, a seaweed body wrap, a facial, and a mani/pedi. There was even free yoga each morning. It was pure heaven.

I started the process of writing this book that weekend. In truth though, it wasn't actually "this" book. Only a few short weeks before this mini-vacation had it ever even occurred to me to consider writing a book at all. But after being knee deep in my own personal healing process and having already learned so much, I was feeling very grateful for my life and felt called to share my experiences—all the methods I was using to heal—with anyone and everyone I could.

I was feeling better and better all the time, so I wanted very much to help other people and to make a difference in at least one other person's life, if at all possible. If my writing a book could do even that, then I would feel that my health issues, and I, had served a greater, higher purpose.

That was May 2011. It started slowly, but I was very excited and determined to do this, and to be of service in this way.

I had no idea that in only two short months from then, "the book" that I had been comprising of my own recipes, health tips, and personal healing modalities, etcetera, would take an incredibly unexpected turn.

I still plan on writing that healing book someday, sharing my healing journey as well as my recipes and fun food ideas, with an emphasis on raising healthy children.

So, *that* book will come at some point, I am sure.

Much to my surprise though, it was not this one. There was a different book I needed to write, and it had to come first, even though before this point I had never even considered becoming an author, let alone sharing such deeply intimate and very raw parts of my own Soul Journey.

Even when I did get the feeling I was to write a book, I only thought I would write one book. It goes to show that we can know so much in some respects, but we don't ever have the entire picture laid out for us.

We have to journey on this path and learn as we go for much of it, embracing the mystery of not knowing, and forging ahead anyway.

CHAPTER 59

The Cosmic Lightning Strike: Discovery of the Vanishing Twins

On July 16, 2011, I attended a regenerative whole foods preparation workshop. A friend of mine was leading it, and I assisted with her demonstrations and clean-up in exchange for the class fees at a local healing retreat center on the outskirts of Sedona. It was here that I met a woman named Sierra, who also attended the day's events. The instant I met her, I felt an inexplicably strong connection with her. I didn't know what this connection was, but I knew it was there.

At this point, I was open to my connection with Anthony again, yet I was still shut down from my Galactic Knowingness. I still viewed all of my experiences as something out of my control, random, and unfortunate. I didn't realize these experiences were even connected with my multi-dimensional work with Anthony. I was still in the dark about a lot of the deepest aspects of myself, basically.

At the end of the day, as I was helping clear the dinner plates, bringing them to the kitchen to be washed, I heard Sierra and two other women who were there that day talking. I heard the word extraterrestrials and I stopped dead in my tracks.

Someone was finally *talking* about "them." This woman I had just met, who stood over six feet tall—this ageless, beautiful Amazonian woman, was sitting here talking about extraterrestrials!

I had to get in on this conversation and see what she actually knew. My hunch was strong that she had some of the answers I'd been searching for years to find. The two other women she was talking with, one being her partner at the time, and the other, a woman we'd met that day for the first time, all seemed to know something, so I raced over to join them, knowing I could not miss this opportunity.

It was suddenly clear to me that this was the real reason I'd been drawn to be there that day. Finally, *someone* I could question and talk with about my experiences! I had waited 15 long and lonely years for this opportunity, and here it was, at long last.

I sat down next to Sierra and was obviously very eager to get in on their conversation. Sierra was warm and inviting. She asked me if I'd had "experiences," and without hesitation I launched in to the last one I'd remembered, which was the dreaded ultrasound day, January 2, 2009.

I also shared with her about my very first conscious experience that had occurred in my dream state, where something was implanted into my left palm and where I'd awoken the following morning with the pain deep inside my rectum.

I was not expecting what she was about to share with me next. She took my palm in her hand, and felt around. Sure enough, there was a small bump in there that was hard, and felt square in shape, and then it all became blindingly obvious. I couldn't believe I had never thought to feel for it before. Clear as anything, I could sure feel it in there now.

This discovery really threw me for a giant loop. Then Sierra started launching into questions, asking me if I knew what the "Vanishing Twin" phenomena was. I had no clue what she was talking about, though it wasn't too difficult to hazard a guess what it involved by the name of it.

I knew deep down in my soul what she was about to launch into, when suddenly, flashes of both my pregnancies began. I had thought I was pregnant with twins both times; certain at one point during both pregnancies that I was having a boy and a girl, only to physically birth one baby each time, both boys. During both pregnancies though, I was "given" girls' names, which I always found peculiar.

Then there was the subject of both sets of ultrasound pictures from both pregnancies "mysteriously vanishing," not to mention the strangest experience with my ultrasound when I was pregnant with Rubin. How both my babies had odd-shaped heads in their own ways, Rubin's being most obvious and prominent, and Noah's simply being very large, much larger than average.

Next in my mind were all those odd noises in our home when I was pregnant with Rubin, synchronistically occurring after my experience in Vancouver. And on, and on, and on the flashes passed before my inner eye.

And how could I forget the fact that my first born, Noah, had become almost obsessed with "aliens" as soon as we moved to Sedona, before I ever knew what Sedona was all about? He even requested his first birthday party at age five be an "alien party" and asked me to make him an alien cake. I did so, and it ended up looking like a green Zeta, or "Grey," which were the only "aliens" I knew of at the time. Rubin was just shy of three months old during these festivities, rocking his beautifully-shaped skull in all its glory. It was so prominent when he was a newborn, an apropos "party gear," I suppose.

My head was spinning, connecting all of these seemingly random pieces together. Then I realized the connection between my health issues and this experience, and it all started melding together, and very quickly. It was almost too much, and I was overwhelmed and started to cry at this overwhelmingly deep recognition of truth.

Sierra, a Shamanic Healer of Cherokee descent, was also what she termed a "Braided Walk-In." I had never heard of a walk-in before.

For those of you who are new to this term, it occurs when an ET "walks in" to the body of a human who is either on its way out or is needing assistance to complete a certain mission on the planet. It is always a contracted agreement made with the soul of the human before incarnating, so is not at all the same thing as "possession."

The ET will step in to the human earth suit in order to carry out a certain mission or missions, and they may remain in the body and live the rest of the life in that particular earth suit.

Other types of walk-ins may be temporary, and will work with a human soul and, either take over for a period of time, or merge or "braid" with the human soul so that the mission is carried out to completion through their joint efforts to complete certain missions. They may stay for minutes, hours, days, months, or even years.

The world I had been living in suddenly started to make sense to me for the first time. Others hearing this kind of information might have had their foundations rocked, but for me, it was like life was finally beginning to make some sense.

My head was still reeling with all of this new information though, as it was a lot to process. Yet for the first time in my life I was meeting someone whom I felt comfortable with that actually knew what I was talking about. I was finally getting some help and long-sought-after answers.

I experienced a feeling of being "home." A whole new view of this world and my life began to awaken, quickly, inside of me. It felt amazing. Though I had no idea what to expect from here, I just knew it all felt right.

Similar to my DNA Activations with Anthony, I could feel it happening here as well. I didn't know about DNA Activations at the time, but I would soon learn about them and come to identify these physical and cosmic experiences as such.

Sierra has her own story to tell, and I won't tell it for her, but suffice it to say, this was a woman who was giving me some serious food for thought to chew on as my own neurotransmitters were firing with waves of truth-recognition like I had never known before. Sierra also assured me that there were, indeed, many others like us here. This is the day I learned about "starseeds."

You see, Sierra was the one who led me to Selene, which I knew instantly was a Divine Appointment we'd set up long before coming here; an appointment I am forever grateful to both her and myself that we kept.

CHAPTER 60

Celestial Healing: Meeting My Pleiadian Sky Children

Two days after meeting Sierra, I had an appointment scheduled with my dear friend and lymphologist, Dr. Tapzyana Thomas. It was July 18, 2011 and I was still reeling from the weekend I'd had, and the new level of consciousness I had been cracked open to.

Once again, my experiences with extraterrestrials were front and center in my waking consciousness, but this time, I could no longer ignore them. I was actually begging to feel a greater sense of connection with "them" for the first time ever. In actuality, what was really happening was that I was begging for a deeper connection with myself.

It was in this session that, not only after a year and a half of trying non-stop to heal myself, did I witness my connection with these majestic beings—*my ET family*. I also witnessed the miraculous, as three blue orbs descended upon me and removed every last mutated cell from my body with one fell swoop. Quickly, effortlessly, and with the greatest of ease, grace, and Unconditional Love.

I went into a lucid state, and it was there that I met my two daughters from both of my pregnancies, neither of which I'd ever consciously met before. My Pleiadian hybrid sky children, Satya and Maya.

They were stunningly beautiful beings standing in front of me, and my eyes transformed into sacred running rivers upon this profound soul recognition of both of them. Tears that were releasing years and years of pain and sorrow from the unrecognized, unconscious disconnection from my own Authentic Soul. It was so very healing for me.

These exquisite specimens were a perfect mixture of beautiful humanistic characteristics, swirled with very subtle shape differences in their eyes; a little larger and more pointed on the outer edges. Their skin was blue and had a golden glow to it. Additionally, they held a very high energetic frequency, with the presence of colours surrounding them that I have no Earthly words to describe other than cosmic.

Both were tall, slender, fully-grown, and absolutely magical to me. Their energy matched perfectly with that of the stars, twinkling, sparkling, and yet incredibly grounded and powerful all at once. These beautiful beings walked together, from what I remember, hand-in-hand, both smiling warmly at me. It was a spectacular meeting.

They told me telepathically to continue to stay open and if I could do so, I would receive all the guidance I needed to continue healing and remain in a consistent state of good health.

They assured me that they were always with me, available to assist me, and both thanked me for helping give them life.

Later on that evening, in my nightly meditation before bed, I was given the information to eat mostly liquids in the form of green juices and pure, raw smoothies, as well as to be sure to ingest plenty of berries, namely blueberries, every day. It was also suggested I begin enjoying grapefruits, and large amounts of water daily.

Then I was shown a symbol in which to place my hands directly over the area of my body most in need of Divine Healing. It was the shape of a triangle, a pyramid. I was informed that I would still be assisted in my healing process regardless if I used this symbol or not, but that if I were to make a conscious effort to create and lay it upon my body as such, this would make the healing assistance I was already receiving much more efficient and streamlined. It was like honing in on the energies in order to make them stronger and much more direct, with faster Earthly results.

I began to religiously implement this healing symbol every single day, every time I would meditate. However, I didn't actually follow the diet regimen for some time; having to prepare food for my family proved challenging for me to eat so minimally and simply myself. When I finally did begin to employ these dietary shifts, I immediately noticed very positive effects begin to take place inside and out. I felt a million times lighter and noticed a significant shift in my digestion, not to mention my overall sense of mental and emotional balance, well-being, energy, and health.

As soon as I shifted to the eating guidelines I had been given, my life shifted rapidly. For the first time, full, integrative, deep, permanent healing seemed not only probable, but inevitable.

I was so incredibly grateful for this new conscious connection with the Pleiadians, my children, *my cosmic family*.

CHAPTER 61

Witnessing Galactic Agreements

I began to unravel a whole new part of my self, and it continued to surprise me and awaken inside of me more and more. Everything began to fall into place. I was making new friends, coming together with "soul family" who were on similar paths as I was. Of course, I was coming into contact with people who knew all about the hybrid children, some of whom were hybrids themselves. I would later find out from Selene I was one as well. Nearly everyone I began to meet seemed consciously aware of their own connections with this particular mission, and were popping up in my life everywhere.

I noticed increased activity in both my children with things they were coming and sharing with me. Very often, this involved telling me of their nightly experiences aboard spacecraft with other dimensional beings and ETs. I hadn't even told them any details of what I had been recently experiencing or discovering. It all just seemed to happen simultaneously, *synchronistically,* almost as if when I got "turned on," so did they.

I began to see my children, as well as myself, in a whole new light. I could see our galactic light. Probably the most accurate light we have ever held. I wasn't "trying to fit us into any sort of mold either. I was simply seeing everything around me with newly activated eyes, and listening with my newly awakened ears, noticing much more intricate layers of Who We Already Were. It was all so beautiful and fascinating to me and I knew my life was never going to be the same as a result.

I received experiential confirmation of these new awakenings in many forms the following November 2011, which was a mere four months after meeting Sierra and learning about Selene.

My galactic GPS started beeping big time, and I was in the fast lane on the cosmic highway of my own awakening.

I had my first session with Selene on September 26 of 2011, where my cosmic DNA crystals just popped all over the place. The confirmations about Who I Am were so empowering and they felt so right, it was a reading like I had never experienced before. After that, I began to fast-track into hyper-space, quite literally.

In November of that year, I was certain that I had become cosmically impregnated, and not through Jeff. I was absolutely certain I was pregnant though, and was also certain that the ET beings I was now aware of doing multi-dimensional work with, had somehow impregnated me. I could feel it in the core of my being. I was also certain this was not the first time; it was merely the first time I was consciously aware of it.

I was internally searching for my own unique Divine Truth, for that inner spark of ancient knowingness that would lead me to personal empowerment in every sense of the word. I had started this journey during my physical healing, and now it continued, on the spiritual healing I was deep in the midst of.

I really tried to accomplish this whilst staying True to myself within my marriage. I didn't want to just throw it away because I was changing. But I certainly was not willing any longer to give up my self, my health, or my truth, for *anyone*—not even my husband.

I had been searching non-stop, day and night for the past year and a half, to discover a way to not only regain my will to live, but the ability to thrive, with greater clarity and strength than ever before.

The Goddess inside of me had begun to Awaken. I knew my life had a Greater Purpose and that I was only beginning to uncover the truth of what that actually meant.

To me, it became all about what was feeding me the inspirational life force, the creativity, excitement and sense of divine purpose that would re-spark my inner flame. Because without this necessary ingredient, what was the point?

From my perspective, this was as high stakes as literally choosing life over death. It was during this time of awakening that I met another Pleiadian walk-in, within days after meeting Sierra and learning about Selene in July 2011. His name was Mynzah.

Mynzah lived in California, and we somehow became social media "friends" when I somehow discovered his page and his artwork during my intense online researching I dove into after being activated on July 16th. One day I felt a pull to connect with him personally, and wrote him a private message, thanking him for his artwork and his messages he shared on his page. It was then he told me he was actually moving to Sedona within a week or so, and trusted our paths would cross.

The very first day he got to Sedona, we both ended up at the same function for a Full Moon Ceremony. I had no idea before I'd committed to going that Mynzah would also be there. It was like some other unseen force was bringing us together.

We did not speak much that evening, but when we all walked the labyrinth, our hands brushed against one another, and he later told me he'd done that on purpose. I did not know then that starseed codes can be passed on through physical touch, but I do now.

Mynzah and I met up again, also synchronistically, at an 11-11-11 gathering at Bracken Cherry and Nina Joy's galactic rainbow dome home in the Village of Oak Creek, where we connected one on one for the first time. We planned to go on a hike together at the Bell Rock vortex on November 14, 2011, right at the gateway of the most activating time for me: November Pleiadian Line Up.

Mynzah quickly became a very significant person in my life at this time. I began spending more and more time with him. I quickly came to realize he was not a "new" friend at all, but an ancient member of my soul family. In essence, he was one of my many soul mates. I don't use the term "soul mate" exclusively to mean a romantic involvement either, though often we experience these kinds of connections with soul mates romantically as well. Jeff is also a soul mate of mine. My connection with Mynzah went beyond these romantic aspects though.

Unseen forces definitely drew us to the same place at the same time, and Mynzah and I both realized that we knew one another already upon our first Earthly encounter. It was definitely synchronistic that we had been brought together and were reunited, this time in the form of a deep, ancient Brother/Sisterhood.

Our connection was so easy and comfortable for both of us; we could talk about our deeply metaphysical and otherworldly experiences in one breath, and then laugh about our dysfunctional or wild Earthly lives and experiences with such a lighthearted affinity and detached amusement in the next. It was purely magical and exactly what my soul desperately needed at the time. More laughter and fun, mixed with the safety and openness of being able to express my metaphysical awareness and experiences, who I really was, without judgment. I was in heaven over this newfound connection and cherished our friendship immensely.

Mynzah's Sun is in Scorpio. This was interesting for me and ignited the blood crystals in my DNA when I found out that he physically embodied the Male Scorpio Sun energy. I had spent a major portion of this lifetime working to clear and purify this exact energy, and I never knew why. This also happens to be Anthony's Sun Sign, so my connection with Mynzah felt healing and activating for me in many multi-dimensional ways. My connection with him helped ground these energies into the physical plane.

What is especially interesting to me now is that Mynzah was already aware of Anthony's conscious connection with the cosmos, of Anthony being *Awake*. He appreciated his band's music and recognized this celestial connection in Anthony's channeled lyrics, which, not surprisingly, often include small (or larger) hints of the cosmically metaphysical and multi-dimensional aspects of Existence.

Mynzah was well aware of this, to a depth that even I wasn't yet, and so, though we didn't really talk much about it, to me our friendship felt in alignment with the work I was doing "out there" with Anthony. It somehow helped ground it more physically for me during this "unfolding of the great mystery" process, being able to share so openly together in this way and with such a profound depth of mutual knowing, understanding, and non-judgment.

Anthony has openly shared in interviews about his writing process, how the whole band writes together actually, and how he literally "receives" his lyrics through the channeled flow of the Divine Cosmos, streaming through him while in his creative "zone."

This is no act of coincidence that this would be the soul I have been so intimately connected with since I was but a young girl. I was being prepped in order to make this connection, to have this awakening, to do this work, since I was a child. And once the pieces began to finally fall into place, it has been like a domino effect all around me. Truly and endlessly fascinating.

It wasn't until I'd started waking up to my ultimate truth in the summer and fall of 2011 though, that I really began to see, from a cosmic and galactic perspective, this aspect of my connection with Anthony.

Of course, it was there all along. It was one of the major missing pieces to the puzzle of my existence I had been searching for so many years. A combination of listening to his music and reading his lyrics may have helped speed up my understanding, but I honestly don't think so. I would never have fully "Known" until it was Time. Until I was ready.

The difference now was that I was finally ready.

Until July 2011, I'd had no idea what the Pleiades were, nor my deep, personal soul connection with them; with this aspect of my self. So there were codes in Anthony's music I may have received unconsciously, but receiving them consciously after I was fully awakened and ready was a wholly amplified experience, deeply activating and soul-purifying for me.

I had not been ready for this type of activation until after I began to consciously awaken to my Pleiadian Soul Origin and my main mission and purpose for being here on the planet now. The root of my cosmic connection with Anthony.

So, when I recognized that familiar feeling of having been impregnated, even though I knew it was not humanly possible, I now *knew* how real these experiments were, and I panicked inside. I knew my friendship and connection with Mynzah was already pushing major buttons in my marriage and creating a lot of discomfort and fear in Jeff. Couple that with feeling sure that my body was now being used as part of an ET genetic experiment at the same time, it was just too much for me to have to explain in Earthly terms to my husband.

I was also honouring my body's need to complete its healing process. I didn't want to even entertain the idea of growing another baby inside my womb space at that delicate stage in my healing and ultimate awakening. Would I be asked to carry this galactic seed I sensed inside of me physically? I knew what Jeff would think, and the kinds of issues that a surprise, "impossible" pregnancy would likely cause in my marriage. After all, how does one explain to their logical, rationally-minded spouse that they feel they've been impregnated by way of extra-dimensional ET frequencies?

Now come on! I really didn't want to have to go there...*yet* anyway. And boy, would I ever be asked to go there, and then some, many months later. But right then, I didn't know this, and it all was so new to me, and I was just trying to hang on to my sanity and my normal life for as long as I possibly could.

CHAPTER 62

The Meeting Room Part II: Bridging the Worlds & Uniting the Races

I pleaded desperately with my sky family, whom I had only recently been newly reunited with, and begged of them that if they had impregnated me, to please consider my situation and to please cut me some slack and not make me have to go through a third dimensional explanation of a "fifth-and-beyond" dimensional experience.

I really needed my own time to understand and process this new way of viewing my world. And though I appreciated the confirmation of my experiences, I wasn't really willing to have to go through any third dimensional drama in order to prove it to myself. That would not serve me, or anyone for that matter.

I asked that if they had impregnated me, then would they please be so kind as to remove the baby as soon as possible to allow my healing body and my unstable home life to adjust to these new frequencies I was quickly inhabiting more and more on the daily. I was still willing to serve in the creation of this being, I simply was not willing to endure a third dimensional experience that may accompany it right then.

The morning following this plea, I awoke to Noah, cute as ever, stretched out on the living room floor all sleepy-eyed, telling me all about his dream from the night before in which he'd been on a spaceship, practicing flying and playing games, surrounded by "all different kinds of aliens" as he described them. I am quite certain now he was playing with, teaching, and learning from, the hybrids.

Noah now refers to them as "extraterrestrials" like me.

When he was as young as six or seven, he'd started telling me about his "sibling," Zola, and his visitations with her. Upon waking this morning of November 15, 2011 though—which also happened to be Pleiadian Lineup, he was talking about and describing in detail, the different races of ETs from his dream the night before, which he also noted felt "very real."

What was really interesting to me, and a perfect example of synchronization being confirmation, was that at the same time he'd been having his experience aboard the ship, I too was also aboard ship in my "dream time," having a similar experience, though in a meeting room. My experience also encompassed many different races of extraterrestrial and interdimensional beings. The exact same races of beings that Noah had just described to me were the same ones present in my own experience.

It was uncanny that, detail for detail, the races he went on to describe to me, I'd had the exact same recollection of having been aboard ship with, on the same night. Only, instead of playing, I was in a board meeting and we were discussing issues related to the Shift in Consciousness we are currently undergoing here on the planet and how each of us were being called in to service, as a collective, in support of this shift.

There was a very strong sense of Brother/Sisterhood in the air during this meeting. It was very respectful, each race honouring the others deeply and what we all uniquely brought to the table for the greater good of the planet, and the Universe as a whole. There was a great sense of peace and camaraderie present among and between everyone that was palpable and strong. It was a very powerfully focused and successful meeting.

I was a representative for the Earth Humans. I did not remember the specific content of our meeting at the time—I was so taken with Noah's parallel experience. I am quite certain now though, especially because of Noah's involvement and experience that night, it most likely involved the hybrid children experiments, both on planet Earth and off, and the bridging of the worlds we were all working to create together. After all, I already knew I was very probably pregnant with a hybrid at that time.

Noah goes through his own training at night in his dream state, and he has often told me about the things he gets to do, and how he trains to fly, flip, and use his body in otherworldly ways, such as creating fire with his hands and learning how to manipulate and use it. He has also told me about training for battle and how to use things such as swords and other non-earthly weapons in the event he ever needs to call on these skills one day.

At the time of this experience, Noah had started sharing these kinds of details with me, even though he was never exposed to these things in the media, and I never spoke about them with him either.

It was only after he started talking about his "training" and "experience dreams" to me that I began showing him certain films (at my parental discretion of course, as he was still technically a child) that I thought might help give him a third dimensional outlet for these experiences in an effort to help curb his frustrations of not being able to do these same things in his waking state.

I have allowed him to see movies such as *Contact, The Last Airbender, The Last Mimzy,* as well as other inspiring films such as *Peaceful Warrior,* which all deal with supernatural or metaphysical content with a positive message in order to hopefully give him that outlet I feel he needs and is asking for from me. And it seems to work! He loves them and gets incredibly inspired by them. They always seem to open him up just a little bit more to himself, which is always a beautiful sight to behold as a mother.

This parallel dream encounter was not the first nor the last time I would consciously dream or go aboard ship together with Noah. I had no idea what was in store for us, and I'm grateful for this, because I'm not sure I could have handled it if I had known.

CHAPTER 63

The Gentle Giant

November and December 2011 was a time that was jam-packed with mystical and otherworldly phenomena. In fact, it had been since right before the 11-11-11 gateway that things really started to accelerate for me.

I'd had my session with Selene on the 26th of September. At precisely midnight on the 25th of October, almost a month to the day after this session, I was awoken from my sleep to a series of non-stop visions clearly penetrating my Third Eye, moving in a pulsating rhythm at what felt like the speed of light. This experience lasted until precisely 4 am. As quickly as it had begun, it stopped.

Four hours of wide awake, continuous visions of my possible "future," of the work I am doing, the work I would do. Visions showing me my friend Mynzah's artwork, of the whales, dolphins and mer-people. Visions of Who I Am, connections to be made in this lifetime, all moving so quickly I can only recall but a few, though my consciousness holds these memories deep inside, etched there permanently on a cellular level, I am convinced of this.

In the moment, these images were so clear. Some were even shown to me multiple times throughout those four hours. All were absolutely incredible and powerful. It was intense and spectacular, and I had no idea what was happening. I had zero control over the experience. All I could do was lie in bed and receive the visions via my Third Eye, or pineal gland. My physical eyes ceased to exist during this time, and only my Third Eye was active.

I remember being in the midst of this experience, unable to see the clock, or anything but the visions, after initially waking up and noting the clock reading precisely 12:00 am. Once I was awakened by this invisible force, I was unable to fall back asleep. I was in a state of such energetic hyper-awareness, that the images I was being shown were all that existed.

At exactly 4 am the visions stopped, my physical eyes were "turned back on" and I was able to go back to sleep. I knew something huge had just occurred, but was not exactly sure what it all meant.

A succession of events would unfold after this that completely shifted me to a much higher frequency, which was why I was able to go on to have other dimensional experiences aboard certain craft at night in the months that followed, and be permitted to remember them.

November 1st has come to be a significant day for me in my awakening process, for reasons that are personal, as well as the fact that they begin what some term The Holy Trinity Months. The Holy Trinity Months begin this day each year, and last until January 11th of the following year. So being activated in time for this, I am sure, was important for me and the experiences I was being prepared to have.

I attended a gathering at the Xanadu domes in Sedona where a big 11-11-11 Gateway gathering was happening from morning until midnight that night. I participated in meditations in the main living space of this home, then occupied by none other than some old and dear friends of Selene's, of which she was present for at least two of their daughter's cosmic births. Talk about synchronicity and "small worlds." Selene lives in another state, not even close to Arizona soil at all. I'd met these friends of hers before I'd ever even heard of or met her.

It was a wonderful gathering, filled mainly with higher consciousness, joy and celebration. There was music, interesting speakers, and this is where I first had the chance to sit and talk with Mynzah, who was also there. I had only met with him in the flesh once before, in the summer time, at the Full Moon ceremony the very day he moved to Sedona from California. I was one of the very first people he met here.

When we ran into each other at the gateway gathering (there were more than a hundred people at this gathering) in the kitchen dome, he left his other friends and asked me to join him where the band was setting up to play.

We listened together and enjoyed some light conversation. I had Noah with me, who was seven at the time, and he came to sit with us as well. After a while, I took Noah home to bed, as he was tired, and it was later than usual for him so he was ready to go.

Before this surprise meeting, Mynzah and I had already set a date to meet up for a hike at the Bell Rock vortex to hang out and get to know one another. We both knew it was time for this.

I had contacted him after my night of visions, since his artwork was a prominent part of this activation, and I felt I needed to share that information with him. It was then that we set the date for our hike, both knowing this activation for me was a call for us to make a deeper connection. I found out a month or so later that Mynzah's birthday is October 26th, so it is extra interesting to me that I was having this experience within 24 hours of his birthday, perhaps even during his Solar Return. Synchronicity working its mysterious magic again.

We arranged for me to pick him up from a small café here in town on a cool, windy, slightly rainy afternoon here in Sedona on November 14, 2011. My family knew where I was, who I was with, and all seemed fine. Jeff said he was fine with it, and I believe he was at the time.

Mynzah and I went to the Bell Rock vortex together. We hiked up to the little side vortex, talking and getting to know one another. It was delightful and we both seemed to enjoy being in the presence of a galactic friend we could feel at ease with and say whatever we wanted to say without the risk of seeming weird or crazy. For me, it was such a breath of fresh air.

When we were in the vortex, Mynzah told me that his guidance was letting him know that I was to have one of the crystals in his medicine pouch he carried. He had them already sitting out on the rocks as we sat in meditation together.

I was surprised by this, but could also feel there was a crystal that indeed wanted to come with me. It was a purple amethyst shaped like a square pillar with an apex at the tip. It was only an inch or so in size, so I could carry it with me in my pocket.

I began to carry this crystal, along with a quartz crystal that Sierra had given to me on July 17, 2011, the day after we first met. Sierra was my initial connection to learning about star-seeds, hybrid children, and most importantly, Selene. Sierra, of course, was also a Pleiadian seeded walk-in.

This day at the vortex was when I learned that Mynzah was too. Two Pleiadian walk-in friends in a matter of a few months came in to my life. And both had gifted me with a crystal.

I slept with both of these crystals each night in bed with my two sons, as Jeff slept in the other room. In essence, the three of us, my sons and I, slept with the crystals. I see clearly now that these energies were only meant for us.

I received information through these crystals while in meditation and while I slept. As synchronization always works, things amped up for both the boys and me. Our connection with ETs and our conscious experience with them was growing stronger each day, and I never once told my children about the experiences I was having, so knew I was not influencing them or creating ideas in their heads. Looking back on this time still makes the hairs on my arms stand on end to think about.

Mynzah and I had shared an instant connection right from the start, as if we had known one another for lifetimes. He was already awakened quite fully, and I was getting there. Being in his presence accelerated my own awakening, which was why I craved to be in his presence as much as possible. I loved what was happening to me as a result of our long conversations and our incredible sense of ease together. I had not felt that comfortable to be fully myself in someone's presence in a very long time. It was helping me heal in so many ways. I even noticed my physical body started to regenerate and I started looking and feeling younger and more vibrant again. It was truly spectacular, and something I obviously wanted to continue experiencing.

The night of November 14th through the morning of the 15th, after having spent the day with Mynzah, is when Noah and I both had our dreams of being on a spacecraft. He was in a classroom or play room, and I in a board room, both of us meeting with the same myriad of other ET races.

I was beginning to feel like I had been impregnated. I wasn't sure if I was imagining this with all of my newfound awareness as far as the ETs and their genetic experiments went, but I knew something inside of me and my womb space definitely felt different.

I hadn't been intimate in my marriage for a long while, so there would be no way of explaining to Jeff if I were pregnant. I knew this much, and was not ready to deal with this. I felt I had been through enough, and didn't feel it was fair to ask me to have to do this, knowing the havoc it would wreak in my marriage and my life.

So, I pleaded with my star brothers and sisters, asking that if they were indeed working with me in this way, if they had indeed seeded a hybrid baby in my womb like I suspected, to please, *please* at least cut me a little slack, and not make me have to explain an unexplainable pregnancy. I couldn't handle one more thing on top of everything else that was constantly being thrown my way. I mean, I was embracing it all as much as I could, but I was drawing the line at a possible physical pregnancy that I could not explain to anyone, except maybe Mynzah or Selene.

I trusted that if I were right, the ETs intentions were not to ruin my life, so I waited, patiently, with all the faith I could muster, that this situation would be handled.

Three nights later, on November 18, 2011, it happened again. Remember, this all occurred during the Pleiadian Alignment, which makes it even more potent and powerful, as this specific alignment is my most activating time, and has been throughout my life. This was when I first experienced the massive mothership in plain sight, followed by missing time. My Moon sign is at 26 degrees in Scorpio, which is the marking for being directly connected with the Pleiadian ships, especially in November during the Pleiadian Alignment with Earth. At the time though, I still had no real understanding of this.

So, there I was, November 18, 2011, in a lucid multi-dimensional dream state, having an experience, and Noah was right there with me. We were in a large empty house in the middle of a countryside, miles from any other houses. It was winter outside, and I recognized the exact home we were in. We had actually viewed this beautiful home out in Williams, Arizona in the summer of 2011. It was night time, and we could see the starry night sky through the 50-foot high wall of windows leading outside. I was watching Noah fly around the room laughing and playing, all the way up to the ceiling and back down again. He was having a ball, proud of his skills, maybe even playfully showing off a bit.

Amongst the stars, a fleet of about ten or more UFOs were zigzagging, very obviously communicating with us that they were about to land where we were. I had been practicing my discernment and protection capabilities in my waking life, and so in the dream, I began shouting out to them, declaring that only if they were of the Highest Intent and of the light, and coming to assist us in our greater purpose here on the planet, would they be welcome to land and make the encounter with us. I was still getting used to the idea that "they" were also "me," or in this case, "us."

Noah, of course, thought my dramatic display was hilarious. He was laughing joyously and continued on with his game, literally flying up to the 50-foot high cathedral ceiling, whizzing around the room like Peter Pan.

Next thing I knew, the fleet zoomed closer and closer to us, until one of the ships landed right at the front door of the house. The entire energy of the house was electrified with a vibration and buzzing not of this world. It was potent and very distinctive. I knew they were right outside the door.

With this, I opened the front door, and there it was. A ship about 60-feet or so in diameter, round and metal. I didn't see any lights on it at this point, but couldn't see underneath it the way it was stationed.

I stepped out the door and the gateway to the ship opened in front of me. A giant blue being began to descend from it, and the next thing I knew, I was jolted awake from the dream, but the experience was far from over.

I lay there, wide awake in my bed in Sedona. I was fully and completely conscious and awake. I felt the familiar feeling of paralysis when a being of such high frequency and otherworldly origin is near. My body felt like lead. My eyes were wide open, adjusting to the darkness in the room, but then I had to fight to try to keep them that way, the paralysis threatening to overtake them.

Rubin, two-years old at the time, was fast asleep to my right. We had slept together this night just the two of us, while Jeff and Noah slept in the bunk beds in the boys' bedroom on the other side of the small hallway. Noah appeared to be fighting off a cold, and we didn't want the boys sleeping together as they usually did, just in case. So, Noah was not physically in the room with us.

I pried open my eyes, fighting their desperate attempts to close. It took all my might to do so as my eyelids were extremely heavy, but I managed finally. Thankfully, I was able to keep them open for what transpired next. I was not fully in control of them though, and it was as if I was being shown where to look. This is when the stakes raised significantly for me.

I felt my night vision kick in, and I could see very clearly the physical presence of the same giant blue being from the dream I'd just awoken from standing directly to the left of me beside the bed, only about a foot away from me. This being appeared to be anywhere from 7-9 feet tall, from what I could tell being horizontal on my bed; perhaps he was taller, I really don't know. He was massive and blue and his head appeared to touch the ceiling, that's all I knew.

Side Note: *I look back now and realize that these blue beings were not new to me. I used to see them in my bedroom doorway as a child, checking in on me. I thought they were monsters. They were the ones who would often stand beside my bed as I pretended to be dead, thinking that would make them go away.*

What I saw next shocked me (as if I wasn't already!), and sent me into a bit of a panic to be totally honest. Seeing a giant being in a dream state is one thing; seeing them in the flesh so to speak, with eyes wide open, standing next to you in your bedroom in a full waking state is an entirely different level of experience. I had never had such a clear and conscious waking encounter with an ET before this.

Words can't describe the energy in the room. To say that it was beyond high doesn't do it justice.

At first, I was suspicious and wondered what this being was doing there, and had a moment of panic when I thought he (the energy felt more masculine than feminine), this gigantic and very muscularly built being, was about to do something to my babe beside me. But then I saw what he was really there for.

About five feet above me and just to my left, I saw Noah's body, hovering horizontally as if on an invisible bed. He was levitated there. His eyes were closed and he looked to be asleep.

It was not his physical body though, as I could see through his flesh, as if he were transparent. I have since learned about the Ka body, also known as the etheric body, and I am sure that is what I was witnessing. But he was there, unmistakably, and this blue being was doing what appeared to be some form of energy healing, similar to Reiki, though something entirely different, over him. It was surreal, and unlike any other experience of my life to date.

The whole scene was peaceful. Yet, to be wide awake, paralyzed, seeing a blue giant beside me, my seven-year old child transparent and hovering over my bed, this mysterious giant doing some sort of energy work on him, well, it was a trip.

This being seemed to be extremely gentle, as big as he was. However, this was all still quite new to me, especially the connection with my son. So as I said, a wee bit of panic set in and my mama bear instincts were ignited in a major way.

As anyone who has ever had one of these experiences can attest to, the mental focus and energy it requires for our human minds to communicate with these beings is phenomenally astounding and can zap every ounce of strength and energy you feel you possess.

Indeed, it did take every ounce of my strength and focus to say to this being telepathically that only if he were a being of the Highest Light, and if he were here with the Highest Intent to support Noah and me with our Missions on this planet, and only if he were fully embodying the highest light from whence he came to be of assistance, then and only then was he welcome to stay and continue working with my son. I gave my heartfelt gratitude for such an act of love and service, if this was his true intent. However, if he was of any other vibration or intent, he would be banished from our home immediately and would not be permitted further contact or access to us.

I managed to get this full statement out somehow, and repeated it at least once, maybe even twice more. I held this communication very clearly and with great command, though it required everything I had to keep expressing it and holding my field strong. I have no idea how long this went on, as time has an uncanny way of ceasing during such encounters. The important thing is that I got the communication out, and he heard me.

Yet he remained, holding his hands ever so calmly and gently over my son, who was still hovering beside me.

Finally, after another minute or two from my perspective, which could very well have been skewed due to the frequencies, Noah vanished, and the blue being cloaked himself. I could still feel his presence there, yet my eyes were no longer able to see him visibly.

He was not finished just yet.

He instructed me telepathically to roll over onto my right side, away from him (towards Rubin), which I did. I was now in a fetal position. I then began to experience the gentlest of procedures occurring in my abdominal area by way of my lower back, and within a few moments, the procedure was complete, and I knew without a shadow of a doubt that I'd just had a baby taken out of me.

I remember saying "*Thank you*" and feeling such an enormous sense of relief, shock and gratitude all mixed together for this gentle giant having heard and honoured my request to not be asked to carry a third dimensional seed I could not explain to anyone at this time. It was such a powerful confirmation for me of all I had been newly awakening to within my self.

This time, thankfully, I was able to have the experience of having served in this way, while learning about one of the ways in which this experiment is carried out in the physical realm. In turn, I too was being served and honoured with great respect and love.

This experience was a much less dramatic one than the suction cup vacuum experience during my second pregnancy. Let's just say it was deeply healing for me, and I ended up being extremely grateful for the entire experience. The mysterious hybrid pregnancy, and then the releasing of it directly to the ETs.

I fell back asleep instantly as soon as he left.

When I woke up and realized the full truth of what had occurred, a name suddenly made itself known to me: *Sannaya.* I believed then, and still do, that the being taken from me that night had named herself *Sannaya*.

CHAPTER 64

The Purge

The following day Noah woke up in the morning in a bit of an altered state and remained that way all day. There was nothing wrong with him, he was simply a little more quiet and introverted than usual. He was extremely calm, which was unusual. No other symptoms accompanied this introspective shift, so I left it alone.

He went to school, had a fine day, and as a mother, I had zero cause for concern, so I allowed him to just be. Besides which, I couldn't forget that I had very clearly witnessed him being "worked on" by a blue giant in my room the night before, so I gave him some significant leeway for being a little unusually quiet, even though at the time he consciously recalled nothing of the experience, or so I thought.

Two months later, in January 2012, Noah recited the entire "dream sequence" to me, image for image to what I had also remembered, telling me about this "dream" he'd had "a while ago." In his recollection though, he did not appear to remember anything about the blue being that had landed in the dream experience, and it was just as well. He remembered right up until the ship landed.

Noah's sharing of his dream, and it being exactly what I had experienced, was more than enough confirmation for me. Even if I'd needed it by that point, which I didn't, I knew that the experience had been, unmistakably, real.

The day after the original experience though, at precisely 6:00 pm and in the middle of eating dinner, Noah stood up. Almost as if he were being operated or instructed to by someone else. In a slightly robotic tone he said, "I'm going to bed now."

Anyone who knows my son knows that these are the last words I'd expect to hear from him two hours before his bedtime. He usually stays up as late as he possibly can get away with, and only sleeps by choice when he is not well, so I asked him if he was feeling alright.

"Yeah. I'm fine. I'm just going to go to bed now," he said to me, almost like he was already in the dream state. It was extremely bizarre. Even Jeff was looking from him to me, back to him, then to me, trying to figure out what was going on here.

I asked him if he needed help getting into bed, and he said, "No that's okay." It was as if he were sleep-walking, which I had never seen him do before, especially in a waking state, and this early before bedtime.

I made sure he got into bed alright and told him that if he needed anything, I would be here and would be ready to help. "Okay Mommy. Thank you," said my boy, but it really didn't feel like my boy speaking. He was in a sort of trance, and it felt eerily as though something or someone else was speaking through him.

At exactly 11:00 pm that night, after not hearing a peep from him until then, out walks Noah from his room. A sense of calm enveloped him, and he didn't look at me or say a word. He turned directly into the bathroom, knelt on the floor, opened the toilet bowl and began vomiting out the most heinous looking substance I'd ever seen come from his beautiful little body. It was so incredibly odd because every single movement was made with such grace and precision, like it had been pre-calculated somehow, or there was a puppet master pulling the strings, guiding him through each step.

A thick black-brown sludge began to pump out of his body through his mouth. This is the only way I can describe what I witnessed that night. It was unlike anything I'd ever seen from him before. This substance had the quality of tar or thick sludgy muck, and it kept oozing out of him in a rhythmical heaving motion. It did not look even remotely like anything he'd been eating for the past few days. There were no bits of food, no other colours or textures. Not even water. Absolutely nothing but a thick, black-brown sludge, oozing out of his mouth.

It was incredibly bizarre. The way he was releasing it from his body was unlike any other time I'd seen him vomit before. He would usually panic or cry anytime he was sick to his stomach, which was very rare as it was. This time though, he was cool as a cucumber--easy, peasy, lemon-squeezy--knocking out some of the vilest stuff I'd ever seen in my life.

But I knew what was happening. I instantly made the connection between this "cleansing" that was happening in front of me, and the energy work our blue friend had performed on his energetic body the night before.

I also knew that Noah was an extra sensitive being, having already watched him become seriously ill when the Fukushima radiation fallout occurred and the radiation cloud made its way over Sedona on March 16, 2011. How this affected my son was truly frightening. I witnessed his skin burning red like his entire body had been scorched, something I hadn't seen in a regular illness for him before. He spiked a fever of 104, accompanied by incessant and uncontrollable vomiting. He was unable to stay awake or even move, having to be carried to the toilet just to use the bathroom or throw up. He couldn't eat or drink. It was my worst nightmare.

I was literally seeing the life draining from his little six-and-a-half-year-old body for more than a week straight. He turned greyish-white, his eyes blackened, and I thought I might actually be losing my child. The doctors could do nothing and didn't have any answers. So I was beyond grateful for the assistance from our blue friend, for Noah's benevolent family stepping in when he needed it most.

I knew it right down to my bones that this benevolent being had come to assist my son in clearing this nuclear damage from his physical body, as well as any other toxicity he'd accumulated over his (by then) seven years in his Earth suit.

I was extremely grateful in this moment, witnessing my son purging these poisons from his body, and realized the profound enormity of what I was witnessing this night.

I put my hand on his back and said, "It's okay honey, your body is just getting rid of stuff it doesn't need and what isn't helping you be healthy. It's just clearing all the yucky stuff out," to which he replied with such presence and grounded purity, "I know, Mama." I was amazed by his grace and display of mature knowingness. It was astounding really. This purging went on for several minutes; that non-stop rhythmical pumping, when finally it simply ended.

Noah sat silently for a few moments, entirely still, head down and eyes closed. This was also unusual, and as if he were coming out of his trance. He then turned to look at me, his skin was glowing, and his eyes and his face were clear and bright again. I could see my child in there fully, for the first time that day. He looked at me, his eyes sparkling and dancing and said with such excitement and life in his voice, "Wow! I feel awesome!"

He had an enormous smile plastered on his face. He got up, almost giddy, and I checked to see if he felt warm or had any other symptoms of unwellness as I had also done before he'd lain down earlier that evening. Again, there was absolutely nothing that indicated he was ill in any way. In fact, I hadn't seen him look so healthy and vibrant in a long time! I was truly amazed.

A year later, in December 2012, while experiencing a Dolores Cannon Method quantum healing session, I learned that this exact kind of ET-assisted purging in a child of Noah's age, who is a starseed and/or is part of the hybridization program, is actually common. That often, around age eight or nine (Noah happened to be seven at the time of his purge.), the child's galactic guardians will come and do a healing on them to help clear their system of any toxins picked up in their physical body through their human experience.

I found this whole ordeal even more fascinating, and interestingly, it brought back memories of my NDE hemorrhage experience after my tonsillectomy when I was nine. I wondered again about the mysterious cloaked being that had also shown up, and who performed arm and hand gestures over my body, as I was losing so much blood amidst being polluted by heavy anesthetics, of which I was about to receive more. I now realize that what this being was giving me was not my Last Rites, but rather Healings.

Whether the two experiences are connected, run parallel, or are similar in any way, or if they are entirely different and separate occurrences, I'm not one hundred percent certain. What I am certain about is the way that sludge was pumping out of his mouth, and that it sure brought back distinct memories of my own experience when I was nine.

No doubt about it, the energies of these purges were very similar, which to me, of course, carries the sweet scent of synchronicity yet again.

CHAPTER 65

Goddess Codes Ignited

> *"The snake symbolized power. A very long time ago, in matrilineal cultures, the snake was one of the symbols for the Mother Goddess, the power of the Sacred Feminine. More recently, in spiritual texts written during patriarchal times, the snake symbolized the kundalini life force coiled up at the base of the spine."* ~ Lucia Rene, Unplugging the Patriarchy

Following all of this Pleiadian Line up ET activity, December 2011 continued to harbor many high strangeness experiences, as well as paranormal activity, activations and more dream messages.

I continued to feel a strong pull to spend as much time with Mynzah as I could, as every time I did, more lost pieces would awaken inside of me. It wasn't anything in particular that he did or said necessarily, though this would also be true, but it was also Initiated by the ancient energy we shared together that stirred so many memories for me, especially after we would part ways. These memories would show up through synchronistic events in my life, and would come in many forms, almost all at once as confirmation for my stubborn ego so that there would be no denying it or trying to chalk it up to "coincidence," even if I'd wanted to. Which I didn't.

I'd learned early in childhood, from my mother, that "there is no such thing as coincidence" anyway. For all her challenges, my mother is actually a walking fountain of wisdom waiting to be discovered and lived by. As I said, I am so grateful for these gems she instilled in me at such an early age.

Mynzah was very open with talking about his Kundalini Awakening he'd experienced a year or so before we met. I remember wondering what that experience must be like, pretty certain I had not had a full on awakening of that kind yet myself. I was still living too much in duality and suffering, so was quite certain my energies had not risen fully.

Energies were *definitely* flowing and shifting inside of me, especially since our first encounter together in the Bell Rock Vortex, which naturally tied in to my newest ET experiences, the impregnation and subsequent encounter with the blue being who'd answered my call. I was feeling empowered by my contact with them, more certain by the day of my galactic work, and feeling ready to embrace it, thus embrace my true Self fully, once and for all. I was actually excited!

I was driving Noah to Flagstaff one morning for school, and as I ascended up the final climb of the switchbacks from the depths of the canyon, I noticed a thread of five ravens leading my car, just up ahead of me. They were flying in a formation that was marvelously unmistakable. Weaving in and out of one another like the DNA spiral, they were flying in the pattern of the rising Kundalini. The two serpents weaving in and out of the Seven Chakras, up the spine. Raven was here now to show this to me, with a message that I was on my way, and transformation was indeed taking place. The image was so crystal clear and so stunning, it brought me to tears. I was beyond grateful for this Divine message from Raven. During the six weeks that I spent a lot of time in Mynzah's presence, Raven would often send me clear messages, but this one was by far of the most powerful.

Higher consciousness communications continued to present themselves to me throughout December 2011, where I would go on to receive a series of cryptic messages upon awakening from the dream state, one of which involved my connection with the Egyptian Goddess, Isis. At the time, I knew nothing about Isis except that I'd heard the name before somewhere.

I was napping with Rubin one afternoon in the first couple weeks of December, and had gone into my nap through meditating before I fell asleep. As a mother of two young boys, I often take these quiet times I have before or after resting for my meditations.

We had a blissful nap, one that lasted more than an hour, which was nothing short of monumental for Rubin once he turned two, so I milked any chance I got to drift off and rejuvenate this way with him, always praying this would be "the one" where he'd stay asleep long enough for me to feel rejuvenated.

Usually, my "alarm" to awaken would be Rubin stirring or climbing on top of me to nurse, but this day I awoke before him to a voice, almost screaming at me: "AKASHIC RECORDS!!"

That was it. Simply "*Akashic Records*" was all the Voice said, loud enough to jolt me awake from my slumber with a start, having to catch my breath. Rubin was still fast asleep beside me, and the voice reverberated inside my head with those two powerful words like an echo, and I was unable to tune it out, knowing this was a message from the beyond. But what did it mean exactly?

I'd definitely heard of the Akashic Records through my little knowledge of Edgar Cayce, and knew enough about them to remember that they were like the cosmic record keepers, akin to an invisible living library, of everything that has ever been—every single thought, word, action, or intention ever created by any and every single soul is what comprises these records, right down to the tiniest, most seemingly insignificant detail. *They are all significant.*

I had never studied these files. I had never even felt the need to research them beyond finding out the basics. Having read a couple of books about Edgar Cayce in the decade prior to this experience, I had learned these bare minimum basics. I knew these records contained information about previous and parallel incarnations, but I hadn't given the significance of that aspect of them much thought upon receiving this message.

It was some giant library, I knew that for certain. What on Earth did it mean for me right *now*, I wondered? I thought at the very least there must be something significant about me that I needed to find out that could possibly assist me with all I was suddenly uncovering about myself. I had a feeling that this jarring cryptic message must be referring to something having to do with my own previous or parallel incarnations, and their possible connections in my life and my purpose *Now*.

I'm almost embarrassed to admit that I still didn't research it further, feeling that if there were something more I needed to know, I would be *shown*.

What I did know was that I felt this message loud and clear, as these words continued to reverberate inside of me for days afterwards. Then, life happened and I conveniently forgot about it, chalking it up to one of those random message dreams that I never really figure out.

At this same time, I began feeling a strong pull to begin learning the art of belly dance. This came on suddenly much like when I was a young child and discovered I'd had a deep and mysterious love for this art form, without ever actually having seen it, as I'd mentioned previously.

The way I could roll my stomach muscles so intricately in more than one direction, while moving my hips in all ways also came naturally to me as a child. I remember standing in front of the mirror and watching my stomach roll sensually, as if something alive was moving inside of me. It reminded me of the motion of a snake, and I was always certain a snake was dancing up and down my spine. I had no conscious awareness of the Kundalini Rising, I was only but a child.

This was coupled with that deep yearning to become impregnated and carry a child inside my womb, as I have also already mentioned. These were the soul longings I experienced as a young child; harnessing my Sacred Sexuality and bringing forth Life and Creation.

It is not surprising to me now looking back, that about a week or so after hearing the "Akashic Records" message, followed by my sudden urge to take belly dancing classes, that it happened again.

I awoke from yet another nap to the Voice. This time it was not quite so jarring or pointed, and not yelling in such an intense manner. It was still very loud and clear, yet this time, with a more calming tone: "You are Isis, Mynzah is Osiris."

It was so clear, there was no mistaking the message. But what did it mean? I was not an avid researcher, and had never put any efforts yet into learning about deities of any sort—Goddesses, Gods, or any other kind of historical fact or figure. In fact, I'd always had an aversion to learning history of any sort, much the same as my aversion to extraterrestrials before I witnessed my first starship back in November 1996.

But I knew this message was significant somehow. I knew Isis was considered a Goddess, and I was pretty sure she was Egyptian, but was not certain of even this fact. I jumped up immediately to see if I could decipher what this next cryptic message meant or if it had any connection with the first message about the Akashic Records.

I hopped on the computer to Google "Isis" and was *floored* when I began to take in exactly who this Ancient Egyptian Goddess truly was, and what she symbolized in an esoteric sense. She was known as the Cosmic Mother, and she was also symbolic as a sort of midwife of the afterlife. *Of death.*

What I discovered was beyond fascinating. I received instant downloads that day when I ingested her story, particularly with how her son Horus was conceived. I discovered that Isis was indeed an Egyptian Goddess, but not only that, she was married to her brother, *Osiris*. Out of an act of jealousy, their brother, Seth, murdered Osiris and cut his body up into pieces.

This gave me chills to read, as I couldn't help but picture myself as Isis, and Mynzah as Osiris as the message I'd awoken to had clearly named us as. And yet, who was Seth?

Isis was devastated by the loss of her Divine Counterpart. She ceremoniously gathered the pieces of Osiris' physical body, and put them back together. There are many different versions to this story, but one of them mentions that the only piece she could not find was the phallus. So she went about crafting one out of gold, and in doing so, she was able to resurrect her Beloved. Then, in an act of Sacred Sexual Union she became impregnated with their son, Horus.

This could be seen as an immaculate conception type of impregnation, and I knew by now I'd definitely had these experiences myself; having been told when I was a child of five that I would become impregnated much the same way that Immaculate Conception works. Besides which, how on Earth had I been impregnated only a month earlier anyway? How else could I explain that one away? I needed no convincing of the validity of this type of impregnation.

Yet I was nearly blown off my chair when I read this information. It screamed to me of a very obvious connection with the story of Yeshua and the Virgin Mother Mary. It was then that I noticed a very intriguing connection between these two deities and myself.

Both of these women had supposedly become impregnated in ways beyond what the human mind could comprehend logically and rationally, beyond what the human being was reported to be capable to do.

I, too, had recently discovered my very real experiences of similar supernatural phenomena when the blue being came in to my room and removed a baby from my physical body. This was still all very new to me, but as such, I had already been given a very clear physical demonstration of precisely how this kind of pregnancy can occur. It was ignited by my connection with Mynzah, or as the Voice referred to him, my "*Osiris*," which my blue being friend had so kindly confirmed for me when he removed the fetus from my womb upon my desperate plea.

It was not a coincidence that I received this level of demonstration within weeks before being given this information, cryptic as it was. So, what did it all really mean? And what exactly was the connection here? Was I really Isis incarnate?

I found this hard to believe, especially when I began to notice all over the internet many women who were actually claiming to be Isis incarnate.

I didn't want to make such a bold, egotistical, ignorant statement, and sure as hell wasn't about to broadcast my personal experiences out to the world via social media in that way.

One woman, who was absolutely certain she was Isis Incarnate, would refer to all of her YouTube followers as "her babies" and put herself out in this way, as if she were "the mama" and everyone else were "hers." It was quite disturbing to me. I remember thinking to myself *'Honey, you may think you're the only one, but I hate to burst your bubble - you're not!'* I knew none of us were really special. I knew that there must be many of us out there.

I watched some pretty unsettling things being exchanged between this woman and her "following," and decided to remove myself and all of my energies from such garbage. Anyone truly embodying Isis would not go about broadcasting it in neon lights, trying to get a following of vulnerable souls on their own inner search. How disempowering. It made me sick to my stomach to see this, so I removed myself completely from that whole nonsense.

Yet, I was clearly being shown some sort of Divine Connection with this Goddess Deity, and I could not deny that.

What to do with this information, I wondered? When I told Mynzah about it, and of all I was learning about Isis and Osiris, he was not at all surprised. There was a lot about Mynzah I still didn't know, as he did not easily divulge this kind of information to people. He kept these sorts of things very private. Though he shared a lot of his personal story with me at the time, this was not the type of thing he walked around doing. He is a Scorpio after all.

Synchronization once again gave confirmation here, as Mynzah often seemed to know things about me that sometimes even I didn't know yet. Yet there was still more of this story to unfold...and I would go on to receive greater confirmation still.

Things escalated to where, about seven months after my receiving this initial message, I was sitting in my living room talking with Mynzah when my left breast spontaneously started to leak mother's milk from it, *completely out of the blue*.

This may not sound all that unusual, but the timing of it was very odd. My son was still nursing, yes, but he was also three years old, and my body had stopped any and all signs of "let down" or leaking from my breasts at least a year prior to this if not more. To top it off, it was coming from the breast that naturally produced the least amount of milk. Rubin sweetly referred to my left breast as "Tiny Snack" (the right side, affectionately nicknamed "Big Juicy" by him as well) because of this, and he always favoured the right side, only nibbling on the left for a minute or two each time he nursed.

So, I was totally shocked when I suddenly felt my shirt begin to soak on the left side, as if I'd just had a major let down. I thought I must be imagining it, but then looked down to find my shirt not with just one little drop even, but indeed, my entire left breast was soaked.

I didn't get it at first, I was simply stunned at what was happening. Mynzah understood it right away though, and shared with me that he had recently seen a picture of a statue of Isis that had really struck him and that it had specifically made him think of me - so much so, it had remained in his conscious awareness ever since. The picture came to him by way of synchronicity, from somewhere completely unexpected. So, it had surprised him, though he knew it was not an accident. He knew at the time there was some significance to it showing up for him that day.

In this picture, the statue of Isis was nursing her infant son, Horus, at her left breast. We both sat in awe and amusement at the high strangeness of this event. I didn't really know what to make of it.

Regardless of what any of this meant, at least in some way, these dream-waking messages were sharing with me something about an energetic frequency I was carrying in connection with this Ancient Egyptian Goddess.

I began taking my belly dancing class called "The Goddess Groove" with a local teacher. The class showed up synchronistically in my social media feed immediately after I'd decided I had to learn this art form officially, which of course was no surprise.

What was also synchronistic was that after I'd received the download on Isis, I posted a picture of her on my own social media feed, only a day before seeing this class advertisement. Out of all the pictures from which I chose, the one that was on the website advertising this class was the exact same picture. And it was not one of the most common images one sees when looking up Isis. So that definitely caught my attention and confirmed for me that I indeed needed to take this class.

I loved it! There were definitely belly dancing techniques the instructor taught, but the focus was not only on technique. It was on the yogic principles, the spiritual side, of the art form. The focus was on the sacred geometric patterns, the esoteric, holistic, healing effects of this sacred movement. I was in heaven! The trained contemporary dancer in me was satisfied completely with the techniques, and the wild artist in me was enthralled with the freedom of expression within the movement that was allotted in this class, which was more about the feeling and intuitive movement, rather than the strict boundaries of the form.

I would be carried away to the Otherware amidst the spiraling and breathing, allowing my body to go on its own journey, taking my spirit along for the ride of its life. It was ecstatic verging on orgasmic so much of the time!

About three weeks in to the class, I had been invited by a local yogi here in town to come to his classes for free whenever I wanted. This invite was quite a wonderful surprise, since I really didn't know this man, and had only been to one of his classes before, about six months prior to this invite. That day was the first time we'd met. Admittedly, there was an instant cosmic connection between us. I simply found him to be humourous and silly and besides which, he was a great yoga instructor. I was humbled and honoured by his invitation.

I showed up at his class one morning sometime in mid-January 2012, about a month after receiving the Isis information. I had been settling down from the energies of this discovery, and simply letting it be, not thinking much of it at all by this point, other than enjoying my new dance classes.

Now I was here in this Hatha class, inside a tiny studio at the resort it was held in here in Sedona. Once again, I found this man's little soft spoken puns and jokes (that no one else was laughing at) quite funny. I giggled to myself as I went deeply in to each asana. It actually helped me get through some of the more brutal ones, and made them more enjoyable. I was pretty out of shape by this point in my life, and too much thigh burning lactic acid ignition was not exactly a comfortable or joyous experience.

We were in triangle pose (interestingly the 3-point pose, the triad, the "holy trinity") with my gaze up to the ceiling, enjoying the wringing of the stretch in my spine, when the most incredible vision appeared before me.

The square vent in the ceiling, which was about 2' x 2' in size and filled with tiny holes, came alive. I saw not merely an image of Jesus looking down over me, but rather, *He was alive—moving, blinking, and smiling at me!*

I blinked quickly, trying to adjust and clear my eyes, assuming I must be seeing things that weren't there. This instructor would often have us hold poses for a long time, so I hung out here for quite a while. I blinked, looked away, and breathed deeply; everything I could think of to clear my eyesight, because obviously, I must be seeing things!

Every time I looked back, however, there He was, smiling down at me, almost as if He were giving me a "thumbs up," minus the actual thumbs. He seemed very pleased with me for some reason. I finally realized I was definitely not just "seeing things." Somehow, He was there. Try as I might to erase Him, I couldn't. Jesus had appeared before me.

I felt such a sense of joy and peace at this vision, as I had never before experienced an Ascended Master in my waking reality. I wondered what I had done to deserve this. The whole thing felt very personal, almost as if we were family, in a way, that Jesus was a dear loved one guiding me from the Otherware. It was moving and exhilarating all at the same time!

Amidst basking in this heavenly realization, I felt a nudge within me to glance at Him "upside down," so I turned my focus to look from that angle, and I was blown clean away with what I witnessed.

There, on the other side of Jesus, as if creating a Yin Yang effect, was Mary. First, it was His Mother, and then She morphed into The Magdalene. I was breathless for a moment, in complete and utter awe, as She Herself smiled at me with the warmest, most tender eyes of Love I had ever seen. My eyes filled with tears.

If I turned my focus back up the other way, there was Jesus; if I turned it around, there was Magdalene. I did this repeatedly for a minute, to be absolutely certain I was not just imagining things.

Indeed, they remained, and I realized that these Divine Beings were acting as a living symbolic demonstration of the Yin Yang, Divine Counterparts of the Sacred Masculine and Divine Feminine. Something inside of me already knew what this meant, though to put my knowing into words yet, I could not do, not until more than two years later, when I finally, and synchronistically, came upon the book *The Magdalen Manuscript*, thanks to Tom Kenyon and Judi Sion for writing it.

What I could form into conscious awareness was that somehow, the two Marys were connected. For the majority of the two years following this vision, I would find myself thinking and even occasionally saying out loud to someone in conversation that I felt the Divine Virgin Mary, and Mary Magdalene—The divine feminine counterpart to Yeshua—somehow shared the same Soul, or at the very least were a part of the same divine spark. I didn't quite understand how this could be, as they had lived at the same time, but I didn't know any other way to describe it other than this. All I knew for certain is that they were deeply connected in some divine and sacred way.

This aspect of the vision was always very confusing for me, because I couldn't seem to drop the strong feeling, the knowing, that there was a soul connection between these two Marys that simply went beyond Christ connecting them by way of one being His Mother and the other his divine counterpart. There was much more to it than that, but I had no context to reference to discover just what that was.

I also realized that The Mother had been impregnated cosmically through what I will call, for lack of a better term and to make it more accessible, "Immaculate Conception." It was in that instant that the light bulb of synchronicity sparked and I realized that Isis and Mary were deeply connected, and that their energies were somehow enmeshed in a cosmic sense.

Instantaneously I was downloaded with the intel that these beings—Isis and Mary, Osiris and Christ—are indeed interconnected quite intimately, and at the time I thought perhaps they were the same souls from different timelines, and that I was one (of many) here now who are carrying their energetic frequencies and codes on the planet, for very specific purposes and missions.

I did connect the Isis message I'd received in December and this sighting of Jesus and the Marys in January. I became certain that the two Marys were somehow both connected to Isis in some way. For obvious reasons, the Mother was, yet I also knew that somehow, Magdalene too was connected with this Ancient Egyptian Goddess.

I wondered if my feelings were merely because Isis and Osiris were brother and sister as well as divine counterparts merged in the act of Sacred Union. That in birthing Horus, and then subsequently entering into sacred union with her own son, that the Mother-as-Lover Archetype was somehow connected with the two Marys closest to Christ.

I knew I was missing a significant piece to this very intriguing puzzle, and yet I couldn't seem to find answers. I tried researching things like "Mother Mary and Mary Magdalene soul connection," or "Mother Mary, Mary Magdalene and Isis connection" but never really came up with anything that helped me understand what I had witnessed spontaneously on that auspicious day in yoga class.

So I let it go, as much as I could anyway. I figured that if I was ever meant to know more, I would be shown when I was ready, in Divine Time. And if not, well then, perhaps there was nothing for me to know, and the intrigue would have to end there.

I did wonder why both of these images and messages were coming to me in this way, and why I had been so clearly told that I "*was Isis.*" Especially since after this, as I have mentioned already, I began noticing many women online claiming to also be Isis reincarnated. That was a bandwagon of which I was prepared to steer very clear. I was not trying to be something, or someone I wasn't, I knew that. Yet I was told in an altered state (between sleeping and wakefulness), without any concept of what it meant or for that matter, that it was me who was really Isis.

I feel that in our own ways, many of us have been told the same thing, because there is a rise of the Divine Feminine occurring on the planet as we speak, in 2015 as I write this, and that at least one of the energies needing to come back to help bring the planet back in to balance are the Isis and Magdalene Codes.

This is a time of huge transformation. So many of us carry these ancient Codes of Mary and Isis, two of the most powerful, sacred and divine goddesses in existence. And many carry the codes of other goddesses, for the same core purpose. We all carry these codes with a strong sense of responsibility to assist with the re-balancing of the Divine Feminine with the Divine Masculine energies on the planet.

Mynzah insisted to me at a later date that he knew without a doubt that I was truly carrying the frequency of Isis, more than anyone he'd ever come across. That I was the "real deal." I knew myself that I was never one to fake things like this or anything for that matter, and it was nice to be seen for this truth. It could explain many things about my life, especially in hindsight. Many interesting and strong parallels, though they were unmistakable, I always took these knowings with a healthy grain of salt.

Whether I was actually Isis (doubtful) or whether I am simply a carrier of the Isis Codes (way more likely) makes not a speck of difference to me. What does make a difference to me is that I follow through as I'd promised, and do my part in assisting the Return of the Divine Feminine to her rightful place on the planet—because *Now* is the *Time*.

In the midst of these Goddess Code Activations, at the end of 2011, Jeff and I took the kids for a New Year's trip to Las Vegas for a few days, just to get away.

I had a hard time in Vegas. The energies there were too scattered and fragmented for me. Being an empath can be challenging in large crowds, and combined with the excessive drinking, drugs, and gambling, I felt absolutely awful the entire time we were there. I had headaches that would not go away, and I felt tired all the time. But I still managed to have fun in spite of these woes, seeing my kids having a blast made it all worth it.

There was much more the kids wanted to do when it was time to leave, so we decided to stay an extra night beyond what we had planned. We couldn't afford another night at the hotel we were in though. It had been the only one we knew of that was non-smoking and clean, since it was also one of the only hotels on the strip without a casino inside. But it was too expensive, so we decided to spend our final night at The Luxor, at my request, since I had only had my Isis "experience" less than two weeks earlier, and was about to start my belly dancing classes in the New Year after we got back to Sedona. Egypt was quickly becoming an obsession of mine.

I loved the idea of The Luxor but was not really a fan of the fact that even our non-smoking room oozed with stale cigarette smoke, caked to the walls, furniture and bedsheets. It was disgusting to all of us, but we decided to make the most of it.

That night, as I was meditating before bed, I felt my attention be pulled in that otherworldly way, beyond my own control. I was led to open my eyes and look out the window. Hovering right outside our window was a silver craft with white lights. It appeared to only be about 20 or 30 feet in diameter, and was round. It was very bright and seemed to be "saying hello." I remember seeing it, feeling its greeting, and then I lost total consciousness. I have no idea what, if anything, happened after this. Very likely another missing time episode.

January came, with my Jesus and Mary vision, and I also had several dreams that I could feel were more than just dreams. Rather, they were other-dimensional experiences.

One of these dreams involved me flying with Eagle and Owl. They flanked me on either side as we flew through the air, over mountains and vast, never-ending landscapes. It was quite spectacular, and I had the feeling they were teaching me something. I felt so free and powerful. I awoke the next morning still feeling their sacred medicine coursing through my veins, and I knew that I was assimilating whatever it was they were teaching me and helping me integrate with all of my recent experiences, and I was grateful.

CHAPTER 66

My Third Eye is Alive

In February of 2012, Bashar was nowhere near my radar. I didn't even know who Bashar was. I'd probably seen random postings by random people on social media, and if I ever watched one of his transmissions prior to this, I have no recollection of it. I'm pretty certain though I had not yet even heard of him.

I had a dreamtime activation by a blue laser-eyed being on February 12th, and developed a significant body rash suddenly the very next day. I knew this huge rash was related to whatever upgrade my body was experiencing as a result of this experience, as I am not prone to getting skin rashes at all, so the timing of this was unquestionably a synchronistic confirmation for me.

It all began when I decided to do a different meditation than my usual daily favourites. I had read about a meditation from Drunvalo Melchizedek where you place the tip of your tongue on the roof of your mouth. As I did this, I immediately began to see green spirals, like a tornado or a spinning vortex that spun me into another dimension of awareness.

When I "came to" from this meditation, I heard a voice say "*Sulannaya*" and knew somehow that that was my Soul name.

Now I know her as my Higher Self, my twin aboard ship. In that moment though, it was a powerful knowing that came quickly, and I immediately needed to ground and clear my energies by putting sea salt on my feet. I was able to sleep then and went to bed.

This same night, I had a dream encounter that I knew was real in an other-dimensional sort of way. Something I was becoming used to.

This experience began in what I can only describe as a cavern beneath the surface of the Earth, or the "underworld." As I walked through, I walked among many women who were grieving. I saw wooden crates all over the ground, and felt that these women were all grieving the loss of their children. What is interesting is, I never did see an actual body anywhere. The crates appeared empty. Before I'd realized the crates symbolized or somehow contained the energies of their children, I stepped on one as I walked. One of the mothers became very upset with me, as if I were dishonouring her child. I felt horrible about being so careless, and not seeing what I was actually doing. I apologized to her and kept walking, knowing that I was there seeking someone, though I didn't know who.

I spotted a young man. He wore only a dark blue metallic pair of shorts, and had dark, short hair. He was a perfect-looking specimen, very attractive with a strong energetic presence. He was sitting at a little wooden table on the ground in the dirt and I felt magnetically drawn to him. I knew this being was The One I was there to see. There were other beings present, but I was there only to see him.

I approached him, as he looked at me for the first time, gazing deeply into my eyes. I noticed he had bright blue eyes, like laser beams. They were definitely other-worldly and held much power in them. I knelt down in front of him, as he rose to meet me. We both knew exactly what to do, and why we were there.

He reached the palm of his hand to my Third Eye and pressed it firmly against it. Immediately, I began receiving incredible downloads, visions of the future, possible future events and timelines. I don't recall now exactly what I saw, unfortunately. However, I do recall that these visions were extraordinary. Upon completion of the download, from such a place of empowerment I said aloud, "My third eye is ALIVE."

Following the activation from this mystical being, I wondered curiously at the timing of it. I was still swirling in my Isis Activation, not to mention my Jesus and Mary Activation, with this particular dream occurring only a couple of weeks after the latter.

As I'd described, it had felt as though this last encounter took place underground or in "the underworld." Interestingly, Isis is the Goddess of the underworld, of birth, death, **resurrection**; and of course, these energies tie in with Jesus and Mary's story. I felt somehow this dream activation was connected with whatever the meaning of these previous activations was all about.

It would be a third activation, the sacred number 3, all occurring in a matter of three months, all occurring almost exactly a month apart. Definitely timed.

Of course, at the time, I didn't notice all of these details, I was so much in the experiences, doing my sleuth work to figure any of it out, to no avail in the moment. The only thing I was certain of were the experiences themselves. How they fit together in the cosmic puzzle though, I hadn't a clue.

With information that synchronicity would bring to my awareness some three years after the fact, I wonder now if all of these experiences and activations were the handiwork of Time Travelers. Specifically Isis, and even Tatos, otherwise known as Hermes or Thoth.

My feeling now is that these time travelers, if that's what they were, were activating me in order to step forward with the information in this book. That perhaps, these "babies and children" were not actually Earth babies. Perhaps the mothers grieving that I witnessed in the underground tomb-space were the mothers who are just like me. The ones who have unconsciously grieved over babies they've lost, or had but they didn't know consciously they'd had due to these ET experiments. Perhaps all of these women were grieving the fact that they had no clue they had hybrid children of their own somewhere, like I did.

Perhaps the seed was being planted in me by the Time Travelers that these mothers were awaiting healing, awaiting salvation from their grief and pain and that the being with the laser blue eyes was sent to me, to activate me and prepare me to be the one, or one of the ones, to offer these women some answers, and at the very least, the solace they have been seeking, knowing they are not alone in this Secret Sacred Sisterhood.

CHAPTER 67

Seeing Through Ayahuasca

On February 18, 2012, mere days after my Third Eye Activation, I had an experience I never in a million years expected I would have.

Jeff told me about a spiritual ceremony that was happening that night in a wonderful space we were already well acquainted with here in Sedona. We both loved this property located out in open land nestled quietly in the red rocks. It had a salt water pool and hot tub, and a giant, under-lit quartz crystal embedded in a cavern in the floor, topped with a glass cover at the hearth of the fireplace in the family room; a very unique and stunning feature in the home. I always feel wonderful in this space, so when Jeff told me the ceremony was happening there, I was excited, and trusted it must be synchronistically presenting itself now for a reason.

I asked him more about this mysterious ceremony and he went on to tell me that it was a ceremony which lasts all night, so my mother would have to babysit the boys while we were gone.

There was just one little glitch. Attending the ceremony meant that everyone in attendance agrees beforehand to take the sacred medicine. I had never even heard of Ayahuasca, as this happened before it started showing up all over the internet, and all over our little town.

Any opportunity to delve into the deep, even dark or challenging recesses of my unconscious mind, bringing the darkness to the light in spiritual matters, has always been exciting to this Scorpio Moon girl. To put it mildly, I am not afraid of doing the shadow work necessary to bring me to the light. I thrive on it. I love the liberation of clearing away the cobwebs and the darkness, delving into the mysteries and discovering whatever richness I have been missing. Purely exhilarating and freeing.

I wasn't sure about taking this "medicine" though. I'd never heard of it, and the fact that Jeff put it out there so hesitantly gave me reason to pause. He mentioned that this particular medicine was known for instigating gigantic purges of the physical body while it simultaneously purged the spiritual body. Basically, a lot of people vomit and get violently sick while taking this medicine.

I hate throwing up, so the thought of this made me nervous, but if it was safe, with a shaman, and in the name of spiritual growth while hopefully helping Jeff and I possibly reconnect, I was willing to let my fears go and delve into the unknown and have a healing adventure. I still hoped and prayed I would not have to become a "barfing guru" though!

Right away, upon entering the home I was so familiar with, something I had never noticed before jumped out at me. There was a portrait of a black jaguar hanging above the fireplace, watching over us all. Perhaps the shamans had hung it there for the purposes of the ceremony, I am not certain. I do know that I took it being there to be part of my medicine for the evening. I was grateful for the black jaguar's presence, and somehow felt safer knowing I was being protected and watched over by this spirit animal.

I find it interesting to note that of all the research I have since done about black jaguar/black panther medicine, some of the most common qualities of it have to do with connections with prophecy, psychic sight, and more accurately, inner knowingness. Some research even spoke of people with this totem holding galactic knowingness that if not held sacred and if not released in Divine Time (if leaked or irresponsibly shared), could be detrimental. Others noted often that women who have black panther/jaguar as their totem find themselves raising their children alone, through divorce or rather by being the ones who primarily care for their children through asserting a kind of dominance in that area of the coupling. Also, connections with sexuality and potential for strong sexual healing, through the portal of darkness and healing sexual wounds was also noted. Black Panther could also symbolize silence and the silent healer. I found every one of these descriptions to be fascinatingly on point with my life as well as the journey that awaited me that evening.

The ceremony began at around 9 pm that evening. We were introduced to the Spirit of the Ayahuasca medicine, and I noticed some strange energies in the room. There were people present who were genuinely seeking a spiritual experience and healing, and there were others there that I sensed were using this sacred medicine as an escape and an excuse to get high. I could feel those energies so potently, it almost hurt me. Being highly empathic in situations like this isn't always the best feeling.

It was time to take the first dose of the medicine. I was nervous as we went around the circle and one person at a time took theirs. As it approached my turn, my nerves activated even more. I hadn't had a drug or drank alcohol in many years leading up to this, and didn't care to ever have the experience again of getting high off of a substance. I heard a voice from above me say to me, ***"There is nothing to fear. YOU are the medicine; the medicine is YOU."***

I had not even taken it yet, and was already receiving divine messages!

I understood what this meant, and it immediately calmed me down. I connected with the Spirit of the plant as I readied myself to receive its medicine. It was then time to receive my dose, and before drinking from the cup, I held it between my hands and prayed over it. I melded my consciousness together with the medicine, and became One with it, as the Voice had told me.

Once I felt this process complete, I drank it.

It was bitter and had a very potent smell, but I liked it as it now felt a part of me, not separate from me.

As I began to feel the medicine affecting my body, I realized that I had to flow with this, as much as I felt myself wanting to resist it. I don't enjoy the feeling of being heavy or being controlled by a substance. I began to feel this way, and panicked inside a little bit when I heard, *"You will never need to do this again"* which I was so incredibly relieved to hear the voice above me say.

Who was this voice? Whoever it was, I liked it. I felt like it was my Higher Self, my Twin, Sulannaya, walking me through this experience. As hard as it was for me to go through, she was right there supporting me which I greatly appreciated.

As the experience intensified, I began to see and feel inside of everyone in the room. This was not something I was particularly comfortable with, as I was hearing the inner voice of each person present; how they really felt about themselves and their lives. It was actually quite painful. I tried to close my eyes and ears and shut it all off, but it was as if something, someone, was keeping them open against my will. Almost as if I needed to experience this as an initiation of some sort and it was beyond my ability to control it.

I heard some of the deepest, darkest secrets of each person in that circle, including the two shamans. I felt like a voyeur, and at first felt guilty for invading their inner space. Then I realized why I'd needed to hear this.

We went around the circle, taking turns holding items from the center altar. When the rattle came to me, something came over me, as if a force greater than me descended upon me and began to move through me, shaking this rattle with such intention, clarity, and power, commanding attention and clearing the dark entities in the space. It was incredible. I didn't feel that it was me doing this, although it was my body being used as the vessel to bring forth this medicine.

As the intensity of the rattle came to a gradual conclusion, with the Navajo shaman now over on my side of the room, there was a moment of piercing silence, and then a collective "Aho." Everyone felt the presence of power in the room. I knew something greater than me was working alongside me and through me that night. I knew I was protected.

The night went much like this, with me sending healings to people in pain, purging and having a rough go of it. My focus was on helping as a silent healer. I stayed in my space, did not say a word to anyone. I sent healing energies to everyone I noticed suffering, including the Navajo shaman after he accidentally spilled some of the sacred medicine on the carpet. Instead of seeing it as a gift and offering to the space, which was how I saw it very clearly, he emotionally got himself worked up over it. I sent him waves of self-forgiveness and gentility.

Things went on like this for hours, with me receiving profound messages (it felt as though all of my guidance came from a voice that was hovering above me) and sending healing out to my fellow brothers and sisters in ceremony.

At around 1 am I began to hear the Voice saying to me, *"Go! Now!"* I was extremely conflicted with this message, as I knew the commitment is that you stay in ceremony until dawn. I didn't want to look like I was running away! Because I wasn't. So, I chose to ignore this one message, thinking it somewhat of a nuisance.

"GO! NOW!!!! Your work here is complete. GO!!!" the Voice insisted.

It would not leave me alone. I couldn't even focus on anything else, it kept chiming in and it wouldn't let up.

Finally, I could ignore it no longer. I could barely stay present with the ceremony with this voice yelling at me to leave. Finally, after feeling the medicine had worn off almost completely, I went to get up.

Jeff must have seen me or felt me, as he came running over to see if I was okay. "Yes," I told him. "I am being told over and over again that I need to leave now, that I am complete here. So, I'm going to go."

He helped me gather my things and walked me to my car. I felt 100% able to drive safely, even though I admittedly did still feel traces of the medicine inside of me. I would never get behind a wheel anymore unless I felt sober. And I felt sober. My reflexes were working normally. It was now after 2 am and it had been five hours since I'd ingested the medicine, and I'd only taken one dose, as opposed to most of the others, who'd had about five or six rounds by that point.

I assured him that I felt perfectly fine to drive and that I knew I wouldn't be told to leave if I was not okay to do so. I trusted this voice above me, whoever it really was. I knew that much.

It was a dark, peaceful night. Sedona shuts down by 9 pm every night, so by 2 am the streets are extremely quiet. I passed two cars at most the whole drive home.

I was just entering in to the heart of West Sedona when my eyes were pulled involuntarily and drawn up and to the left, right where Thunder Mountain stands—the tallest, most powerful mountain in Sedona. It was then that I saw clearly a black triangular ship with a singular red light on each tip, and it was flying next to me! It was merely hundreds of feet away from me, and it literally *flew beside me* all the way home, almost as if I were being escorted personally! I remember I kept looking out the window, thinking it would be gone and maybe I was just imagining it. But no. All the way home this ship rode beside me.

I feel it's important to note that not once in the entire evening had I had any hallucinations of any kind. I *knew* in my heart and soul that I was not imagining this. It was also then that I realized who had been guiding me all evening throughout the ceremony. Of course, Sulannaya was present, and yet, I also knew that the beings from this ship were supporting me in this journey as well.

I thanked them, knowing that whoever they were, they'd made sure I'd gotten home safely. In that moment, I assumed this was the reason I'd had to leave the ceremony, so that I could see this ship. But when I got home and went to climb into bed with my boys, I noticed that my youngest son, who was two-and-a-half years old, was on the floor, which was odd. My mother was fast asleep on the bed and had not noticed what was happening. I went to pick him up and put him back in bed, and realized he was burning hot.

I took him to the bathroom and took his temperature. It was 103 degrees. Wow! This was the reason I was being shouted at and nagged to come home, and this was why I had been personally escorted by the ship; to make sure I got home safely to take care of my son! He needed me more than the people in ceremony at this point.

I gave him some homeopathics, got a cool, wet bamboo cloth and snuggled up in bed with my little feverish angel. Once again, I thanked these guardian beings for sending me where I was needed most. I am fairly certain that this was Bashar's ship, and that this incident was to become the start of a whole new level of connection with the Galactic Hybrids and me.

***Note: I have since learned that it is imperative for Shamans taking on the enormous responsibility of leading people through an Ayahuasca journey to also be responsible for the safety of the participants. Since my experience, which I went into totally blind and naïve, I have learned of people dying while using this medicine. I have come to realize that when the Shamans are in their full integrity, the ones wishing to take part in the ceremony should be given a mandatory interview by the Shaman, and assessed to see if they are indeed ready to take on such a powerful form of healing and initiation.

This did not take place in the ceremony I attended. Jeff and I merely showed up, paid our money, and the Shamans never once even asked us our names or anything about ourselves. They didn't even personally speak with us. I now find this protocol to be highly irresponsible and questionable. It also goes to show why I had the experience I had, though at the time, I felt the Shamans were in integrity, as far as presenting the medicine as sacred and wishing everyone a positive experience. I do not feel now, however, that they were in their full integrity or power. Perhaps they were a little naïve of the serious position they held, as no care was taken to prepare anyone present for the journey.

Personally, I had zero clue what I was getting myself into when I walked into that room. Perhaps that was for the best, from a higher perspective, for what my own personal experience was to be. Yet knowing what I know now, I do not agree with nor condone this approach. It's no wonder I heard and saw the things I did there. Surely a healer was needed to be present, and that night it just happened to be me.

Years later, I am hearing publicly through social media how Sedona has become a place where Ayahuasca, among other Sacred Medicines, are being abused, which makes me sad. At the time, I'd had no idea that what I had been a participant in that night was already quietly happening under the guise of "spirituality" and "healing" even though some innocently approached it genuinely.

I do not recommend dabbling in these or any other powerful medicines (including marijuana) lightly or for the sake of getting high or having a "cool" experience. When taken *unconsciously* and *irresponsibly*, these medicines have the power to do more harm than healing, both to the ones taking it as well as anyone who comes in close contact with them. It's about taking these medicines consciously as a sacred tool, with integrity and an up spiral and clear intent, never to be abused. As soon as consciousness and responsibility are out the window, most often so is the medicine.

CHAPTER 68

Sisters of Frequency and Galactic Babies

About two months after my experience of seeing Bashar's ship in February 2012, things started to really fast-track for me. I had begun receiving energies connected with Anthony through some very synchronistic events. I didn't exactly know what to do with them, but did my best to channel it all into the book I was still struggling to write.

I'd had a long, painful year of trying to work on my book any chance I got, which sometimes went weeks, even months, between sessions. It was brutal. I would totally lose my flow and forget where I was at with it. I would write stream of consciousness, but every time I sat down to write, I was in a completely different space within myself and my understanding of things.

I never even finished it, but kept plugging away nonetheless any chance I got. I was like a hamster in a cage spinning inside the wheel, never really getting anywhere. In the midst of this process though, much was happening within, beyond the veil of my physical being.

It was March 21, 2012, the Spring Equinox. I have since learned this date is also connected with Selene's tracking of the Goddess frequencies, specifically including Athena and the 96 Goddesses, and Mary Magdalene. It was on this day that I contacted Selene for a second reading. I'd had an initial session with her on September 26, 2011 that was brief and detailed my personal natal chart star markings, and how they pertained to my life, how I chose to come here directly from the ships, and a sampling of some of the ET experiments I came here to work with. Basically, it was a hint of what I'd chosen to be involved in during my time here on the planet in this incarnation. Just a hint. I was still a baby when it came to consciously comprehending the enormity of what I'd truly signed up for here.

We had spoken then at length about my health issues and their connection with my galactic work, but I now felt ready to delve more deeply into questions I'd had that had yet to be answered. Questions a part of me was afraid to know the answers to, yet I needed to know the answers to in order to move forward with my life, and my missions, most effectively and honestly.

This was an inner struggle for me, as these were questions I never really wanted to admit that I even had, because then that would mean admitting to my own potential insanity or state of delusion. Whoever really wants to hear that they are making things up? Things that feel so real, things that can confuse our minds and mess with our sense of equilibrium, simply by being so "unbelievable" in the eyes of the Muggle world?

I was still trying desperately to be normal in certain ways, and it was really beginning to hinder my ability to be happy and to feel whole inside. I was trying to fit into a box, into a mold that I was squeezing myself into with the hope that I would become comfortable and feel right eventually.

All the while knowing this was never really going to happen, unless of course I could get some outside counsel that I could trust completely who would be able to tell me without a shadow of a doubt if I was full of shit or really on to something here.

I knew Selene was that person.

First of all, I knew she understood where I was coming from, metaphysically speaking. She had seen practically everything, visible and invisible, and had lived through it all. She knew of the unspeakable and the seemingly unbelievable. She was also blunt, honest and didn't sugarcoat anything. She would kick you in the pants lovingly to wake you up if that's what was needed. She would help confirm your authentic experiences with her own intuitive and experiential Mastership, *especially* when it came to ET contact, experiences and the types of experiments taking place on the planet.

I knew I'd had some experiences that were questionable. I really admired this woman and her strength and courage. I admired her galactic track record and her unwavering commitment to being available to those of us seeking support on our own paths and missions. And I was scared of looking like a love-crazed celebrity stalker, even though I knew in my heart that was never the case with me. But from the outside, if anyone had known what I was really experiencing, it sure could look that way at times.

I decided I had nothing to lose. I would never know for sure if I didn't muck up the courage and just ask already. If anyone would be able to give me some clear, honest insight, with a reliably accurate otherworldly wisdom, it would be this woman.

I had been having experience after experience since November of 2011. I had many questions. I had not had so much ET activity in years and I knew Selene could help me sort out exactly what was happening. Plus, my life was in the usual disarray it had been for some time, and I wanted a clear sounding board for my direction in life, and knew she was the one I could count on for council.

So, I contacted her in March to set up an appointment as soon as possible, but she was totally booked for the next two months. '*Damn!*' I thought. But then she said, "I'm sorry, but my next available appointment isn't until May 24th."

Bang. There it was. The synchronicity I was waiting for. May 24th was my 37th birthday. I knew right then that this session was going to be significant. *Huge*. But what on Earth did that even mean?

I waited patiently for this session, trusting in the divine timing of it, knowing that I was to wait for it for whatever reason. At the time of making the appointment, I knew I wanted to talk with her and ask about certain experiences I'd been having, yet I had no idea how much we were going to get into about Anthony, if at all. Of course, I wanted to ask about our connection, but was still unsure I would have the guts to really go there and "out" myself to this person I so admired. I knew that regardless; I would get some invaluable information through the session that I needed.

Then it happened.

In the early part of 2012, right after my intense awakening times with Mynzah, he moved back to California not knowing when he might return to Sedona, and I felt lost and in need of finding others "like me" again. I found myself surfing social media sites and something brought me to a group page I had recently joined, which focused on Ascension information, starseeds, and people sharing information and tips about their own metaphysical experiences, which I found fascinating for a short while.

As I said in the beginning, this road can get lonely sometimes, and I was certainly lonely now. I had someone in my life who finally understood me on a soul level, and now he was gone. I have grown a lot since then though, and no longer feel the need to seek others who understand me, thankfully. But when I found this online group, even though I was still feeling isolated in my home life, at least I felt like there were people out there I could relate to, which I still needed at the time.

I had surfed this page almost obsessively and non-stop for a couple of months, taking in all the information, though quickly realizing I was rarely gaining any wisdom I didn't already possess myself. I really wasn't getting much information that was new to me. I also realized it was much more important for me to be present in my own *Now* life, with my kids. So, I had stopped clicking on every single interesting-looking article or video that pertained to ETs and other people's experiences. I almost became bored with it. This was actually a great relief to me. I wanted to be more present with my children, and wanted to step away from the hypnotic gaze of the computer.

And then one day in mid-April 2012, while scrolling through this same group page, I clicked on a video, only half-aware of what I was doing.

My eyes had been drawn to this video posted by a young Swedish woman who had only just become a member of this group, if I recall correctly. There was nothing remotely appealing about the look of the video still shot. At the time, I was inundated with videos from other members of this group of starseeds and lightworkers, as I had been hungry for information since learning of my own Galactic Heritage. I was already "video-ed out," but for some reason, I clicked on her video anyway.

The title didn't even pull me in. I had seen and heard so many ET contact stories by then, and besides which, I was living my own. I really wasn't looking for this kind of information. Yet this one, I simply could not walk away from. Something in me, *beyond me,* clicked on her link.

When I realized I had just clicked on a link to a video entitled *"My ET contact experience,"* I almost closed the tab, but something inside stopped me. I couldn't close it, even though I wanted to, and had no real interest in hearing this story or watching this woman's video. It was a ten-minute long video, and I could hardly believe I was committing myself to listening to it.

Yet I found myself compelled to keep listening to this Swedish woman's voice. I wasn't exactly sure why. It was quite beautifully made, as this young lady shared the depth of her experience in as clear a way as she could. It was lovely actually to hear her speak of times where she had questioned her own sanity due to her experiences. Yet, she was not saying anything I hadn't experienced or heard before. It was nothing new to me. Still, I couldn't bring myself to turn her off. I realized that she and I had something else significant in common. In the last two minutes, I discovered the reason why I had not been able to turn it off.

My jaw dropped as I listened to her speak of how she was beginning to have experiences that would leave her in a state of confusion and "not-knowing," and being a mother of three children, she decided the most responsible thing to do would be to check herself in to a hospital and get some help, as she thought she just might be losing her mind. She was trying to do the right thing for her children.

I felt deep empathy for this young lady, getting to the point of committing herself after having these experiences, in order to get some support in figuring out what was happening to her. She was in fear, which of course, I could whole-heartedly understand. She was a young mother with three children and she wanted to make sure she was not losing her mind. What courage it must have taken to do this.

What she shared next hit me right in the gut. She started talking about her time in the hospital, undergoing hypnosis sessions, and when her friends and family would come visit her. They would later share with her that during this time she would talk about being taken aboard spaceships and being impregnated while aboard *"them."* To this day, she has no recollection of saying this to anyone while she was in there. She didn't know what they were talking about, but heard it from several of her loved ones.

Of course, this information pricked up my ears. I began to listen to this transmission with renewed interest, hanging on the edge of my seat. Here was a cosmic sister who was talking about these experiences I knew I'd also had. And I knew they were true and that she was sane. I wanted to hear what she had to say about this as I was still uncovering my own memories and was shocked someone else was talking so publicly about it.

I knew exactly what she was talking about, and thought to myself, *'Oh, wow, another one like me.'* But how similar were our stories, I wondered?

By this time in my life, I had known for a little under a year about my deep personal involvement with the ships. And in that time, I had pretty much lived and breathed contemplating and researching this phenomenon since I'd discovered about these genetic experiments the previous summer when I met Sierra and consequently had had my first reading with Selene.

I had also recently finished watching the Stephen Spielberg television mini-series, "Taken," which also depicts the story of this type of phenomenon in a fictional, yet to those of us who "Know," eerily accurate and detailed way. So, this timing was synchronistic to say the least. I had never heard of a mainstream media series delving so deeply into such taboo phenomena that is generally ridiculed anytime someone comes out to speak of the validity and truth of such experiences actually existing.

This woman had me totally riveted by her honest, detailed and courageous sharing of her unusual experiences. I felt like *'Wow, there are others out there like me who are talking about this.'* I felt an immediate sisterly bond with her, even though we had never met, and likely never would, not in this dimension at least.

And then my heart stopped for a moment. I was not expecting what came next. I'd thought she'd already blown my mind clear out of the water, but I was wrong. I was not at all prepared for what was coming to me.

In the last minute or so of her video, she starts talking of waking up from a nap while she is in the hospital. She describes her television being turned on, and "coming to" to a music video playing of a song by a band she didn't really know well. She had never heard the song before.

What I saw and heard next was shocking beyond belief for me. She recognized the band, but not the song. She inserted a few moments of this video at the end of her story, and there he was. Again. *Same band. Same singer.*

My jaw dropped to the floor. My throat closed up, the blood in my veins began to do its notable vibrational coursing of intense activation, so I felt like I might explode. Instantaneous DNA upgrade, *big time.*

There he was again. There was Anthony in front of me.

This was a video to a song I didn't know well at all, but recalled it being a real "Activator" for me back in 2006 when I'd first re-recognized Anthony and began researching anything I could find out about him to help me understand what I was experiencing. It would be years before awakening to my Galactic Missions, or gaining a true understanding of my connection with extraterrestrial intelligence in the first place. By now I knew, and when I saw the clip of Anthony's video during this young woman's story in April of 2012, especially after hearing her personal connection with hybrids, I nearly tipped over the edge again.

I was dumbfounded as I saw the lyrics displayed on the screen. She had only included the last 45 seconds of the song, with the lyrics spread out in order to deepen her message. In this particular clip of the song, Anthony sings of being taken aboard spaceships, and he even goes so far as to mention being taught about the Pleiades by the beings aboard the ship.

It was not the same song and video I had seen when I was seventeen. It was yet another song I had heard only once before, and to which I had a very strong physical and emotional response. In 2006 though, I really didn't understand why this particular song struck me so deeply. I'd had tears streaming and a pumping in my veins that was so very powerful. The moment I saw this clip, I finally understood why, some six odd years later.

I remember feeling an energetic drive in this particular song that would sit in my resonant field long after it was over, and several of the lines always hit me on a deeply profound level I didn't quite understand, and could not explain to myself, other than I knew exactly what he was talking about.

I had always connected with the line, "Can't stop the spirits when they need you; This life is more than just a read through," but what really hit it home for me now was something I had never consciously picked up on in the song before, as at the time I'd first heard it, in 2006, I was not at all consciously thinking of ETs or that my connection with Anthony had anything whatsoever to do with anything extra-terrestrial in nature, let alone spaceships, ET agendas and experiments, or by golly, different star systems beyond Earth.

Yet when I saw these words written clearly across the screen, talking about "the spirits" and the phrase that they were "coming from space to teach you of the Pleiades" I lost my breath momentarily.

I had only recently learned of the Pleiades as well as my personal connection with the Pleiadians through Selene a few months before seeing this woman's video. I had not known, not consciously at least, about the Pleiades *or* the beings from there before meeting Selene, or the fact that I was directly connected with them and their ships when I'd first heard the song six years earlier.

This synchronistic experience took my connection with Anthony to a whole new octave of "real" for me in the blink of an eye.

What was this? Here I was, witnessing another woman's otherworldly connection with this man. And right after she'd finished talking about her impregnation aboard ship to boot, which made it even more intense for me. This was surely confirmation of something huge.

It reignited my need—that deep soul need—to figure out what the hell had really been going on between me and this man on multi-dimensional levels for all these years. I felt I was receiving confirmation that I couldn't possibly be making it all up.

But what was it then? What was I still not "getting"?

Immediately after seeing the video, I wept. I wept at the enormity of this realization as it sank in deeper and deeper for me. I wept at the soul recognition and the knowing of this ancient connection I shared with this man, which felt growing and becoming more real by the minute. I could no longer deny it to myself; there was some connection here, and it was potentially much bigger than I might ever comprehend on my own. But what was it, dammit?

I began to dig a bit, to see if I could uncover another clue, the next obvious puzzle piece. I was now more deeply rooted in my awareness of his knowledge and experience with extraterrestrial beings and I was trusting synchronicity. This wasn't just some random, silly riffing in a song. These were lyrics cosmically downloaded straight from the ships, and I knew it. Whether he realized it or not consciously, I didn't know. But I knew this is what it was.

For the record, this young woman has never publicly claimed to have been aboard ship with Anthony that I know of. Considering my own vivid experiences, mostly connected with this same man, hearing her describe the impregnation download while waking up to this song, spoke indirectly to me of her very possibly having had similar experiences. This is a conclusion I came to on my own. Let's just say that it would not surprise me in the least if I heard her recall experiences of this nature with him specifically at some point.

My entire world opened up to a whole new level of awareness from that one video I had synchronistically happened upon that day. I was already on YouTube, so in the midst of reeling from this electrical jolt to my system, I began a search for any sort of video that might help me connect the cosmic dots even more specifically with Anthony. In that instant, I got a "hit" and started trying to find out if he'd ever mentioned anything about these kinds of experiences in any past interviews. I was frantically searching for more confirmation. I didn't hold out much hope of really finding anything, but I knew I had to try. Something in me, beyond me, was insisting I do this.

It didn't take long either. Almost right away, as if it was handed to me, was waiting for me, up popped a YouTube video I had never noticed or seen before. One that would surely confirm, yet again, this connection for me.

It was a fairly old video, a clip from an interview Anthony had done decades earlier, in which he is being interviewed about a woman, another singer, a quasi-famous celebrity from Europe he was intimately connected with at the time, and whom in the interview, he states is aware of things on levels most people aren't.

They flash to her portion of the interview, and she starts talking about her child, and being impregnated by way of a spaceship, and how her daughter was "delivered" to her from the ship, and my heart is really pumping now.

How had I missed this interview, in all of my researching of this man, trying to figure out this connection that I could never seem to fully grasp? Yet here it was, showing up in my field of awareness at the precise moment I'd needed it to.

'He already Knows about this stuff,' I thought to myself. *'He already knows. He is already aware.'*

This synchronicity blew my fucking head off, quite honestly. By now, with the lightning bolt of energies running through the blood in my veins, I was shaking like a motherfucking leaf.

The video not only confirmed what I had just seen in the other woman's video, by having this female musician talking about her bizarre experience of how her daughter had come to her by way of a spaceship, but here was Anthony being interviewed about this woman, a close friend of his—a former lover—talking about how amazing she is, how she is aware of things beyond what most other people are usually aware of.

Now I knew that he knew. At least on some level of consciousness, he already knew.

This confirmation was so empowering for me. I knew, for absolute certain, that this information, this book, whenever it was divinely timed to reach him, would not be new information for him. In fact, he may even already know more than I do about it all. Perhaps receiving this book, whenever he does, will not come as a surprise or shock to him at all.

All along, I hadn't ever really speculated as to how much he may be aware of his own participation in these otherworldly galactic experiments, but I was beginning to feel fairly certain through this gigantic synchronicity that at the very least, unconsciously, he had a pretty damn significant clue.

Had I ever doubted myself before (*often*), had I ever doubted that there was some connection between us, having felt it from the first moment I recognized him on the television screen at seventeen? I was becoming increasingly more convinced by the minute that I was most definitely not a delusional maniac, nor would he think I was if and when our paths were destined to cross.

Finally, I was given the confirmation I needed that, not only had I truly recognized this man's soul all those years ago, but that when the divine timing was right, when timelines were aligned and we were given the opportunity to be in the same room together, there was a very real chance that he would recognize my soul essence just as powerfully as I'd recognized his.

The vast awareness of this enormous truth took place in a matter of milliseconds, but the impact on me was beyond gigantic and everlasting. I was frozen in time and space by the weight of this knowing. The synchronistic message was undeniable. The energies had gotten so strong at this point I had to go lay down.

I remained in this field of activation for weeks, knowing that my session with Selene was approaching, wondering how on Earth I might go about asking for her council on all of this. I wanted to know if she could intuit anything psychically, and also wondered if anything "showed up" astrologically between us. I wondered if she would be able to get enough information for me on this, as we had a two-hour window of timing for his birth, and all the other details were accurate, as he had included them in his book, interestingly enough.

I also knew that Selene might tell me to step off this notion and get a grip on reality. I really didn't care. I needed to know once and for all where to focus my energies. I was tired of wasting my precious time and energy if that was what I was doing. By this point, I was ready, and more than willing, to hear anything that would either help me understand the greater purpose to this connection, or be the catalyst that would snap me out of something that was not serving me or the planet in any positive way.

Was I just desperate and seeking some kind of self-importance through this? I didn't really think so when I searched inside my heart, since I had truly tried to ignore this man, his energies, and this unbreakable connection I felt with him many times before. I did try, for months, even years at a time, to no avail in the end. And when I did manage to successfully disassociate for a time, as I said, it nearly led to my own demise.

So, what was she going to be able to tell me?

Selene was no stranger to any of this. Nothing much, if anything, could surprise her. I knew she was highly trained in galactic matters concerning the roles celebrities play on the planet where the ET experiments are concerned. I knew she had lived through her own experiments with certain celebrities and people in the public eye, and here she was, "just a little farm girl from Oklahoma" as she always so candidly puts it. She is far from that, but most people would never know from looking at her. Selene has been a hidden treasure for decades. Through all of her own galactic adventures and assignments, never once did she seek out notoriety or fame. In fact, she deliberately kept it from happening to her for many decades.

I trusted this woman, her unwavering integrity, and her strong galactic wisdom, with every cell in my body. I knew she was the key to the next step for me in my own assignments and missions on the planet.

I decided to wait to write to her about all of my synchronicities concerning Anthony, knowing she was on a Sacred France Quest with a group of starseeds she had put together of certain clients of hers with specific markings on their natal charts she had been tracking that tied them to Jesus and Mary Magdalene, their bloodline and their teachings. These markings also included the Cathars, of which I now know I was a part.

I found out about this quest she was on only days before our session. The fact that I decided to write to her while she was there to tell her my story is absolutely synchronistic, since I feel quite strongly that Anthony most likely also shares a deep connection with that sacred place, the bloodline and moment in history.

I finally sent Selene the email detailing nearly everything I had ever experienced in connection with him on May 18, 2012; synchronistically when the Pleiades were in direct alignment with the Earth. I knew she was coming to the end of her trip, and that our session was scheduled six days later. It was now or never, and I couldn't live with "never," so the only time was Now. I stepped out of the cosmic closet and confessed everything.

I threw caution to the wind, knowing that I might not get the response I hoped for, but I had to do it. I spilled the beans. I told Selene all about my other-worldly experiences with Anthony in all different dimensions. Other-dimensional experiences where I would receive confirmation through synchronization in my waking life, such as what I had just experienced with the videos. Though I didn't always know what it was that was happening, I knew through countless synchronistic and high strangeness experiences that whatever was going on was very real.

At least I was sure it was, but I was also at the point where I was ready to let the cat out of the bag and risk being told by someone of her galactic caliber that I was delusional and obviously making these stories up in my mind. I was finally ready to hear this, especially if it were true. I was surrendered. After all, I couldn't go on any longer with one foot in each world when I was still questioning if one of these worlds was all I was certain it was. I was tired and finished with doubting myself.

In my own experience, which I'd had too many to count, I had started to feel that these "other worlds" were usually much more real than this "reality."

I needed answers. I needed to set my pride and ego aside in search of the Ultimate Truth. I was willing to shatter every image I'd ever had of myself in order to uncover this truth.

I wanted someone to have the opportunity to tell me that I was wrong, so that I could give it all up, and put my focus on what was right in front of me. A part of me actually craved this.

I have since learned that the best way to adhere to one's calling is to be in full surrender to where we're at now. To be present with "what is" and this includes being fully involved in my own physical life, the reality I am living, day in and day out. Being mother to my sweet children is most important of all. They have always come first for me, without question.

So, I put it all out there to Selene, in case she had any insights or wisdom to offer me during our upcoming session. I waited on pins and needles, as I didn't hear back from her until the day before the session, when she emailed me to get ready and centered and to be prepared for a huge session.

Holy shit! I wondered what I was about to hear, and quite frankly, what I'd gotten myself into. But this was my moment, and I was prepared to have to let this connection with Anthony go if it was what was best, especially if it turned out to all be some fabrication in my own mind. I really didn't think it was, yet I also didn't want to fool myself, so knowing the truth from an entirely neutral perspective was so much better than forever wondering and questioning myself. That had become boring. It was time to move forward, and either way, I was ready.

As the timing for our session drew closer, my heart pounded in my chest. It beat a million miles a minute, and I knew I was about to have my socks knocked clean off. I meditated like never before, attempting to ground myself so that I wouldn't accidentally fly away as the bag of jumbling nerves I had suddenly become. I concentrated on deep breaths and worked on mastering the art of patience until it was time for our reading.

On my 37th birthday, the phone rang at exactly the moment I'd expected it to. It was Selene. And the most intense and informative Galactic Transmission of my life commenced.

CHAPTER 69

The Cosmic Equation

May 24, 2012 - Solar Return Reading with Selene:

As our session began, Selene called in Divine Protection and the Galactic High Council to oversee this communication, invoking our personal Galactic Guardians to help guide the session and support the transmission that was about to take place. It was already super intense, and the energies running were beyond high.

Without going into the entire session in full detail, as I do not have the authority to do so at this time, and even if I did, it is still so very personal for me, I will share certain details Selene provided me with that day concerning this connection with Anthony I had asked her to help me clarify.

Assuming that she was likely going to tell me to let it go, I held my breath and prepared for the worst, though deep down I knew that I was about to have my world rocked.

I had given her Anthony's birth information, as much as I knew of it anyway, from what he'd shared of it in his book. We did not have the exact birth time, so she could only tell me about 75% of the information, but it was enough for her to get some major hits.

Selene is one of the forerunners in astrology, and she is definitely the only person I've ever heard of doing Galactic Astrology. She is the one who made the discovery of star markings in natal charts after learning directly from ETs aboard ship how to track these energies and astrological aspects in connection with galactic forces. It was also Selene herself who coined the term "starseeds" back in the 1970s that we see all over the planet now, as well as being the one who was behind the scenes in much of Shirley MacLaine's metaphysical training and experiences in the 1980s when she started stepping out in this way, bringing forth an entire metaphysical movement that swept across the planet as a result.

This particular synchronistic connection between Selene and Shirley is immensely significant for me, as once again, Selene was the one who introduced Shirley to Chris Griscom, the woman I became so focused on working with back in 2001 after reading "Dancing in the Light" where Shirley shares about her multi-incarnational sessions with Chris. This is the same place in Galisteo, NM that I would end up visiting in December 2001 after 9/11 for sessions of my own at her institute to received major awakenings and DNA upgrades; the same trip where I willed the plane to fly even after we were told it was not going to.

This Three Sister Spin, though not actively spinning any longer, was significant in my own journey to where I am now, and I know none of these events and meetings were accidental; that these connections were pre-arranged before I came down to the planet, and all of it, every connection I made with these women, were set up to lead me directly to Selene.

You see, I've been training for my meeting and work with Selene my entire life here. I know this with absolute certainty.

So, on this day of our session, I knew that whatever Selene was to share with me would hold deep Galactic Truth, and I was ready for it.

What was she going to tell me?

She spoke to me about bloodline experiments and how my involvement in them dated all the way back to Atlantis. This did not surprise me at all. She also verified that I would be writing about these experiments at some point. That before I incarnated here, I put my hand up and said *"Yeah, not only do I want to help facilitate the birthing of a new consciousness on the planet, but I will be part of a hybrid group."*

Okay. This definitely made sense to me!

Then she went on to tell me that Anthony and I were "genetically the same," and that when she looked at both of our pictures, she could see this clearly. This sort of jarred me. She talked of us being like twins in a way, brother and sister, and that her feeling was that "they" were working with our bloodlines and have been fine-tuning us both for a very long time.

The idea of bloodlines had never been in my radar before I met Selene, but synchronistically, ever since 2006 and the reigniting of this multidimensional connection between Anthony and me, I always found myself talking about blood being of some very important significance to our connection, not knowing what I even meant by my own words. I simply knew it was true. I even went so far as to buy two bloodstone gems at one point as a symbol of our work in the higher dimensions, and I worked with these stones physically for a very long time. Each stone represented one of us. Then I learned about the cosmic connection with our bloodlines, and it all finally made perfect sense to me.

Selene explained how the ETs, specifically the Pleiadians, whom she has had direct conscious and physical contact with daily for over 30 years now, decide they are going to weave bloodlines back and forth in order to bring in a new hybrid civilization to the planet.

She also explained to me that in her own experience and awareness, of which she has an abundance of both, that many people of celebrity status are being used in these experiments because the ETs know that, when the time comes to finally release this part of the story, not only will it reach further, but the public will be more inclined to absorb the information and believe it. In other words, it will help deliver the message that is needing to be received by the world at this time. I understood this as truth immediately.

She also made sure to clarify for me that "I was not the only one." Though I already knew this, I'd needed to hear it from her, as again, she was able to provide more detail and clarity of just what that meant.

We spoke of the woman who had posted that video of her own story, and she told me I would begin to learn of other women who have similar stories to tell.

We spoke about how Anthony has probably been used to impregnate thousands of women on the planet aboard ship, which did not surprise me in the least, especially after hearing this other woman's story a month earlier.

She said that sadly, many of the women who have these experiences are not able to cope with it. Like the woman in the video, many end up in mental institutions, perhaps never to come out. Many turn to drugs and alcohol in order to try to cope with the incredible stress of such unexplained high strangeness and the loss of control one can feel when undergoing these kinds of experiments.

My heart gets heavy thinking about this, because I have been there more times than I care to count, teetering on the edge of my own sanity, not knowing what was happening to me, not able to tell anyone, and not understanding then that I had made this agreement long before coming here. I had no idea that, on a soul level, I was a willing participant. When these important pieces of the puzzle are missing, it can be enough to drive almost anyone to turn to drugs or alcohol, sexual addiction (all of which I experienced), even suicide (which more than once I, too, thought about).

That is the extremely unfortunate side of agreeing to this level of galactic work from a human perspective with the mass consciousness being what it's been for so many thousands of years. Thankfully, this is shifting now.

During our session, Selene gave me the cosmic equation for ET experiments: They send it down to 1000; 100 pick it up; 10 run with it; but only 1 gets to do it.

Wow. This really got me thinking. '*Was I possibly the one, the "1," in this particular cosmic equation who would actually get to do this—to write about this experiment?*'

I did not consider this possibility lightly.

By looking at our natal charts together, Selene confirmed for me that Anthony and I had indeed shared many, many lifetimes together. This seemed to confirm my feeling that we had at the very least been in France together during the times of Jesus and Mary Magdalene and the Cathars. It would not surprise me in the least to learn that we have shared lifetimes in Atlantis and Ancient Egypt also.

I was so relieved to receive this kind of confirmation from someone who was sought after by some of the most prominent names in entertainment and politics for her crystal clear accuracy, as well as being able to see even greater than the "big picture." Selene can see the *Galactic Big Picture*, beyond the veil of this reality and on into the others.

This was all the confirmation I needed. Someone outside of myself who had the skills, with no agenda, telling me what I already knew, and then some.

Selene read the parts of Anthony's chart that were available for her given the information she had (no exact birth time). She spoke of his Venus at 26 degrees in Scorpio being *"the galactic breeding signal!"* Of course. And then she said, "Boy, is he ever starseed!"

She spoke of his Mercury in Libra, and how this indicated that he is striving for balance in his music and lyrics. This also made a lot of sense to me, given the codes I, and many others, have recognized and been activated by in his lyrics, especially since I had been guided to begin listening to them for this very reason in 2008. It floored me when I actually started listening and hearing the codes, two years after seeing him again on my television. Up to that point, I had mainly only worked with the energetics of our connection. Once I added in his lyrics and music, things began to make so much more sense to me. Selene only confirmed this.

It was when she asked if I would like her to look at our combined charts that things clicked even further for me. My Moon at 26 degrees Scorpio is in the same place as his Venus at 26 Scorpio. She translated this to me as "indicating lifetimes of knowing one another and being hooked up to the creative power of the sexual experience of impregnation." I needed to breathe very deeply after hearing this.

And this same combination, she said, was also connected with the Goddess frequency, which also held great significance for me, since I would often receive messages about the Goddess whenever I asked Spirit about our connection. Now I was beginning to understand this message of the Goddess in a deeper, more cosmic way.

It was so much to take in, it was almost overwhelming for me. My eyes filled with cleansing tears, which rolled down my cheeks as she said all of this. It was more than I could have ever expected as far as confirmation went.

The next connection in our natal charts was in the 11th house of Aquarius. Selene noted that my Saturn at 16 degrees Cancer is in direct alignment with Anthony's Athena at 18 degrees

Cancer, as well as my Venus at 16 degrees Cancer also being in alignment with his Athena at 18 Cancer. She emphasized here how this combination was "one of the very, very, *very* strong Goddess experiments on the planet" (there was that Goddess connection again).

What she said next about this alignment nearly knocked me over. She described that through this connection, he and I were both saying, *"Yes, I'm here to show how hybrids are produced and brought here to this planet."* Yet more synchronistic confirmation for me about my mysterious, other-worldly connection with this man and the intense need I felt to write this book.

The final alignment Selene noted in our charts was that his Pluto and my Ascendent are both in Virgo, are both at 11 degrees, and are both in the first house. She described this connection as being one of *"co-creation"* to the extent that it has the ability to **change my life**.

I remembered a vision I'd repeatedly had back in 2006 when I first became re-acquainted with this man's energies. After working with them for a while, I began seeing myself handing him a book. At the time, I racked my brain trying to think of what book it could possibly be. I knew it was something metaphysical in nature, and I knew that there was a message he needed to receive through me by way of this mysterious book. I had no idea what it was, or why I was the one to give this to him. Of course, now I know, and will detail this more specifically in The Fourth Activation chapter coming up.

During my reading, Selene told me something else of great significance: that I would begin to start seeing other women step forward and share these same kinds of experiences, specifically with Anthony. I wondered at the probability of this, and also thought about how validating that would be for me. Admittedly though, even after all this mind-blowing confirmation, I still had a twinge of self-doubt—in a way it all just seemed too huge. Yet deep down, I knew she was right.

I wondered how this was all going to eventually present itself to me, as I wasn't in the habit of obsessively researching anything about Anthony or anyone else for that matter. I decided all there was to do was trust that synchronicity was on my side, and that if I was meant to become aware of more women, they would somehow find me. Up to then, synchronicity had a pretty good track record with me. It appeared to always have my back, so I trusted that this would be no different.

Our session confirmed so much for me about what I had already suspected. By being gifted the ability to be shown the unmistakable connections reflected in our combined natal charts. This also made me realize the significance of the massive undertaking I was agreeing to carry, and the weight of this responsibility. This realization actually scared the living shit out of me for months afterwards. I admit it. This session was way more intense than I had even imagined it was going to be. Seeing it laid out right in front of me, like a cosmic roadmap, almost as if we had both preplanned this all on a soul level was enough to make me have to go sit down for weeks—or rather months - afterwards.

The enormity of the fact that I was very potentially going to be the "1" out of the "thousands" of women given this assignment who might manage to stay sane and centered enough to be able to even write this story nearly paralyzed me for some time. I am not even sure I would have been able to write it without Selene and her wisdom, mentorship, and her enormous capacity to hold the point for me during all the ups and downs of life and the process of writing it as I navigated my way through coming forward with this information, and that is the truth.

In some ways though, I feel that it was always going to be "me." I had to withstand much galactic training and many grueling Initiations in order to get me to a place where I was truly ready to step out with this story.

There was a strong message Selene kept repeating over and over to me that day: that I had to be smart about writing and releasing this information. That the timing of its release and the way in which it is presented would be crucial, as it had the power and potential to destroy lives rather than help them if any of the alignments, within myself, the book or the timing of its release, were off.

That day, I also received confirmation from Selene that my son, Noah, is definitely an integral part of this story somehow, and that Anthony's son will also likely be instrumental along the way, which wouldn't surprise me in the least.

Although I'd needed to hear the information about the potential dangers of coming out with this story, for a time I became paralyzed with the fears of doing something wrong, and heaven forbid, that me coming forth with my story might have repercussions in other people's lives, mainly my family's as well as Anthony's. That was not what I wanted for any of us.

I loved and cared for Jeff and the boys too much to risk anything. Was it worth it? I didn't know anymore, and so I couldn't progress with the book at all for the longest time. Anytime I tried, it was like I was attempting to move through quick sand or run through water. It felt painful, impossible, and like it would never end. It was all too much.

I would still attempt to sit with it and be productive, yet more often than not, I felt like I was spinning in circles, going nowhere. I was still such a mess that, by winter of 2012, I'd ended up with a 700-page document that was impossible for me to decipher what the hell I was doing or what I was even writing about.

It was extremely frustrating, but I still could not just throw it away entirely. Somewhere deep within my soul, I knew I would have to somehow find a way to move past this fear and write the damn book, because deep down in my heart, I knew I had agreed to do this before ever coming here, so I simply had to find a way.

In September 2012, I had started feeling that I may be ready to begin taking initiative again; this time from a newer, lighter perspective in regards to finishing the book. It seemed to wash over me one day, a feeling of '*Of course I can do this, and I don't have to hurt anyone in the process if I make certain I approach it always from the purity of my Heart space.*"

It was at this time I began to feel re-inspired and opened myself more fully to synchronicity again, which I'd realized I had closed myself off from through the screen of all my fears. I knew it was now time to move things to the next level and get on with it, so I did. Even though I ended up with a 700-page document, I knew it was important to release all the emotional baggage that had been holding me back so that I could eventually write the actual book that was always meant to be; the one you hold in your hands now.

This reading with Selene was huge for me. It was far beyond what I had expected to hear. After processing the enormity of it, with periods of time where I wanted to forget the whole damn thing, *more* high strangeness experiences began to present themselves, and undeniable synchronicity would smack me in the face and yell at me to get the hell back up and get in the game, because this damn book needed to be finished already.

The entire process provided a deeper clarity for me to where eventually, I was able to ground, center, and align myself enough to complete this part of my mission, thank the fucking Goddesses. Sometimes we need to fall on our asses for a bit and regroup before standing back up, stronger and more resilient than ever.

CHAPTER 70

The Labyrinth Activation, 20 Feet, Bouts of High Strangeness, & The Law of One

I was in the shower one beautiful sunny day in September 2012, clearing my energy field and consciously cleansing my chakra system, when I heard a mantra begin to run inside my mind on repeat: "I transmute all energies into The Law of One."

I didn't yet have a clear understanding of what The Law of One was, though I thought perhaps I may have read someone mention it online somewhere before. That was my extent of conscious awareness on this subject.

It simply felt right, *in alignment*, to begin repeating this mantra out loud as I cleared each chakra, and watched everything that was not aligned with me or my missions on the planet be cleansed out of my body, and run down the drain. This process felt amazing, and I wasn't entirely sure where I had pulled it from, but I knew it was working for me.

I stepped out of the shower and immediately felt the urge to dress myself entirely in white clothing, go outside on my back porch with a white sheet laid down in the dirt, and lie there, supine, soaking in the rays of the sun. While sun-charging, I asked for Divine Protection and Guidance to lead me through this unknown experience.

I learned later that "The Law of One" is also known as the RA material. In Ancient Egypt, RA is the god of the Sun.

I had grabbed my Star Gate quartz crystals that Selene had gifted me months before and placed them on my sacral, heart and third eye chakras, as well as above my crown and just below my feet. These crystals were one of Selene's biggest missions, during which they had been encoded by the Pleiadians while Selene held the point inside the Queen's Chamber of the Great Pyramid in Giza for three days non-stop back in November of 1983.

These crystals are tiny and powerful—holding at least 7,000,000 times celestial power compared to any other crystal on the planet.

I lay on my white sheet for about a half hour, breathing deeply and soaking in the sun's rays. This sort of ritualistic intuition had become unusual practice for me, yet I felt extremely guided to do it and had to honour that feeling. It felt so freeing to be in the flow of synchronicity again.

When I got up, I realized that I was menstruating, and felt to do something I had never done before. I took some drops of my blood, and mixed them with the red earth and a bit of spring water, and placed this mixture inside a glass bowl with some of the Star Gate quartz crystals. I then ceremoniously offered them up to the Earth underneath the apple tree in my backyard.

I wasn't exactly sure why I was doing this, but it felt like I was making an offering to our Earth Mother and every Goddess and God on the planet, setting my intentions for Clarity, Highest Truth, Divine Manifestation, and Unconditional Love. I prayed over the glass bowl containing this Sacred Alchemical Mixture and set my Intent on the Highest Light, the Highest Love, the Highest Truth and the Highest Outcome for All aspects of my life, every Mission, including the writing of this book. I was elevated after this and felt absolutely amazing, clear, and ready for whatever came my way. Then the synchronicities began to increase in frequency and the stakes began to rise significantly.

Within days, I was led to the information that Anthony's band was going to be in Phoenix within a few weeks. *'Of course,'* I thought. I looked into ticket prices, and saw that there was a seat in the fourth row floor that happened to be priced at the exact amount of money, to the dollar, that I had saved for the purposes of working on my book.

The price also happened to be a number that was significant energetically in my work with Anthony, so I decided I needed to pay attention and seriously consider attending this performance even through my obvious resistance. Synchronicity was knocking loudly, and I knew enough to pay attention.

I would never have paid for a ticket to go see any band in a huge stadium, especially at this point in my life. I'd left that life in my early twenties, after my ET experiences started and I no longer enjoyed the whole gong show these types of live events can turn in to. I'm no longer interested in being in a gigantic room with thousands of other people loaded to the gills with alcohol, drugs, and all too often misguided aggression. To top it off, I knew I wasn't a true "fan" of this band, even though I had come to appreciate them and the beautifully strong sense of integrity of the band as a whole. I had come to love and appreciate some of the music, especially for the codes they carried. But to go and submerse myself in that zoo-like atmosphere was overwhelming for me, being as empathic as I am.

Yet something in me kept saying *"Go!"*

This was not an easy decision for me to make, and I sat with it for a couple of days before finally committing. After all, I would have preferred to use the money for a healing massage or a day at the spa rather than a two-hour drive to Phoenix, only to end up in a huge stadium filled with drunken frat kids, the smell of booze seeping from their pores; a room filled with smoke and other people's bodily fluids splashing on me! I was thirty-seven, completely sober, and *so over* that kind of 'fun'!

I wasn't too excited about any of this frankly, but realized I had a higher calling and that I needed to listen to the voice within, who'd never seemed to steer me wrong before, so why would it start now? I surrendered, sort of half-wittedly, thinking of that massage I would have to begin saving for again.

The day of the concert, one day shy of it being exactly a year since my first reading with Selene, I was mere hours away of coming within feet of this man for the second time, also, almost exactly six years after the first time. This time though, I was to be inside the concert hall. I knew I had to do it.

Before heading in to the stadium, I decided I would meditate to shield and prepare myself as much as I could for being around such a massive number of people, many of whom I knew would be intoxicated. Meditating was the only thing that would center me and keep me focused. I knew I was not a true fan. I was not even sure I wanted to be there. But I *was*, and it was time to face the music, pun surely intended.

I finally entered the stadium and took my seat in the fourth row about ten or so minutes before Anthony's band was scheduled to come on. I continued to hold the energies through meditation and deep breathing to stay present. Holding my field was crucial, and the only way I would make it through this experience. I'm sure it's possible I stuck out like a sore thumb, and I didn't care.

The band took the stage, and my heart began to pump wildly. I continued to breathe deeply, not knowing what I was really in for, but here I was, and there was no undoing it now. I was riding this wave as far as it was going to take me.

And then there he was. Anthony was within about twenty or so feet of me, and the blood in my veins proceeded with its usual rush and my eyes welled with tears. I wasn't exactly sure why, but I didn't question or judge it. Whatever it was I had come there to do or experience, I simply allowed it to be.

Of course, it didn't surprise me that they played the two most activating songs for me and probably many others there that night, one of them being the third song in their queue—3 is the most significant number I have worked with since this connection had reignited for me years ago. This was also the song from Lynda's video experience from the hospital. And speaking of 3, if I wanted to track way back, I'd been working with the number 3 my entire life, even as a child.

I remember I had an almost obsessive/compulsive need. I had to do everything in threes. Even before ever seeing Anthony, being aware of his existence, I carried this vibration deep within my soul. Though since I have come to recognize it as a symbol of our multi-dimensional connection dating way, way back—even before this incarnation. More on the number 3 perhaps at a later time, in another book.

The third song started, and at first I didn't even recognize what it was until about half the way into it. That's how much of a "not fan" I am. I actually became frustrated with myself about it when I realized what song it was and that I had failed to recognize it. I felt I had missed a part of whatever activation I might be there to receive by way of its "live" encoding, though now I'm sure my cells soaked it up anyway. Immediately I summoned an extra force field of Sacred Space around myself, and sat down in a meditative state, breathing deeply in my seat while everyone else around me stood.

I could no longer see the stage. This didn't matter to me. I put all my focus on holding my own field and sending only positive vibrations onto the stage and around me, most specifically to Anthony.

It was intense. Seeing Anthony so close to me, within twenty feet, was interesting. I noticed right away that Anthony's energy that night felt a bit strange. I wondered if he might be sensing my presence. I felt ridiculous for wondering such a thing. Was my ego that inflated?. Of course, he was receiving and sensing a ton of energies; there were thousands of people there. Though I also knew he was used to performing in front of this many people by now.

I simply couldn't help but wonder: *Can he sense my presence?*

I didn't want to interfere with his experience at all. I began to doubt my own guidance that had so clearly led me there, as I was hoping it was not negatively affecting him in any way, even unconsciously. I tapped into my true reasons for being there, and it honestly was to simply "be" in the energies he helped create in *present* time and space. To help hold that space Sacred, and to do whatever "Cosmic Work" presented itself to me, without any attachment to what that might look like, if anyone would even notice, or to any sort of outcome whatsoever. I was totally in the flow.

I could do this! I began to send the entire band my love and appreciation for having created such magic for so many people throughout the world and presently in this giant room we were all gathered in, *right here, right now*. I telempathically sent the entire band this message of gratitude for always doing their best to make a positive mark on this planet. I "told" them all that I understood what they were doing, and was there to help hold this conscious space with them, in whatever way I could.

I was there in Divine Service.

I actually enjoyed sitting in meditation for the duration of the show, as one who was co-creating consciously with this beautiful, heartfelt band. I didn't know most of the music, though, over the years of having been aware of my connection with Anthony, I had come to respect him as a cosmic artist and divine messenger channeling whatever the cosmos wishes to send to the planet via his lyrics.

As the night came to a close, I noticed that Anthony had not uttered but a word or two the entire show, which seemed extremely odd to me. Perhaps it wasn't, but I felt he had seemed somewhat distracted, not entirely present on stage. It could have been a million different things that might have caused it, I simply couldn't help but find it peculiar.

I only recalled him saying "Thank you" at the very end of the show as he was leaving the stage—a common courtesy. I'm still quite certain he said nothing else the entire show. The other bandmates had carried a minimal amount of banter between songs. I was surprised by this display. For a group of usually goofy guys, I couldn't help but notice and wonder.

I wondered if perhaps Anthony may have felt or experienced anything different or odd that night to have instigated this seeming disconnect from the audience, or was it simply an *'I'm getting so tired of touring'* sort of night? Also, very possible. One could speculate forever about it if they wanted to. I really didn't know, and would not assume to know why. It was all simply peculiar to me.

I had brought some of my Star Gate Giza crystals with me. If I'd had the opportunity to give the crystals to Anthony, I was going to. I knew the likelihood was slim, but I brought them just in case. You never know. At one point, I even asked a security guard to take them back to him either during, before, or after the show. I wasn't asking if I could see or meet him personally, and I sure wasn't attempting to get backstage. The guard looked at me like I was just some silly fan, which felt really strange and honestly pretty gross, so I let it go. I realized this was not the place to do any visible galactic work. I had to stay quiet about it, so I did. It was a very strange experience all around and I am still not exactly sure why I'd had to be there. But I did. And I was. There must have been a reason for all of this, even if I would never know what that reason was. I felt at peace with this.

The activation I experienced from him and me being in the same room and at such close proximity led to another string of high strangeness, providing me with even more confirmation of this cosmic connection.

More High Strangeness.

Exactly one week after the concert, I was drawn to take a bath in my usual alchemical cleansing mixture of baking soda, sea salt (or pure Epsom salt), organic essential oils, and of course, crystals. I was meditating and enjoying this clearing release happening in my field. I felt very relaxed and calm, nearly falling asleep, when all of a sudden, a warm rush filled my entire body.

It intensified quickly, these energies pulsing through my body. I was in the middle of a meditation when I began physically vibrating and became sexually aroused. It took me something by surprise, it had come on so suddenly. I knew it was not coming from me, but rather something coming into me from the outside. That much was very clear.

What happened next was also surprising and unlike any other conscious paranormal experience I could remember. I felt my seed being taken from me. I experienced a physical energy reach in and remove some of my ovaries. It was a strong physical sensation, though not what I would label as painful. It was also an energetic sensation that left me feeling elated.

The energies subsided the moment the seed was acquired, which happened to be the same moment as orgasm, I might add. Once the seed was taken, I was finally able to relax again, and complete my meditation.

Immediately, I had the conscious thought that *'Wow, so this is what it feels like when they come and take your seed'* and I left it at that.

I was already so used to high strangeness, this was simply another notch on my galactic belt. I let it go, though still reveling somewhat in the intensity and fascination of having witnessed this sort of event in full consciousness.

I have since learned from Selene that this is exactly how the seed of the human "donors" are taken in the context of these types of genetic experiments, and she has also since confirmed for me that indeed, this is how every extraterrestrial species extrapolates the ovaries of women—at the moment of orgasm. This made so much sense to me, and of course, confirmed much for me about my own past experiences as well.

After this particular experience, I got out of the bath feeling rejuvenated. Something brought me to the computer to check for new messages and to take a quick peek at Facebook. I was stunned at what I saw a "friend" post during the exact time this high strangeness had been happening with me in the bathtub.

It was October 3, 2012, and this Facebook friend, Jocelyn (who turned out to be a Quantum Healing practitioner and who later facilitated a regression session for me), posted in all upper-case letters in her status that she had just *witnessed a UFO over top of Coffee Pot*, which is the exact area I lived in! And she was not the only witness, as others began to chime in and comment that they too had seen it, and that additionally, five military helicopters quickly swept in and chased it away.

Now there was a synchronistic confirmation if ever I'd had one! What would be the odds of a UFO sighting in my neighbourhood, in broad daylight, precisely as I was experiencing something that I was *absolutely certain* was extraterrestrial in nature!? In that moment, still not knowing how these experiments worked, I was convinced that my intuition of these strange energies that had taken me over were directly related to whomever was in that craft spotted at the exact same time near my house.

About two weeks after this experience, I felt drawn to get deep into my work on the book again. I realized the significance that the concert had been only a day off from my very first reading with Selene, a year earlier in September 2011. Then this unusual seeding experience exactly one week after that. What all of this meant, or if they were even connected, I didn't really know for sure, other than it was all interesting timing, and synchronicity appeared to be in the driver's seat again.

Within days of Anthony's concert, I'd found myself in New Mexico, back full circle at The Light Institute—more than nine years after the last time I'd been there and 11 years since my initial powerful sojourn there. I had not been there since that second trip I'd taken in April 2003 with Paul where we both did a series of multi-incarnational sessions. This trip was about a half a year before I became impregnated with Noah, my eldest son.

On my trip in 2012 though, I didn't have the money to do a session series, which would have been amazing, but I did go and receive a cranial session, and then took part in their fire walk.

I stayed in town for the weekend, with the intention to begin my book anew. I wanted to write it as a fictional novel, as I felt it might reach more people that way. That was my goal that weekend, as well as to walk on fire without chickening out. I was absolutely terrified to do this, yet I knew that if I could actually overcome my intense fear of being "burned alive," releasing the cellular memory from other incarnations where I had experienced this, it would help me overcome my fears of being burned in this lifetime for simply being who I am, and for writing and releasing my story to the world.

I never thought it possible that me, the one who jumps in panic whenever I light a match and start to feel the flame even slightly burning my finger, would ever walk on fire. Cellular memory of witch burnings and the Cathar genocide, I wonder? Never in a million years had I thought I would be able to handle walking with my bare feet across burning red hot coals, unscathed. Sure, I'd wanted to try it for years, simply because I knew how consciousness-shifting it would be. Yet that nagging self-doubt didn't believe fully that I would actually ever be able to bring myself to do it.

It was exhilarating. I remember standing underneath the vast starry night sky with a group of people, one woman that I had remembered from my very first stay there in December 2001. She was one of the five of us from the Sexuality workshop I had taken part in, where I'd met the man who had spoken about being a "galactic seed."

We both remembered one another, and the whole night was a wonderful experience with many amazing people. Chris Griscom was also there, the founder of The Light Institute. She pointed out the Pleiades in the starry sky to all of us, and a few spoke matter-of-factly about our Star Brothers and Sisters. This time, I finally got it. 11 years prior, I hadn't a clue what they really meant when they spoke of "galactic" anything. I didn't realize that there is no "us" and "them," but rather, "us" and "us."

I was really nervous, still nursing my left-over traumas from having been burned to death in parallel realities, or previous incarnations. I was breathing deeply, helping hold the Sacred Space in our circle around the fire pit as, one by one, people would walk the fire and speak a prayer or incantation aloud.

The woman I'd met in 2001 must have run across those coals 20 times before I ever managed to muster up the courage to go for it myself. I'd been standing there breathing deeply through my fears, when all of a sudden I heard Sulannaya's voice say to me *'This is your chance! Are you going to seize the moment and the opportunity, or are you going to let it slip away? We are all ready, whenever you are!"*

I giggled a bit to myself at how silly my fears seemed, and how patient she was with me, whilst simultaneously giving me a very deliberate kick in the rear so that I wouldn't blow this opportunity.

Then I did it! I walked across those red-hot coals, and I'd never felt more alive and ferocious and powerful! It was incredible because, at the same time, I felt such a profound sense of peace and joy, and wanted to walk those coals over and over again. I ended up walking them about 15 times, walking in honour of miraculous, instantaneous healing, walking in honour of my children—both Earth and Sky. Walking in honour of Divine Motherhood, walking in honour of the Goddess, walking in honour of Divinity made Manifest, walking in honour of the Great and Mysterious Unknown, walking in honour of my Self, walking in honour of the Souls I was sharing this magical experience with, walking, walking, walking in honour of BE~ing a part of this incredibly auspicious time here on the planet.

That fire walk was highly activating, and I could feel deep healing of so many aspects of myself taking place. It was one of the most incredible sensations I have ever experienced.

I was buzzing for the rest of the night and all the next day. My feet felt absolutely amazing. They tingled with a life force I had never known before. They were pink on the bottoms, yet I had zero pain or discomfort. In fact, they had never felt so good. I swore then that I would bring my kids one day to have an experience like this, knowing that especially Noah, my little Fire-Moon Child, would be highly intrigued and excited by it.

CHAPTER 71

The Fourth Activation: Prophecy Fulfilling

A few weeks after my journey to New Mexico, I finally felt the call to visit Angel Valley in Sedona. I'd known about it for more than three years, but had yet to step foot on the land.

I'd just finished a session with Tapzyana, during which I talked about wanting to go somewhere to focus on finishing my book. Somewhere away from the distractions of being a mother, even for a few days. She mentioned Angel Valley to me, and told me I needed to go talk with Michael, the man who stewards the land and runs the retreat center there. Apparently, Dr. Masaru Emoto had tested their water and said it was one of the purest sources on the planet he'd seen. I was definitely intrigued to go there, and at the very least, drink some highly activated sacred water.

When I left Tapzyana's office, I headed directly over to Angel Valley in hopes of arranging a work trade with them in exchange for allowing me to complete my book there. When I arrived, I was told that before I would be permitted to speak with Michael I needed to walk their labyrinth. A little strange I thought, but I complied, wondering what the deal was, but more than happy to walk the stunning spiral pathway.

Their labyrinth is an exact replica of the one found in the Chartres Cathedral in France, built by Mary Magdalene and her people. This definitely pricked up my ears as I'd had my own personal vision of and connection made with Mary Magdalene at the start of 2012. In an attempt to understand this connection further, I had also since listened to the audio recording of Kathleen McGowan's book, "The Expected One," which details the relationship and sacred work between Jesus and Mary Magdalene.

I was reminded that the main character, Maureen, who in the story travels to France, investigating this relationship after receiving messages from her own dreams, has a powerful experience when she walks the Chartres Cathedral labyrinth for the first time.

I "heard" before entering the labyrinth, before I was even aware of there being a cloaked ship hovering above me, that I was to walk this path barefoot. Probably in an effort to slow me down, be present and take it all in, now that I look back and recall the gigantic galactic activation I would experience during this walk.

It was quite exhilarating, once I got over the intensity of hundreds of tiny red rocks digging into my feet. At one point, as I felt a pang of regret for surrendering to this guidance, I was "told" that this was the best acupressure treatment I could ever hope to receive, as it hit every single point on the soles of my feet. It was helping open up all my channels, in order to receive the massive energies that were to come, forcing me to walk slowly and deliberately, meditatively, and receive the heavy downloads that awaited me.

During the entire journey, I felt very strongly the presence of a craft hovering about 30-50 feet above me. Though it was not visible to my eyes, I could feel it there with every cell of my body, and knew I was not imagining it.

As I delved more deeply into the experience, the pain in my feet morphed into energized open portals ready to receive information. Then I heard a voice, and felt a consciousness from above, download me with sacred symbols and vast amounts of information about my connection and planetary work with Anthony. It was pouring in so fast, there was no way to consciously decipher with my tiny human mind each download individually or to remember it all in detail, though somewhere inside of me, I knew I would retain the information in the DNA of my cellular structure.

I was being activated to the max. Not what I had envisioned when deciding to come that day, yet definitely a welcome surprise.

It took me 45 minutes to walk the entire labyrinth, and when I was done, I breathed deeply, taking in the enormity of what had just occurred. I then proceeded up to Michael's office. I had to focus on the task at hand now and would process what had happened in the labyrinth later. I'd never had an experience like this before and certainly had not been ready for such an experience that day.

I should note that this day also happened to be Anthony's 50th birthday. More cosmic synchronicity.

I quickly realized after talking with Michael for a few minutes that this was probably not the place for me to write my book. We were not really an energetic match. So why had I been drawn here? To receive the download in the labyrinth? And what was the significance of that, I wondered.

And then I saw something. I noticed a book up above Michael's seat and to his left. There was a drawing on the cover of a being that looked like an ET to me. My heart started to race, and I realized that there might be a connection here between the ship I'd felt above me and this ET in the picture.

I finally couldn't stand it any longer and after our meeting which lasted almost an hour, I said to Michael, "I noticed that picture beside you. I have had experiences myself," and I left it at that.

You see, I hadn't told him what my book was even about.

He jumped up and ran to the table behind the chair I was sitting in and took a brochure off of it. There on the brochure was the labyrinth I had just walked with a picture of a triangular space craft photo-shopped over top of it. And it looked *EXACTLY* like the ship that had escorted me home after my Ayahuasca experience the night of February 18th earlier that year!

My jaw dropped and I was speechless for a moment. I realized quickly that there was indeed a very strong ET/otherworldly/galactic presence on this land. Finally, I managed to blurt out, "I've seen that ship! It followed me home one night!"

Michael went on to explain to me that they had built the labyrinth in honour of the Chartres Cathedral labyrinth in France, an exact replica, with the intention to have it become a landing pad for ET craft, specifically during first contact.

He said nothing to me that day about the hybrids or Bashar. I had no idea until a year later that the being in the picture beside his desk was Bashar, or that the landing pad was specifically created for the landing of the hybrid children. I likewise didn't tell him that day about any of my experiences, so he had no idea just how connected to this mission of his I was. That I may even be holding a part of the key for him.

My feeling remains that he and I are definitely not an energetic match, so no love-loss there. Simply interesting synchronistic details. And the fact that he'd built a structure based on The Magdalene created specifically as a bridge for connecting the hybrid races with this planet, I do find intriguing, and parallel to my own Sacred Path.

I left Angel Valley highly energized that day, and I was not exactly sure what had happened to me there, but I was certain something had. It was indeed no accident that I'd ended up on that land, on that particular day. I had experienced the very tangible presence of a ship above me, and had definitely experienced a major download. All the while, until meeting with Michael, I'd had no idea that Angel Valley's quest was to create a safe place for the integration and reunion of our Sky family with their Earth family.

This bridging is a very large part of my own mission, and my main reason for writing this book.

I'd had no clue that Angel Valley was doing any of this when I went there that day—on Anthony's birthday. And yet, the ship I had very clearly sensed above me was real. So real in fact, that when I awoke the following morning, I had two large puncture marks in the palm of my right hand, that looked fairly deep, though were not at all painful. I didn't notice them straight away, as it had taken me a while to come to that morning. But they were unmistakable. I had done nothing the day before nor that morning that would have caused these markings on my body.

When I did notice them, it was simply more confirmation for me about the happenings of the day before, and I walked around in a sort of cosmic daze at this physical evidence. In my ungrounded state, I showed my hand to Jeff, and his response was so nonchalant, almost bored, as he was getting used to, and probably tired of, me and my encounters with high strangeness.

"I think you already know what that is," he muffled. Of course, I knew what he meant. He meant that I'd been aboard ship the night before.

So, I checked my sources within to see if this were true, as for some reason, I was admittedly surprised to hear this coming from Jeff of all people. I felt deep inside me the truth of Jeff's statement, yet I was not used to him being open to any of this, so had to consult my own inner guidance system.

I felt and heard the response, immediately: 'Of course you were aboard ship last night. You and Anthony celebrated his birthday together.'

WOW. Talk about high strangeness. And what did that even mean?

I knew in my heart and soul it was the truth though. I knew that my connection with this man went far deeper than anything my logical Earthly mind could muster as an explanation. I knew that our souls were unmistakably interconnected in some way. I knew that we were doing important planetary and galactic work together.

I knew then, as I had always known.

I had felt the need to come clean with Jeff the day we were legally married, on August 20, 2008. I shared aloud with him one of my most frightening "little secrets." I was prompted by several of Anthony's songs coming on the radio synchronistically as we drove. I took it as a sign that I needed to pay attention to, and finally, in an attempt to start our life together off on as honest a foot as I could (as much as one can disclose this sort of bizarre information anyway), I did my very best to explain the situation to him. I still did not have nearly even close to a clear understanding of it all myself, so I simply said what I knew to be true.

"Jeff, there is something about this man I need to tell you. I have been doing work with him in other planes and dimensions for many years now. I am connected with him beyond my human, third dimensional self and comprehension.

"I know that one day I am going to meet him. I know that we are supposed to meet in person. I know that somehow, he is connected with Noah's birth, and that somehow, I am connected with his own son's birth.

"I know that there is something important we are going to have to do together once we meet, and I know that the purpose of it all is to help people on the planet through our work together and through this multidimensional connection.

"I do not know exactly what this is going to look like, but I just need you to know this. One day, he and I are going to meet, and my life will never look the same again."

I truly could not believe what I was hearing come out of my mouth, yet I knew it was the truth.

As I mentioned back in The Cosmic Equation chapter, beginning in 2006 after having become re-awakened to Anthony's significant presence in my life, I was witness to a recurring vision that has stayed in the forefront of my consciousness, even after all these years. I always knew there was something very significant about this vision. It felt huge for me because it persisted in presenting itself for many years, even without any rational or otherwise understanding of it.

In this vision, I'd witness myself standing in Anthony's physical presence, and each time, I was handing him a book. I knew this mysterious book was "the thing" that was going to bring us together in the physical realms, and that it would serve the purpose of grounding our multi-dimensional connection into the earthly dimensions, and that it was all for the Greater Good of the planet.

I received this vision multiple times, and continued to misinterpret it.

At the time, I began looking at every single metaphysical book that I felt even remotely drawn to, wondering *'might this be*

The Book?' I knew that I was to somehow get The Book to Anthony. Yet no book I saw ever seemed to be "the one" that I, he, was searching for. It became rather tedious and frustrating after a while, as this vision would never seem to let up, and continued to nag at me by showing up over and over again.

I knew somehow without a doubt that this *book* I was gifting him in every one of these visions was going to hold very important Key Codes of Activation and cosmic messages for him, as well as for myself. I knew that on some level, whether consciously or unconsciously, he was awaiting the moment when he would receive this book from me.

I knew that the book I was handing him was going to change both of our lives. I knew this same book would assist him, as well as myself, to open up in ways in which neither of us had ever quite experienced with another person on this Earth plane before. And I knew that this book would irrefutably connect us, always, through all aspects of time and space. I knew that in the physical exchange of gifting him with this mystery book, it would activate, for both of us, whatever our assignments were together on the planet, at this particular time.

I could not have fathomed all those years ago that the nook I was gifting Anthony in every one of those visions would be written by me.

This is The Book. The Seed of it All.

And *NOW* is The Time.

It is here that I jump off the edge of the cliff into the Great Unknown, wings ablaze, free as a bird, into the realms of Infinite Possibilities, inspired by the mystery.

About a week after my highly charged event at Angel Valley I had a strange incident where I began seeing cars driving slowly in front of my home. I started to feel a bit strange, as not only did this start suddenly, but it was accompanied by other bizarre things that began happening around me at the same time.

This one particular day, I got stuck driving behind a black sedan in Oak Creek Canyon on the way to pick up Noah. I noticed this car had a personalized license plate: "*MNINBLK.*" What were the odds? By far one of the strangest things I'd ever seen connected with timing and synchronicity. This car seemed to be deliberately driving 20 miles an hour in a 40-mile-an-hour zone.

I became mildly suspicious, thinking that someone in there was messing with me. The car was moving at a snail's pace, and I couldn't find a safe place to pass it amidst the winding roads and very few passing opportunities. I finally passed that car and its tinted windows the first chance I got, which was nearly at the other end of the canyon. Then I took off as fast as I could, feeling a very strange energy present. It could have simply been paranoia, or it could have been authentic. I can only hazard a guess, and for the record, my guess is on the latter. But who knows for certain.

This occurred a mere two days before I would be heading to Phoenix to attend my very first writing retreat with the full intention of writing this entire book in that one weekend. It turned out that I spent the weekend purging my entire life story out of me, so that the following summer I would be able to start again fresh and focus the information more clearly.

The intention to write my story was definitely there, and the timing of this car showing up directly in front of me was uncanny, especially after the strange full-body orgasmic ovary-heist I'd experienced only a short couple of weeks before, as well as my ship reunion with Anthony mere days before this.

All this high strangeness nonsense had become old hat.

CHAPTER 72

~ELLENA~ ET Experiments Hijacked

In my session with Selene on my birthday in 2012, she told me that I would start meeting other women who had similar experiences as me. With Anthony in particular.

I wondered how this could possibly manifest, especially before I was speaking out about it publicly with anyone other than her.

And then it happened. When I least expected it, it surely happened.

It was November 8, 2012, one week after my Angel Valley experience, and I was at the local organic grocery store, gathering my stash of raw food snacks to take with me to my writing retreat in Phoenix.

I had known Ellena as one of the staff members in charge of the raw foods section in the store, and also knew she was a mom. I was always sort of attracted to her energy. Something about her resonated the frequency of sisterhood, though we had not yet developed a personal friendship by this point.

Though if I happened to come by there as she was doing her inventory or stocking shelves, we would always chit chat, and we seemed to speak the same internal language. We could sense we were similar in ways. She had a very real, sort of hard-core truth about the way she spoke which I instantly appreciated and even found humourous. I think the feeling was mutual.

I liked her. I knew what I was getting with this woman. There were no games or hidden agendas with her, ever. It was always clear to me that whatever her story was, she had lived through some very real shit.

On November 8th, I was standing in the raw foods aisle gathering my snacks for the weekend when we started chatting. I ended up telling her I was going to a writing retreat to write my book and finally get it done. She asked me what I was writing about, and I gave her a vague description, something about "experiences I've had and where they've led me" or something cryptic like that.

Right away, being a highly skilled intuitive, she picked it up and said, "You mean like with spirits or aliens or something?" She took me totally off guard. Usually people stared at me blankly when I gave this kind of description and then changed the subject. Not Ellena. Somehow she knew at least the essence of what I was referring to.

"Yeah, there is definitely stuff about that in there," I confessed. "A lot, actually."

"Oh, girl, let me tell you, I know all about spirits. I've been messed with for so long, I don't give a fuck anymore. I just tell them, 'You aren't messing with me, that's it, and give me my fucking stuff back already.' Oh yeah, they take my shit all the time, and they've tried to take me down, but I didn't let them."

I was standing there, listening to this woman who I knew somehow understood me. Her experiences seemed much more intense than mine. I knew she had walked the initiatory path of a warrior who had been messed with and had had to pull herself out from the trenches and burning embers more than once, even in this lifetime.

We ended the conversation with her telling me we should get together when I got back from my retreat to discuss my new raw food line that I was still developing and attempting to get into her section of the store. She was already reserving a shelf space for me and my products for whenever I was ready to launch them, and she wanted to help support me in getting my business up and running as soon as possible. We agreed to meet and talk about some ways she might be able to help me make that happen.

So, I went to the retreat. I began the book from scratch that weekend, and was the only person there that did not finish my book. I was at 70,000+ words, nearly 700 pages, and still huddled in a corner as everyone else celebrated finishing theirs.

Writing this book continued to be a long, painful, drawn-out experience, especially because I was still, after all that writing, avoiding one of the most important storylines in it. Anthony. I was not giving up on it though. I knew without a doubt by that point that I was meant to write this damned book. It was only me standing in my own way and that was the most frustrating aspect of it all to be honest.

After I got back from the retreat, I called Ellena and we set an appointment time to meet at her home on one of her days off to talk about my business.

I was looking forward to it, as I had started feeling a deeper sort of connection with this woman once I'd realized we spoke the same language, metaphysically. I didn't find many people I could fully be myself with, so this was a promising connection, perhaps even a friendship, I was making.

I showed up at her home the morning that we'd scheduled. She lived in a small town outside of Sedona. When I showed up, she was a bit frazzled as her husband just couldn't seem to understand her spiritual path, which she lived and breathed daily, committed to fully. So, this caused friction in their relationship. This particular morning had been a hard one for her.

Ellena jumped in the shower, and once she felt settled a bit, we went into her kitchen. We sat down for some tea, and things took an interesting turn.

She asked me how writing the book had gone. I told her it wasn't done, and that the experience was amazing but intense. I told her that there was a section of it that I knew needed to be written, but that I was avoiding it because I was afraid of sounding crazy. I told her I was working up the courage to get over that and write it in.

Ellena asked me what I was afraid of people calling me crazy for. Then, in an attempt to set my mind at ease, she ended up sharing some of her own experiences with extraterrestrial types of energies—and as she sometimes would refer to them—*spirits or beings from other dimensions*—that would follow her, give her directions about what to do, where to go, even sending angels and shapeshifters in her path to support the assignments she was being sent on. It was then that I felt compelled to share a little bit of my own story with her. Something inside me told me it was time to tell someone, and that for some reason, Ellena was an important one to tell.

I still played it safe though. I told her that there was a certain connection with a person of "celebrity status" that I had had many experiences with throughout my life that I could never fully explain nor understand. I told her that I was coming to terms with the understanding, and that I knew it needed to somehow be a part of my book.

I did not name the celebrity; I didn't give a first name. Nothing. I didn't even say what he did.

This is when Ellena started *really* opening up with me, and *nothing* could have prepared me for what she was about to share!

First of all, she shared with me that she had had dreams of a certain Native American celebrity, and that within a year of these dreams beginning, she met him in L.A. in line at a local health food store. She met him on Father's Day 2010, and they ended up spending a lot of time together for the next couple of days. He had just finished filming a movie that, interestingly, involved aliens, which she noted to me, and together they shared an intense, otherworldly connection, similar to what she had been shown in her dreams a year prior.

She ended by saying that she always wondered if the two of them had other work they were to do together, and wondered if their paths may cross again someday.

Ellena then asked me if the celebrity I'd had "experiences" with was an actor, and I said no, that he was a musician. Things really heated up then, as if they weren't already.

Ellena launched into another story about how she'd had a whole "thing" with a certain celebrity as well, back in 1992, and that this man was also a musician. She told me that this experience lasted for two years. The difference with this connection was that she never was able to physically make contact with him. And then she told me who it was.

We both nearly dropped to the floor when I gasped for breath and told her that this man I was to write about was the same person. It was Anthony!

We both sat there in a state of awe and shock. Of all the musicians out there she could have been referring to, it was him.

'Selene told me this was going to happen!' I thought to myself. And boy, was it happening!

Ellena went on to confide in me that, at one point, she found out that Anthony was in Hawaii on the same island she was, writing the album that would go on to include the song that activated both of us, and most likely thousands of others, at exactly the same time that Ellena had felt a strong calling to travel there and stay for a period of time herself.

Apparently Ellena had had an experience in 1992 with a guy claiming to channel aliens. After this she started hearing messages and codes in the lyrics of a certain band's music—Anthony's band. She was hearing subliminal messages encoded in the music, and at the time, she was certain the vocalist was talking to her and that the messages were "meant for her." Sound familiar? Around the same time, she noted that people from her past lives started showing up in her current life again, and she was able to recognize them.

She was searching for him and trying to make a physical connection with him for two years. She even moved there, convinced she was meant to be with him, because of these experiences she was having. Hearing even this much of Ellena's story was a gigantic confirmation for me. What were the odds I would come across such a detailed story of another woman having such similar experiences as me? The only difference being she had been younger and, in her confusion in trying to make sense of it, took drastic actions in an attempt to figure it out.

She was showing me the path I could have taken in regards to my own experiences. I am so glad I had the Voice always gently telling me *"It is not yet time,"* instead of thrusting myself in front of him when I wasn't ready or grounded or centered in my knowing of what this cosmic connection truly is.

Back to Ellena though. She described these experiences, and her "following" the Spirits' call out to Hawaii, as if she had been in a hypnotic state when she did it. That the spirits as she referred to them, had led her there. Who knows what it really was. It could have been a number of things, which is still a mystery to her. I found her whole hypnotic fixation on him in response to the codes she began hearing after "the ET channeler" experience highly interesting. And the whole connection with meeting with him in her dreams parallel in so many ways to my own story.

It was August 16[t], 1992 when Ellena received this activation or otherworldly message which sent her on her wild goose chase to the tropical islands. I am not certain what was happening for me specifically at that time in my life, but I know I was seventeen then and that it was within mere months of the age I was when I'd first seen Anthony on my television screen.

These activations occurred for both of us at relatively the same time. I wonder now how many others were a part of this gigantic experiment. My guess would be thousands, if not more.

There was also a connection I began tracking with the ages seventeen and twenty-two, as these were both significant ages for both myself and Ellena, we realized that day. At age seventeen, we both underwent a gigantic Activation which led us to big shifts at the age of twenty-two. Seventeen was when I first saw Anthony and didn't understand what was happening to me, and twenty-two was the year 1997, when I was deep in the trenches of my initial ET experiences which totally rewired and changed me and how I viewed myself in this world.

My interaction with Ellena was too wild. Here it came to pass, as Selene had said it would: I had actually met another woman who'd had very similar, and dare I say even parallel experiences as me. It was so incredibly intense. More confirmation of my own experiences, and with someone I personally knew and could talk with about it.

I marveled that within the span of only a few short months, I'd personally, and unknowingly, connected with two other women who shared this sort of connection with Anthony that involved otherworldly experiences.

'This guy is really getting around,' I jokingly thought to myself. Because when faced with such intense and undeniable Galactic Truth, you've got to keep a little humour about it all, or you're in trouble.

Ellena told me that she finally left Hawaii after two years of searching for Anthony, and more importantly, after surviving an attempt on her life. Were the two connected? And was she being tracked through this, and if so, by whom?

This poor woman was manipulated through different methods of mind control for being open to the wrong people about her experiences. Talk about a hard lesson in discernment. Eventually she broke free, and came back to the mainland, settling back on the reservation in Northern California. She still often found herself driving to L.A., following the messages she was still receiving through the encoded lyrics in Anthony's music.

Also during this time, Ellena was admitted by her mother (who couldn't understand her otherworldly connections and was concerned about her) into several different mysterious institutions for "government testing," and endured some very intense and unpleasant experiences involving mind control and secret agents who ended up trying to use her for her spiritual gifts. She would give them none of it. If nothing else, this woman is unwavering in her strength and power and is not afraid to stand up for herself, against anyone.

At one point during this time, she found herself waking up on a table, strapped down to it, with about 30 or 40 others in the room, strapped down on identical tables just like her. She recalls vividly that a massive person, a "government official" standing in front her, had a large tail. At the time, she didn't know what it was, but she knew without a doubt that he was strong and powerful. She said he was very large, that he made clicking sounds, and his energy seemed to feel dangerous.

Ellena feels now that this was potentially a malevolent reptilian being, working in cahoots with the government, though she has never stated this for absolute certain, as they did have her heavily drugged at the time. Though make no mistake about it, she was definitely coherent. She does remember forcefully questioning this strange authority figure, after which incident she was immediately transferred to the psychiatric ward.

She feels quite certain that this all happened because of her time in Hawaii, and she felt that the spirits, perhaps aliens, were the ones trying to get her committed.

There is so much more to this story, but it is Ellena's to tell if she ever chooses to. I am simply laying out a picture of when these kinds of experiences and experiments can possibly be harmful to the women unfortunate enough to have to endure them. The women who experience this level of sinister mindfuckery repeatedly often end up fractured, sometimes permanently, or worse, dead.

I am so relieved that Ellena lived to tell me even a fraction of her story, as it confirmed what I had already been learning, yet here was a woman who had lived through aspects of these experiments that had the very real potential of becoming a living nightmare.

This woman is so strong. Her strength and courage amaze and inspire me.

At the end of the 1990s, Ellena was finally able to let this whole experience go. She had to, for the sake of her own sanity and life. She stopped searching for answers where, at the time, there weren't any. She didn't want to be seen or labeled as crazy any longer. It was not serving her in the least, and was only hurting her. The people and the answers she was seeking were not available, and she realized that all she wanted was to simply live a normal life. This is when Ellena finally married and gave birth to her daughters, and started to turn her life around. She was able to put her past experiences behind her and focus on her new family.

Ellena made peace with perhaps never knowing what it truly was that was driving her to find Anthony and seek answers through her bizarre and otherworldly connection with him.

She shared with me details about her DNA Activation on August 16, 1992, and we talked about the two of us being only two amongst many, many women who have survived this strange experiment and come out of it with our minds and souls still intact, thank God.

We paid homage to the women who have not been so lucky, who have been used for these same or similar experiments and who, without proper discernment intact, have said the wrong things to the wrong people, been locked up for it or turned to drugs on their own as a way to cope with the weight and confusion these intense energies can cause, only to overdose or worse, intentionally take their own lives out of utter desperation, confusion and loneliness.

It is time for this nonsense to *stop*. It *does not* have to be this way. If we can only understand what is really happening, and trust that none of us is ever alone in this game of galactic chess, and that there are so many others out there who have had similar, and sometimes even identical, experiences. Then we can begin to help save many more hearts, spirits, minds and even lives from such unnecessary suffering.

Ellena still questions why she was "chosen" for this particular experiment, and hopes to gain more clarity for greater peace of mind one day. Unfortunately, I could not really offer her that answer at the time, especially since her personal story is so wrought with outside interference and so much darkness. She did say, however, that it was immensely helpful to receive such strong confirmation of her own experiences with her celebrity connections, and perhaps why they occurred, and so powerfully, in the first place. I was happy I could help give her some answers to at least that.

When more women begin to realize they are not actually alone in these often confusing experiences, and they begin to step forward with courage, so much more clarity will come for all of us. Until then, we've simply got to have each other's backs.

More and more, these confirmations were showing me that my own experiences have been as real as the air that I breathe. Even though I no longer need the proof for myself, it is incredible for me to hear these women's stories. Both uniquely different from mine, yet both similar enough at the roots to be a strong, common thread.

There are many of us out there taking part in these experiments unknowingly, many connected with Anthony alone. So many other "celebrities" are also taking part in this experiment and others like it whether they realize it or not. It is all part of the Divine Galactic Plan for the most part, and in its essence, it is perfect.

I know that each story, each experience, will vary depending on each woman's specific assignments and piece to the galactic puzzle, yet in this, we are unified, all part of the same cosmic family, *all a part of the same ultimate plan*.

I found this whole interaction and relationship with Ellena to be quite fascinating in all honesty. I am so grateful to have met her. Of course, it was synchronicity guiding us both, and our connection served each of us in positive ways.

I also find it endlessly fascinating that there most definitely are cosmic encodings within Anthony's music that must activate those of us with compatible or pre-coded DNA who await them to trigger our own wakening. These encodings serve us in such a deeply galactic and spiritual way. The divine messages coming through the channel of his music, and of others' creative offerings in the public eye like him who are reaching millions upon millions in this way, connect us all in a most divine, multi-dimensional cosmic dance.

What a gift he is to the planet, being such an open and willing channel for these messages. A kind of galactic shaman in a way. I am so very grateful and blessed to have awakened enough to receive these gifts and then keep myself centered and calm enough to be able to offer up publicly my own small personal piece of this fascinating cosmic puzzle.

This is our collective cosmic dance with synchronicity. For those with the ears to hear.

CHAPTER 73

Quantum Healing & December 2012 Activations

That first writing retreat I'd attended November 9-11, 2012 was only a first step in the process of being ready to actually write the book I was to publish. There was so much pain and fear and suffering to purge in those earlier versions. I also kept avoiding certain aspects of my story. I was still playing it safe, especially with the information regarding Anthony. Besides which, I had a whole lot more in store to experience before I would really understand what I was actually writing about. I still didn't fully understand the energetic frequency of the message I was to share, so I was not yet able to successfully write about it. I didn't know this yet though, so I kept plugging away at that giant manuscript after my writing retreat. I was like a hamster spinning in my wheel.

In the meantime, I kept digging into my inner work.

I had previously been offered a quantum healing session by a woman in town I'd met on social media, after an exchange we'd had in an online forum a couple of months prior. In fact, this was the same woman, Jocelyn, who had witnessed the UFO near my home when my eggs were extracted and had posted her sighting online. This all occurred before we ever actually met.

We finally synced up our schedules and on December 7, 2012 we had our session. I mentioned something before we started about her social media posting about the ship near Coffee Pot Rock. She remembered exactly what I was talking about.

Jocelyn had studied quantum healing directly from Dolores Cannon. She was passionate about these regression healings, and had seen many people heal and benefit as a result of them. She knew I had been on a major physical healing journey for the past two years and she wanted to help me receive answers to some of my questions.

In our session, I asked to be given information on how the ET experiments I am involved in on the planet really work, because I felt strongly that if I was writing about it, I'd better be certain of the information I would be sharing, and I wanted to be as clear a channel as possible in this sharing. My goal was to help people, so I wanted to be absolutely certain that what I was writing was precise and accurate.

I was intrigued and admittedly somewhat nervous about the session. I'm always a bit unsteady when facing the unknown, even though I inevitably muster up the courage to dive head first in to it.

There's always that small moment of hesitation, that feeling of not knowing where the edge is, or where there might be a surprise drop-off, a cliff. There is that feeling that I might suddenly drown in a pool of my own darkness if I dive in too deeply.

But I have a Galactic Scorpio Moon. I crave that kind of depth; I need it and need to embrace it in order to grow and be happy and do the galactic work I came here to do. I always manage to find the light inside even the deepest, most dreaded darkness. I knew I would be better than okay after this.

Yes, I trusted I was there for a reason. I never really let these kinds of uncertainties scare me off in any of my experiences, this one included. I was more than ready to delve into the darkest depths of mystery that day. I was ready to go as far and as deep as possible, knowing that nothing in this world can actually "kill" me, so what was there to lose?

It's that rush of adrenaline that comes with uncovering the truth for me that really gets me excited in times like this. I was nervous, but also very excited by what I might learn about myself in this session.

Quantum Healing Session with Jocelyn - December 7, 2012:

"I am in a land that is warm. It is sandy. There are pyramids and lots of people. Strong sense of community.

I live in a large castle in the hills. I am of royal bloodline, though enjoy spending time with the community, dressing in disguise so that no one makes a fuss over me, and quietly passing out treasures for people to find, to help them, as I know they work very hard and most of them have families to feed. I love being able to do this, with no one having to know.

I have a good family. My father, the King, is kind and generous in his own ways. I do prefer to spend most of my time alone though. I walk alone on our land, and go off the grounds where people can't see me. I commune with elementals and other dimensional beings when I am out here, and it is where I feel most at home. I commune with the animals, butterflies, fairies, and also a special Being that I visit with daily.

He comes down on a ship and we teach each other about the worlds that we live in. He is an off-world being.

He is green and looks like an insect, but he is not an insect. He is insect-like, yet still humanoid. He has arms, legs, a torso and head, and walks upright. He is extremely gentle. He is also somewhat of a shapeshifter, as he can become different sizes at will.

The ship he travels on is very large and round. There are lights, but once it lands, the lights disappear so as not to draw attention to our secret meetings. The ship also changes, and cloaks itself. It is a living organism and can expand or contract as well on the outer dimensions. Inside, it always stays the same size.

On board the ship, there are doors and portals that open and close. There are bright purple lights, and white lights in a lounging area that feels more social with comfy chairs to sit in.

There is a meeting room with chairs and a large table. The chairs are silver and white. The silver chairs have a device on them like an open hole on the chair overhead. The white chairs do not have this.

I have been visiting this craft since childhood. My mother and father also know about this ship, as my mother grew up on it also. It is our secret. This is how no one worries about me when I am gone. They always make certain of this, to allow me my experience and to do the Work I am here to do.

I am in charge of bridging the worlds, and uniting people of both races through the Love frequency. Bridging together the differences, releasing fear and misunderstanding.

The Beings are helping me with this. It serves them as well. It serves us all. The more peaceful we can be with one another, the more accepting we are with them, the more access they have to the riches and beauty of the Earth. This also allows them to share parts of their world with us.

My mother knows what I am doing, as she has done the same. My father has come to learn as well, and he has agreed that I may bring these teachings to our people. As I grow and mature, he welcomes my opening our doors to everyone, and to share my experiences and what I have learned with others. I am also given reign to share our gold with all who come. We all realize that everyone is better when we are all taken care of by one another. My father understands this, so we have a very peaceful palace and kingdom.

I go on to experience preparing to birth my own child. I am becoming a Mother. I am 9 months pregnant, and I am about to birth my child in my special place on our land where I meet my other-worldly companion each day. My mother is there with me in support of this Sacred Rite of Passage and Initiation. A small group of women from the village are there as well. A circle of Sisters to hold the space as I birth this child into Being.

There are butterflies present. Hundreds of them. And my Beloved Companion from the ship is there as well. He is emanating such a deeply profound Love as I prepare to birth this child. He is indeed the child's father, and we have been married for some time.

I birth my baby in a state of joy and ecstasy, and as she emerges, it is obvious that she is not of this world entirely. She is a beautiful mixture of my Beloved and myself, and yet completely her own unique Being. She is so soft and warm; I melt as I hold her for the first time. She has a large head, and giant blue almond shaped eyes. Her skin is grey-ish green in colour. She is absolutely breathtakingly beautiful to me. She is a very balanced essence of male and female, though clearly holding the form of the feminine.

Her hair is brownish red.

I call her Sheneala.

My father is so proud of me, as is my mother. I am successfully helping bridge the worlds by bringing this child into physical form. She is a healthy baby, with bright all-seeing eyes. She is wide awake, and squishy and cuddly as a newborn baby all at the same time.

My daughter grows more quickly than other children. She matures at a rapid rate. It is as if she is grown, yet still a child. In her "adolescent" time, she begins to teach larger groups of people. She enjoys working with children, to help them hone their skills and abilities. She practices with and gives guidance to the elders in the village and on the ship in order to help them understand their own children and to be able to work with them. She also helps the elders on Earth to activate their own DNA, and with the Earth children, she is helping them learn how to keep their DNA intact and activated.

Most of the children in the village, if not all, are now hybrids as well. The merging of the worlds has been successful. Women tend one another's birthings in much the same way I was supported. There are young children that my daughter works with from the ships that look much like her also.

Sheneala has taken over my work, as I have fulfilled my purpose. I am free to go live aboard ship with my Beloved now, and leave the Earth. My Earth family stands around the spot in the land that has been my Sacred Space, and I walk aboard the ship.

As I leave Earth with my Beloved, my body is illuminated, and I am Light pulsating from the inside, radiating out exponentially. I am able to hold the form of my physical body, but am now translucent. Hand in hand, my Beloved and I enter the ship together, and my Earth family knows I am always with them, and they will see me aboard the ship now."

The session was very powerful for me, and at the end of it, before coming out of the hypnotic state, I was able to ask my Higher Self some questions and receive some long-awaited answers.

One of the major questions I asked about was the process of being "taken" and what my part in the hybridization experiments looked like; basically "how it all goes down." I wanted the nitty-gritty answers in detail so that I could be very clear in the book I was writing.

The funniest thing was that right away, Sulannaya, my Higher Self, told me to make sure I was absolutely certain that I wanted to know this information. She told me to be very aware of what I was asking for.

In my naïveté I affirmed that yes, I did indeed want this information in my conscious awareness. Well, let me just say that I had no idea what I was in store for! One can never be fully prepared for knowing such details, even if one thinks one is. Boy, was I about to learn a major lesson.

For the record though, I would not change the experiences coming my way as a result of this innocent request for anything. I did get my wish after all, and it did help me to see with much clearer vision and a deeper wisdom how these ET experiments work on this planet, which I felt was essential and beyond valuable.

All that said though, be careful what you wish for!

Quantum Healing Session with Jocelyn - Questions for Samantha's Subconscious/Higher Self/Sulannaya:

Q: What work does Samantha do aboard ship at night?

A: *Many different roles are played aboard this ship. First and foremost is she is working with the hybrid children, both of Earth origin and Sky origin. Secondly, she is a member of the Council of Love, who work to restore the frequency of Unconditional Love on Earth, so that this frequency may vibrate and reach out to the cosmos. Other civilizations will learn from it also. This is very much needed.*

Q: How often is Samantha taken aboard the ships?

A: *Almost nightly. There is a lot of work to be done.*

Q: Who is Samantha working with primarily?

A: *The Pleiadians and The Venusians mainly. Also the Sirians, the Lyrans, and the Zeta Reticuli.*

Q: Can you help her have more conscious memory of the work she is doing aboard the ships?

A: *If this is what she wishes for. So long as she knows what she is wishing for. It is imperative that she stay centered. It is also important that she exercise her physical body to help move the energies. It is very important that she mind what she puts into her physical body in order for her to keep her center if she is to recall what she is doing interdimensionally. She is almost ready.*

Q: What is Samantha's specific role in creating these hybrid children?

A: *She provides her seed and houses the fetuses in the nurturing environment of her womb-space. Also aboard the ships, she visits with her children as well as other hybrid children who are in need of the Love they require. She is Mother to All.*

Q: How many children does she have?

A: *Currently aboard the ships, she has 17 children. 7 male dominant, 10 female dominant.*

Q: What are the ages of these children, if in fact "ages" are equal to how we measure age on Earth?

A: *There are different experiments. Generally, these children age much quicker, but then plateau at a certain stage and remain there, much like humans. This process usually happens more quickly than humans though.*

Sometimes the experiment has to do with slowing this process down in order to discover the difference between how development takes place in a slower aging process, down to a more Earthly timeline. Oh, those wee ones, very precious!

Q: Is it because of her work as a hybrid mother that Samantha has experienced some health challenges with her physical body in the past?

A: *Yes. This work can indeed take a toll on the more physically dense Earth body, but we have been attempting to tell her to care more for this aspect of herself in order to lessen these burdens or release them altogether. It is possible, you know. She can be stubborn and does not always listen though. We have told her what to do to relieve this.*

Q: How does the experiment of creating the hybrid children from two earthbound beings who do not know one another in the third dimension take place, and is this at least one of the experiments Samantha is taking part in, specifically with Anthony?

A: *Yes. Both beings are brought aboard ship. They know one another on a soul level, and have made the choice together to do this work. Even if there is no conscious memory of such, these agreements are contracted with full awareness by both parties on a soul level.*

It works much like mating in the third-dimension works. There is a blending of energetics and genetics through the act of intercourse. We are then able to insert extra DNA if needed or desired into the seed. Sometimes this takes place, sometimes not. There is also technology capable of extracting DNA from the parents of a hybrid child directly from them, without the need for intercourse, though sexual merging is most often how it is done. Subsequently, it is not uncommon for there to be more than two DNA donors for a hybrid child. We are able to mix the DNA of many donors together.

Q: What does the name Sulannaya mean?

A: *It means "seed."*

Q: What star system or planet is Samantha's Soul from?

A: *Again, eternity has no beginning and no ending, so this is not a relevant question. She has her strongest Soul ties with the star system known as the Pleiades, if this helps.*

Q: What is Samantha's connection to Native American culture?

A: *She is of the same star origin and so resonates to the same frequency. There is a blood connection in which the crystals in her blood are of the same resonance as the crystals in the blood of the Native Americans. This connects them on multi-dimensional levels of consciousness held by the ones you call "Native Americans."*

Of course, in this session I had already seen much having to do with mothering hybrid babies, mostly with the mantis beings. I was regularly going aboard their ships, and was able to create a hybrid child and birth this child physically, as its mother. I was able to raise the child, and it was a very beautiful, moving experience. I was one of the bridge-builders between the races and worlds, and my child became one as well. This child became a teacher, and an exquisite, loving being all around.

I have since remembered my sessions back at The Light Institute in December of 2001, and finally realize some of what I had witnessed during my multi-incarnational sessions there pertaining to my role in these programs spanning many, many lifetimes.

I specifically remember one lifetime that was not the most positive or uplifting, but it's worth mentioning because of the kind of being I was. At the time of this session, I'd had no idea that it was even possible for our souls to have existed in other worlds, on other planets, in other dimensions.

Of course, I was always deeply metaphysical by nature and was always aware of the existence of all of these things, yet I had also spent a lifetime forgetting my true identity. So, by the time I began to consciously do this inner work and deep soul-searching, I had completely forgotten that any of it was possible, especially for me.

I remember seeing myself as a mutated "monster" of a being. I remember my family rejecting me at birth because I looked different—"like a monster." I wonder now in hindsight if perhaps I was experiencing a lifetime of not being fully human. Perhaps one of the early experiments with hybrid beings. Who really knows?

The point is that in viewing this lifetime, I witnessed firsthand that being born this "different" scared others, which is why they rejected me and left me to starve and die on the top of a hill by myself.

It was heart-wrenchingly painful to relive and witness this experience. I remember being stranded on the hilltop. I could not move on my own. I had no real arms or legs, and the animals began to chew and peck away at me until I withered away and died, after which they ate my body. It may have been simply a case of mutation, but I really can't help but wonder now if there was indeed not more to it. I certainly did not have a normal-looking face or head.

I have since learned that earlier on during these hybridization experiments, sometimes things would go horribly awry, and the babies would be born with severe mutations. I remember when I heard that, I instantly recalled this particular incarnation I had seen back in 2001. Is this what had happened to me in that lifetime? I wouldn't rule it out now, that's for sure.

So, I'd asked in my session with Jocelyn to remember more of how these experiments work so that I would be able to be as precise as possible in my writing. Then I had let it go, with all that was going on in my life and in the world after that. December 2012 was a pretty powerful month for me. A lot was going on for both me and my children, and though I'd had a great session, once it was over, I let it go, and for the most part, forgot about it.

*

December 12, 2012 came and I remember that day (12-12-12) being very powerful for me, energy-wise. It was only five days after my session with Jocelyn, and I knew I was being prepared for something. I could feel it in every cell of my body.

A few days after the 12th, as I was making dinner in the kitchen, I was struck with a sudden urge to show my kids a really cool breakdancing video I'd seen on YouTube earlier that day. I knew they'd love it.

It was only a five-minute video, and at the end of it Rubin, who was three years old, blurted out in an excited voice, "I know that guy! I *know* him! The guy from the submarine!"

I had no idea who he was looking at, so I went over to see. He was *so* happy to see whoever it was.

"What guy honey?" I asked him. "Who do you know?"

And he pointed at the screen where the little suggestion videos pop up after a YouTube video is finished. Most of the little icons were of videos about breakdancing, but there was one that had nothing to do what-so-ever with dancing.

Rubin was pointing at a Mayan Elder named Ac Tah, and a video that was circulating on YouTube about the 12-21-12 prophecy. I had seen this video myself many weeks earlier, so I knew who this man was and the message he was sharing.

"You *know* him?" I was shocked, but I really shouldn't have been, as exactly a year earlier, on December 18, 2011, this same child, then two, would not leave the house that day, and kept talking about "staying in his cave." He didn't want to come out from his bottom bunk, which very much resembled a cave. We had all been trying to go out to a fun family event dancing in town, and Rubin simply would *NOT* get out of "his cave" that day. He had never done this before, and interestingly has never done it since.

I took Noah to the party while Jeff stayed with Rubin at home. He had never refused to leave the house before, so we took his refusal to leave as a sign he was not to go. Later that evening, I found out from a man who was there that at that same time, the Hopi Elders were retreating to caves in preparation for the energies of 12-21-12. Also curious to note that during this time, Rubin often insisted that he was seeing Buddha every day.

I learned later that also during this time, there was some connection happening between the Tibetan Monks and the Hopi tribe, which was interesting to me, since these were the two "energies" my two-year-old was clearly picking up on and expressing.

So, when he told me that he "knew" Ac Tah, especially with such a familiarity in his voice, I wanted to believe him.

"Yes! He's the guy on the submarine! He's really nice!" He was certain they were pals. Funny that the only name I got as a possibility for Rubin before he was born was "Maya."

I felt the submarine he was talking about must be a craft of some sort. I didn't say anything to him about this being true or false, as it was his experience, not mine. How could I judge for certain if it was true or not? I knew one thing though, this child was certainly in tune with the energies of the native tribes to some extent, and it was part of his path for whatever reason, at least at that time. I still don't know exactly what all that was about, but I did find this incident to be timely and interesting nonetheless.

December 21, 2012 also came and was very significant for me. I should preface this by saying, I didn't share any of my quantum healing session with my husband or my kids. I talked about it with no one. I wouldn't even listen to the recording of it until December 2013, a year later, when taking notes for the purposes of sharing those sessions in this book.

When 12-21-12 arrived, it was my elder son, Noah, who surprised me this day. We had gone to a reverent little school ceremony with the boys that evening, and when we came home, we decided it would be nice to honour the energies of the solstice and the Mayan calendar with a meditation inside my copper and quartz crystal pyramid.

The boys, each of their own accord, got out their bowls filled with crystals, and began making crystal grids with them, which I had not taught them to do. I found it all very fascinating, of course.

Next, we sat in the middle of the pyramid, underneath the apex of the clear quartz crystal pyramid tip and went silent into meditation. Jeff, Noah and I had formed a little circle, while Rubin danced around us. Being only three years old, he was unable to sustain such focus yet. But he held the energy with his dancing, and did not distract from what we were doing. I'm sure his movement was his version of the meditation and it was perfect.

There was silence for a few moments, as we all closed our eyes, and then I heard Noah, then eight, begin speaking in a low voice, but he was not speaking English. He was speaking in a language that I recognized as the Language of Light, or Light Language. I had heard many starseeds speak in a very similar way, but he never had, which made this all the more fascinating to me. It was almost impossible for me to focus on my own meditation as I witnessed my son really stepping in to his own. It was so beautiful; it took all my strength not to stare at him! His eyes were closed so he didn't notice me peek at him once or twice.

When he was finished, I waited until I knew he was "back" fully, and said in a very nonchalant voice, "I noticed you were saying something, but I don't think that was English."

"Yeah, I know. That was my first language. The one I knew even before I knew 'baby gaga' language. It's called Lysha." There was such a knowing in his tone that I didn't ask any more questions and allowed it to simply be. I wanted him to keep whatever that gift was without tainting it with my own ideas or too much heady questioning.

He and I went outside together then to star gaze, and we noticed a beautiful halo around the moon. It encircled the moon here in Sedona like a giant golden ring. Noah's response to it was, "That's a Mothership."

Hmm... We went inside to grab the camera because it was so beautiful. It was quite odd what happened anytime we tried to capture its beauty. Whether with the flash on or off, the halo would disappear and all we could see were light squiggles coming from the moon. Maybe this is normal; I have no idea of the science behind how or why this might happen when taking a picture of the halo moon. Perhaps there's a perfectly logical and scientific explanation, but for Noah and I that night, it seemed quite strange, and we were intrigued by this seemingly different phenomenon.

After the boys were in bed that night, at exactly 11:11, I went deep into meditation on my own. I knew there was something I was to download. I now strongly suspect I was being prepared for the gigantic demonstration I would encounter exactly one month later, and boy, did I need to be prepared for that one.

CHAPTER 74

Galactic Negotiations & the Daughter that Wasn't

January 2013 started the year off in a very interesting way. I was activated in a newer way than ever before. I wasn't the same person, but I didn't realize it yet. Upon looking back though, I am certain that all of the events leading up to the end of 2012 were catalysts for what would transpire in the months to follow.

I had forgotten detail for detail what I'd asked about during my quantum healing session with Jocelyn regarding my involvement with the ET's. Inwardly, I'd assumed at the time that it wouldn't actually be possible to really know how the experiments work. Probably another testament to my lacking sense of self-esteem which I was still struggling with to some degree. I didn't really expect to get tangible answers. I *wanted* them desperately, but I had also been wanting answers to a lot of questions for years and for the most part had never fully received them. What made this time any different? I was so used to not knowing in full detail.

I wasn't prepared for what was to come. Or so I thought. Looking back, of course I was prepared—as prepared as I could have been, considering what awaited me. There's only so much preparation allowed in these heavy galactic matters. After all, they are still "experiments," and in some way we are the guinea pigs. If we always knew what to expect, most of us would likely never finish our assignments! In all probability, we would run like a bat out of hell in the other direction.

Within a 24-hour period in the first week of January 2013 I became aware of two groups on Facebook called The Hybrid Children Community and The Phoenix Lights. Out of the blue, I felt compelled to look at both of these pages, almost obsessively. The woman who started The Phoenix Lights Facebook page is a woman who channels people's hybrid children. I had no idea at the time there was such a significant connection between the Phoenix Lights and the hybrids. There were many others "coming out" about their connection and experiences with the hybrids.

We all had our own take on it, so reading and hearing their perspectives was refreshing and inspiring. I felt relieved and excited to have found these sites. However, I still decided to remain silent publicly, while these people were all out in the open.

On The Hybrid Children Community page, there were many daily posts. Fun and silly comics about ETs, some beautiful artwork sometimes accompanied by a blog post, all created by Bridget, one of the administrators for the page. Occasionally she would post a YouTube video with hybrid children content.

Both of these pages were being run by people residing in Los Angeles, California. This was interesting to me, because not only did I feel a strong connection with L.A. now through this otherworldly aspect of my life and experiences, but Anthony is also from there.

I found myself scrolling down the Hybrid Children Community page daily, and through this, I found an interesting Bashar meditation. I had not heard much about Bashar before, and if I had, I certainly hadn't been ready to truly hear him or allow him to penetrate my reality in any significant way. For whatever reason though, it was now Time.

This was a 15-minute long audio and visual meditation, which consisted of looking at certain symbols that had been channeled from Bashar through Darryl Anka, the man who has been known for channeling him for decades. The audio portion was a soundscape intended to go with the symbols, and the combination of the two were meant to activate and prepare the meditator for ***more conscious contact***.

The link to this meditation can be found here:

http://galacticconnection.com/15-symbols-originating-from-the-sirians-can-bring-you-improvement-and-enhancements/#sthash.qfrNeyuV.dpbs

I started doing this meditation every single night before going to bed, without fail. I simply had to do it. I continued this pattern for at least a week, and wasn't exactly sure why, other than I'd felt I needed to. I was usually doing Pleiadian-channeled meditations at that time, and yet had switched on a dime to this Bashar meditation all of a sudden. Some nights I still did my Pleiadian meditations as well, but the one I could not go to bed without was the Bashar symbol meditation. I was being prepared.

And then, something happened.

I was going to stay with my friend, Larry, in town to work on my book the weekend of January 18-21, 2013. It was all arranged. I had Jeff and the kids hooked up with a lot of healthy yummy food I'd made for them to help Jeff have an easier time and for the kids to feel my love for them through some of their favourite foods while I was away. I wasn't far from them, only a 10-minute drive, which was nice, but I was needing to focus on getting this monstrous, now nearly 100,000 word book, finished. Home can be too distracting for me, so occasionally, I would take a day or two or a weekend to work on it.

I saw Rubin after he finished preschool that Friday the 18th right before he and Jeff headed up to Flagstaff to pick up Noah at his school. As they pulled away in Jeff's white Subaru, a sinking feeling struck my gut as I waved at my baby and blew him kisses and called out "I love you!" to him, dancing my usual silly jig to make him laugh as they pulled away.

As I watched the tail end of Jeff's car leave my sight, I felt a sudden foreboding sensation wash over me, and heard the Voice say, *"You have no control over what happens to them once they are out of your sight."*

That was a very strange thing to hear and know, and it really shook me up for a few minutes. But the Voice was right, I realized. I truly did have no control over anything when I wasn't there. At least not that day. And the Voice was reminding me of this.

It was all too eerie, but what could I do? I'd already had my car packed up to go, and they were on their way to Flagstaff. I did what I knew I could do and sent angels of protection around them and the car. The only other thing I could have done was try to catch up with Jeff and follow him which seemed ridiculous, so I chose to let it go, and decided I was being overprotective and needed to trust Jeff to keep them safe and do my best to forget about it.

I chose to focus on myself and the book, which was the whole point of the weekend. When I got to Larry's, I set up my computer space for a productive weekend. Before I settled into the book, I sat down to check my emails and noticed a message from Jeff. I clicked on it and saw in all caps:

"PLEASE CALL ASAP. WE HAD AN ACCIDENT. PLEASE CALL ME NOW."

I was flooded with the awareness of the message I'd received, along with that sinking feeling of my children being in danger as I'd watched Jeff and Rubin pull away from me only a few hours before. My heart dropped to the pit of my stomach and I began to panic. Shaking, I pulled up Skype and dialed him as I do not own or use a cell phone, so this was my only way to call him directly.

Everyone was fine. But what had happened was still a total mystery, and in my opinion, a very clear message from "*the beyond*."

Halfway through Oak Creek Canyon, right near Slide Rock, a large loaf-sized rock fell from on high through Jeff's windshield, directly on top of him. This meant it was aimed directly *AT JEFF.* Rubin was fast asleep during the whole ordeal. He had windshield glass all over him in his car seat, but was otherwise unscathed. He didn't even wake up until about an hour after the accident.

Looking at the pictures of his car was eerie as well, as it was obvious to me that this was no "accident." This was a message of some sort, and to me, it felt "otherworldly" in origin. It was clear to me that this was a galactic demonstration meant for Jeff to experience, and for me to simply be aware of.

The energy surrounding the smashed window was that of deliberation. The hole was perfectly placed over the driver's seat, and when it smashed through the glass into the car, it hit Jeff in three distinct places. In order, they were the chin (communication), the chest (heart), and the groin (creation/sexuality).

I knew that there was a Higher Power who had orchestrated this event, no doubt about that in my mind. Although at the time, I thought it was only about Jeff, and that this experience was a sort of a calling to him, a message from Spirit. For what, only he would know the answer to that, if he was capable and willing to dig deep enough within himself. But it was clear to me that something beyond him was behind this incident, and I told him as much. I was quite certain that it was ETs at the helm of this strange and synchronistic "accident," especially given the date—while the sun was at galactic degree in Capricorn.

I offered to come straight home and forget my work weekend. I could hear it in his voice and see it in his eyes. He had been faced with the prospect that his life could have been severely altered by this incident. At the time, I thought it was because he was recognizing his own mortality, which I still believe was part of it. But there was definitely more going on with this accident than I knew at the time, but would later put together on my own.

Somehow, the rock through the windshield striking him had shaken up his energy and auric field, and for a few days at least, he seemed like a completely different person. Meaning that to me he seemed to be existing in several different realities all at once. I didn't realize this at the time. I only knew that something about him seemed easier for me to connect with. Something I welcomed greatly.

Looking back now, I can see how something else was orchestrating a connection between Jeff and me where the door to intimacy would be opened, and unbeknown to me, I would become almost miraculously impregnated. We didn't even think it was humanly possible, because physically speaking, there was a slim-to-none chance that this could have happened from this one experience together—the only time we had been intimate in many months. The bright side was that this made it very easy to track dates later on.

Out of nowhere, we started to come together magnetically, and it was here that we realized we had to be together in that moment. As I look back, it's very interesting how it all played out. I was ready for intimacy, which I had not felt in ages. My body was screaming for this, seemingly out of nowhere.

Then the oddest thing happened. As he undressed, and I was ready and waiting, almost jumping out of my own skin, I heard the words come out of my mouth, but was very aware that I was not the one saying them: "Don't wear a condom. Please. Don't wear a condom."

Jeff did a double take when I said this a few times, because it was very unlike me, especially in those days. I had been so protective of my body for the year and a half leading up to this moment that if and when we ever did get intimate, which sadly was very rare, we would always use protection. There was never a good enough reason not to, so of course this surprised him. It surprised me just as much, because truly, it was not me talking, and I knew this.

But, who was talking then? I wondered.

We made love passionately. I was starved for this. I had multiple orgasms in only a few minutes, my body so ready to receive. What happened next was strange. Jeff could not ejaculate. He could no longer sustain himself and we had to stop. It was out of nowhere, and we didn't make a big deal of it at all. I was still squirming but pretty satisfied, though not entirely. I wanted more.

We went to bed, and the next morning, miraculously we had the house to ourselves, which was a very rare thing to come by. Jeff had taken the kids to school and I was napping from our late night rendezvous, when Jeff crawled into bed with me.

Suddenly, there we were again. I was ready to go, and so was he.

We continued what we had not finished the night before and it was going great. I was climaxing repeatedly, when suddenly, Jeff winced in pain and had to stop. It was a very odd moment, as normally men do not experience physical pain with intercourse, especially since we weren't in some strange position.

He told me that he had to stop, that "it was hurting him." He never explained it to me right then, but it was definitely the first time I could remember this ever happening. I was still squirming inside but also understood that he was in pain and was able to settle myself down eventually.

As far as he or I knew, he had not ejaculated. There was no evidence of it anywhere, neither that morning nor the night before. So, we left it alone. And that was it. Life went on as usual, busy with work and kids, and everything fell back to the way it had been before.

Then, about a week after our night of intimacy, I had a dream. I had not had a dream encounter so vivid or real in about a year, but this one was extremely vivid for me. Again, the multidimensional experience of witnessing, being a part of the experience, all while my physical body slept in my bed; holding multiple states of consciousness all at once.

In this dream sequence, I was in a house with a bunch of my friends from high school, who I hadn't seen in years. One friend in particular is a woman whose birthday happens to be November 18th, which interestingly is one of Selene's main tracking dates for starseed. I wouldn't be surprised if most of my closest friends from then were also starseed.

I noticed a UFO that had landed in the backyard of the home we were in. We all went outside to see it. Most people ran away from it, no one approached it that I knew of, except me. I remember saying out loud, *"There they are. They are here for me."*

Suddenly I was the only one there, and started walking toward the craft, whose entrance door was open and truly, they were waiting for me. It was all so very familiar to me, actually.

I took note as the "conscious dreamer" that this was the first ET experience in a dream state that I had ever willingly participated in that I knew of. At least from the ones I was conscious of. And besides which, I had not had a dream of a craft with ETs in over a year, when I had met the blue being who healed Noah and removed my baby in 2011.

I wasn't afraid. I took note of my calm demeanor and readiness as I approached the craft and gave myself an internal pat on the back.

I entered. Inside was a vast rounded entrance, with somewhat of a lobby feeling to it, and I was not alone. I looked to my right, and beside me was standing, precious as ever, about 17 ET children, all looking up at me with wonder, awe and love in their eyes. They were my hybrid children, and I knew this.

There were so many of them, and there were varying degrees of expressions in their energy fields. Some were waving at me, eyes smiling and twinkling, excited to see me. Some just sat there, watching me, almost expressionless. But they were all definitely watching me, even greeting me. One or two had a sense of longing that was almost devastating, but most of them seemed happy and healthy. I couldn't believe the love I felt for these precious little beings.

I spoke with them telepathically and said, *'Hi my sweethearts! I have to go and do my work, but when I am finished, I will come back and see you all. As soon as I am done, I will be back here to spend some time with all of you.'* I felt an immense swelling in my heart of unconditional love for all of them, accompanied by a very strong sense of responsibility and needing to get inside to take care of business.

I am pretty certain this exchange happened telepathically. I could feel their understanding of me, and sensed that they would happily wait for me to finish my "work."

I walked through a short corridor inside the ship, which felt partially made of metal, and partially "alive." When I got to the other side, I entered a room that felt welcoming and warm. In front of me stood two beings; the one directly in front of me was female, the other, in front of me and to the left, male.

Their energy was soft and kind, and as I entered the room, they had their hands pressed together at their hearts in prayer, as they bowed slightly to me. For some reason, these two beings were making a gesture of honour and respect, grateful that I was there. I remember taking note of this as the dreamer, thinking, *'Oh wow, this is something I don't remember seeing before!'* Whatever "work" I was there to do with them must be important, I thought.

It was all very exciting actually.

They both wore very intriguing clothing, not what one would expect an ET to wear. The female had blonde hair and was wearing a very colorful sari type of fabric. It was quite beautiful, exotic even. It looked ethnic in some way, and seemed to have an African tribal feeling mixed with a Middle Eastern theme flowing through the combined fabrics.

The male, who I remember as having no hair on his head, was wearing a button-down shirt with a tropical island print of some sort, much like an authentic Hawaiian shirt. Again, very unusual for ETs, I thought. In my past experiences, they were always in fitted suits where you could see their body shape. These two were wearing human-esque clothing, in odd combinations. It was almost humourous. I knew it was time we get to work. They had been waiting for me to get started. It's always like this aboard ship, as we are often on a tight schedule.

Next thing I knew, I had to pee, and badly. It came on all of a sudden and felt as though if I didn't go right then, my bladder would burst. We were about to start our session together, but I had to relieve myself, so I said to them, *'I know we have to get started, but is it okay if I just quickly use the restroom first please?'*

What a thing to ask! I remember feeling sort of silly for asking, but it was crucial! I really had to go. I could feel my bladder ready to rupture all over the ship floor.

Their response was the oddest thing to me. They responded telepathically with, *'Not now. Actually, it would be best if you were able to wait until our work has been completed if you can. It will be beneficial for what we are doing.'*

I was a bit confused as the dreamer hearing this, though my self inside the dream experience seemed to understand precisely what this meant. Before I knew it, displayed in front of me via hologram or living image, I was shown a fetus inside a womb that was also inside of a jar. This was no ordinary fetus either. It was large, and was only partly human. It looked almost like a fully-grown human body but with very long arms and legs, and a larger than average head.

At this image, I gasped for breath, and woke myself from sleeping to the most excruciatingly full bladder I had ever had before. I ran to the bathroom to finally get some relief. Just as it had been in the dream, my bladder was completely full, and indeed, more than ready to burst. I knew then that my question from my quantum healing session back in December 2012 was being answered. I still had no fucking idea at what cost though.

*

I remember thinking to myself, *'Okay, I asked to know how it all works, and that was a pretty clear experience showing me,'* so I was grateful. It still hadn't dawned on me that I could actually be physically pregnant. I have no idea why not, as it seems painfully obvious now. The entire demonstration, from the rock through the car windshield to the strange lovemaking scenarios, all seem so obvious now in hindsight. Yet in the midst of this experience, I simply felt that my question from my session with Jocelyn had been answered through my dream and I was content with that.

I was still not seeing the bigger picture here. Though I knew that the dream encounter was real, I thought that its purpose had been to show me my lesson: a pregnancy where simultaneously a fetus resides inside the physical womb as well as aboard ship in a jar—perhaps "twins," one in each dimension, sharing DNA even. I was shown this as a sort of "school lesson." After all, I'd asked to be shown how it worked, hadn't I? I had no clue that I was currently living it—that I was actually embodying this truth.

About a week or so after this first dream of being aboard ship and seeing the fetus, still feeling utterly drained of all energy, I had a second "dream."

This dream sequence had a completely different essence from the first one. I would vouch to say it was the polar opposite, in fact. In this sequence, I was in a home again, but this time alone. There was a knock on the door. I answered it, and there standing before me was a man, or at least he appeared to be a man. He was wearing a beige uniform, and I knew he was a part of the military in some way. He told me that he had a recording on an audio cassette and that he needed to come into my home and use my cassette player to listen to its contents.

This sounded like an odd request to me, but he was clearly not asking for my permission. He was telling me what he was about to do. This much was clear, though he did not appear to be forcing his way in. On the contrary, he was almost monotoned and when I looked back afterwards, I was almost sure he was not fully human, perhaps not human at all.

When I say this, I hear Selene's voice ring in my ears, *'Is it real, or is it Memorex...''* and I can't help but giggle to myself.

I let him in, most likely under some form of mind control, and showed him to the room with the cassette player. We both sat down on the floor. He did not speak to me, but I could feel him trying to get physically near me. There was something about him that felt like he was deliberately trying to make physical contact with me, but why?

He pulled out the cassette tape we were to listen to, and on it I saw scribed in handwriting that looked exactly like my brother's (whose birthdate is December 16th and who I have felt for some time is a hybrid himself)—which in itself I found odd and took careful note of—*'ET hybrid experiment.'* After I read those words, and what appeared to be my brother's handwriting, the man in the beige cargo suit started to lean his body into mine slowly...slowly...slowly...I felt him almost melt in to me, and remember absolutely nothing after that. *Blackout.*

I awoke from this dream and felt very strange. I didn't know what to make of it, and still had no idea that I could possibly be carrying a child, maybe even twins, inside of me. This still did not occur to me on my internal radar somehow. From the two dreams, it felt to me that the first one was of benevolence and mutual agreement, and the second one had something seriously fishy going on.

I continued to feel strange, still feeling that I was fighting off negative entities and dark forces, especially after that second dream sequence. The New Moon came and went and I did not begin menstruating. It wasn't until then that I started to become a bit suspicious. I took a pregnancy test on February 18th, exactly one year after seeing Bashar's ship, and also, synchronistically for whatever it's worth (if anything), Yoko Ono's birthday—and received confirmation that indeed, I was carrying the seed of a child inside my physical womb.

Jeff and I were absolutely floored. On the one hand, I was relieved because I had seriously started to become concerned about my health, and now found out I had nothing to worry about, other than the fact that I had very obviously been set up and mysteriously impregnated.

I say mysteriously even though I realize it's possible to impregnate a woman without fully ejaculating inside of her. I use the term "mysteriously" because when I realized I was pregnant, I replayed the series of events that led to the only possibility that would have allowed me to become pregnant in Earthly terms.

Intercourse would have never taken place without the strange accident with the rock that happened first. Then, to have me robotically tell Jeff not to wear a condom, while inside I was practically screaming to tell him otherwise but couldn't seem get the words out. I knew that voice coming from me was not mine. Then, the fact of having intercourse with no hint of ejaculation. *Twice.*

Only after receiving the news that I was indeed pregnant, Jeff shared with me that when we had been intimate that only time in months, he'd felt something being "yanked out of him" the second time we made love, like something had been "extracted" or "pulled out" of his penis. It made him so uncomfortable that he had to stop because it was physically painful for him, not to mention way too strange.

At the time though, he did not share this information with me, as he could not explain it and couldn't have imagined what it would turn out to be. It was too strange for him to even say anything about it at the time.

It was in his sharing that I was able to fully see how it had all unfolded. Let's just say that I got my wish—to know first-hand how these experiments work—and then some! (Lesson learned here is: Be careful what you wish for. You just might get it!)

WOW, thanks for the lesson in hybrid baby creations. But now, there I was, *pregnant* without a clue what to do about it.

Jeff and I were both in a state of shock for several days. After the shock wore off, I could see that Jeff had become almost happy about this news. I didn't know yet how I felt. Mere moments before making love, we had been talking about separating, and it hadn't been our first discussion on the subject. Now here we were. *Another baby*.

Besides all that: where the *hell* did this baby *really* come from? I wondered.

Part of me was exhilarated to be able to see so clearly how it had all played out, knowing that this soul must be doing me a huge service by teaching me exactly what I had asked to learn about only two months prior.

But what was I to do now that there was an actual baby involved? I sure hadn't banked on this being a part of the equation, and I was feeling incredibly torn.

I loved this soul already. Firstly, because she was now merged with me; my body was feeding her little human body, and nurturing her physical growth inside of me. Secondly, because she was a teacher of mine, and very obviously a generous and powerful one at that. Somehow, I knew she was a girl, and my heart ached for a baby girl. A big part of me wanted to know her. I wanted to meet her. I wanted to hold her, love her, and thank her.

But I wasn't sure Jeff and I having another baby together was the best thing to do for either of us, especially knowing where we were at in our marriage, which was in a constant state of limbo, frustration and confusion and downward spiral. I wanted to make absolute certain that if we decided to keep working on our marriage and stay together, we were doing so for the right reasons—out of our love for one another and our commitment to walking through this life together—not because we "should" due to the fact that we were having another baby, so staying together seemed like the "right thing to do" and what was "best for the kids." I don't think that's ever a healthy reason for two people to stay married.

I felt so torn. So I went inside in meditation and spoke with this beautiful soul. We communicated so very easily, it was magnificent. I was even more in love with her!

What she said to me was profound and incredible. First of all, she giggled the whole time. Here I was, stressed out about the whole thing, and yet there she was, ready to roll with however the dice rolled, with zero attachment to any of it. She told me that it was my decision, and that was what the real lesson here for me. To be able to make the decision that I felt was best for me. To empower myself by choice.

WOW. That in itself was a huge gift for me as I still didn't know how I truly felt about all of this, and didn't want this soul to feel unwelcome in any way.

So, I called my friend and Master Ayurvedic physician, Nuva. I told him that I was pregnant and not sure how I felt about it. He gave me some strong Ayurvedic herbal medicines to take that would strengthen my uterus that I could take to support this pregnancy and baby.

He wanted to meet with me after I told him that there were unusual circumstances surrounding this pregnancy. We met for some raw chocolate and fresh organic vegetable juice, and I told him the story of how I had become pregnant. I knew he would understand, as Nuva is not really of this world either. He seemed to become a bit giddy for the first time since I'd known him. He seemed fascinated by the whole thing.

That day, he ended up sharing with me some of his own experiences. Nuva had never told me anything about himself before this, yet suddenly, we both realized what our connection was; a cosmic brother and sister of sorts.

We only had a short time to meet before I had to go pick up Rubin from his preschool. Nuva suggested we go out to Angel Valley, of all places. I told him that I'd had a HUGE activation there the previous November, only three months earlier. I hadn't seen the room he was suggesting we go to, which is where they have their crystal skulls and hold live channeling events. He wanted to take me there right away.

We hopped in his car and he high-tailed it to Angel Valley. I wasn't sure what I was supposed to receive there, but obviously it was something for Nuva to be this insistent on going.

Our relationship jumped up about 10 notches in those two hours alone.

We arrived at Angel Valley, and no one was there. Nuva took me directly inside, a measure of how familiar and comfortable he was there, and he brought me to the "private" room where the Bashar channeling events happened. I had not engaged in anything having to do with Bashar since that week in January 2013 when I was doing the symbol meditation every night right before being impregnated. So, this was interesting to me that Bashar was coming up in my life again in relation to this pregnancy.

At this time, I still didn't know that the "landing pad" created on the land there was meant specifically for Bashar and the hybrids either.

Nuva did tell me about Bridget, the woman who had started the Hybrid Children Community Facebook page, and how her artwork was in this room we were sitting in, and that she channels the hybrid children through her artwork. Not only that, he told me that she was on her way to Sedona, as we spoke, to live at Angel Valley, and that this move was connected with the hybrid children.

We got to the room, which was small but held a lot of energy. There was a grid of crystal skulls of all different sizes in one part of the room. We sat next to them, beside all of the Bashar material, with Bridget's painting directly in front of me.

We sat there in complete silence for about 15 minutes. In energy like that, 15 minutes felt like an eternity! I knew I had to go and get Rubin and we were cutting it close. Nuva knew it too, so at one point, he said, "Shall we head back?" and we did.

I didn't realize that day how significant that one seemingly "little" excursion would be to me later on.

It turned out I did not need to carry the baby to term in a physical sense, as it was merely a demonstration for me, since I had asked so kindly to be shown. I was shown all right. Ultimately, I lost the baby. It was a mixture of emotions for me surrounding this experience, but I knew the soul of this baby knew what was best for all of us, and I trusted her.

I knew I needed to nurture my body for me alone a little while longer, knowing that if I had had to carry a baby to term, the giving wouldn't stop at birth. I would be responsible for providing everything for this child by way of nutrients and health for at least a year, and I knew my body was not ready for that yet. I knew I had to be strong enough physically to trust that my body was really ready for such a huge feat. I can honestly say, a part of me was very saddened that this pregnancy did not get the chance to go full term. That's why I say be careful what you ask for, because it's so very true. You never know what heartache might accompany such wishes being granted.

I knew precisely when impregnation had occurred. It was technically on January 22, 2013. I went for my first ultrasound after my home test results, to get a sense of where my body, and this baby were at, even though I had no question as to the conception date.

When the doctor read the ultrasound results, she got the date of conception exact. She said that conception occurred January 22nd (yup!), and that put me at six weeks, and she figured out the due date to be October 14th.

Due to my unusual circumstances with health and my age, I decided to set up another ultrasound that was scheduled for only eight days after the first one. I knew I would only be 7 ½ weeks by the time I went in for that appointment, but wanted them to look further in to my physical reproductive health and my ability to carry this baby.

While I was having the second ultrasound, things took a turn from strange to stranger. The great news was that my physical health looked perfect in the ultrasound which was a huge relief for me. Where it turned strange was that this woman was apparently "one of the best" ultrasound readers, the most accurate reader as she and everyone in the office told me in my questioning confusion afterwards.

This doctor looked at the size of the fetus and said to me, "So, your baby is measuring at 10 ½ weeks."

What??? That's impossible!!!

"There must be some mistake, or you're reading it wrong. I'm sorry, there is only one day that this could have happened, and that is January 22nd. There was no other time. Can you read it again? There is definitely a mistake."

"No, this clearly reads that the size of this baby is measuring to be 10 ½ weeks, almost 11 weeks in fact."

"This can't be! I just had an ultrasound eight days ago, and it read perfectly, and the date was exact! Can't I send you a copy of that one? I know that one was correct, since it was the only day I could have possibly become pregnant!"

This went on for about five minutes, and she insisted over and over again, even showing me the baby and her measurements. It made no sense to me. How could the fetus grow more than four weeks' worth in a matter of eight days? There was no way I could say to her, look, this is not a normal pregnancy, I was impregnated by ETs through my husband. I need you to measure this again.

But in the end, I lost the baby anyway. What I did take away from this ultra-high-strangeness pregnancy experience was that I will never have to walk that path again. Lesson painfully learned. Be careful what you ask for, because you just might get it.

I lost the baby on March 19, 2013. Selene knew about the whole situation, and she had already had the Galactic Secret Service on hand and ready to act if strange circumstances arose around me within this situation. She knew how torn I was, and that I needed some galactic sisterly support.

I had suddenly begun to feel sort of numb about this baby. About a week before this date, I had noticed the soul of this child retreating from my energies. I wasn't sure I could still feel her inside of me. Her life force and her love seemed to have vanished completely. In the end looking back, I was grateful that she did this for me.

I will never forget the moment. It was at 3:33 when the gush of blood came flowing out of me. I took note of the time, as I looked at the large red numbers on the digital clock beside me, knowing this was significant somehow since 333 is the main number that I work with most directly in my metaphysical and galactic work.

I was in this moment stepping more deeply into my role as a galactic healer, and cosmic Mother. I breathed deeply and let go of this energy, the physical cells that had once housed this beautiful being, my daughter that wasn't, as well as the energies of unconscious conception and the past pain and grief of not knowing or understanding my place in this genetic experiment program. I felt I was helping release this pain and grief from the collective consciousness of the planet as a whole. I knew I was not the only woman who had ever experienced this kind of loss.

In the moment of this intense release, I was in deep gratitude of the greater galactic gift I was given through this experience, and this made it all worth it for me, honestly. Plus I knew in that moment, I would never be asked to participate in these matters in such a dramatic and painful way again, and for this I was most grateful.

CHAPTER 75

Bashar

I felt called to attend the Bashar channeling event at Angel Valley on April 13, 2013. It was less than a month since my pregnancy had ended and I needed that connection with spirit and to be surrounded by others like me; my galactic brothers and sisters—even if I didn't know them. I needed a little pick-me-up and inspiration, and to feel sort of normal within my high strangeness life.

I noticed Bridget there, but remember feeling a distinct and strong "*no*" to this connection, so I didn't introduce myself, and decided to keep quiet and simply absorb the energies of the transmissions being offered. This day was for me and my healing. She told me that on that day that she was having a challenging time, which confirmed for me the message I'd received about holding off on our physical connection.

I knew I was called to the event for a reason, I just wasn't quite sure why yet. And then, Darryl Anka entered. It was when he stood at the front of the room on his platform that I noticed his shirt. It was a button down Hawaiian shirt, and I was immediately flooded with the memory of my experience aboard the ship with the beings who were working with me and impregnating me.

THE MALE BEING ON THE SHIP WAS BASHAR!

My eyes began streaming at this recognition and synchronistic confirmation. Here he was, Bashar, in the third dimensional form of Darryl Anka, *right in front of me*. The same being I had been working with from the ship. I also realized then that the female being on the ship must have been Anima, Bashar's female counterpart. I felt a resounding "yes" jolt through my blood at this realization.

I was in complete shock, absorbing the enormity of the information I had just received. At one point during a break, Darryl was walking out the door of the building to get some fresh air. Like people in the public eye often experience, he was being bombarded by people from the audience. I am never one of those people. I stayed at my seat until he was able to exit.

Just as he was about to leave the room, our eyes locked. We were about 40 feet away from each other, and there were people on all sides of him, wanting a moment of his time. But it was my eyes he was drawn to. Time felt like it ceased in that moment, though I would hazard a guess that our eyes locked for what felt like five seconds.

There was an instant recognition between us. He smiled at me from across the room, and then continued on. That moment was all the confirmation I'd needed.

This synchronicity was what I had come there to experience; momentary physical contact, eye-*SOUL*-contact, with *Bashar*, to complete the connection from my own experiences and bring them full circle.

Now I understood. I had been called there to find another piece to my personal soul puzzle. I was to connect the dots that it was Bashar, and consequently, his female counterpart, Anima, who were the ones that had heard my call; the ones who came through for me, to teach me, as per my request, about how the ET/human hybrid experiments work on this planet.

In the meantime, I was learning more and more about the hybrid species and realized through a Bashar channeling that The Phoenix Lights ship is where the Shalinaya reside, apparently right over Sedona, which is the hybrid species mixture of humans and greys many, many years into our future.

After learning this, I Googled the date when the Phoenix Lights made their most documented appearance, and found it interesting that they showed up March 13, 1997, which was precisely when I was smack dab in the midst of my initial year of encounters and experiencing profoundly physical symptoms (being impregnated and closely monitored through implants) as a result of them.

There had been a lot of galactic activity for me at that same time. Even though I was living in Canada during this massive UFO sighting over Phoenix in '97, the timing of this spectacle versus what I was going through in my own life at that exact moment in time is more than intriguing to me.

CHAPTER 76

The Daughter That Was

I remember times in this life that I have had dreams of babies being born, not necessarily through *me,* but sometimes through people in my life. These beings would contact me, tell me they were on their way, some even asked for my assistance once they were to arrive here, saying I would be the only one who would understand who they really are. Interesting that all three of these babies have birthdates that coincide with Selene's discovery of star markings in their natal charts, two out of three in the sun.

This confirms they are all starseed, and that somehow, in some way, I might be the only one in their lives that would be able to know and acknowledge this. None of these children are in my physical life now. It will be interesting to see if an opening of communication with any of them presents itself down the road.

*

About a week after I lost the baby, in March 2013, I had a dream.

In this dream, I saw Paul's girlfriend Natalie, and she was pregnant. I woke up feeling this message very strongly, but did not want to tell Paul about it. He had never really thought that having children of his own was in his future, even though he knew that he would make a great dad. I knew he had never really felt ready for such a responsibility, hence all the times I turned to parsley infusions and Vitamin C - "just in case" - all the time I was with him.

However, the message of this dream stayed with me. It was potent and strong, but the last thing I was going to do was tell Paul about it. I didn't want him getting freaked out, and besides, what if it was "just a dream." Why worry him over nothing? So, I kept it to myself. I told Jeff about it, but that was it.

June rolled around, and I was again heading out to Larry's to work on my book for the weekend.

A couple days before this, Paul had started calling me and writing to me with a sort of urgency, saying that he really wanted to talk with me. I knew something must be up, because we didn't just call each other up about anything anymore. It hadn't dawned on me yet what it was about, since I'd had that dream back in March and it was now June and I was focused on my own life.

I told him I would be able to Skype when I was at Larry's for a little bit if he really needed to talk. When he took me up on it in a nanosecond, I knew something was up. We got on Skype and Natalie was sitting beside him. The first thing he says to me is, "Natalie's pregnant. We're having a baby."

My immediate response was to blurt out was, "*I knew it!* I had a dream that Natalie was pregnant back in March! But I didn't want to tell you!"

Paul laughed out loud, then turned to Natalie, who was wide-eyed, looking somewhat shocked, not knowing whether to laugh or not, and he said, laughing hysterically, "*See?* I told you the first thing she'd say was that she had a dream!" And he kept on laughing. By that point, we all were. Well, at least Paul and I were. Natalie was smiling, perhaps giggling nervously, not certain what to make of it all. I realize to her it probably sounded a bit strange. Then I told them that I was serious, and he said, "Oh, I *know* you are!" He and I laughed some more.

I asked them when they had conceived, if they even knew. Of course, I was looking to track this news. Paul replied, "Well, we 'did it' a lot the weekend of March twenty-second, didn't we?" He laughed. She looked a bit uncomfortable but giggled shyly.

That's when it *really* hit me.

Oh my gosh. Paul, the most careful man I knew when it came to not getting his girlfriends pregnant, was sitting here telling me that they had conceived within ***three days*** of my losing my baby, and most likely ***exactly*** two months from when I had conceived.

My mind was officially blown.

One of the things that flooded back to me about my baby was that, when I was talking with her about whether or not I would get to have her physically this time, or wait for another opportunity for her to come in, one of the things she said to me, with a giggle in her voice even, was, *"If I can't be with you and I want to come into a body sooner, I will find a way, don't worry! It will be okay, it doesn't have to be you and it doesn't have to be now."*

It could have been mere coincidence, but quite honestly, I gave up believing in coincidences long ago. I now live by recognition of synchronization as my guide. Which would mean that there was a very real possibility that this was potentially the same soul who had been trying to come through me.

I asked Paul if he knew their due date, and he told me December 18th. Of course, a galactic star date. I had a feeling she (I just knew the baby was a girl) would probably come before that, but wasn't quite sure when.

I was in awe of this entire process, as I now watched it continue from the outside, and in a much less personal way for me. It was fascinating indeed. I was learning "how it all goes down" and it was beyond what I could have dreamed up by myself. It was truly a wild ride.

I was beyond excited to meet this baby one day, and to see if we might recognize one another and if down the road, we might even become friends. I sure hoped so!

I was overcome with my connection to this baby, and I finally had to cut it off and detach, telling myself that this was *Paul and Natalie's baby, not mine,* and to remain focused on my life and let them enjoy this miracle for themselves. If this was the same soul, it was now time for me to get out of the way. I could be ecstatically happy for them all, which I was, but I certainly didn't need to project my own experiences or information onto them, especially when no one was asking!

I wasn't the one having her. They were having her. I could be happy for them, and perhaps even be a part of her life one day, but until then, I was to focus on what was right in front of me. My own children. And my work.

Still, I was incredibly fascinated with the idea that this could possibly be the same precious, funny, light-hearted soul I had carried and loved only a few short months earlier.

*

In November 2013, I started having dreams of Paul and Natalie's baby, sometimes a couple of times a week. They were always of her being born small, or early, and I finally had to share it with Paul, because it seemed that she was trying to tell me something and relay a message through me. I hated doing it and feeling like I was butting my nose where it didn't belong. But I had to. She just wouldn't leave me alone and it was starting to concern me.

I didn't know how to approach the subject so simply told Paul outright that I was having dreams, and that if Natalie was trying to eat light or not get "too big," to not worry, that the baby was asking for more, or at the very least, telling us that she might come early. I also told him to use his discernment and that if he didn't feel it would help her, to not share this information with Natalie. After all, he certainly knew her better than I did, and the worst thing to do to any pregnant woman is worry her with false fears about her baby. There's nothing worse than some arrogant person thinking they know more about a baby than the mother. I trusted Paul would know and would do what was best for Natalie and their baby.

As it turned out, little XO (they named her Xyla Oaklyn) was born a bit early, quickly and quite easily—also something I'd "seen," in one of my many dreams of her where she literally slid out quite effortlessly in one breath—on December 14, 2013.

Another little interesting synchronization was that my "due date" was October 14th, *exactly* two months before. Couple that with the conception dates being exactly two months apart also, and it made me go "hmmm..."

Personally, I found the synchronization in the dates to be fascinating, whatever they mean.

Xyla is such a doll. Paul and Natalie are totally in love with her; she couldn't have chosen better parents. Natalie adores her so much and is a doting mother, and Paul has surrendered to fatherhood in such a graceful, beautiful way. He loves that child like I've never seen him love anyone before. It's such a gift to witness, and I'm so grateful I am able to do so, even if it's only from a distance. They are a perfect little family of three and I couldn't have imagined it any more beautiful.

CHAPTER 77

Stepping Out of the Closet

On August 21-23, 2013, right after the anniversary of the Harmonic Convergence of 1987, I attended another writing retreat to finish my book. Little did I know I would start from scratch, writing the entire thing in only three days.

Two days before the retreat, I finally met Bridget, another hybrid mother, in person for the first time. She had contacted me through Facebook out of the blue and told me she was back in Sedona and would love to meet with me.

This took me by surprise as we had not been able to connect when she was here in March or April, as I'd gotten a "no" for going to talk with her at the Bashar event in April. So I'd let it go, thinking it was simply not in alignment at this time.

She came over one morning, and we hit it off right away, as if we were long-lost sisters. I really liked her and we really connected. We were both honest, upfront tell-it-like-it-is kind of people, and we both seemed to enjoy that in each other.

We talked a lot, she shared some of her ET experiences and how she came to start the whole hybrid children community online forum, and I shared pieces of my story with her. She tells me now that after our meeting, she couldn't even talk, and had to go lie down for the rest of the day, and for a couple of days afterward because she was still processing it. I'd had no idea my story had had that kind of effect on her.

I don't think it was an accident that when I went to the retreat two days later, I started over and the whole book effortlessly streamlined in through my crown chakra, Divine Guidance. I cried when I finished it. Here I'd been "trying" to write this book since 2011, and here it was August of 2013, and in three days, it was *done*. The sense of relief that washed over and through me was enormous.

I do still feel that our meeting somehow activated me to be able to write the book so quickly, and am grateful for Bridget calling this meeting forward.

*

I knew it was imperative that I not fuck up the writing of this book in any way. I didn't want to mess with Anthony; I wasn't trying to ruin his life (or anyone else's who I'd thought it might affect). In fact, I only wanted the opposite for him.

I wanted Anthony to be able to receive this information one day through me. I'd felt more strongly than ever that if I was receiving all of these incredible synchronicities pointing to this work and the cosmic connection I was certain we shared, and the fact that I was feeling such a strong need to write about it and share it with him, as well as the others on the planet who needed it—*the vision of the book gifting from 2006 long before I ever knew I would one day write one!*—that on some level of his consciousness, he must also be awaiting this information, to the same degree that I felt compelled to share it with him.

This upped the stakes for me, big time. I really had to get this information right. I knew that other women who were having these experiences out there needed to read my story, and in a way, I felt like some of them were depending on me sharing this information through my own story. I felt a gigantic sense of responsibility to tell it as accurately as I could.

I also had to somehow find a way to share my story directly with Anthony one day, the entire reason for which I would never know unless and until I was able to do exactly that.

CHAPTER 78

Women Healing Women – The Goddess Connection

I attended a weekend women's retreat in mid-April 2014. This retreat focused on the empowering ways we as women can help heal ourselves and one another through the embodiment and essence of the Goddess in Sacred Sisterhood. This was also the place where I would discover "The Magdalen Manuscript," which would go on to become an enormous Activator for me in so many ways, and I will share more about that later.

The retreat was a three-day intensive life-altering circle of Sacred Sisterhood for all who heard the call, mustered the courage to dive deep, and showed up ready for expansion on all levels.

The two women who co-create the container for this work and hold the sacred space necessary for us all to explore the depths, as well as the ecstatic bliss of our own inner marriage of the Divine God and Divine Goddess within, are Cheryl Good and Crystal Dawn Morris. These are beyond powerful and inspiring women, and synchronistically, both starseed. They thrive on co-creating and co-facilitating these kinds of healing and celebratory spaces for the goddess within us all. And the best part is that they both live it, daily. These women exude what it means to truly exist in the goddess state, in all its beauty, bliss, power, and intensity. I adore and honour them both immensely.

I had worked with Cheryl the summer prior to this workshop briefly, with one session where I worked with her one-on-one. We moved deeply into physical tantric healing, which opened me up in a way I had never quite experienced before. It was so incredibly powerful, at the same time making me vulnerable beyond what I ever imagined. I was busted wide open. So, I went in to this weekend with a pretty clear idea of what I was taking on, and I was ready for it now.

I experienced the gamut of emotional experiences in the course of that weekend, from ecstatic elation, to full-fledged, guttural mourning and grieving on a cellular level of the feminine energies I had lost, suppressed and been robbed of through certain choices and experiences beyond my control in this life, past incarnations, as well as through generational imprints inherited through my ancestral lines.

Pretty heavy stuff.

Every woman there went as deep as they could. An instant sisterhood was established the very first night and continued through to the closing circle. It was quite magical really.

As we all arrived to gather and meet that first night, Crystal Dawn had set out a deck of Goddess Oracle cards from which she invited each of us to draw one card. With these oracle cards was a separate small deck of seven Chakra cards, which she also invited us to pick one of to see which chakra we would be working most directly and intensely with for the weekend.

As we all arrived in the circle, drawing from the decks one by one, I began noticing a pattern. *Every single time* a woman drew a card from the chakra deck, we each drew a *different chakra*. No two of us drew the same card.

Interestingly, synchronistically, there were 7 women who had signed up. 7 women (aside from Cheryl and Crystal Dawn), 7 chakras. It was a wild observation.

When we were down to one last woman who had not yet arrived, the six of us sat there drawing more cards from the larger deck. I kept proclaiming out loud as we sat together in our circle, "Look at us! We have all pulled different chakra cards! There are six of us, and six different chakras have been pulled!" I knew that so far, each one of us present there was there specifically representing a chakra of the greater collective to be healed and celebrated in the sacred space of sisterhood.

I was amazed, and also surprised that no one else seemed to have noticed this stunning revelation until I'd pointed it out, and even then, it seemed as though I was the only one truly excited and astounded by this demonstration. If they were, they sure weren't showing it. I was certain that a greater hand was moving the chess pieces on the cosmic chess board here.

The seventh woman came in. She sat down to my right in the circle, apologizing profusely for being a few minutes late because of her work. We all welcomed her warmly, and I said to her, "Go ahead and pull a card from each of these decks." I knew something greater was happening here, and I knew without a doubt that she was going to pick the only chakra that was left to pick in the 7-card deck—*the Root*.

Sure enough, *she picked it,* and I almost jumped out of my skin! I yelled out, "She got the Root! Of *course,* she did! We've all got one of the seven chakras, no two people drew the same card!"

In this moment, there was an unspoken energy that quite literally "rooted" us all deeply together in the space of Sacred Sisterhood, each of us knowing now that what was about to take place here this weekend was to be sacred, magical and beyond any of our expectations, as there were clearly other energies at play here.

I had drawn the Sacral Chakra. Orange. *Sexuality. Creative expression*. I was not at all surprised by this, and knew I was in for quite a ride!

I knew I was about to be busted wide open, and I was ready to do this for me, my ancestors, and for my Goddess Sisters.

Immediately that first night, my awareness was drawn to the shelf of books of Goddess literature Crystal Dawn had made available for our perusal that weekend during breaks. This was when I spied a particular book that rattled me to the core simply reading the title of it: "The Magdalen Manuscript: The Alchemies of Horus and the Sex Magic of Isis." It took me the first two days of the workshop before I was even able to pick it up, actually.

The title alone nearly brought me to my knees. I could feel the energy emanating from this book without even touching it.

I was not ready yet. I waited until the last day of the intensive, and during our lunch break, I sat alone in this room where such deep sexual healing and activation had happened for me and every woman there, and I held the book in my hands. I was trembling gently inside, enough to know that if I opened it and read its contents, I would never be the same again.

I looked at the table of contents. It was all I could do to start with. I wondered how this book would weave these two powerful goddess priestesses together, when instantly, the title alone confirmed for me the visions and experiences I'd been gifted more than two years prior to setting eyes on these pages.

I knew this book held the key to some long sought after answers for me. I knew it held a wisdom and the gift of clarity, especially around my own energies of sexuality and the power of alchemy—the highest form of creation. I had no idea at the time how significantly these revelations and synchronistic events would come to empower me and further etch into my consciousness what I already knew, yet had no words for.

I was about to be shown—rather *granted*—the clarity of Divine Wisdom and Sacred Initiation I had been seeking my entire life, specifically from the time I was five and was shown through various Visions and Voices information about who I was and what I came here to do on this planet, *Now*.

I had to be ready or the activations would not be able to be fully embodied. *I was ready,* I told myself.

I opened up directly to the section containing the Manuscript itself, and though modest in length, it was poignant and clear. No extra words. No beating around the bush. Straight from the hip—the *heart* - and to the point.

This text is a sacred, beautiful and very telling story of the tantric and alchemical relationship between Mary Magdalene and Yeshua ben Joseph, or Jesus the Christ, written in the words and voice of the Goddess Magdalene herself, through the channel of Tom Kenyon.

That day in the healing room, I was only able to get through two paragraphs of this manuscript before I had to put it down, breathe, and release some deep emotion within. Perhaps ancient emotion and knowingness were behind those tears.

I was already blown wide open, after a weekend of opening up to the Sacred Feminine channels within my physical, etheric, and emotional vessels. I had opened up to receive this information, in the most fitting of environments. I was to finally receive answers, coupled with *tangible, concrete* research by highly credible sources, as to what I had come to know deep within my own psyche, heart, and soul two and a half years earlier.

I was not the only one who recognized the powerful connection between Isis and Magdalene. In fact, here was an actual source, *gifted* to me no less, so that I would be able to integrate what I already knew to be true. Until now, I had no reliable or respectable resources to back me up.

It was overwhelming, and again, confirmation of practically all the visions and messages I had continuously received my entire life. Often at the time of receiving a vision or message, I am not told or shown the whole picture. Only snippets. It can be frustrating as it often feels like there are endless riddles to solve.

I have always been a fan of decoding, right from my earlier days with mathematics, numbers, and even languages, so there is some sort of drive for me to remain aware and always open to the synchronicities around me that give me clues.

In essence, these types of experiences have been a form or training for me, so that I would one day be able to decipher the cosmic riddles and puzzles placed before me, despite some of them taking years to solve.

This was no different. Though it feels like it is one of the truths I have trained my entire life in order to uncover. This is one of the big ones. Big Girl Panties were required for this one.

So, I simply breathed, knowing that I had to get my hands on a copy of this book so that I could take my time with it. I knew it was about to open up a whole new world for me. One I had been *waiting for*. One I had been *preparing for*. One that I was *made for*.

My awakening to these ancient truths all started for me with a major series of activations I spontaneously received in the summer of 2011. From when I first became aware of the term "Starseed," to when I'd first heard of Selene and her synchronistic connection with Shirley MacLaine as well as Chris Griscom, and the significance that that alone held for me.

Upon learning about Selene, I also learned through her, once we were connected, that it was indeed possible to be impregnated in ways beyond our human understanding of conception and creation of life. An Earth mother and a Galactic father. The visions I'd had, the knowing from deep within my own soul I'd carried throughout my life right from early childhood—that I would be impregnated and have babies "in a way that Earth humans do not usually experience"—were suddenly clarified and confirmed for me as truth.

I wasn't crazy. In truth, I'd always known this, though admittedly I had questioned my own sanity many times, usually as an attempt to play my own devil's advocate. I had to, as there were often no other Earthly explanations for my experiences. No frame of reference, and seemingly no one else who understood or had the same experiences as me. What else was I to do?

I was awoken to the concept that perhaps all those times in my life when I'd thought *'I might be pregnant,'* a new possibility existed for me: *I very likely was.*

Upon learning of Selene and her own experiences that summer, I started to pay more attention to synchronicities showing up in my awareness again, and I took special notice of people that came into my life in that same timeframe. I received visions, then I would contact these individuals, and make the connections. I would always experience a recognition and familiarity with the souls I felt drawn to spending time with. They were all "sent" to me as I opened up to my divine path, and to understanding more holistically who I really am.

I began to change rapidly. I was inspired about life in a way I had never quite experienced before. My dream life became more vivid again, full of revelations, messages, and divine encounters. I was experiencing connections with others in my waking life that went beyond time and space; people who knew and understood me on a cosmic soul level, rather than just what they saw of me in the third dimension. I felt myself desiring to move further away from my dense, challenging, third dimensional existence, while finding a way to continue being present in it somehow. I knew I no longer wanted it to drag me down.

I became happier as a mother. I was more patient, loving, and attentive beyond what I had been able to access within myself prior to this awakening.

But my relationship with Jeff was becoming more strained, as we did not see many things from the same vantage point any longer, and this was becoming painfully clear to both of us. I realized that perhaps we had never really viewed life in the same way, ever. I had adjusted my version of "reality" in a desperate attempt to live a normal life, and he most likely did the same, but for his own reasons.

This was a devastating realization, though exhilarating in its own way at the same time. At least I was able to witness my own truth more clearly, and this is what was exhilarating. Yet the realization that I felt like I was living in a different universe than my chosen life-partner was the absolutely devastating part.

He could feel me slipping away. I was used to not 'feeling' him, as through any and all crucial and painful moments for me in our time together, which unfortunately there were many, his pattern was to escape emotionally, and often even physically with his work, exercise and work, and other vices.

In so many ways, he was already gone from my field. Now I was desiring—*needing*—to spend as much time as I could engrossed in this new world inside which I found myself dwelling, both in my waking and my dream state; exploring these new connections, which for me, felt so much closer to the world I had always been searching for in relationship with others, yet always seemed to fall short. I had assumed before this that it was not humanly possible to share such an inter-dimensional connection with another person in my physical life, other than perhaps with my own children.

And now here I was. I finally felt at home in my own skin, truly and holistically. It was as if I'd discovered a significant piece of paradise within.

There were people around me who spoke freely of things I had never *dared* talk about publicly or at all. There were people around me who could understand me if and when I spoke of my own experiences, and in turn, they could share their unique or similar stories with me. It seemed like a miracle, and I never wanted it to end. I craved more and more of this, as these interactions brought inspiration and excitement back into my life.

CHAPTER 79

The Isis Initiate & Decoding the Goddess Codes of Mary Magdalene

As I stated in the previous chapter, in April 2014 I was finally ready to begin knowing how all of these puzzle pieces; my early abductions, the blue beings I would see in my room at night as a child, multiple "false-flag" impregnations, hybrid children, my Earth children, my Sky children, my marriage to Jeff, my sexual partners, Anthony, my obsession with finding my Divine Counterpart, and my deep desire to experience True Sacred Union fit together cohesively.

I set an intention to attempt to put all of these puzzle pieces I had been given over the years together, random and disconnected as they seemed. I was now more aligned with my own essence and soul vibration, combined with the synchronization I needed in order to once and for all connect them together as One, if that was even possible. Of course beyond figuring it out, I would come to realize the deeper meaning of how the whole of it fit into my present existence, in the Here and Now.

I need to say that anyone feeling the soul tug to know more about Magdalene, Jesus and their relationship would do well to read "The Magdalen Manuscript" and study it themselves. There is so much richness in the book itself apart from the actual manuscript, I highly recommend reading it from start to finish.

As I previously stated, only one small section of it is Mary Magdalene speaking and giving teachings, which in itself is one of the most powerful scripts I have ever come across. Also however, the "One Woman's Story" chapter, where Judi Sion, co-author of the book, shares her very personal story and journey is truly riveting and brings the entire meaning of the Manuscript full circle, alive in the world today. It may even serve to awaken a part of your own soul that has been waiting to be revealed.

What I will share, are the aspects of the Manuscript which finally gave me the confirmation and clarity that I had been searching for, for more than two years; and truly, my entire life.

Both the Mother Mary and Mary Magdalene were High Initiates of Isis. According to the Manuscript, at the age of twelve, Magdalene was sent to Egypt to study with and become a part of a Secret Sisterhood of Initiates, "under the wings of Isis" where she was trained in the secrets of Egypt, as well as the Alchemies of Horus and the Sex Magic of Isis, as the Mother Mary had also done when she was a young girl coming of age, both of them in preparation for their great cosmic assignments.

I just about stopped breathing, as my mind was immediately blown upon reading about this, which was stated within the first two paragraphs of the Manuscript. This was confirmation of a deep wisdom I had somehow already known.

According to the Manuscript, Magdalene was training in preparation to assist Christ with His Sacred Mission on the planet. It was known that becoming an Initiate and entering into Sacred Union with Yeshua would allow Magdalene to help him be fully prepared and ready, both spiritually as well as physically, for his gigantic assignment here on the planet.

Without the piece of the Goddess, he would not have succeeded. The assignment needed both God and Goddess to be complete. The Yin and the Yang.

Through the act of Sacred Union, Yeshua's Ka body, also referred to as His etheric body, was strengthened to the point where it was equally as physical as his flesh and blood. Through the act of Sacred Sexuality with a chosen Initiate, The Magdalene (you see, she was chosen long before her lifetime as Magdalene), Christ was able to fulfill his mission successfully.

She was so much more than a "whore."

This is a taboo message to be sending out into the world, and with great admiration and empathy, I honour Judi Sion and Tom Kenyon for bringing this message forth so that people like me could begin to understand fully the whisperings of our own souls, as fellow and potential ancient Initiates.

In the channeling, Magdalene shares that when the two Marys first saw one another, there was an unspoken recognition that they both understood—as fellow Initiates of the Goddess.

You see, the Mother had also been trained in the temples in Egypt as a High Initiate in order to be able to bring forth the Sacred Seed of the Divine Father God into physical embodiment. This was no small feat. Only an Initiate of the Highest Form would have been given such a divine assignment.

This completely explains the vision I'd had more than two years prior, when Mary The Mother literally morphed in front of my eyes into Mary The Magdalene before remaining as The Magdalene. Before Yeshua was ready to enter into Sacred Union with His Beloved, his Mother held the Divine Feminine Goddess frequency as a balancing beam for His Divine Masculine frequency with him, and for *him*.

So, The Mother was the first Initiate, bringing forth the God Seed. The Magdalene was then passed the flame to ready Yeshua to fulfill his divine mission. Both were needed in order for His Work here on Earth to be successful. Both goddesses were necessary, and it had to come about through these Initiations and alchemical trainings.

Bingo!

This also explained why I had been given the cryptic message about Isis exactly one month before receiving the divine vision of Jesus and the two Marys.

Isis was at the helm of it all!

The Voice screaming at me "*You are Isis*" finally beginning to make some sense.

It has never been important for me to try to find proof of whether or not I am actually Isis reincarnated. I say not a chance. In fact, some researchers say that she may never have even been physically embodied. Though others, such as Dr. Bruce Goldberg, claim she was a Time Traveler, and spiritual partner to Thoth, and that she was most definitely embodied, all the way back to the times of Atlantis. There are so many different accounts of the details of her existence, and all hold and carry some aspect of truth. Discernment is always a must when navigating these kinds of subjects.

To be frank, I will go on record to say that I do not feel anyone out there today that claims to be the reincarnation of Isis actually is. And I have seen all over YouTube and the like that there are a few. I do, however, feel that there are many of us carrying the Isis Codings within our DNA. I might stretch it further to hazard a guess that the ones who feel very connected to Isis and Mary may perhaps be embodied Initiates with important work to do and assignments to complete in the name of The Goddess while they are here on their tenure on this planet.

As for me, I am finally at peace with this cryptic message I'd received back in December 2011. I couldn't grasp then the magnitude of this message, though now, it holds a powerful message for me that I am no longer able to ignore.

I am an ancient Isis Initiate. I came here again, now, to reclaim this Divine Birthright, and thus, I stand as One who is forever changed by this information, as one who is committed to becoming the living embodiment of The Holy Initiate.

I feel in many ways I had already been unconsciously walking this path my entire life. Always feeling the internal tug to be doing this Divine Work, yet since the awareness of this knowing was mainly living in the unconscious realms of my being, as the pull I felt towards this path was unexplainable, I found myself never feeling fully ready or able to "go all the way" with it. Always holding myself back just a little, or in truth, a whole heck of a lot.

I'd always felt that a piece to my personal Soul Puzzle was missing, because I understood the power in what I felt inside myself, especially within relationship and partnership, but I didn't yet fully understand why I felt this way, what it meant, or how to use it in a positive, non-destructive way.

I often believed that I must just be too difficult a person to be with for very long. Not because I create drama or anything silly like that. In fact, in those ways, I often felt that perhaps I might be much easier to be with for many men. I could see them, for real, and allow them whatever freedom they needed in order to express themselves, even if that meant they strayed for a time. I could handle that if it meant their Soul was getting the answers that were needed. In fact, I usually encouraged this.

I also knew that I expected a lot, spiritually speaking, from the men I have been with. I have expected them to be awakened enough to see the game. Awakened enough to step out of the game and enter into Sacred Relationship with me. I am definitely not pointing fingers here. I also was not fully ready for this, fractured from myself and not yet fully embodying the true goddess within, which is why the divine counterpart I so desperately longed for was not able to fully show up in my life.

These men have been my mirrors, showing me what I was ready for, and perhaps, what I was not yet ready for as well. They have mirrored so perfectly for me where I was at, and where I still needed to go within myself to become whole again. Balanced within my own sacred Inner Masculine and Feminine energies, which by divine right of passage, is my natural state.

Now I see it clearly, and understand. This is a huge part of my mission here at this time; to embody the role of the Ancient Initiate. To embody The Goddess; to embody the Wisdom of The Priestess. I am certain I have been an Initiate many, many times before. Perhaps I have been for "all time" and have simply been waiting to remember and get on with it!

This would explain to me my highly awakened sense of sexuality as a young child. My natural pull to the sacred art of belly dancing, also as a young child, and even how it was that I already knew how to do it. My insatiable propensity to seek out orgasm at almost any cost, knowing that there was nothing more divine or holy, and not yet knowing of other ways to channel this massive creative life force energy.

I went on to become confused when I learned that sexuality was something to be ashamed of, as well as something that was abused, misused, forced and judged. The anguish that this painful discovery caused me for decades, and the self-numbing I felt necessary to execute in order to simply maintain a semi-functional relationship, was exhausting and challenging, not to mention self-destructive. I was especially confused about my own sexuality, and eventually, this confusion, anguish, and numbing created energetic blockages and deep cellular trauma, enough to ignite physical dis-ease in my Divine Temple.

I had already been grieving for decades emotionally, mentally, and most of all, spiritually, over this confusion all around me and within concerning my sexuality, a divine gift I'd always felt was to be held sacred, yet which so rarely seemed to be. I came to embody this universal dysfunction within myself. I was then gifted a final attempt at waking me the hell up; awakening within me my Divine Calling. I had to first be given the choice to face my own divinity and embrace it, or let it all go, and ultimately, destroy myself.

Of course, I chose to embrace it all. This is why and how I sit here now sharing my own story with you.

I chose Life. I chose Love.

I chose the way of Divine Guidance and Synchronicity.

I chose the Sacred Divine Path of The Goddess.

Now all that's left to do is to keep showing up for myself.

Because *Now is The Time.*

CHAPTER 80

The Crystal Bed

During one of my regression sessions, I was shown a piece of a lifetime and timeline where I'd lived in either Atlantis or Ancient Egypt. I am not certain, since I only witnessed the inside of the pyramid, and the energies felt otherworldly and very ancient. I did not think to ask for clarity in the moment.

Regardless, the important point is that this regression took place in November 2013, many months before I would discover "The Magdalen Manuscript" and receive confirmation of a connection between the two goddesses I'd always seemed to connect most with—Mary Magdalene and Isis.

I was being asked to go back to a lifetime I'd shared with Anthony. Immediately, I was inside of a temple with pyramid structures inside of it and around it. There were crystals *everywhere*—their otherworldly vibration permeated the entire sacred space.

Inside the Temple, there was a crystal bed which was used in Ceremony for Sacred Sexuality ~ *Sacred Union*. The frequency of the bed was so high; it was actually alive. The bed itself was like a conductor, a machine; an inter-dimensional portal. When two Whole beings entered into Ritualistic Ceremony together in this bed, it would transport them through time and space, while their energies would meld together as they made love.

This was known as the highest form of Alchemical Creation, whether creating an energetic manifestation of healing together, whether it was to set the spin for some other up spiral creation for the planet, or quite literally, the creation of the life of a higher being in the form of a child.

This bed could be used for any form of Sacred Alchemy or Initiation. Whatsoever was created while in this crystal bed, with the cosmic forces of the powerful alchemical spin that it held, was a Sacred Creation. Babies born of this type of union carried this alchemical frequency within their DNA, and whether or not a physical child was borne from this Union made no difference. Merely the joining of such energies created such a powerful alchemical frequency on the planet that it would pulsate out into the universe, setting the tone and frequency for perfectly balanced energies of the Divine Masculine and the Divine Feminine. These balanced energies would assist in the realization of a true sacred re-union in the form of divine sexuality, and this would greatly assist in *all* divine creations on Earth, *and beyond.*

A Sacred Alchemical Creation.

In this regression, I was shown that there are 144,000 pairs of these Whole Beings on Earth at this time who are all capable of anchoring in and shifting Earth's frequency if they so choose to, in order to raise the vibration of the entire planet through this form of High Alchemy. This level of alchemy has the potential to assist all shifts taking place on the planet at this time.

Some of these pairs will experience this union while aboard ship together, though most have no recollection of doing so, which makes the alchemical process taking place unconscious. It still works this way, however. When in full alignment with this magical process, it allows a greater margin of possibility for certain physical timelines to cross and thus, allows for the potential of a physical re-union.

The power of such alchemy is strengthened significantly as physical evidence of such a union is witnessed by the masses. This allows the alchemical creations that result from this Divine Union to be magnified and rooted more steadily into the physical dimension. This exponentially increases the impact as well as the capacity for what is alchemically possible on this planet.

It must be held in sacred space, however, as this sort of power is mighty. Thus, both partners must be fully ready for such a co-creative experience. Many now are in preparation, few are living it just yet.

When full alignment takes place, and sacred union alchemy is created, it assists with bringing the rest of the planet into greater alignment for creating possibilities for a more peaceful, loving, ecstatic existence for All.

The bells of synchronicity rang again when I was reading "The Magdalen Manuscript" about six months later. The section entitled "One Woman's Story," where Judi Sion describes an aspect of her own Initiation where Isis and her Priestesses would show up every night for quite some time, and bring Judi in to different temples, where the Priestesses would lead her to pools of oil, and dip her in each night, anointing and initiating her. This went on for many, many nights, with many, many Priestesses, in many, many pools of oil. She says her skin got softer and softer during this process.

For several nights, she says, the Priestesses would lay her on a crystal bed with giant pointed crystals penetrating each chakra point. They would change the crystals depending on what type of healing was required at the moment, and Judi claims that though she expected the crystals to hurt her, she was never in even an ounce of pain.

One night, she even experienced a giant cobra slither under the sheets as she lay there. It wrapped around her legs like a "human Mobius strip." She noted that after this experience, how she related to The One who was a dear friend, yet would become the man she would enter into Sacred Relationship with, *changed*.

The experiences on the crystal beds were healing Initiations which led into her readiness to enter into Sacred Union with her Beloved.

My experience in the regression from November 2013, though not exactly the same, holds many similarities in the essence and purpose of lying not on just a regular bed intended for Sacred Work, but one composed purely of silica—*quartz crystal*. These crystal beds were used as healing chambers, portals into other dimensional frequencies, emitting the vibrational codes needed for absorption and integration within the energetic fields of the Ones called to them for the purpose of Divine Service and Sacred Union.

CHAPTER 81

Meeting My Hybrid Children

Meeting Angel.

I first consciously met Angel in my regression session with Bridget on November 26, 2013. Angel walked right up to me with the sweetest energy and said with great clarity and conviction: "I might come down and be your Earth baby, but that's up to you."

She proceeded to download me with non-verbal information about herself telempathically. What she showed me was that she is able to exist in multi dimensions at once, *fully consciously*. That even if she decided to come into a third dimensional Earth body, which tends to be accompanied by long periods, or even lifetimes, of amnesia that, given the opportunity, she would come in with full awareness and remembrance of Who She Is. She would arrive fully awake and aware of her multi-dimensionality right from the get-go, and would maintain this knowingness throughout her time here.

Angel told me that she too is a "world-bridger" and that she is ready to step into an earthsuit if and whenever I wish her to.

"I'm ready whenever you are!"

She is a very bright light and I feel blessed to have met her in this way, even if only briefly.

Meeting Mahwin.

"I see a boy. He is tall, and looks to be about fifteen or sixteen years old, in human terms. He looks quite human, but with larger eyes than a regular human. He has hair that is long-ish and golden brown in colour. Though it would be easy to mistake him for being fully human, his frequency is unmistakably otherworldly. He is beautiful.

This young man is a guide and teacher to me. He watches out for me and is helping navigate the writing of this book and the intersection of the timelines needed to bring it forth successfully into the world. This is what he has been trained to do.

This is his purpose.

He is 'The Calendar Keeper.' He makes the divine appointments with us, and does whatever he can to help us keep these appointments. For instance, when either Anthony or I receive an intuition pertaining to our multi-dimensional work together, it is this child who is assisting us in noticing it and assimilating it. Of course, we both have Free Will, so there is only so much he can do, but this is the essence of his 'job.'

He is a wise sage, and was created to be our guide along this path to this particular part of our mission. His words to me in this meeting were:

'You will know when it is time. Be there and be ready. Show up. When time ceases to exist, it is Time. You will know what this means at the appropriate moment. Be there. Stop worrying. You cannot do this 'wrong.' Events will unfold as they should. You will see.'

I was clearly shown through hypnosis that I have been being prepared for this work since infancy—in fact, for many lifetimes leading up to this one. I have been on this Mission and preparing for this incarnation quite literally for eons.

I was also shown that during my main episode of experiencing missing time, which ignited my DNA codes and blood crystals holding these frequencies relevant to this Mission, that I was taken aboard the ship that night and underwent a massive upgrade. It was as if they flicked the switch inside me, and set it on high. They had been working with me and my physical body already since birth, but during this encounter, they "turned it up."

I quite literally became a "baby machine," and this was the plan. I would have to quickly learn to adjust to this new frequency, not knowing or understanding what the hell was going on with me, and why I was chosen and for what purpose. I had no idea about the hybrid babies, or the hybrid children back then. I didn't even know it was possible. I had not a clue that I, myself, was one.

I never even found out about any of that until a year after my diagnosis, when I was thirty-six, 15 years after this switch had been turned on inside of me. Until then, I was floundering around, trying to stay afloat, trying to make sense of my unusual experiences, including relationships that were riddled with so much pain and confusion all the time.

I would have to learn to adjust, to trust myself, to hold these frequencies, or to exit this life, essentially. I had to wake up. My sanity, and my life, depended on it.

There was a reason I was allowed to remember so much of what I experienced back in 1996 and 1997, though stubborn and fearful as I was. I was meant to put the pieces together one day, and to once and for all, understand the meaning of it. I was meant to write this book. I was not meant to take these experiences to the grave, though try as I might have to keep it that way, I couldn't. Running from it, rejecting it, was what nearly destroyed me, honestly. I was meant to follow the many sparks all leading me to complete this assignment and fulfill this aspect of my mission. Not only did it matter for me and my children, but there were others out there who were depending on me to step forward with this story as well.

I am never shown everything about my life or my path. I am shown little bits and pieces, and then left to move forward and figure out what it all means as I go. I am left to discern what the truth is, and what best serves me and my purpose here, which is ultimately being in service to the planet.

Discernment has always been one of my biggest, and most challenging lessons.

I have been left swimming, nearly drowning at times, but eventually I learned to trust the current, always doing my best to stay awake, to stay on my path of Highest Intent and Purpose. Sometimes easier said than done, having so much Gemini trickster energies in my natal chart. Oh, I have encountered Trickster often, and some of these lessons burned me to the core to learn.

Carrying such an enormous cosmic responsibility, I have nearly fallen off the tracks more than I care to say. Finally having people in my corner who understand what I am doing and Who I Am has been enormously helpful and a massive blessing in my Life most recently. I am eternally grateful for every single one of them. You know who you are.

CHAPTER 82

Awaken the Sleepy Seer

I was generously gifted an all-inclusive weekend pass to the Sedona Yoga Festival in February 2014 by a new friend Eva who I'd met as a "chocolate client." I had been running my own raw chocolate business, selling organic raw chocolate whole food puddings and nut butter cups in local stores here in Sedona. Synchronistically, I met Eva during my very first delivery.

She seemed so excited about my product, and my labels, on which I'd used some sacred geometry digital art by Mynzah. He'd titled this particular piece "The Seed," which I thought entirely fitting for me and what I was creating and putting out into the world, as I was already deep in to the creation of this book as well. And of course, it fit perfectly on my labels.

These labels were truly cosmic, and I even included my sons' artwork featured on the bottom label of each product. The idea was to inspire other young children to eat healthily, and know that raw food could be rich, delightful and delicious. I had the bigger idea to eventually have children from all over submit their own artwork, and I would feature a different "artist" each month, then send the child who was being featured a little package of treats in the mail with their artwork on it. Eventually, I wanted to start a charity to raise funds and create art scholarships for children in need of financial support to realize their own dreams while also learning to eat healthier. It was a large vision but one I still hold.

So, when I met Eva, she seemed so excited about the puddings, I decided to gift her one. These were not cheap products. I used only the best in packaging too, so each pudding was packaged in a glass mason jar, perfect for reuse and repurposing, which was precisely the idea behind it.

Eva was so grateful; I could feel her gratitude and excitement. It was such a promising moment for my business! When I got home, I noticed on the local social media bulletin board a picture of my product. Eva's review of it was so touching. I hadn't realized this would even happen when I gave her the pudding, but it was perfect. This was a woman spreading positivity and love wherever she went, and she did it all the time, I began to notice. From then on, our friendship blossomed. Of course, she is also a starseed, her birthdate is October 17, when the sun was at galactic degree in Libra.

I continued to message Eva and give her chocolate whenever I had some extra, because I knew she appreciated it, and it made me happy to see her excitement and joy in eating it. She is a great receiver which I think is an amazing gift. Her light is so bright, and from then on, I felt I needed more people like Eva in my life.

One day, totally out of the blue, she messaged me that if I wanted it, I could have a free weekend pass to the yoga festival here in town, which I had been pining to go to, but didn't have the resources to make it happen. And then there was this angel, offering me not only a day pass, but a ticket to the whole enchilada!

I'd managed to be gifted a day pass the year before, and had enjoyed it thoroughly. I felt so blessed to once again be handed a ticket with zero strings attached. I must be doing something right in the world to have such gifts bestowed upon me! I felt very grateful.

The sad thing was that I could barely use the ticket. I told Eva up front that I could only go on Sunday, because Jeff was out of town working that weekend and wouldn't be home until late Saturday night. She didn't care. She told me if I only made it to one class, it would all be worth it. She is amazing like that.

So I practiced my receiving with no guilt, and looked on the Sunday schedule to see what I could make it to. I was torn, because the class that pulled my awareness most was not even a yoga class. Here I was excited to finally take a yoga class, with so many different teachers (though by Sunday afternoon when I could actually go, most of the great yoga classes were done), and I was drawn most to a class where we would sit and listen to someone speak. I still had this idea in my head that I should do a physical class, since I'd been craving it so badly having not done a full yoga class in ages.

Yet I couldn't ignore the class that was pulling me the most, with a woman I'd never heard of before, named Sunny Dawn Johnston. It was a class that apparently focused on tapping in to our own intuitive knowingness, learning tools about how to tap in, what different ways work for each individual, that sort of thing. I was worried that I would go to this class, be disappointed, and wish to God I'd just chosen a yoga class for goodness sake! Even though I have had many experiences of vast awakening and awareness, I am also by heart a skeptic, especially after having tested my own discernment with various charlatans and tricksters on my own quest for the truth, learning by default how to hone my discernment skills.

I took the chance though. The worst that could happen was that it was a fluffernut class and it wouldn't teach me anything new. At worst, I'd be disappointed. I didn't want this to be the outcome, but something in me told me not to worry.

I brought my yoga mat hoping that at least we might stretch or meditate on the floor, breathe deeply, something that resembled a yoga class, even slightly.

Nope.

I walked into a small carpeted room filled with chairs. Sunny sat on a chair on a small podium at the front, and she had a woman "on stage" with her with a guitar.

I wondered what I'd gotten myself in to here.

Sunny's energy was quite stunning. She radiated a beautiful light about her, that felt peaceful, warm, welcoming and calm, though I could also tell she had a fiery spirit about her, which I liked. I always enjoy a bit of a rebel in someone, being one at heart myself. I could feel that she was her own person, and I could feel her truth, so started to get excited for the class. I had front row seats.

When she began talking, I instantly took to her. I had been to see Allison Dubois in Phoenix when I'd first moved here in 2008. I had been really excited to see her, and though what I witnessed that day was beautiful, and I did like her, she had a bit of a harder edge to her that was a little too much for me. Way less warm and personal. Much more "business." I suppose she's been at it longer, and in the middle of the spotlight thanks to the television series, *Medium*. Perhaps she merely set clearer boundaries. I'm sure she would be overly bombarded by people if she didn't, so I do understand.

But Sunny still had this pure, warm and caring way about her, while also having that edge which I suppose one develops when they are in a constant state of practicing discernment as a result of receiving messages from beyond the veil so regularly.

I was nervous when, after Sunny had guided us through some fun exercises to boost our energy, helping us each achieve a state of joy and lightheartedness within, she told us to go find a partner and that we were going to do readings on one another! *WHAT?!*

Of course, all of my old programming about "*What if I do it 'wrong'; What if I'm exposed as a fake or a fraud; what if I can't do it...*" Blah blah. The tedious and irritating self-doubt from my culturally programmed monkey mind creeping in again. I was so over it.

I decided to remain in the state of high vibration that I'd just achieved and ignored the voices from within attempting to sabotage my experience.

It worked! They got quieter, especially when I came face-to-face with the stranger I was going to have to read. And she wanted me to read her first! *Eek!* The first exercise was to be done by simply holding hands facing one another and simply "dropping in" as an open vessel to "see" what messages or images might come through, while focusing inwardly on my partner. We did not speak together beforehand at all.

Immediately, I began to feel a throbbing, almost stabbing pain, like a stitch or something, in my gut. I tried to "make it better" but then realized since I am an extreme empath, this sensation may actually be one of the messages, and not to discard it as something about me, separate from the reading I was to give. I simply breathed through the sensation, as it was indeed quite uncomfortable.

I kept hearing the word *"move"* over and over. *"Needing to move."* Turns out, there was a "move" that this woman was resisting that would actually be good for her. I felt it strongly as a physical move of location. Then I saw the head of a man. He was handsome, with dark wavy hair, and blue-ish eyes. He was very clear, but I could only see his face. He was smiling.

It was time to share with her my messages. I was nervous that none of it would make any sense. But Sunny had also told us not to worry about that, that even with experienced mediums and intuitives, at times the messages are not immediately clear, and maybe they never would be. Our job as an intuitive is not to interpret the information. That most of the time, what we get and how we get it is exactly as the receiver is meant to experience and receive it, and that most of the time, it will make complete sense to them. And if it doesn't, that's not our job. It's their job to stay open and receptive in their own lives, and to remember the reading if and when the confirmation does show up later on.

The intuitive's job is merely to give the information as it is received through the psychic channels. It is not to be judged by the reader. Sunny told us that once one is experienced enough, that the intuitive will be able to decipher general images they are shown, that give a specific message for the person.

For example, if an intuitive sees the image of a baby, it may come to be shown to them every time they are intuiting a pregnancy. So, the intuitive learns that this image shown to them always symbolizes a "baby" or a "pregnancy."

I decided that I needed to trust these seemingly random hits, and took a deep breath. I began to share with her what I had experienced while holding her hands, dropping deeply into receiving divine messages for her, and I was *amazed* at how comfortable and confident I suddenly felt.

She didn't fully understand the pain in the stomach, which I had interpreted myself as a possible digestive or health issue to be taken care of, but didn't project my interpretation onto her. She said that her abs were sore from the weekend of doing yoga nonstop. Later she shared with the group that the second woman to read her also mentioned the stomach pain. So, after hearing it twice, she wondered if perhaps it might be something she needed to pay attention to with her diet. That had been my own intuitive sense about it, but I hadn't said that.

Maybe I should have but I was trying to let her make her own connections.

I was glad nonetheless to hear her say this, because it was the only one of my messages for her that she didn't seem to fully comprehend, though by the end of the class, she did.

She totally understood what I was talking about with regards to "moving." Apparently, her husband had been trying to convince her to move, and she was resisting it. Funny that with the man I described to her, she said it sounded exactly like her husband. Even the shape of the face I described to her was the same, so neither of us had any doubt it had been her husband coming through to assist her with letting go and trusting more in the idea of moving.

It felt incredible to receive such confirmation on my reading for her!

The next exercise we did was to get with a different partner, and this time we played around with psychometry. Psychometry is the art and science of being able to read the energies psychically from an object that has been worn or held regularly by someone. The energies of the person can be transferred into the personal object. One can use psychometry to give a psychic reading on someone.

I had first heard of psychometry in about 2002, and had experimented with it in the first meditation group I'd ever been a part of, back in Vancouver. This is the group in which I had met my friend Angela.

In this meditation group, we'd explored psychometry with different crystals. It was really interesting, as it was the first time I'd ever heard a crystal speak! I remember finding it utterly fascinating, as it came very easily to me.

So, Sunny's class was the second time I had ever worked consciously with psychometry for the sake of it, as an exercise. I know I've done it all my life naturally. I have consciously received messages and information through objects, yet I hadn't ever had to *tell* anyone about it, never mind give a complete stranger a psychic reading while doing it!

I was very nervous, and yet again, I whisked those unhelpful, dense thoughts away, and focused on the bracelet this woman had given me to hold. I tapped in to its energy.

Right away, things started coming, and quickly. At first, I was judging what was coming in because it seemed too random to be connected. Some of it was embarrassing for me to have to say, because it sounded utterly ridiculous and nonsensical to me. I tried to forget the things I was judging as "stupid" and useless information, assuming my mind was trying to trick me, being a total jerk, and would make me look like a fool if I dared say what I was seeing and hearing out loud.

Basically, I was totally caught in a battle with my ego. Though, I suppose I shouldn't really say totally because somehow, I'd managed to quiet these judgments. I realized that whatever was being shown or told to me, was all appropriate. I remembered Sunny's sage advice, saying that it was *not* up to the reader to interpret what they received. In fact, a reading could be utterly *ruined* by an egotistical reader thinking that they know what the meaning of the message is for their client.

So, I shut my analytical mind up and allowed everything to flow, even the seemingly ridiculous stuff.

When the time was up, I felt like I'd barely gotten anything for this poor girl, simply a bunch of gibberish. I felt somewhat guilty for spending so much of my time fighting with my own ego, instead of allowing a "good" reading to come through for this woman.

I breathed deeply, and began sharing what I'd received from her bracelet.

The accuracy of nearly every message was astounding to both of us.

Right to her personality, to specific messages concerning her relationship with her brother, I received accurate information. And when I shared with her the very strong image of an "angel" I kept seeing, who was close with her at all times, she told me that her mother's name was Angel, and that they were indeed very close, and that she feels her with her all the time. It was beautiful and touching to be able to pass this information along to her.

There were about ten different, obvious hits, which was absolutely incredible to me. The final one, which I almost didn't mention as it was one of the most embarrassing and confusing messages I'd received, was seeing a very clear image of her eating an amusement park hot dog. Like, the absolute worst hot dog one could eat for their health, yet for hot dog junkies, perhaps the yummiest kind. She enjoyed this hot dog *so* much.

When I shared this with her, she stared at me in astonishment for a moment, then started laughing. She explained to me that she had been vegan for a couple of years, and what she actually missed the very most were amusement park hot dogs! She told me that just that very morning she had been complaining to a friend that she wished she could have one! I never would have guessed that, and most certainly could not have made it up more perfectly!

The most obscure image I'd received ended up being one of the strongest messages to confirm for both of us the validity and accuracy of the reading. Who knew? I'm really glad I shared it all with her though. An excellent demonstration of synchronization at play.

After this day, I felt like I had received at least some confirmation for all the feelings and visions I've had about seemingly random things throughout my life, especially the ones that would consequently come to pass in the physical realm. It was verification for me that try as I may wish to sometimes, with the responsibility it can require, at times quite a *heavy* responsibility, that I was intuitive, perhaps a little psychic even, like it or lump it, and I had to start owning this aspect of myself and begin to truly trust it as it would come to assist me greatly in my work here on the planet.

This class arrived in perfect synchronistic timing for me. At the time, I'd been having a very challenging time in my marriage, more so than ever before. I was to the point of questioning myself constantly, becoming afraid to continue on with my galactic work here—especially in regards to writing this book.

This empowering experience, thank heavens, altered me in a very positive way. I received confirmation of at least some of my gifts, and received the confidence booster which helped me begin believing in myself again. I was able to start picking up the pieces of myself I had grown terrified of owning, for fear of a potential retaliation or attack that could ruin my life, or the lives of my children.

It had been really hard for me to move past this fear, and the class with Sunny on February 10, 2014 was a key moment in my life where I was presented with the permission slip that said not only was it safe, but in fact it was necessary for me to fully step in to myself again. Perhaps more important than ever before. I realized that day that to simply be "me" without apology, without fear, was a gift to this planet, as is the case for everyone. I realized right then and there that I held the responsibility to own this Truth completely.

Thank You forever to Eva for assuring the door to this incredibly empowering experience was available for me, especially before she really even knew me.

I'm so grateful for her impeccable timing, and am ecstatic that I made the conscious choice to walk on through to the other side, from the darkness to the Light. I became witness to the truth yet again: that on the other side of this debilitating fear, I had actually never stopped shining.

CHAPTER 83

Activations of The Next Generation

The First Blood Moon – April 15, 2014

The eve of the first Blood Moon of the year, which we would see a total of four in a one year period, had our little home filled with anticipation. In Sedona, the night skies tend to be immaculately filled with clear, cosmic wonder and beauty most nights, so we were quite certain we would be able to enjoy this phenomenon to the fullest.

Noah, being nine and ever rebellious, always pushing his edge, wanted to keep up pace with the adult lifestyle rather than be a regular kid. The peak of the Blood Moon was to happen around 12:45 am, and he wanted to stay up for it to witness it in all its cosmic glory. As parents, we had to be discerning with his bed time, knowing the lack of sleep would throw him off in the coming days. But we did agree to wake him up when it was time to come see it. He agreed that this was fair, and made us promise, repeatedly, to wake him, no matter what.

We kept up our end of the bargain. At least, we tried.

And we have done things like this before. When Noah is deep in sleep though, it will often take a moment to get him coherent enough to wake up, yet, he will always wake if there is something he wants to experience, and he was hell-bent on seeing this Blood Moon that night.

Jeff went into the room to wake him and Noah would not wake up.

He tried several times the five minutes he was in there. Noah sat up on two occasions, went to get up, eyes refusing to open, and then lay back down. Jeff told him it was time to see the Blood Moon, or he would miss it. Noah slumbered on, unable to open his eyes or move from the bed.

Jeff came out, dumbfounded, laughing at the comical scene he had just witnessed. He had tried several times, repeatedly. Noah even became conscious enough more than once, yet he simply could not do it.

I thought it rather bizarre, knowing how adamant he had been to see this moon. I went in and tried myself; same thing. He wouldn't wake up for me either. So we left it alone, what else could we do?

The Blood Moon was absolutely stunning. I am so glad I was able to witness it. It was some kind of magic, that's for certain. I counted my blessings and expressed my gratitude for this experience and for my life.

The next morning, without realizing yet what had happened, Noah started telling us about a really incredible dream he'd had during the night. He was at Bell Rock, one of the infamous rock formations here in Sedona, especially known for its cosmic powers and connection with ETs and other dimensional activity coming and going.

In fact, one time, while Jeff and the boys were out at Bell Rock waiting to meet me after I'd spent a weekend in Phoenix working on my book, they all heard what the three of them to this day are certain was a ship sitting behind the mountain. I remember the boys running to tell me about it when I arrived there, and Jeff confirmed it.

But back to the Noah story. In this dream, he described to us the morning after the Blood Moon, he was accompanied by an elder man, whom he described as a "wise man." He said he remembered him to be a monk.

This monk was attempting to open a portal in Bell Rock, but was having difficulties. He could not remember how to do it, and kept trying in vain.

Finally, Noah pulled out a Book. He described it as a Book that he himself (Noah) had transcribed, and in it contained many codes. It was filled with them, and he said that they were written in many different extraterrestrial languages. He handed the Book to the monk in order to help him. The monk found the code that he needed to open up the portal in the red rocks. Noah described this event as "awesome," with lights appearing all around it.

As he finished telling us about this experience, he finally realized that we hadn't woken him to see the moon, and was severely irritated with us. Jeff and I laughed and told him what had happened. He couldn't believe it.

I found out several days later randomly from some acquaintance in town that apparently, during the Blood Moon, a portal had been opened up in Sedona. The synchronicity set in like a light bulb flicking on in a flash, and in that moment, I was in even greater awe of my young son.

Could it really be?

I can't help but remember one of Selene's many timely and powerful messages: "Synchronization is confirmation." If this is true, which I know in my heart that it is, what exactly does this mean about my son, and who in the world is he?

Introducing: "*White Lightning*" – Early May 2014

Noah came to me one evening sometime in the first week of May, 2014. He had been brushing his teeth when all of a sudden, he heard a very clear voice say to him, *"Stop thinking NOW."*

His thoughts ceased, instantly.

As he was looking at himself in the mirror in front of him, he began to see himself transform. He was still the same size, as he recalls, but his entire body was filled with light. He was Light. He was so bright in fact, that he was transparent, though he recalls he had a solid outline "shaping" him, containing his brilliant light body.

As he described to me, he appeared to be wearing a mask, "though it wasn't a mask," as he put it. I asked him if he meant that he looked different, perhaps *not human*. He said "yes," immediately and clearly. He was *not* human.

Then he proceeded to tell me that his hands emitted a great deal of energy, and that they were very large. He said that he could shoot lightning from his hands, and that his name was "*White Lightning*."

Once he was shown this, and witnessed his transformation in the mirror, and then proceeded to be told his name, he heard the voice say to him very clearly again, *"You may think once more."*

And with that, the image in front of him returned to the nine-year-old boy we know and love as "Noah."

Noah was very excited and energized by this experience. I had not told him how to do this, nor had I taught him any such tricks to seeing these types of things. This was not his first metaphysical experience and it sure wouldn't be his last, I knew that. This experience was all his own, and it was so very empowering for him.

Interestingly enough, only a few days later, we were camping and Noah was admiring a friend of the family's new car she had just bought. It was a white Volkswagen, and Noah with his great fondness for cars, was inspecting every inch of it with sincere and focused interest.

Out of the blue, our friend says, "Guess what her name is, Noah?" He tried a few guesses but none were correct. Then she told us. "I named her 'White Lightning.'"

This friend had no knowledge of Noah's experience a few days prior to this, and he and I both almost fell over hearing this. He started laughing in shock and astonishment, and I sat there, somehow not surprised in the least, basking in the synchronistic amusement of it all.

CHAPTER 84

Mission Inevitable

Both of my children have continued to talk with me over the years about their experiences with extraterrestrials, and there are far too many to share here in this book. Suffice it to say, I have no doubts as to their, or my own, soul origins. I find witnessing them grow, becoming more of Who They Are, embodying these truths more and more as they get older in their earthly existence, to be a fascinating and humbling experience.

Yes, my children are in human bodies as is the case with most of the starseed here now. They are living human lives. Most likely, the majority of the children being born now and in the past several years have different, more advanced DNA than even we do. There are more starseed being born on the planet, because they are needed now more than ever, and whether they use the term or not, everyone knows it.

There are scientists and geneticists tracking the DNA changes in these "new children," and it truly is not "*new*" nor is it contrived propaganda. There is scientific proof of these DNA changes. It is happening all around us. It is happening within ourselves and within our own families. And we always have the choice to consciously upgrade our own DNA to a certain extent, which is another topic. Nor is it something I claim to be an expert in. I am only an expert at my own life, and my own experiences. Nothing more, nothing less.

I have personally been witness to my own multi-incarnational and parallel lives, in many of which I also witnessed myself Ascending. I have witnessed many incarnations in which I was involved in these same assignments, particularly with the hybridization programs.

I have been preparing for this time and this mission for many lifetimes, and I have been working with some of the same souls, Anthony being one of them, for eons. It just so happens that in this particular lifetime, in order to support my mission most effectively, there is also a further connection between our physical children regardless of having ever met in a physical third dimensional sense, which to me, is a synchronicity I cannot ignore.

My connection with Anthony is most definitely not accidental or random. Rather, it is significant and purposeful. Synchronistic even. The mystery now is to witness how it all unfolds from here...which could truly be any which way through the Law of Free Will.

CHAPTER 85

Tapping in to the Crystal Skull Consciousness and Meeting 'Synergy'

At the end of May 2014, I started attending a meditation group with Eva. This meditation group was led by a couple in Clarkdale, Arizona named Jeanne Michaels and Dr. Jaap van Etten, who are the current caretakers of hundreds of crystal skulls. Jaap is Dutch and has a very strong scientific background and education. He has written several books in the past years, many focusing on the history and wisdom of crystal skulls and their messages, The Sidhe, as well as other cosmic information. He is very connected with the energies of Gaia. At the time of this writing, I have only been to their meditation space a handful of times, but each time has been powerful in its own unique way.

The first time I attended was on May 28, 2014 and I was there with both Eva and another friend of hers, Taniah. Taniah had told me about this meditation they were going to, and so I tagged along with her and Eva, not sure what I was getting myself in to exactly. It could have been anything really, I do live in Sedona after all. But for some reason, I felt a gentle calling to go and check it out. I'd worked with the tiny fluorite crystal skull that I'd carried with me when I was pregnant with Rubin back in 2008/2009. The one I ultimately offered up to the Grand Canyon. That entire experience was quite powerful, and bizarre, so I was quite certain something interesting would happen here.

Walking in to their meditation room full of skulls, I noticed they were each placed consciously as a grid in a sacred geometric pattern by Jaap himself, complete with each section or petal of the flower being attuned to a specific group vibrational frequency relating to a vortex area on this planet, a star system, and a general life theme. For example, the first time I went, all other seats were taken, and the seat that was "waiting" for me was connected with Mexico, the star system was Zeta Reticulum, and the frequency of the skulls were most aligned with the energies of "Change."

This particular night turned out to be quite a powerful one for me. I can't remember most of what the skull relayed to me, but it was a LOT. One of the biggest messages I received from it was that the being working with me through the skull was going to "enter me" and work with me, supporting me through the changes I was currently undergoing in my life and helping me synchronize with limitless.

Honestly, this concerned me slightly based on the Zetas' (or "greys'") bad rap, which in large part, they earned themselves. Not all, but many. I know there are benevolent Zetas who truly do have our best interest in mind. But this time, I was a bit nervous. Enter me? Work with me? I wondered how this might present itself.

After this experience, things really did begin to shift for me in a positive, progressive forward movement. Within a month of this experience, I set the plans in motion to go meet Selene for the first time in person. And less than three months after this evening, I was in her presence, hugging her like she was one of my closest family members, and it was such a joyous reunion, and a trip which I have since made another six or seven times.

This Zeta being was extremely helpful in assisting me in being open to synchronicity, to seeing things from a different perspective and to help keep me open to things I wouldn't otherwise be open to. At the time, magic did continuously seem to be happening all around me. I was definitely placed into a significantly increased up spiral after meeting this being and allowing a temporary merging to take place between us.

Due to life circumstances, it was about a month before I was able to make it back to the weekly meditation circle. I made it back on June 25, 2014 and once again there was only one spot left for me to sit at when I arrived, and it was directly between Jeanne and Jaap. This time, the petal in front of me was the Sedona petal, which was connected with Sirius and the theme was "Knowledge/Understanding."

This particular night, a woman named Sherry Whitfield was there. Sherry is the current Guardian of the ancient crystal skull named Synergy. Everyone seemed excited about Synergy being present in the circle this evening, and at the end of the meditation, Sherry offered each person in attendance a few moments with Synergy if they chose to.

As the group meditation started, I had not yet selected a skull to work with. I went into meditation and listened. At once, I could feel that a black-coloured skull was requesting to work with me for the evening. This skull showed me the location in the circle I would find it in, and it was not in my petal, but rather, from Jaap's. It is okay to reach a little bit for a skull, so long as one isn't walking around the circle or dropping them. When I opened my eyes, I saw that this skull was easily reachable. It was next to another larger black skull, but I could feel which one had been contacting me, and so I brought it to me. A few moments of breathing and connecting with this skull, a few deep breaths, and instantly, it began speaking to me.

"You are the Keeper of the Keys."

'What in the world does that mean?' I thought to myself.

This statement was repeated by the skull over and over until I realized what it meant. I finally figured it out after it also proceeded to share with me that anything that touched my own vibration, my own energy field, was able to only because I had allowed it. This skull was adamant that absolutely nothing that occurred from outside of me that has ever affected me, could have done so if I hadn't allowed it on some level.

And I had done this much in my life unconsciously, and had suffered great consequences because of this grave lack of discernment. But the inspiring aspect of this message, the thing that empowered me, was that if I learned to practice discernment and learned to create healthy, strong boundaries, that nothing of discord could *ever* touch me or affect me negatively again.

The skull relayed to me an image with the energy of resistance attached to it. It told me that it would not work to resist something I did not wish into my field. That merely by the act of resistance, that I would automatically create a field of discord, since resistance holds the frequency of fighting, or pushing up against. Therefore, it also holds the energy of destruction.

Of course, there are times when destruction is necessary in order for creation to blossom, but it is about learning to discern when destruction is actually necessary, as opposed to when it might be harmful, and then navigating the energies of this so as to stay in an upward spiral, naturally leading to new creation.

But in general, simply resisting something creates more strength in the opposing force, and inevitably, which it showed me, an explosive form of destruction occurs. That which we resist, persists; we get the exact opposite effect from what we actually want.

The skull shared with me that by holding one's field with an empowered awareness of allowing or disallowing whatever resonates or does not, that things which are not in alignment with what we choose simply bounce off of our frequency and resonant field, and as a result, no drama or destruction is necessary. One is able to remain in a state of allowing alignment to guide them, which always leads to creative expression of some form.

This is what we are *all* aiming to master.

The skull kept showing me images of a phoenix bird burning up in flames, disintegrating to ashes, only to rise up again. It told me that I was the phoenix rising, and that that which does not serve me gets burned away. Even though at times it may feel like I am dying or that death is inevitable, that I always have the power to rise and become greater than before.

We are all capable of this.

It showed me an image of our beautiful Oak Creek Canyon that only one month prior to this experience had lost more than 20,000 acres of forest due to carelessness; a fire that was man-made and not extinguished properly. That even though this scenario was indeed devastating, the growth and beauty that will arise from the ashes will be even more lush and magical and beautiful than they were before the fire. That sometimes, things need to burn away in order to fertilize and then birth a newer, fresher, more magical version of itself.

I really enjoyed my time with this skull. It shared much valuable information with me, and though none of it was really "new news," it was indeed helpful to be given the visuals so clearly. I know the messages sank deeper into my consciousness, and I am grateful for this. This skull very much took on the role of teacher for me this night, and I appreciated my lesson immensely.

At the end of the evening, Sherry held a space in the room where anyone who wished to have time with Synergy could do so one at a time. She sat opposite whoever was in the chair. She would place our hands on the skull, with hers maintaining the frequency, an action I'd guessed was her protecting Synergy's frequency as its current guardian. I'd already had a powerful experience with one skull, so I was curious about this one as well.

I set my hands on Synergy and breathed deeply in an effort to connect with the energies. Immediately, I saw an image of Buddha flash before me, and then Synergy began laughing like a Buddha. It was quite comical, and I couldn't help but smile and giggle to myself. Then I heard Synergy say to me, "*Laughter brings us to our center. We always get closer to the truth through the gateway of laughter.*"

This powerful message and experience was synchronistically validated for me when later that night, after my experience with Synergy, I looked up information on this skull, as I had known absolutely nothing about it before going in to the experience. The message that jumped out at me, happened as if placed precisely on the screen in that moment, meant for me to see:

Synergy is also called the "Skull of Joy and Laughter" or "The Laughing Skull."

Well, I definitely experienced Synergy's message and medicine of laughter that night!

I was not given this particular tidbit of information about Synergy before this experience by Sherry either. She had said surprisingly very little about the skull in fact, apart from her own personal high strangeness experiences being Synergy's guardian, including the story of how that came to pass. She wanted us to have our own unique experiences with Synergy, without attachment to what that might, or is "supposed to," look like.

Reading this information online was definitely validating for me that I had no doubt tapped in to the messages and wisdom of this crystal skull quite accurately.

This experience was beyond powerful for me, as someone who needs laughter and always has, simply to get me through life; laughter and lightheartedness is often how I cope with stress, and how I enjoy celebrating the magic of life as well. I come from a family with great senses of humour. We can laugh at ourselves when we need to, and we stay (relatively) sane and healthy through our ability to laugh at life as much as we possibly can.

I was able to feel deeply and personally the truth of my message from Synergy that night. I had already begun to rediscover my own sense of lightheartedness, laughter and joy, and to take responsibility for it in my life, knowing I cannot count on anyone else to be the source of my peace or joy, or even to necessarily want to go there with me and explore it. This was a strong revelation for me.

My state of Joy is completely and entirely in my own hands.

It's purely a state of BE~ing. We *choose* laughter; and we choose to allow joy and laughter to penetrate us, no matter what the world may look like on the outside. Or we don't. I knew I only had one true choice here.

I had been moving closer to my joyous Natural State, and Synergy only helped me confirm that laughter indeed would be the gateway to rediscovering my ultimate truth.

Laughter and Joy. Who knew that was all I'd needed to choose all along?

CHAPTER 86

"50 Shades of Alien Grey": When Failure to Discern Destroys

Joy is one thing, discernment is another. Both are equally important, as we need both to keep us in a constant state of up spiral energies, which is what helps one remain focused on their assignments and missions.

Let's just say discernment has not always been my strongest attribute. By nature, I am overly trusting and even naïve with people, always wanting to believe that their integrity is intact and their intentions are pure. Talk about walking around with a sign on my forehead saying, "Fuck me over, please!"

I would say that learning to discern successfully is still something I am working on, and may have to continue to my entire life. It would be nice if I could master this fine art sooner rather than later, as it's certainly wreaked more than its fair share of havoc in my world; most strongly in my psyche and my physical body. There have been many instances in my life where I know it was my failure to discern that landed me in boiling hot water. I have been hurt, abused, and messed with psychically, physically, mentally and spiritually. Wearing these earth suits can be risky business and we all need a little perspective sometimes.

A major lesson in discernment occurred recently, which stung quite a lot. Because, by this point in 2015, I thought I'd had this discernment thing in the bag. Boy, was I wrong!

It started with spending hours on end on the computer, writing my book, researching, and admittedly, surfing way too much for my own good. I was about to find out the hard way how detrimental this really was to me.

I was so hungry for metaphysical information, and went through a phase of a month or so when my friend Jen would send me e-books to read that were blowing my mind and filling me with valuable galactic and metaphysical knowledge. How could this hurt me?

I forgot to protect myself.

My always perfect eye sight, even at thirty-nine, started to blur intensely within a matter of weeks of this constant reading. I had never liked reading books online, but at the time, I'd had no other choice if I wanted this information, and I wanted it badly. Much of it was research I was doing for this very book. I thought no harm could come to me. I was being careless. Talk about naïve.

My eyes started to blur, then suddenly at work one day, I slipped a disk in my lower back which was excruciatingly painful, and though that was healed through chiropractic care thankfully, my eyesight continued to remain blurry. I wasn't too concerned, as I was turning forty after all, and isn't that common for us in the over forty club? Hmm...

I coasted in this "I will see an eye doctor soon to get a prescription, and research how to naturally heal eye sight." I knew healing it was possible. After all, I had now had many bouts of healing the "impossible" in this life, and I was certain I could lick this eye problem naturally. I know I carry the power of resurrection within my soul records, however, this issue took a sinister turn.

To be fair, I am not actually certain that "sinister" is the correct word, but any other term to accurately describe what happened to me next escapes me, so sinister it is. The energies sure weren't coming from a benevolent force, wherever they were coming from, I do know that much.

Working as a raw and whole foods chef six days a week to support me and my boys, as Jeff and I had officially decided to separate, I was working myself very hard. I am by nature a hard worker, no matter what I do. I don't believe in doing things half-assed. So at work, I am super focused and produce high level work, with integrity, beauty and love. To me, there is no other option.

Jen and I had decided that on October 10[t], 2015, when Jeff was scheduled to take the boys to stay with him in Flagstaff, we would get together at my new place and I would finish my book, and she would begin writing hers, as she has a stellar one living in the ethers waiting to be written that I cannot wait to read one day.

As it turned out, Jen had a new roommate coming to move in with her, and she would be arriving in Phoenix from California that same evening, and Jen felt it only right to be there when her friend arrived. I understood and agreed. So we decided to push our writing date back two weeks. Besides, Mercury was just coming out of a retrograde that same day, and to me, this timing of waiting a little bit for Mercury retrograde to fizzle out seemed like a better plan anyway.

I decided to enjoy my day alone, with silence and peace, even stealing a nap here and there, which I desperately needed. The day was low key and glorious. I had no responsibilities except to myself. I hadn't had that freedom in months, it seemed.

For fun, I began watching episodes of the X-Files on Netflix, as I'd heard a new season was going to come out, after all these years. I was not interested in it when it had first started airing decades ago, plus, I thought this would be fun. I'd only started watching it with my past boyfriend I'd mentioned earlier, Darrell, after my missing time episode and all the strange ET activity that followed it in 1996-97.

I had also begun reading a new book I'd ordered by an author and researcher named Nick Redfern, and the book I was really into reading was his book *The Real Men in Black* which details who these mysterious men are, how they show up in people's lives, and the mysterious happenings and high strangeness that often surrounds these encounters. After all, I was still trying to figure out if I'd had authentic connections with them in the past myself. Somehow I always came back to "yes" though this was strictly an intuitive feeling from strange experiences I'd had. I was looking for answers for myself, and especially for the writing of this book. I wanted to make sure anything I wrote about was as on point and accurate as I could make it.

I was blinded, almost literally, by my own curiosity filter.

I found while reading this book, I could only read a page or two at a time before I would be "hit" with an extreme heaviness, and I would have to go lay down, unable to keep my eyes open. I noticed on this particular Saturday, that heavy-eyed extreme fatigue began to be accompanied by a mild headache, which built to quite a significant pressure in my head as the day wore on.

I chalked this up to not drinking enough water that day. Perhaps that was part of it, who knows. What I do know is that the headache grew worse as the day passed, and when I woke up from a short nap, I had a sudden urge to burst out of bed and go contact a woman I'd heard speak at the library only a few weeks prior about MILAB cases and her research on MILABs—or *military abductions*—including her own experiences with these intense types of abductions.

This lady seemed like a sweet woman fearlessly exposing these operations, even though "they" had made attempts to steer her away from outing this information on many occasions. She seemed courageous to me, and when I asked when her birthday was and she told me August 19th, foolishly I presumed her being a starseed with her Sun at galactic degree in Leo meant I could safely confide in her and talk about some of my experiences with her. I figured with her knowledge, I might find some missing pieces to my own puzzle where military-feeling encounters were concerned. I somehow convinced myself this information would enhance my book, and that this is what it was missing, and needed.

I now wonder, was I under some form of mind control as a result of reading this book?

Though our meeting was friendly and mostly enjoyable, I did notice that she seemed very quick to shoot down or poo-poo my experiences as most likely "next to nothing." At least that's what it felt like. I didn't feel the need to be right about my experiences, but by now I do know when something is really happening as opposed to simply using my imagination. I knew at least some of my experiences I was questioning had some significance to them. I have had enough experience to know this much. But to be fair, all she was actually saying was that most of these possible MILAB experiences I'd had could have been something other than MILAB encounters. Fair enough.

So, perhaps she was not exactly shutting me down completely, though I could not shake the feeling that something felt unmistakably off about this meeting for me, and I could not quite put my finger on it right away. What I did notice was that she did not seem all that interested in listening to any of my stories, and was way more interested in talking. Which was fine, I told myself.

Usually those of us with these kinds of otherworldly encounters and experiences are chomping at the bit to find people we can tell our stories to, who might understand us, or at the very least hear us without thinking we are nuts. But did she do this with everyone she talked with? She seemed to enjoy the sound of her own voice and stories way more. It even seemed like she didn't want anything to do with mine. Also fine. I was not attached to her approving of me, I was simply looking for answers from someone I thought might be able to help me. Or, whose thought really was that in the first place?

I should have gotten the hell out of Dodge when I realized she was not hearing me. I should have walked out the door. But there was an invisible force that seemed to be holding me in the chair I sat in. I noticed a light behind her that started to feel way too bright, like it was shining directly into my eyes, and really disturbing my sight. I began to shield my eyes from it, it was that intense. Yet I still did not leave.

What was going on here? My only thought process was that the light in the room was too bright. I was ignoring my intuition all over the place, a BIG red flag if I ever saw one. I definitely suspect at this point that some sort of mind control was at play here, even if that was not her intention. After all, didn't she say at her talk now that I remember: "anyone who talks to me about this stuff surely will be watched by them as well." I am not necessarily inclined to think she had any ulterior motives, but I do know from her many stories she shared, both at her talk and our private meeting, that she is closely monitored by secret forces, and most likely connected with the MILAB agents.

Where had my discernment gone? What the hell had I done to myself? I wanted to get up and run out of there, and yet, something, *something* was holding me in that chair like I was bolted to it, the light assaulting me and continuing to blind me. It was so strange and eerie now that I look back on it.

I was in that chair for four hours. I could not believe it when I realized that. Where had the time gone? Was I missing time, perhaps? I really didn't know. I just knew I wanted to get out of there and get home. The whole thing had felt like a huge mistake.

We got outside, and still, I had trouble getting out of there, as she kept talking to me, telling me stories of how she's been watched and monitored by these agents for a long time. Finally I got to my car, and high-tailed it home. All I wanted to do was forget that night, it had felt like such a huge letdown. I never did find any answers to my questions, and I had wasted hours of my time and energy on this, but for what?

I am not blaming this woman at all. Let me be clear about that. I simply feel that the game she is playing at, her point of focus, is in a way darker field than I care to play in anymore. I think she is courageous in exposing important information, but she is also being tracked and watched because of it. Which means that anyone coming into contact with her, especially having to do with these kinds of experiences, is also tracked. I feel like an idiot that I didn't have better judgment when it came to this. I have no idea what was pushing me to meet with her that day, but like I said, I do feel now in some way, I had been accessed through some sort of mind control outlet. I was simply the dummy who took the bait.

I couldn't get home fast enough that night. I sat down, in my so rarely empty home (the boys were spending the weekend in Flagstaff with Jeff), with my one day a week off work, and decided to watch some more episodes of *The X-Files* on Netflix.

As I watched, I noticed I was having a hard time looking at the computer screen. It was several feet away from me, but still, my eyes felt sensitive after that damn light in her office had assaulted them earlier that evening. I was wearing my blue-blocker glasses, yet I could still not stand to look at the screen for very long. I found my eyes wandering all over the place, and finally decided I needed to turn it off. I wasn't even paying attention to the story anymore by then.

I went to bed around 11 pm, to rest my eyes as I wanted to put that strange day to rest and start fresh the next day. Big lesson learned. Don't be so curious about finding answers, especially to the detriment of your own discernment. *Big, fat* "check."

My eyes had trouble resting that night, but I thought they'd simply had too much, and I wasn't too concerned. I finally fell asleep and woke up the next day. They were a bit blurry but I decided to ignore it, as I had to work. I assumed this too would eventually pass.

Well, it didn't. In fact, it only got worse.

Within a few days, something strange started happening. I had a very unusual headache smack dab in the middle of my forehead, right where the pineal gland (the "third eye") sits. My eyes were feeling strained and started doing a sort of twitching motion, and I began to have trouble focusing them on anything for longer than a second or two. It was very odd.

Once again, I thought this would pass. I was in denial. I believe now that I experienced some sort of mind swipe which kept me from connecting the dots. I simply thought I had a strange headache, and wasn't certain why, or why it would not go away. I very rarely get even mild headaches, and this one, starting in the center of my forehead, progressively got more and more intense over days.

Finally, I began to notice that my eyes were becoming unable to even *look* at any source of light. I couldn't even stand to have them shining around me. It became increasingly difficult to drive, as the light of day was blinding me, even when the sun was behind me. Lights on cars, lights in my home, and absolutely *no* computer screens. Suddenly, I was unable to work on the last parts of my book. I would open my laptop, and be blinded, painfully, by the screen. It was horrific, really, as after days and days of this, I started to notice that not only was I unable to communicate anymore by email (my main source of distance communication), I was beginning to notice that everything around me was becoming blurred. I was having to strain just to look at my hand in front of me.

Work became nearly impossible. My production slowed significantly as I fumbled around the kitchen and bumped in to things and kept dropping things out of my hands. I didn't say a word to anyone for at least a week, hoping and praying it would get better.

All the while, sleeping at night was a waking nightmare. I barely slept at all. My eyes were constantly in motion, and felt like they were going to pop out of my head. Whenever I would close my eyes, they would immediately cross, and look up into the center of my forehead, and feel like they were pushing their way out of the sockets. It was maddening, painful and terrifying.

This went on for THREE WEEKS. I was terrified. My boss began to get short with me, saying things like "It shouldn't take this long to do such and such..." I was totally stressed and by this point, I was certain I was on my way to going blind, and fast.

'How on Earth did this happen?' I thought to myself over and over all day long until I was almost crazy.

Actually, I felt like I was going crazy.

The hardest part was when I would get home at the end of the day with the kids. After a stressful day, I had to drive us home from school and work, which was becoming a nearly impossible feat. Never mind come home, put lights on in the house, make dinner, and get them ready for bed. I was becoming unable to function at all, especially in the evenings.

I remember one evening Rubin asking me to sit with him and draw each other pictures, which is something we enjoy doing together. I was crushed when I went to draw him something and realized I could not even bear to look at the white blank paper in front of me; that alone was much "too bright," never mind attempt to focus my eyes for more than a split second on anything I might attempt to draw.

I was devastated. But I tried anyway. I only managed to make about seven stars with my eyes basically closed, because they couldn't handle looking at the white paper and yellow marker I was using.

I went to the bathroom and broke down on the floor, crying.

I lay in bed that night, as I watched him fall asleep as best I could with the lights out, his sweet little six-year-old face still hanging on to the last bits of baby fat on his adorable cheeks. Looking as beautiful and perfect as I'd even seen him. It hit me like a knife in my gut that I was losing my ability to see the beauty of everything around me. My children. I began to weep, as the pain of this realization washed over me.

What if I lost my eyesight completely, which is what it felt like was happening? What then?

How could I not see with my eyes, the beauty of my children, as they grow to become young men? What about everything they do and create? Rubin's drawings and art work? Noah's silly slapstick comedy routines and infectious, mischievous smile? Their crazy, unkempt long wild hair? Rubin's hilarious dance moves? The sweetness of their "brother hugs"? Rubin learning to ride his bike? Rubin's equal parts pride and nervousness at his school play? Noah's silly side notes and doodles on his school assignments and work, always cracking jokes or drawing ridiculous pictures? I mean, the list went on and on and on. What if I would one day be in total darkness, and saw no vibrant colours or exotic shapes in the world anymore?

Their soft, perfect skin.

I cried myself to sleep. I was going blind, and I knew it. But I didn't know why. *Why?*

Finally, I reached out to Selene and Jen, and told them what was happening, and that I was getting very scared about it, as it was not improving, but rather, getting worse by the day. My line of vision was blurring more each day, and I could no longer focus my eyes on anything for even a split second. In my waking life, I was being driven slowly insane by this madness. And I was in such a state of fear and helplessness.

Then one day Jen contacted me and said that in a few days, she was coming up to Sedona, and we were going to take care of this. She told me that she'd set up a session with a woman named Stormi for me, who might be able to help me. After all, it was Stormi who "saw" what I was going through while working with Jen's roommate over the phone one day. Jen had never told her about me, and Jen's roommate had only met me briefly once before this. There was no way Stormi could have known anything about me. Jen had never even told her my name or that I even existed.

During her roommate's clearing, Stormi stopped and said, "Wait! Jen has a friend who is having a serious problem with her eyes. She needs a clearing badly!" With that, Jen did not hesitate, and she set up the appointment for me for that Saturday and I could use her phone to do it, as I don't have my own cell phone, and still had not hooked up a landline in my new place I'd only moved into weeks before.

Before the session that day, we called Selene to see if she had any suggestions for me, or any wisdom as to what might have brought this on so suddenly and intensely. I was almost afraid to hear what she might say.

"You need to see an ophthalmologist right away. Do not mess with your eyes. I want to rule out anything physical before we move forward with galactic help. If they don't find anything wrong, then we will send in the galactic secret service and take care of it. My thought is that it could be an implant if the doctors can't find what's wrong, but you need to rule that out first."

Implanted? By whom? Who would do this to me?

I knew right then what had happened. At least I strongly suspected. I had failed in my discernment, and put myself in the line of fire. My curiosity and need for information nearly cost me my eyesight. I wondered if this could even be true.

I started taking high doses of vitamin D3 that day, as per Selene's instructions, and began looking up local ophthalmologists, to make an appointment by Monday.

In the meantime, it was time for my session with Stormi. I was not certain she would be able to help me, I had no clue what to expect, but I trusted Jen's judgment on this one, and obliged, thinking there was no way it could hurt me. If anything, even if it helped me clear things that were holding me back in life, aside from my eyesight, I would be grateful. But of course, I was desperate and praying that whatever she did might help clear my eyes too.

Stormi was an interesting woman; very sweet, and she got right to it. She had me lie down on my bed, with Jen's phone on speaker beside me. She had instructed me to get one glass of water to drink, and one glass of water that I would not drink, but that would energetically take in and hold all the energies we would clear that day. I got them ready and lay down with my eyes closed.

She went into a past life I'd had as part of the Asante tribe in Africa. She talked about how powerful I was, standing up against slavery and fighting for equality. How fearless and like a warrior I was, yet graceful at the same time. She talked of the drumming, dancing, and richness I enjoyed, both in spirit and physically, adorned in gold.

She went on with the clearing after sharing much of this lifetime with me. My body was beginning to vibrate, I felt a strong buzzing in my hands, up my arms and in my toes, up through my legs. My third eye was extremely alive, the crown of my head bursting open, my core felt like it was being lifted from the bed, in levitation. The energies were surely very high here.

In the clearing, Stormi would check in with her guidance as well as mine (I did not need to say anything or give any feedback, she was in direct connection with my guides). She went through my entire energetic system, physical and non-physical. Without going in to all of the details, two main points stood out for me, which I filed away in my memory banks as interesting.

At one point, she asked aloud if I had any cords from this lifetime and/or previous lives that were holding me back and keeping me from accessing and expressing my highest, lightest version of myself. Jen told me afterwards she was floored at how many I'd had. Apparently when Jen had had her session with Stormi, she'd had something like two million cords that needed clearing, which had seemed like a lot to her, and I would agree. When Stormi asked how many I'd had, the answer that our guides told her was twenty-three million!

WOW. That was a *lot* of shit weighing me down! She cleared these and I felt like I was going to float right off my bed! It was amazing!

The other thing that came up in the clearing which I found *very* interesting was that at one point, she asked our guides if there were any implants in my body that needed clearing, and the answer they gave her was *yes!*

She cleared whatever these were, and I was still lying on the bed, but wondered if I might notice any difference with my eyes once we were done. I was not holding out a ton of hope, but I was holding out some, especially since Selene had suspected implants as a likely cause of this strange condition.

The session was over, and I felt amazing, but still wondered if I would notice any difference with my eyes. I opened them, stood up, and realized I could see with clarity for the first time in weeks. I also realized it was only mid-afternoon, and the real teller would be in the evening once the sun went down, and of course, at night, if I was able to close my eyes and actually sleep without them driving me absolutely crazy jumping around all night long...

I waited for night to come, nervously anticipating the outcome.

I slept! I could close my eyes without any moving or popping, crossing or fidgeting, *all night long,* without the need to open them even once, on the edge of insanity. I slept like a baby for the first time in almost a month! When I awoke, my eyesight was *crystal clear*!

Whatever this woman did, it was incredible. Not only was my eyesight restored, but it was even sharper than before. I couldn't believe it.

And then the reality dawned on me. Yes. I was now 100% certain that someone, somewhere, somehow, had implanted me with a chip to make me lose my eyesight, as I simultaneously (and conveniently) lost my mind. What kind of person (or being) would do this to me? And how badly must they have wanted to stop me from doing my work and completing my assignments—like this book?

It was then that I realized how dangerous discernment, or lack thereof, can actually be. Something so innocent and seemingly harmless as curiosity has the potential to destroy our lives if we are not on top of it at all times when playing on the galactic chess board. In this moment, I realized that graduating from Spiritual 101 into Galactic 404 without having mastered discernment is not something to joke about. There is no room for curiosity once you play in the higher galactic realms, or you could very well be burned beyond recognition or repair. I realized this day that I could not afford to be curious anymore if I wanted to complete my assignments and make it out the other side with my life and my sanity still intact.

That was one hard lesson learned, thankfully before it was too late.

CHAPTER 87

Beyond the Limb – A New Day Dawns

In the summer of 2014, I discovered another meditation group Jeanne and Jaap were starting to offer once a week, separately from the crystal skull meditations, and this one was focused on the notion of working more intimately with the subtle realms; basically, opening ourselves up in an effort to increase our receptivity to them. This meditation would not be focused on the crystal skulls.

I had no idea what to expect, but this time, though had been to their meditation space twice and had had positive experiences both times. So, I decided to go with Eva. This was on June 29, 2014.

Jeanne and Jaap introduced this class as an "open space;" not where they were leading or teaching but rather where we would all hold the space for exploration, each of us bringing to the table our own unique connection with the subtle realms.

During the first meditation Jaap led us through, we were all invited to open up to our unique benevolent connections, and help ground them into the room. The skulls, though not necessarily used in these meditations, did help anchor in a more focused and organized frequency, as before we did this, there was an ungrounded overflow of different subtle energies in the room, all excited to be given this opportunity to connect with us more consciously.

During the meditation, I witnessed a benevolent presence reach in to my pineal gland, or my "third eye," and immediately, I began to see it transform into a deep purple, almost indigo, crystal. I knew I was being prepared for something, and that my "subtle eyes" were being opened more fully.

I wondered what I was being prepared to receive. What sort of subtle realm was about to show itself to me? I was open and ready to receive it, whatever it was.

The next meditation was led by Jeanne, and she had us connect with our heart center to allow Source in—to allow the energies of Unconditional Love for ourselves to flow freely. Once in this state, we were invited to discover which aspect of the subtle realms wished to communicate with us.

Immediately, I saw a stunning blue being in front of me. She felt to have a strong feminine aspect, so I will refer to the being as "she" and "her." Her skin was very smooth, with a shine to it, and her forehead was larger than an average human head. The tone of her skin was blue, but a very light shade, almost pearly white. Her eyes wrapped around in a point to her temples, and were stunningly beautiful.

She looked much like my mother from the ships I would visit through my closet portal as a young child, though I could only see her from about the chest up. I wondered why this was so. I tried to look beneath this, but felt the sense that I needed to be prepared to see what was "down there." I wondered how bad or shocking it could possibly be. I had already seen her face, and she beamed with such love, and a gentle calming peace that I felt safe with, though her presence was undoubtedly also quite strong and otherworldly.

I breathed deeply, and prepared myself for the unknown. I felt safe, I felt ready for whatever it was she was to show me.

And then I saw her, standing much shorter than the blue being; a little girl. I recognized her as my hybrid daughter, Angel. The same hybrid daughter I had seen in my regression session with Bridget in November of 2013. And now here she was, right in the room with me. She was beautiful, sweet and full of love. I was overwhelmed by her presence at first, not having expected this at all.

Angel spoke to me telempathically. She told me that we could touch one another, and she reached out both of her hands. I saw her two long arms stretch out to meet mine. Her hands had four fingers on each side, and were long and thin, as were her arms.

She held my hands, and her fingers reached past my wrists, onto my forearms. Her hands were warm and cool at the same time somehow. Her touch was gentle. I felt an energy run through us like an infinity circuit, and we were sharing information and love this way. It was quite incredible.

After I got used to her enormous energetic frequency, she began to speak to me through thought-form communication. She told me how excited she is to come more directly into my physical life; that she is excited to be a part of it soon.

And then she told me that she could hardly wait to taste the food that I would prepare for her. That all of the blended foods, smoothies, juices and liquid foods I had suddenly been interested in exploring were in part inspired by her. In a way, these foods coming more front and center in my life were brought in to my consciousness upon her personal request!

Then she shared with me something extraordinary. She told me that the one I used to spend so much time with as a child in nature, the reason I was so happy to supposedly spend so much time alone was because I was actually spending time with *her*!

I became confused by this, as back then I too was a child. She giggled and said to me, *"I am a Time Traveler, a Time Jumper, and so I am able to go to any moment in your life and be with you. I have been with you since the day you were born. Even though you are my Mother, I have been able to be with you, always."*

I so enjoy making food for the ones I love, and so between these two messages from her, I was melting as my heart expanded about a million times over.

How could I have ever guessed that my own hybrid daughter, Angel, had also been one of my life-long companions? What an enormous concept to wrap myself around.

A whole new level of consciousness opened up for me that day, and I was left with only one, inevitable, question:

What else was possible?

My mysterious world of infinite possibilities suddenly became a whole lot vaster and infinitely more magical. In that precise moment, I renewed my commitment to myself to love and relish every single blessed moment of this mystical, adventurous magic carpet ride of Life, guided by synchronicity after synchronicity, filled with unexpected twists and turns, loop-de-loops, and ascensions often followed by gut-wrenching drops before rising up again...and again...and again.

In that moment, I was overjoyed to discover that for the most part I am now enjoying this ride immensely. At some points on what has often felt like a long and painful journey, I have literally begged the heavens for relief and a way out. Now though, I find myself completely ready to embrace this radical journey to its fullest, with great excitement even.

As many experiences from this lifetime flashed before my eyes, I reveled in the mystical path I have chosen to walk during this life and so many others before and parallel to it. It was safe to say that I was now fully excited to witness how the fruits of my Earthly and Galactic trials and tribulations, my triumphs, failures, joys, pain, suffering, and ecstasy—turned Cosmic Awareness and Deep Inner Knowing—would manifest within and around me as a result of my own courage to step out beyond the limb, suited up, inspired by, and embracing the deep cosmic mystery of it all.

In short, these big girl panties are on, are a perfect fit, and are *definitely* here to stay.

"And I know that I have seen you there.
We travel even when we're not aware.
Through the portal we go, come on don't be scared.
Because I'll be there, yeah we're everywhere,
In parallel universes."

~ Anthony Singing Bear – "Molecular Transport"

"I believe in everything until it's disproved. So I believe in fairies, the myths, dragons. It all exists, even if it's in your mind. Who's to say that dreams and nightmares aren't as real as the here and now?"

~ John Lennon

ABOUT THE AUTHOR

Samantha Lyn Dickson was born May 24, 1975 to Daphne Williams and Darwin Dickson in St. Catherines, Ontario, Canada. Her mother's family came from generations of fishermen in Newfoundland. Her father's family farmers from New Brunswick.

Samantha's parents say that she always marched to the beat of her own drum and was sweet, funny, impish, and bubbly as a child. As a teen, she was a hardworking 'A' student, high school student council president, and a beautiful dancer and musician.

Samantha studied dance and theatre at Brock University in Ontario and Studio 58 in Vancouver and toured North America as an actress and dancer. Samantha always moved with grace, presence, and purpose. She expressed her art through dance, baking, cooking and the way she lived her life.

Samantha Lyn was an amazing mother, wife, daughter, sister, and friend. As her mother said, she brought joy to her family and all who knew her. She was always a seeker throughout her whole life and The Seed continues her legacy of bringing love and light to those who have the honor of knowing her. .